the complete
# KUBRICK

the

# KUBRICK

complete

## David Hughes

This edition first published in Great Britain in 2000 by
Virgin Books Ltd
Thames Wharf Studios
Rainville Road
London
W6 9HA

Reprinted 2001 (twice)

A catalogue record for this book is available from the British Library

ISBN 0 7535 0452 9

Typeset by TW Typesetting, Plymouth, Devon

Printed and bound in Great Britain by Mackays of Chatham PLC

# Dedication

To Stanley K, Zahida K,
And my dear old 'P' and 'M'

# Contents

# Acknowledgements

Stanley Kubrick once likened film directing to 'trying to write *War and Peace* in a bumper car in an amusement park', but added that, 'when you finally get it right, there are not many choices in life that can equal the feeling'. Working on this book was like trying to write *The Complete Kubrick* while holding down a day job, fronting a band, working for a dozen monthly magazines – and still getting home in time to read the kids a bedtime story.

Obviously, I couldn't have done it alone.

Therefore, my thanks are due to Peter Darvill-Evans, who gave me a shot; Joanne Brooks, who picked up the baton handed to her and then ran the rest of the way by herself; the redoubtable Chelsey Fox; Jonathan Clements, for introducing me to Chelsey and for a last-minute wash and rinse; Dane, whose McMastery of the Internet rivals that of Bill Gates; Angus Spottiswoode, who provided 1,001 useful facts about *2001*; Peter Bogdanovich, Luke Golden and William Peiffer; Christopher Fowler, who taught me how to write good; Susie Webster, Julia Delmas, Mimi and Kat for immoral support; Alex, Seamus and Lee for tea and sympathy; Michael Barrs; Andy and Helen, who delved into the BBC archives way beyond the filing cabinet marked 'BEWARE OF THE LEOPARD'; Adrian Hughes and the rest of the BFI buffs; the relevant people at Virgin Publishing, Warner Bros, MGM, Columbia, Universal and *Empire* magazine; my interview subjects and everyone else I've quoted; the bright spark who invented DVD; and all the talented *droogs* and *devotchkas* at Picture Production Company – especially David Willing, who didn't mind my working on the book during those rare slack moments. (Then again, perhaps I'm fired.)

And, above all, to the great Stanley K, without whom film might still be an art form in its infancy.

# Foreword
## by Peter Bogdanovich

When Stanley Kubrick died in his sleep of a heart attack on 7 March 1999, even the New York tabloids reported the news with an auteur slant, headlining the director's generally bleak view of life. Words like 'secretive', 'reclusive', 'strange', 'mysterious' and 'cold' were repeatedly used to describe him.

It's true that the thirteen feature-length films he made over forty years present a disenchanted, sardonic and generally pessimistic view of humanity, but his lifelong friends, intimate associates and family members conjure a far more complicated picture of a man who could be deeply reserved but also outgoing, meticulous and laid back, loving and self-absorbed.

The precocious son of a Bronx doctor, Kubrick became a staff photographer for *Look* magazine at seventeen, but from the start he was captivated by the movies. He began as a kind of one-man band, financing, directing, producing, writing, shooting and editing three short documentaries – *Day of the Fight* (1951), *Flying Padre* (1951) and *The Seafarers* (1952) – and then doing virtually the same thing for his first two extremely low-budget features, *Fear and Desire* (1953), backed entirely by an uncle, and *Killer's Kiss* (1955).

In 1954, having already run through two marriages, Kubrick moved to Los Angeles and formed a production company with his friend James B Harris, through which he made his first two professional pictures, the film noir *The Killing* (1956), with Sterling Hayden, and the powerful antiwar drama *Paths of Glory* (1957), starring Kirk Douglas. While shooting *Paths of Glory* Kubrick fell in love with and wed the German painter and actress Christiane Harlan, with whom he would rear two daughters, along with Christiane's young daughter from an earlier marriage.

*The Killing* and *Paths of Glory* did not make money, but they did make Kubrick's reputation as a budding genius among critics and studio executives. In 1960, Kirk Douglas hired Kubrick to replace another director on *Spartacus*, the only all-Hollywood production Kubrick would ever make, and his first box-office success. He hated the experience. Disenchanted with the industry and having developed a phobia about flying, the director soon afterwards moved with his family to England, never again to travel far from home.

Over the next 38 years, he made only eight more films. Between his controversial adaptation of Vladimir Nabokov's notorious *Lolita* (1962) and his grim but popular Vietnam War film, *Full Metal Jacket* (1987), Kubrick achieved a kind of mythic status in world cinema with three hugely successful pictures: his black comedy of the Cold War, *Dr Strangelove or: How I Learned to Stop Worrying and Love the Bomb* (1964), the mystical science-fiction saga *2001: A Space Odyssey* (1968) and his ultraviolent investigation of violence, *A Clockwork Orange* (1971), based on Anthony Burgess's novel. (While *Clockwork* won the New York Film Critics' Circle

Award for best picture, it was wildly criticised in England for inspiring copycat crimes. Kubrick, wounded by the attacks, withdrew it from circulation in the UK.)

The gigantic and enduring box-office appeal and critical enshrinement of these three films, coupled with the slimness of his output and his distance – physical and emotional – from the Hollywood mainstream, fuelled a kind of legendary aura of integrity and perfectionism that gave Kubrick enormous power in the industry he avoided. Still, he was troubled by the fact that *Barry Lyndon* (1975), his costume drama adapted from Thackeray, though much admired in certain quarters, did not have a box-office response commensurate with its cost. His next work was his most openly commercial: *The Shining* (1980), based on a Stephen King horror novel and headlining a major star, Jack Nicholson.

When he died, at seventy, he had just completed *Eyes Wide Shut*, based on Arthur Schnitzler's *Dreamstory*, a project he had been thinking about for more than thirty years. The film, which deals candidly with sexual relations between a contemporary New York married couple, played by the husband-and-wife team of Tom Cruise and Nicole Kidman, opened in the United States on 16 July 1999.

I cannot say I knew Kubrick, though we spoke briefly on the phone two or three times in the early seventies. He was preparing to shoot *Barry Lyndon* and he called me out of the blue. His voice sounded extremely youthful, with a subdued but definite Bronx accent and a kind of reticence and self-effacement that was disarming. He asked what I thought about Ryan O'Neal, whom I had directed in *What's Up, Doc?*. Kubrick's young daughters were fans of the movie and now were lobbying their father to cast O'Neal in *Barry Lyndon*. Even in that brief exchange, Kubrick's obsessions – film and family – were twinned.

They would remain that way until the end.

Peter Bogdanovich

the

# KUBRICK

complete

**David Hughes**

# Strange Love
## or: How I Learned to Stop Worrying and Love Stanley Kubrick

Stanley Kubrick did not have much to say about his own films. He allowed them to speak for themselves, which they invariably did. Explaining his reticence to discuss his work, he once said that the *Mona Lisa* would have lost its mystique if da Vinci had written 'she's smiling because she has a secret lover' underneath. Nevertheless, Kubrick also said that 'the very meaninglessness of life forces Man to create his own meanings', and that 'however vast the darkness, we must supply our own light'.

Hence the existence of this book.

I count myself privileged that I saw more than half of Kubrick's thirteen feature films – namely *Paths of Glory*, *Lolita*, *Spartacus*, *Dr Strangelove*, *A Clockwork Orange*, *Full Metal Jacket* and *Eyes Wide Shut* – for the first time on the big screen. *The Complete Kubrick*, however, is aimed primarily at those who didn't. Those who may have seen *The Shining* or *Full Metal Jacket* on their first run releases, and almost certainly caught *Eyes Wide Shut* at the cinema, but have probably seen most of Kubrick's oeuvre on television, on video, or DVD. Those who are more interested in the films than the man behind them. Those who may have detected a *Dr Strangelove* reference on *The Simpsons* before they ever saw *Dr Strangelove*. Those who, like millions of Britons, have never seen *A Clockwork Orange* – or at least not without Swedish subtitles.

The specific format of this book makes it particularly well suited to being read out of sequence, favourite films first. In most cases, seeing the film *before* tackling the associated chapter is the wisest move – I would hate to spoil any endings for you. (Suffice to say that *Dr Strangelove* ends with a bang.)

In the style established by *The Complete Hitchcock*, each entry features such basic information as format, running time, cast and crew (based on the opening and major end credits – additional credits can be found in the Appendix), as well as drawing on the following categories as appropriate:

**UNCREDITED CAST/CREW:** Belatedly giving credit where it's due.

**TITLE SEQUENCE:** Including title styles, music, opening shots and sometimes narration.

**SUMMARY:** The bit that, in the interest of completism, gives the plot away.

**SOURCE:** Almost all of Kubrick's films were adapted from one source text or another. Here's the story behind each of them.

**WORKING TITLES:** Just think – in another universe, Kubrick's filmography might have included the following titles: *Sky Pilot* (1953), *Shape of Fear* (1953), *The Nymph and the Maniac* (1955), *Clean Break* (1956), *Two Hours to Doom* (1964), *How the Solar System was Won* (1968), *The Luck of Barry Lyndon* (1975), *The Short-Timers* (1987) and *Rhapsody* (1999).

**PRODUCTION HISTORY:** The making of the movies.

**CASTING:** Who's who among the cast, and how they came to be there. Plus, how James Mason might have played Colonel Dax, Noël Coward nearly nabbed the role of Humbert Humbert, and Steve Martin might have starred as a New York doctor on an erotic odyssey. No, really.

**THE USUAL SUSPECTS:** For a director who reputedly didn't care for actors, Kubrick sure was a loyal employer – and a great many actors came back for more.

**THE PURSUIT OF PERFECTION:** Kubrick's stock in trade: the quest for absolute authenticity in all aspects of his film making. He demanded perfection of himself, and expected it from everyone else.

**CLASSIC QUOTES:** A personal choice of the most relevant, repeatable or resonant quotes from each of Kubrick's films.

**THEMES AND MOTIFS:** An attempt to unravel some of the mysteries, meanings and multiple layers in Kubrick's masterpieces.

**MUSIC:** From key changes to sex changes, the stories behind Kubrick's music choices are always fascinating, and this section tells you the score.

**POSTER/TAG-LINE/TRAILER:** From the very beginning, Kubrick was as adept at movie marketing as he was at movie making, often designing his own posters, suggesting his own tag-lines and editing his own trailers.

**WHAT THE PAPERS SAID:** A representative cross-section of critical responses to Kubrick's films, from both sides of the Atlantic.

**CONTROVERSY:** Credit wrangles, lawsuits, boycotts, bans, Commies, death threats, 'X' ratings, orgies, and the old ultraviolence – there was never a dull moment once one of Kubrick's films hit the cinemas.

**BOX OFFICE:** American and/or worldwide grosses, in US$ for easy cross-referencing.

**AWARDS:** How Kubrick narrowly missed winning an Oscar – 56 times.

**TECHNICAL ACHIEVEMENTS:** Those inventions and innovations that kept Kubrick at the forefront of the technical side of film making throughout his entire career.

**INFLUENCED BY:** Although there are few obvious influences on Kubrick's films, hence the brevity of this section . . .

**DÉJÀ VU:** . . . he quite often repeated ideas and images from, or made reference to, his earlier films.

**INFLUENTIAL ON:** 'We are all the children of DW Griffith and Stanley Kubrick,' the director Martin Scorsese once said. Here's why.

**SEQUELS AND REMAKES:** The French remake of *The Killing*, the feature-length homage to *Killer's Kiss*, the sequel to *2001*, *The Shining* mini-series, *A Clockwork Orange 2004* . . . who says no one would dare remake a Kubrick film?

**KUBRICK GOES POP:** From *The Simpsons* to *Father Ted*, 'Space Oddity' to Heaven 17, there are enough pop-culture references to Kubrick's films to fill, well, at least this section . . .

**CUT SCENES:** Probably the first director to recut his films *after* they were released, Kubrick is also one of the few film makers who would release a 'director's cut' thirty minutes shorter than the original version. This section covers deleted scenes, alternative versions, censor cuts and any other changes Kubrick may have made to his films.

**TRIVIA:** Bore your friends! Be a pariah at parties! Win film quizzes! It's all the stuff that wouldn't fit comfortably into any other section.

**APOCRYPHA:** Did you know that Kubrick filmed a particular actor every month for ten years for a secret film project? No, and neither did he. Like the rest of us, he just read it on the Internet. Here, the urban myths and legends surrounding Kubrick's films get their hair mussed.

**AVAILABILITY:** A 'pan-and-scan' copy of *2001*, a version of *The Shining* shy of about thirty minutes, and barely a sniff of *A Clockwork Orange* since the seventies? It's never been easy being a British Stanley Kubrick fan – unless you have an all-regions DVD player, in which case you can take advantage of this section's US availability details as well . . .

**EXPERT WITNESS:** A key figure close to the production recalls an experience from one of the films on which they worked.

**FINAL ANALYSIS:** My own two cents, for what it's worth (about two cents).

**KUBRICK ON KUBRICK:** Finally, a few *bons mots* from the late, great man himself.

Please note that there is an index of quotations, giving all sources, at the end of this book.

# Day of the Fight (1951)

**(B & W – 16 mins)**

**Produced and Directed by Stanley Kubrick**
**Produced by Jay Bonsfield**
**Screenplay, Photography, Sound Recording Stanley Kubrick**
**Assistant Director Alexander Singer**
**Narration Script Robert Rein**
**Film Editor Julian Bergman**
**Music Composed and Conducted by Gerald Fried**

**WITH:** Walter Cartier, Vincent Cartier, Nate Fleischer, Bobby James, Eva Cartier, Bobby Gleason, Judy Singer, Douglas Edwards (*Narrator*)

**TITLE SEQUENCE:** The opening of *Day of the Fight* is preceded by a full-screen caption/panel bearing the following legend: 'All Events Depicted In This Film Are True'. There follow two further single-panel captions: 'Day of the Fight' and 'A Stanley Kubrick Production', before the image dissolves through to a shot of New York's Madison Square Garden, with 'TONITE BOXING' boldly displayed on the marquee.

**SUMMARY:** Walter Cartier, a middleweight boxer from New York's Greenwich Village, awakens at six in the morning in the double bed he sometimes shares with his twin brother Vincent, a New Jersey lawyer who also acts as his manager. After a visit to the local church, attending a compulsory medical, and generally preparing psychologically for that evening's fight with Bobby James, Cartier heads for the Laurel Garden stadium with his brother. Pre-fight preparations continue in the dressing room until 10 p.m., when the fight begins. Cartier wins by a knockout – the first fighter to defeat Bobby James by this method – and returns home, bloodied but unbowed, one step closer to his dream of becoming champion.

**SOURCE:** Stanley Kubrick was twenty years old, and had been a staff photographer at *Look* magazine for three and a half years when, in late 1948, he was given the biggest assignment of his career: a photographic feature based around a day in the life of a young middleweight boxer named Walter Cartier. This involved Kubrick's following the 26-year-old prizefighter's routine on the day before a big fight: waking up in his Aunt Eva's Greenwich Village apartment; meeting with his twin brother, Vincent, a New Jersey lawyer who moonlighted as Walter's 'second'; weighing in; conferring with his manager, the legendary Bobby Gleason; spending the afternoon with his girlfriend, including a trip to Staten Island and Yankee Stadium; fixing a toy sailboat for his young nephew; final preparations for the fight; and two actual fights: one that Cartier lost to Tony D'Amico on a technicality, and another that Cartier won, beating Jimmy Mangia by a knockout.

Published in the 18 January 1949 issue of one of America's most widely read periodicals, the long-running *Look* magazine, the 'Prizefighter' spread featured nineteen of Kubrick's photographs, covering a total of seven pages. One of the article's headlines read 'THE DAY OF A FIGHT'. A little more than a year later, in an issue of the same magazine dated 14 February 1950, Kubrick's still camera covered a day in the life of a more famous middleweight boxer, Rocky Graziano. Entitled 'ROCKY GRAZIANO, HE'S A GOOD BOY NOW' – referring to the controversial boxer's erstwhile suspension – the spread included a caption that recalled Kubrick's earlier boxing photographs: 'The Day of the Fight Is a Long One'.

In retrospect, these photojournalistic features might be seen as the storyboards for Kubrick's first film.

**PRODUCTION HISTORY:** *Day of the Fight*, the twelve-minute documentary that effectively began Kubrick's film-making career, was a virtual rerun of his 'Prizefighter' photo feature, covering another day in the life of Cartier, culminating in a boxing match with the black middleweight Bobby James. 'Stanley's concept of using the photojournalist story on *Day of the Fight* was inspired,' Alexander Singer recounted. 'Not only were the drama elements of it marvellously compressed, but the subject himself, Walter Cartier, was a textbook hero. Walter Cartier was good-looking and able. He surely looked good – and his brother, Vincent, looked good – and the two of them together were quite marvellous figures.'

Kubrick jettisoned such peripheral elements as Cartier's girlfriend and nephew, but kept his twin brother Vincent and added a humanising element of his own: a dog. Kubrick used the savings from his tenure at *Look* magazine, along with whatever money he could borrow from friends and relatives, to finance the film, which cost a total of $3,900 – around $1,000 to shoot the film itself, and the rest to finance post-production. It was filmed on a 35mm, spring-wound, silent Eyemo camera rented from Burt Zucker's Camera Equipment Company at 1600 Broadway – a building in which, incidentally, Kubrick would later open a production office.

As filming began, Kubrick allowed Cartier to lead him through his daily routine, deciding upon which events to capture on film in much the same way as he had done using his still camera. 'He didn't really rehearse it at all,' Walter's twin brother Vincent recalled. 'It was just so quick. Once he did it, it was done. It wasn't retake, retake, retake. He was photographing – not manufacturing the day of a fight. Walter had a high regard for Stanley,' Vincent added. 'Walter used to say, "Stanley comes in prepared like a fighter for a big fight. He knows exactly what he's doing, where he's going and what he wants to accomplish." He knew the challenges and he overcame them.'

For the climax of the film, the fight itself, Kubrick and Alexander Singer took their rented Eyemo cameras to Laurel Gardens in Newark, New Jersey, where they took turns loading hundred-foot rolls of film as they struggled to capture the live event on celluloid. 'With me on one camera and Stanley on the other, it was pretty busy and pretty hectic,' Singer recalled. 'We had to get it. It had to be down on film – there was no picture without getting this fight.' When Cartier landed the knockout blow and Bobby James hit the canvas, it was Singer's camera that captured the moment.

With *Day of the Fight* complete, Kubrick hoped that it could be sold to Time Inc.'s successful series of cinema-distributed documentary newsreels, collectively known as *The March of Time*. Although Kubrick and Alexander Singer were disappointed to learn that the producers did not pay for documentary shorts concerned with sports, they felt sure that they could improve on the current level of sophistication and artistic merit of such films, and command a price for theirs. Turning down a derisory offer from *The March of Time*, Kubrick shopped the film to RKO-Pathé, one of the few companies that still distributed the occasional documentary short-film subject. RKO bought the film for $4,000 – giving Kubrick a mere $100 profit – and screened it as part of its long-running series *This is America* at the Paramount Theatre, New York, where it opened on 26 April 1951 – a full month *after* RKO's release of Kubrick's second short subject, *Flying Padre*.

**THE PURSUIT OF PERFECTION:** Unable to stage any element of the climactic bout between Cartier and James, Kubrick managed to capture one 'Kubrickian' shot – of the two fighters viewed from the canvas, lit from above – by lying down and extending the arm holding his Eyemo camera. A staged version of the same shot appears during Davey Gordon's fight in *Killer's Kiss*.

**CLASSIC QUOTES**

Narrator: 'This is a fight fan. Fan – short for fanatic. There's a legion just like him in the United States. Each year he shoves his share of ninety million dollars under the wicket for the privilege of attending places where matched pairs of men will get up on a canvas-covered platform and commit legal assault and lawful battery.'

Narrator: 'One man has skilfully, violently overcome another – that's for the fan. But KO, name of opponent, time, date and place – that's for the record book. But it's more than that in the life of a man who literally has to fight for his very existence. For him, it's the end of a working day.'

THEMES AND MOTIFS: As with two of Kubrick's subsequent features, *The Killing* and *The Shining*, time was a key element of *Day of the Fight*. The film begins at six o'clock in the morning, as Cartier wakes and prepares for breakfast. Subsequent events are given chronological identity with ever-decreasing intervals:

- at 4 p.m. (interval ten hours), Cartier lays out the tools of his trade – towel, shoes, ice bag, Vaseline, bathrobe – and takes a last look in the mirror;
- at 8 p.m. (interval four hours), Walter prepares for the fight in his dressing room, as the narrator tells us, 'Walter isn't concerned with the hands of the clock now, just his own hands';
- at 9 p.m. (interval one hour), Vincent covers Walter's face and body with Vaseline and takes his brother's St Jude medal for safekeeping;
- at 9.45 p.m. (interval 45 minutes), Walter is called to the ring;
- at 10 p.m. (interval fifteen minutes), the fight begins.

This effect of accelerating time in order to increase suspense was used equally effectively in *The Shining*, where the time spans shorten from months to weeks to days and finally hours.

MUSIC: Although Kubrick had not initally considered music to be a necessary element of *Day of the Fight*, his friend and assistant director Alexander Singer convinced him otherwise, and suggested a young Juillard-trained musician named Gerald Fried to compose a musical score for the film. 'They asked me to do the music,' Fried explained. 'Why me? Because I was the only musician Kubrick knew . . . I had ten months to a year to learn how the hell to do it. There were no courses, [so] I went to a lot of movies and took notes.'

In the sleeve notes for Silva Screen Records' compilation *Strangelove . . . Music from the Films of Stanley Kubrick* (FILMCD 303) – which includes a three-minute track from *Day of the Fight* entitled 'March of the Gloved Gladiators' – Gerald Fried recalled his first collaboration with Stanley Kubrick: 'Among the many memories brought back by Silva Screen Records re-involving me with the five Stanley Kubrick films I scored was the incident which almost prevented my career from getting off the ground. My first professional recording as conductor/composer was the scoring of *Day of the Fight*, at RCA's New York Studios. I hired the best musicians I knew, all of whom were about my age, twenty-two, which was also Stanley's age. But, the burly guard would not let us in! "You kids can't go in there," he bellowed. "We've got a professional recording scheduled."'

Fried, as gifted and enthusiastic an amateur in his chosen field as Kubrick was in his, would impress Kubrick so much that he continued to write music for his next short subject, *Flying Padre*, as well as his first four feature films, from *Fear and Desire* to *Paths of Glory*. Aside from his contributions to Kubrick films, Fried went on to carve out an impressive career composing music for several feature films, including *The Killing of Sister George* (1968), and numerous television projects, including *The Man from UNCLE*, *Gilligan's Island*, *Star Trek* and *Roots*.

**WHAT THE PAPERS SAID:** Although *Day of the Fight* was widely distributed through RKO-Pathé, there tended to be few comments in the press about short films. Retrospectively, however, one of the more intriguing looks at *Day of the Fight* was offered by Richard Combs, who wrote, in 1980, that the film was 'not so much a rough draft as a perfect miniature of the feature films that were to follow ... The time-lock structure anticipates *The Killing*; the deserted, early morning streets are as haunted as the similarly used locations in *Killer's Kiss* ... Kubrick's images lend more than a hint of apocalypse, and of a genuinely agonised determinism, to an hour-by-hour account of Cartier's wait for yet another encounter.'

**TECHNICAL ACHIEVEMENTS:** 'I was cameraman, director, editor, assistant editor, sound-effects man – you name it, I did it,' Kubrick later remarked of his experiences making *Day of the Fight*. 'And it was invaluable experience, because being forced to do everything myself I gained a sound and comprehensive grasp of all the technical aspects of film making.'

**INFLUENTIAL ON:** Nowhere was the influence of *Day of the Fight* more obvious than on Kubrick's second feature, *Killer's Kiss*, in which the film maker returned to the story of a prizefighter, fictionalising it and adding elements of crime and film noir.

Cartier's appearance in *Day of the Fight* evidently influenced his future career, for, although he never achieved the status of middleweight champion, he followed Kubrick's film with a creditable career as an actor. After appearing with Paul Newman in Robert Wise's *Somebody Up There Likes Me* (1956) and Elia Kazan's *A Face in the Crowd* (1957), he appeared in several popular and long-running television series, including *Crunch and Des* with Forrest Tucker and *You'll Never Get Rich* with Phil Silvers. He died in 1995.

**TRIVIA:** Not content with securing his place in the history books by appearing as both the subject of a photo-assignment by Stanley Kubrick the photographer, and of a documentary by Stanley Kubrick the director, Walter Cartier achieved the distinction of the quickest knockout in Boston Garden history, flooring Joe Rindone in just 47 seconds in October 1951.

**EXPERT WITNESS:** 'He did that sports short as if he were doing *War and Peace*. He was meticulous with everything, from scripting to editing. Stanley was a full-blown filmmaker instantly.' – assistant director Alexander Singer, quoted in *Stanley Kubrick: A Biography* by John Baxter, 1996.

**FINAL ANALYSIS:** Replete with images from Kubrick's *Look* magazine spreads, and foreshadowings of *Killer's Kiss*, *Day of the Fight* is fascinating both as a documentary about the sport of boxing in the fifties, and as a clear indicator of Kubrick's future accomplishments behind the camera. Above all, the film has dated far less than one might have expected, arguably enduring rather better than Kubrick's first two fictional subjects, *Fear and Desire* and *Killer's Kiss*.

**KUBRICK ON KUBRICK:** 'I was aware I didn't know anything about making films, but I believed I couldn't make them any worse than the majority of films I was seeing. Bad films gave me the courage to try making a movie.' – quoted in *Stanley Kubrick Directs* by Alexander Walker, 1970.

# Flying Padre (1951)

**(B & W – 8½ mins)**

Directed by Stanley Kubrick
Produced by Burton Benjamin
Screenplay, Photography by Stanley Kubrick
Film Editing Isaac Kleineerman
Music Nathaniel Shilkret
Sound Harold R Vivian

**WITH:** Reverend Fred Stadtmueller, Bob Hite (*Narrator*)

**SUMMARY:** The Reverend Fred Stadtmueller, a priest at St Joseph's Church in a tiny rural region of Harding County, New Mexico, flies his single-engined Piper Cub aircraft, the *Spirit of St Joseph*, to a small mission church, where he is to conduct the funeral service of a ranch hand. After the funeral, Stadtmueller flies the plane back to his main parish, where he conducts the evening services. The following day, the priest has breakfast at his parish, and reconciles two young friends who have had a quarrel. Later, after spending some time working to ensure his aircraft remains airworthy, tending his pet canaries, and practising his marksmanship, Stadtmueller is told of a sick baby on an isolated ranch fifty miles away, and immediately sets off to help her. Collecting the mother and baby, he flies them to an airport, where an ambulance is waiting to take them to hospital.

**WORKING TITLE:** Kubrick's preferred title for the project had been *Sky Pilot*, a pun on a slang term for 'priest'. RKO evidently did not see the joke.

**PRODUCTION HISTORY:** Kubrick's second short subject was commissioned by a rising producer called Burton Benjamin, then managing the *Screenliner* series for RKO, the distribution company that had bought his first short film, *Day of the Fight*, as a *fait accompli*. Benjamin offered the young director $1,500 to make a one-reel human-interest documentary about the Reverend Fred Stadtmueller, a New Mexico priest who, in 1949, had borrowed $2,000 from a friend to purchase a small, single-engined Piper Cub aircraft, which he intended to use to keep in touch with his parishioners, who were spread across eleven separate churches covering an area of 4,000 square miles. Although the film offered Kubrick, who had been a qualified pilot since 15 August 1947, the opportunity to combine two of his greatest passions – film making and flying – he later described the film *Flying Padre* as 'a silly thing about a priest in the Southwest who flew to his isolated parishes in a small airplane'.

Despite the advance from RKO, *Flying Padre* did not make a profit for Kubrick, owing to the unforeseen expenses of filming on location. Nevertheless, it was theatrically released in March 1951 – a full month *before Day of the Fight*'s debut on 26 April – and for Kubrick there was no looking back. The completion of the two films gave him sufficient confidence to resign his post as staff photographer at *Look* magazine and, at the age of 23, concentrate on film making full time. 'It was tremendous fun for me at that age,' Kubrick recalled of his experiences at *Look*, 'but eventually it began to wear thin, especially since my ultimate ambition had always been to make movies.'

**MUSIC:** *Flying Padre*'s musical score was the last composed by Nathaniel 'Nat' Shilkret, a veteran composer and musical director of more than fifty films during the twenties, thirties and forties, who had received an Oscar nomination for *Winterset* (1936).

**FINAL ANALYSIS:** It is tempting to look back at Kubrick's earlier films and seek foreshadowings of his later output; indeed, in several cases, I have not managed to resist doing so.

To me, however, the only remarkable thing about *Flying Padre* is that it is credited to a director named Stanley Kubrick, for – aside from the detail with which the Piper Cub aeroplane is covered – there is precious little of Kubrick in *Flying Padre*. The only sequences that employ more than a rudimentary imagination, let alone what might comfortably be called 'Kubrickian', are these: a shot taken by mounting the camera on the undercarriage of the aircraft; a low-angle shot looking up at Stadtmueller in the cockpit (echoed later in the cockpit of the *Leper*

*Colony* of *Dr Strangelove*); the closing shot, taken from the ambulance as it drives away from Stadtmueller and his aircraft.

Overall, *Flying Padre* has none of the sophistication of *Day of the Fight*, and, in the unlikely event that anyone in New York in 1951 noticed that both films were credited to the same director, they would have almost certainly have assumed that they were made in the order that they were released: *Flying Padre* followed by *Day of the Fight*.

**KUBRICK ON KUBRICK:** 'Even though the first couple of films were bad, they were well photographed, and they had a good look about them, which did impress people.' – quoted in *Eye*, August 1968.

# ? (1952)

**(B & W – ? mins)**
**Directed by Stanley Kubrick**

**PRODUCTION HISTORY:** Little is known about this short documentary film, which Kubrick directed for the US State Department while busy with post-production chores on what would become *Fear and Desire*. Although neither the title nor the length of the film is known, it is believed to be a film about the World Assembly of Youth, a forerunner of John F Kennedy's Peace Corps, which may have had its origins in suggestions by two Democratic Senators, Hubert H Humphrey and Henry S Reuss, that, in the absence of conscription, young men and women of college age might be encouraged to travel overseas to carry out socially worthy projects. No known print of the film survives.

# The Seafarers (1952)

**(Colour – 30 mins)**
**Directed by Stanley Kubrick**
**Produced by Lester Cooper**
**Photographed by Stanley Kubrick**
**Written by Will Chasen**
**Technical Support by the staff of the Seafarers'**
**International Union**

**WITH:** Don Hollenbeck (*Narrator*)

**SUMMARY:** Members of the Seafarers' International Union are shown enjoying the various diverse benefits that membership of the union offers them. Such benefits include assistance in finding employment; access to a library; legal and trade-union representation in grievances relating to work; welfare for ageing and/or injured seamen; and so on.

**PRODUCTION HISTORY:** Kubrick had completed the filming of his first feature-length movie, *Fear and Desire*, and was busy with post-production chores when he was commissioned by the Atlantic and Gulf Coast District of the American Federation of Labor to make a promotional film about the Seafarers' International Union, an organisation that provided welfare, legal representation and various other services to East Coast seamen from all walks of life. The film would be produced by Lester Cooper of Lester Cooper Productions, Inc.

Filming in colour in June 1952, Kubrick's camera followed the day-to-day workings of the organisation, with locations including the busy harbour; the Union cafeteria; a retirement home where veteran sailors gratefully receive their pension payments; the Union Hiring Hall; the Welfare Headquarters of Beefs & Dues; the office of the Union newspaper, the *Seafarers Log*; the Port-of-Call Bar where members play bar billiards; a barber's shop – including an incongruous, even gratuitous, shot of a naked woman featured on a calendar for a produce company; and so on.

Kubrick had no editorial control over the arrangement of the footage he shot, and library music was added to the silent material, along with Don Hollenbeck's reading of Will Chasen's script.

**TECHNICAL ACHIEVEMENTS:** Those looking for trademark Kubrick shots would appreciate a continuous dolly shot, almost a minute in duration, which tracks through the Union cafeteria.

**FINAL ANALYSIS:** Regarded by Kubrick as a simple piece of work for hire, *The Seafarers* would warrant no mention in motion-picture history if it had not been directed by Stanley Kubrick, and had not marked his first foray into colour cinematography. Stranded with an uncharismatic presenter/narrator and a stultifyingly dull script, Kubrick somehow manages to sustain the viewer's interest beyond the caption that credits him as director, although the final scene – which features dramatic interplay between the speaker and audience at a union meeting – is almost worth the thirty-minute wait.

Overall, despite presenter/narrator Don Hollenbeck's assertion that this was 'a story simple but dramatic', *The Seafarers* is simplistic and largely undramatic, and Kubrick understandably wished to have nothing more to do with it beyond cashing his pay cheque.

# Fear and Desire (1953)

**(B & W – 68 mins)**

Director Stanley Kubrick
Producer Stanley Kubrick
Associate Producer Martin Perveler
Screenplay Howard O Sackler
Photography Stanley Kubrick
Editor Stanley Kubrick
Music Gerald Fried
Art Direction Herbert Leibowitz
Unit Manager Bob Dierkes
Assistant Director Steve Hahn
Make-up Chet Fabian
Title Design Barney Etengoff
Dialogue Director Toba Kubrick

CAST: Frank Silvera (*Sergeant Mac*), Paul Mazursky (*Private Sidney*), Kenneth Harp (*Lieutenant Corby/Enemy General*), Steve Coit (*Private Fletcher/Aide-de-Camp*), Virginia Leith (*Girl*), David Allen (*Narrator*)

UNCREDITED CREW: Al Grimaldi (*Re-recording Mixer*)

TITLE SEQUENCE: Music swells over a long, slow panning shot across a wooded mountain valley, as a narrator sets the scene with a spoken poem. 'There is a war in this forest,' the voice tells us, 'not a war that has been fought, nor one that will be, but any war. And the enemies that struggle here do not exist unless we call them into being. For all of them, and all that happens now, is outside history. Only the unchanging shapes of fear and doubt and death are from our world. These soldiers that you see keep our language and our time, but have no other country but the mind.'

SUMMARY: In an unspecified war, four soldiers – the handsome, philosophical Lieutenant Corby, the tough, no-nonsense Sergeant Mac, the battle-weary Fletcher and the youthful, inexperienced Sidney – are regrouping after crashing their plane behind enemy lines. Corby outlines plans to elude the unnamed enemy by building a raft and escaping by river, but the appearance of a general in the distance and the passing overhead of an enemy aircraft send them back into the forest, temporarily abandoning the completed raft.

In the woods, the men surprise two enemy soldiers eating in a shack, and kill them with trench knives – along with a third soldier, who responds to the attack – before fleeing into the forest once more. By the river, they come across an attractive young woman whom they capture and lash to a tree with their own belts. Corby, Mac and Fletcher return to look for the raft, unwisely leaving the panic-stricken Sidney to guard the woman. After a fumbling attempt to seduce her, he loosens her bonds, and, when she tries to escape, he shoots her dead before running into the woods, the killing having sent him over the edge. Meanwhile, as the others wait for the cover of nightfall by the river, Mac devises a new plan. He suggests taking the raft to draw the sentries' fire from the enemy command post, while the others kill the general and escape in his plane. Corby agrees to go along with Mac's plan.

Mac punts the raft downriver, while Corby and Fletcher approach the enemy command post, seeing that the general and his aide are drunk. As Mac begins firing at the enemy soldiers, causing them to desert their posts, Corby and Fletcher attack the general and his aide, wounding the former and killing the latter. The general surrenders, but Corby shoots him at point-blank range, just as he realises that the general's face is identical to his own, and the aide's to Fletcher's. As the general's plane takes off with Corby and Fletcher aboard, Sidney joins the badly wounded Mac on the raft. After the raft has drifted along the fog-shrouded river overnight, the four are reunited again on the river bank, all of them changed by the experience: Corby and Fletcher disillusioned, Sidney incoherent and probably insane, Mac dead or dying.

**SOURCE:** *Fear and Desire* was based on a screenplay written, at Kubrick's suggestion, by Howard O Sackler, a poet friend of his from Taft High School. Sackler would later win the Pulitzer Prize for Literature for his acclaimed 1969 play, *The Great White Hope* and write an early draft of *Jaws* (1975).

**WORKING TITLES:** Sackler's original screenplay was entitled *The Trap*, a title that – like Jean Renoir's *Grand Illusion* (1937) – was intended to relate more to a general view of war than to the soldiers' immediate situation. An alternative, *Trapped* – as in 'behind enemy lines' – was suggested by Richard de Rochement, who pointed out that *The Trap* had already been used for three previous features, the most recent in 1947. Production commenced under the name *Shape of Fear*, a title that stuck until 1953, when the distributor Joseph Burstyn finally released the film as *Fear and Desire*.

**PRODUCTION HISTORY:** When Kubrick asked Sackler to write the screenplay that evolved into *Fear and Desire*, the Korean War was barely a month old. Kubrick himself was eligible for the draft at the time of America's entry into the war, and might have fought had he not, according to his friend and collaborator Alexander Singer, been 'turned down by the army on some oddball thing'. Yet, although the soldiers' uniforms and weapons resemble those of the Second World War, the setting for Sackler's screenplay was, as the opening narration asserts, 'not a war that has been fought, nor one that will be, but any war'.

Kubrick knew that it would cost him a mere $25 per day to hire a 35mm Mitchell film camera, complete with four lenses, and that if the project was meticulously planned, shot on location in California woodland, and made with a minimal cast and a skeleton crew, Kubrick could make the film for a few thousand dollars. 'I went to the Camera Equipment Company at 1600 Broadway,' Kubrick recounted, 'and the owner, Bert Zucker, spent a Saturday morning showing me how to load and operate it. So that was the extent of my formal training in movie camera techniques.' In the style customary to directors like Alfred Hitchcock, but for very different reasons, Kubrick proceeded to map out or 'storyboard' the screenplay, shot by shot, so that when he came to shoot the movie, barely one frame of precious film would be wasted. The problem of sound, for which the Mitchell camera provided no recording facility, would, Kubrick supposed, be addressed in post-production.

Already an impressive self-publicist, Kubrick managed to persuade the *New York Times* to write a feature about his ambitious endeavour even before the cameras started rolling. Thus, on 14 January 1951, under the bold headline 'YOUNG MAN WITH IDEAS AND A CAMERA', Thomas M Pryor became the first of a select few journalists to whom Kubrick would, over the next five decades, grant an interview. 'Stanley says he has figured out every camera angle and that after he finds the proper location "in some wooded area of Southern California", shooting should run smoothly and be concluded in fifteen to twenty-one days,' Pryor reported. Subsequent cinematographers engaged by Kubrick over the years might have done well to take heed of Pryor's closing paragraph. 'The one requirement', it said warily, 'is that the cameraman must agree in advance to follow the blueprint laid out by Stanley, who will direct and produce the film.'

Bolstered by the boost to his credibility and ego that the *New York Times* piece conferred, Kubrick was able to persuade various family members – including a rich uncle, Martin Perveler, and his own father, who had encouraged young Stanley to take an early interest in photography – to invest a total of $10,000 in the production. Having cast the film, Kubrick assembled a thirteen-strong crew, which included four of his friends – Bob Dierkes, Chet Fabian, Herbert Leibowitz and Steve Hahn – and an equal number of anonymous Mexicans to act as grips. Even his wife of three years, Toba Kubrick (née Metz), was enlisted to act as 'dialogue director' – a rather glorified name for a script girl. The already fragile marriage would, however, be over before the film was completed.

Shooting commenced in woodland on the outskirts of Bakersfield, Los Angeles, a Boy Scout camp in the San Gabriel Mountains in the summer of 1951, the cast and crew sleeping in log cabins on location. 'At the end of four weeks we were still shooting,' the actor Paul Mazursky recalled in his autobiography, *Show Me the Magic*. 'Stanley told the cast he had to drive down the mountain to get a few thousand more from his uncle. Frank Silvera and I went with Stanley [who] drove the car down the mountain with his usual intensity. "I'll get the money out of that cheap bastard!" He actually spat on the window to emphasise his point. He was livid. It was Humphrey Bogart driving with Ida Lupino in *High Sierra*. I knew Stanley was determined since we had already shot for a month.'

Kubrick inveigled another $5,000 out of his Uncle Martin, and, after a further fortnight's filming, returned to New York with 15,000 metres of film, which, when developed and viewed on a Moviola, more than met even Kubrick's own high expectations. Another area where his expectations were exceeded proved more problematic, however, as Kubrick realised that he had drastically underestimated the cost and complexity of creating a complete audio soundtrack comprising dialogue, music and effects. The absence of synchronised (or 'sync') sound – none had been recorded on location, owing to the limitations of the camera and the lack of a sound crew – meant that each and every line of dialogue had to be re-recorded by the actors, and 'post-synched' to their own mouth movements captured on film, a process known today as 'looping'. The process, added to the ballooning cost of music and sound effects, called for yet more expensive studio time, swelling the budget to $53,500. Despite allowing himself a salary as director, cameraman and film editor, Kubrick still needed more money – and his uncle was tapped out.

To raise the necessary finance to complete his opus, Kubrick resumed work in what he later described as 'miscellaneous television and State Department trivia' – in reality, a US State Department documentary about the World Assembly of Youth; a better-known effort from the same year, *The Seafarers*; and as second-unit director for a five-part series about Abraham Lincoln. Ploughing the payment he received from these projects into the post-production on *Shape of Fear*, Kubrick completed the 66-minute film in June 1952, and screened it before a carefully selected group of friends and associates whose sympathetic critiques he would need if he was to secure distribution.

Thus, in November 1952, Kubrick wrote to the independent film distributor Joseph Burstyn, quoting such respected former critics as James Agee and Mark van Doren, who called the film 'brilliant and unforgettable' and earmarked Kubrick for future greatness by asserting that he was 'worth watching for those who want to discover high talent at the moment it appears'. Kubrick's letter, coupled with such recommendations, immediately fuelled Burstyn's interest. With a return on his money looking increasingly likely, Kubrick's uncle agreed to increase his initial investment, giving him an Associate Producer credit in addition to a share in the film's profits. With a new title, and two minutes of opening titles courtesy of Barney Etengoff, *Fear and Desire* was previewed before several New York critics on 26 March 1953, five days before the film's opening at the city's Guild Theater. Kubrick had arrived at last.

**CASTING:** Paul Mazursky – a twenty-year-old Brooklyn College senior at the time still known by his birth name, Irwin – was cast as Sidney after Howard Sackler spotted him in an off-Broadway production of Leonid Andreyev's *He Who Gets Slapped*, and suggested that he audition for the part of Sidney.

Mazursky met Kubrick at his Fourteenth Street apartment the next day. The actor recalled: 'A rumpled young man with black hair and intense eyes is standing in a corner. He's in his early twenties. "Hi. I'm Stanley Kubrick. Would you please read for me?" No small talk, barely a handshake, and before I know it, I'm reading with this Kubrick guy. He's not much of an actor, but his eyes are blazing right through me. I lose myself in the part. I figure things must be going well since we're reading the entire script. I don't try anything fancy, just a very emotional, borderline psycho performance, complete with hysterical laughter.'

Impressed, Kubrick told Mazursky that he had the part, and that he would be required to leave for California the following Monday. 'Monday?' Mazursky responded. 'But I have school on Monday!'

Although Mazursky's acting career continued sporadically in the coming years – as a juvenile delinquent in *The Blackboard Jungle* (1955), and in his own *Enemies, A Love Story* (1989) – he later achieved greater fame as the director of such socially conscious comedy dramas as *Bob & Carol & Ted & Alice* (1969), *Moscow on the Hudson* (1984), *Down and Out in Beverly Hills* (1986) and *Moon Over Parador* (1988).

The Jamaican-born actor Frank Silvera, whose swarthy looks led to numerous feature-film roles as Indians, Mexicans, Cubans and Romanies, was cast as Sergeant Mac. When filming began, he had already appeared in *The Cimarron Kid* (1951) and *The Fighter* (1952), and he was about to appear with Marlon Brando and Anthony Quinn in Elia Kazan's *Viva Zapata!* (1952). 'I had seen Frank play Nat Turner in the theatre so I knew what a great actor he was,' Mazursky noted later. '"What do you think of Kubrick?" said Frank. "I know he's a great photographer, but I don't know what he knows about acting." "You're right, kid. But I can help with the acting."' Silvera returned as Vincent Rappalo in Kubrick's next film, *Killer's Kiss*, and went on to appear in *Mutiny on the Bounty* (1962), *The Greatest Story Ever Told* (1965) and the television western, *The High Chaparral*.

The parts of the other two soldiers were filled by such unknown actors as Kenneth Harp and Steve Coit, while the fashion model Virginia Leith was cast in the sole female role (compare Kubrick's subsequent war films, *Paths of Glory* and *Dr Strangelove*) as the unnamed (and unspoken) young woman who is captured, terrorised and finally killed by Sidney. Having made her acting debut in *Fear and Desire*, Leith would go on to star in such films noirs as *Black Widow* (1954) and *A Kiss Before Dying* (1956), the latter adapted from the story by Jim Thompson, co-screenwriter of *The Killing*.

## CLASSIC QUOTES

**Mac:** 'Sidney must have gone out of his head. Something about a magician . . .'

**Fletcher:** 'There's gonna be more room on that raft than I thought.'

**Corby:** 'There's nothing so refreshing as a day outdoors in enemy territory. It's too bad the sun doesn't turn us green instead of brown – camouflage, you know.'

**Mac:** 'How far is it to the line?'
**Corby:** 'Only a short distance – the distance between life and death.'

**Fletcher:** 'I'm not built for this.'
**Corby:** 'Nobody ever was. It's all a trick we perform, because we'd rather not die immediately.'

**THEMES AND MOTIFS:** 'Its structure: allegorical. Its conception: poetic,' Kubrick wrote of *Fear and Desire* in a letter to Joseph Burstyn dated 16 November 1952. 'A drama of "man" lost in a hostile world – deprived of material and spiritual foundations – seeking his way to an understanding of himself, and of life around him. He is further imperilled on his Odyssey by an unseen but deadly enemy that surrounds him; but an enemy who, upon scrutiny, seems to be almost shaped from the same mold . . . It will, probably, mean many things to different people, and it ought to.'

Kubrick's effusive description of the themes behind his film are, in many ways, as overwrought as the film itself. In effect, *Fear and Desire* is a simple antiwar polemic disguised as a complex treatise on existentialism and how war deprives man of choosing his own destiny by preordaining him for death and doom in pursuit of the illusion of glory and self-fulfilment. The futility of rationalism is also explored, most notably by Lieutenant Corby, who initially states that his sole reason for living 'is to hunt for a reason', but ultimately realises that pure reason has no place in a war.

Kubrick would subsequently revisit the device of having a single actor play multiple roles in *Lolita* (Peter Sellers/Clare Quilty's quick-change personality shifts), *Dr Strangelove* (Sellers again, in three distinctly different roles) and *The Shining* (Jack Nicholson as Jack Torrance and his 1920s counterpart). Here, Kenneth Harp and Steve Coit both play dual roles, so that, symbolically, they are killing themselves when they shoot their enemy counterparts. The theme behind the device, vocalised by *Full Metal Jacket*'s Private Joker as 'something about the duality of man', was explored more fully in this later war film, in which Kubrick demonstrates that the soldier must effectively kill the most human part of himself in order to be able to kill others.

**MUSIC:** Having composed original music for Kubrick's short subject *Day of the Fight*, the 23-year-old composer Gerald Fried was called upon to score the director's first feature film. 'The music was supposed to mourn the world's innocence,' Fried recounted later. 'Fear and desire are the two dominant forces of our species . . . So it had to be important, profound, meaningful, touching, despairing but yet triumphant. I thought it was pretty good at the time.'

Two tracks, 'A Meditation on War' and 'Madness', comprising more than nine minutes of music from *Fear and Desire*, were re-recorded for Silva Screen Records' Kubrick compilation album, *Strangelove: Music from the Films of Stanley Kubrick* (FILMCD 303).

**POSTER:** Kubrick's background as a stills photographer made him the perfect choice to photograph the advertising material for *Fear and Desire*, and the sexually charged photographs he took of Virginia Leith for the poster perfectly captured at least the latter half of the film's title. 'They were without question the best photographic record of a picture ever put on the front of a movie house,' Alexander Singer enthused. 'This was to me a mark of what this guy would do – that everything he touched would be special.' It would not be the last time that Kubrick decided upon the poster image for one of his films.

**TAG-LINE:** 'The wolves are breathless about Virginia Leith,' the influential broadcaster Walter Winchell – later referenced in *Full Metal Jacket* – said in connection with *Fear and Desire*. Although he had almost certainly not seen the film, he was persuaded by the distributor Joseph Burstyn to provide a quote for use in support of it, despite the fact that several others were available that were more positive – and more coherent.

**WHAT THE PAPERS SAID:** Perhaps encouraged by the dearth of new films from American independents, most of the critics who saw *Fear and Desire* reviewed it sympathetically. The *New York Times*, while admitting its review was slanted by 'the need for encouragement of fresh talent', said that '*Fear and Desire* evolves as a thoughtful, often expressive and engrossing view of men who have traveled far from their private boundaries.' *Variety* called the film 'a literate, unhackneyed war drama, outstanding for its fresh camera treatment and poetic dialogue . . . a blend of violence and philosophy, some of it half-baked, some of it powerfully moving'.

Several other critics praised Kubrick's efforts – most notably in the photographic department – while acknowledging that the enterprise was fatally flawed, most often by Sackler's pretentious dialogue and a number of inept performances. Only a few reviewers were entirely hostile towards Kubrick's feature debut. The New York *Herald Tribune*'s Otis L Gurnseley suggested that Kubrick had been 'carried away on the wings of [his] own zeal into images too revolting for useful dramatic purposes, into hyperbole too elliptical to grasp in the form of movie dialogue and action', while the *New Yorker*'s John McCarten – Pauline Kael's equally intractable predecessor – stated that 'Mr Kubrick, setting out to demonstrate that he disapproves of war . . . proceeds to talk his prejudice to death'.

Although the film is not widely admired, except as a rarely screened curiosity that signalled the beginning of a brilliant director's career in feature films, *Fear and Desire*'s harshest critic is arguably Kubrick himself. In 1960, he told *Horizon* magazine that the film was 'a lousy feature, very self-conscious, easily discernible as an intellectual effort, but very roughly, and poorly, and ineffectively made'. A decade later, interviewed by Alexander Walker, Kubrick dismissed *Fear and Desire* as 'a serious effort, ineptly done'; by 1994, he looked even less favourably upon the film, describing it as 'a bumbling amateur film exercise' and 'a completely inept oddity, boring and pretentious'.

**CONTROVERSY:** By 1951, Kubrick knew enough about the powerful unions who controlled the professional aspects of film making to tell the *New York Times*, prior to shooting, that he intended to hire a professional cinematographer so as not to run foul of the cameramen's union. This did not, however, prevent him running into trouble with Local 802 of the American Federation of Musicians, who threatened to blacklist the film unless the 23 professional musicians hired to record Gerald Fried's score received payment. Richard de Rochemont, producer of the *March of Time* series, agreed to pay $500 from his own pocket in order to placate the union, subsequently recouping the sum from Martin Perveler, Kubrick's rich uncle.

**BOX OFFICE:** Despite the lurid advertising campaign and largely positive reviews, *Fear and Desire* failed to make any impact at the box office. Although Kubrick has often stated that all of his initial investors eventually made their money back, it is unlikely that this was achieved through box-office receipts for *Fear and Desire*.

**TECHNICAL ACHIEVEMENTS:** Severely limited by such key film-making resources as time and money, Kubrick was forced to resort to ingenuity when it came to creating the fog-shrouded river bank through which the soldiers' raft drifts towards the climax of the film. Unable to afford to rent even the most basic smoke-generating machine, Kubrick improvised a similar device by filling an insecticide sprayer with soluble oil and water, creating an impressive miasma to rival any Hollywood equivalent.

Kubrick also managed to manipulate the prevailing weather conditions in other equally ingenious ways. According to *Modern Photography* magazine, 'twilight scenes were obtained in bright sunlight by placing a red filter over the lens and underexposing the film three stops'.

**INFLUENCED BY:** *Fear and Desire* is perhaps the only one of Kubrick's films in which it is possible to separate the themes driving the story and dialogue (Sackler's) and those expressed in image and composition (Kubrick's). Sackler, an emergent poet still almost two decades away from his best work, was clearly influenced by Eugene O'Neill and, most obviously, Joseph Conrad: the fact that Mac's existential journey downriver can be likened to a similar trip made by Martin Sheen in *Apocalypse Now* (1979) is because Conrad's *Heart of Darkness* provided the inspiration for both.

Exploring the influences on Kubrick's photography and editing – the two areas of the film over which he exercised absolute control – is more interesting, even though the influences on his style at the time are equally obvious. Several critics likened the film's photography – particularly the lights and shades of the opening scenes in the forest – to Akira Kurosawa's *Rashomon* (1951), which certainly would have been fresh in Kubrick's mind at the time *Fear and Desire* was lensed. Other scenes – most notably the quick-cut montages of faces – resemble the work of Sergei Eisenstein, another early influence on the young Kubrick.

**INFLUENTIAL ON:** While it cannot truly be said that *Fear and Desire* directly influenced many more films than Kubrick's own later antiwar polemics, *Paths of Glory* and *Full Metal Jacket*, the idea of mixing poetic and philosophical musings with battle-weary soldiers formed the basis of Terrence Malick's acclaimed World War Two drama *The Thin Red Line* (1999).

**TRIVIA:** Although the prolific Dutch Guyana-born director Pim de la Parra made a Dutch-language film entitled *Fear and Desire* in 1992, the similarity between the two films begins and ends with the title.

**APOCRYPHA:** Although it has been said that Kubrick personally oversaw the destruction of the original negative of *Fear and Desire*, several archival prints are known to exist. Indeed, the film was screened at Colorado's Telluride Film Festival in 1991, and reappeared three years later as one half of a 'Young Stanley Kubrick' presentation, also featuring *Killer's Kiss*, at New York's Film Forum. This latter screening prompted Warner Bros, at the request of Kubrick, to issue a press release declaring that Kubrick had 'asked to let you know that if it had been up to him, the film would not be publicly shown'. Subsequent screenings scheduled for Los Angeles, New York and Ohio were cancelled, with the distinct possibility that Kubrick, the sole copyright holder, had threatened legal action if the film was shown.

**AVAILABILITY:** Perhaps unsurprisingly for a film he had virtually disowned, and did not wish to be seen in the context of his later career, Kubrick made a considerable effort to withdraw *Fear and Desire* from circulation. Although a new negative could be made from one of the archival prints currently in private circulation, copyright apparently remains with the Kubrick estate, and, as a consequence, it is unlikely that the film will be made available on any accessible format in the near future.

**EXPERT WITNESS:** 'Conditions were never easy. The crew consisted of four Mexicans who moved the equipment and did a little building; Steve Hahn, a friend of Stanley's who recorded the dialogue (no sync sound); Bob Dierkes, a former coworker with Kubrick at *Look* magazine who handled follow-focus on the Mitchell camera; Skippy Adelman, the stills photographer; and Toba Kubrick, who served as the script supervisor. There was no dolly track, just a baby carriage to move the camera. Stanley did all the shooting. No matter what the problem, Kubrick always seemed to have an answer. To me there was never a question that Stanley was already a master of his universe.' – the actor Paul Mazursky (Sidney), quoted in his autobiography, *Show Me the Magic*, 1999.

**FINAL ANALYSIS:** Today, it is almost impossible to view *Fear and Desire* without the benefit of knowledge that familiarity with its director's later work provides; if it were possible, it is more than likely that the film would be dismissed with barely a second thought, except perhaps for the exceptional photography. For, although the screenplay was written by a poet, the true poetry of *Fear and Desire* lies in Kubrick's camera work, a clear indicator of things to come.

As ever, Kubrick emphasises lighting and composition over performance and dialogue, and it is possible that the film would work as contemporary photomontage if viewed without the cumbersome, pretentious and unwisely allegorical blank-verse poetry that serves, rather inadequately, as a script. The incident with the (admittedly photogenic) young woman, while providing the catalyst for Sidney's descent into madness, feels like a tacked-on attempt to appeal to the sexploitation market, rather than a serious part of the storyline, and bodes ill for Kubrick's treatment of women in his future films.

Nevertheless, despite the sometimes abrasive quality of the post-synched dialogue lines, the overstylised editing and the overwrought manner in which the story unfolds, there are images in *Fear and Desire* that endure in the mind even as they resonate in the soul. Certain themes explored in the film were to prove worthy of re-examination by Kubrick, just as *Fear and Desire* would prove worthy of re-examination by Kubrick fans – if only a print were more readily available.

**KUBRICK ON KUBRICK:** 'The ideas we wanted to put across were good, but we didn't have the experience to embody them dramatically. It was little more than a 35mm version of what a class of film students would do in 16mm.' – quoted in *Stanley Kubrick Directs* by Alexander Walker, 1971.

# Killer's Kiss (1955)

**[B & W – 67 mins (release version), 80 mins ('complete' version)]**

Production Manager Ira Marvin
Camera Operators Jesse Paley and Max Glenn
Chief Electrician Dave Golden
Sound Recordists Walter Ruckersberg and Clifford van Praag
Assistant Editors Pat Jaffe and Anthony Bezich
Assistant Director Ernest Nukanen
Love Theme from the Song 'Once' by Norman Gimbel and Arden Clar
Ballet Sequence Danced by Ruth Subotka
Choreography by David Vaughan
Story by Stanley Kubrick
Music Composed and Conducted by Gerald Fried
Produced by Stanley Kubrick and Morris Bousel
Edited, Photographed and Directed by Stanley Kubrick

**CAST:** Frank Silvera (*Vincent 'Vinnie' Rapallo*), Jamie Smith (*Davey Gordon*), Irene Kane (*Gloria Price*), Ruth Subotka (*Iris Price*), Jerry Jarret (*Albert*), Skippy Adelman (*Owner of Mannequin Factory*), David Vaughan (*Conventioneer*), Alec Rubin (*Conventioneer*), Mike Dana, Felice Orlandi, Ralph Roberts, Phil Stevenson (*Hoodlums*), Barbara Brand, Arthur Feldman, Shaun O'Brien, Bill Funaro.

**UNCREDITED CREW:** Howard O Sackler (*Screenwriter*).

**TITLE SEQUENCE:** The sound of a puffing locomotive over black signals the start of the film, which fades up on to a shot of Davey Gordon standing in the centre of Penn Station, smoking a cigarette. With no music, only the sound of the train and the announcer as accompaniment, the titles appear in stark white letters over Davey, smoking and pacing nervously around his bags. As the opening titles conclude, Davey's voice-over begins: 'It's crazy how you can get yourself in a mess sometimes and not even be able to think about it with any sense – and yet not be able to think about anything else. You get so you're no good for any thing or any body. Maybe it begins by taking life too serious. Anyway, I think that's the way it began for me. Just before my fight with Rodriguez three days ago . . .'

**SUMMARY:** Davey Gordon, a welterweight prizefighter, stands at Penn Station, pondering the events of the past three days, beginning with his preparations for a bout with 'Kid' Rodriguez at the City Arena. From the window of his apartment, he sees a young woman, Gloria Price, in the apartment opposite, getting ready for a night out. They leave the building together, where Gloria is picked up by Vincent 'Vinnie' Rapallo, who runs the dance hall where she works as a 'taxi dancer'. Rapallo recognises Davey, and suggests that Gloria and he watch the fight later, on TV. On the subway on the way to the fight, Davey reads a letter from his Uncle George and Aunt Grace, inviting him to stay on their ranch, just outside Seattle.

The fight goes badly as Davey is knocked out. Gloria fares a little better, managing to fight off the unwelcome advances of the repugnant Rapallo. That night, Davey is awoken from a bad dream by Gloria's scream, and sees her being accosted by Rapallo. Racing to the rescue, he gives chase to Rapallo, who eludes him, and returns to comfort Gloria. The next morning, she tells him of her relationship with Rapallo, and of her dead sister, Iris, a ballet dancer who put aside her ambitions to nurse their sick father. Declaring his love for Gloria, Davey persuades her to come to Seattle with him, once they have both collected their money – she from Rapallo, he from his manager, Albert. While Davey waits outside the dance hall for Albert, Gloria goes inside to collect her pay from Rapallo, who threatens to kill her out of jealousy, before throwing her out. Outside, Davey runs after two drunken frat boys who steal his scarf, and is absent when Albert arrives, only to be mistaken for Davey and killed in a nearby alley by two of Rapallo's hoodlums.

Returning to the apartment building to pack, Davey finds Gloria gone, and watches as the police search his own apartment for him. Taking a gun, he follows and confronts Rapallo, demanding to be taken to Gloria. At the loft where she is being held, Davey is beaten up and, hearing Gloria declare her love for Rapallo in a bid to save her neck, breaks free and runs away. After a rooftop chase, he catches up with Rapallo in a mannequin factory, where a violent fight ends with Rapallo's death. Later, at the station, Davey reflects upon the events that followed, and assumes that he will never see Gloria again. Nevertheless, she arrives just in time to make the train to Seattle.

**SOURCE:** Kubrick had long admired hard-boiled crime writers such as Mickey Spillane, saying he 'knows all there is to know about reaching audiences', and Jim Thompson, author of *The Killer Inside Me* and *The Grifters* and, later, co-screenwriter of *The Killing* and *Paths of Glory*. He was less enamoured of the rash of urban crime thrillers made in the forties and early fifties (which the French christened *films noirs*), but he knew that the genre was popular and that a story about criminals was one that could easily be filmed in New York, and might easily be sold to a distributor.

Looking for a subject for his second feature, he explained to *Esquire* magazine that he made a list of all the action scenes he could conceivably film within a short distance from his apartment on 10th Street. Locations included a dance hall at the junction of 49th Street and Broadway, a boxing gym, the Greenwich Village Theater de Lys (now the Lucille Lortel Theater), a mannequin factory in the Garment District, and various other backstreet and rooftop locations where a film maker without a permit might work relatively undisturbed. Having compiled the list, he gave it to the *Fear and Desire* screenwriter Howard Sackler, who, in Kubrick's words, 'hacked out' a screenplay called *Kiss Me, Kill Me*, which allowed the director to revisit some of the settings of his earlier short subject, *Day of the Fight*, and ingeniously included scenes set in all of the locations listed by Kubrick. According to Kubrick, the script 'had some exciting action sequences in it, but the story was written in a week in order to take advantage of a possibility of getting some money'.

**WORKING TITLES:** Although Sackler's original screenplay was entitled *Kiss Me, Kill Me*, Kubrick would, at times, refer to the project as *The Nymph and the Maniac*. The punchier, but rather less poetic, *Killer's Kiss* was almost certainly Kubrick's idea.

**PRODUCTION HISTORY:** Armed with Sackler's screenplay, Kubrick persuaded a wealthy family friend, Morris 'Moe' Bousel, to invest $40,000 in the project, for which Bousel would receive a producer credit along with Kubrick. He also managed to borrow, with the promise of deferred payment, two cameras from a New York camera-hire company: a hand-held Eclair camera and a BMC Mitchell. Although Kubrick would often operate them himself, he employed two cameramen, Jesse Paley and Max Glenn, the latter working for the Titra Films subtitling company at the same building, 1600 Broadway, at which Kubrick's Minotaur Productions rented office space. Kubrick initially asked Glenn to shoot a single scene, but he remained with the production, and agreed to lend his apartment for the scene in which Rapallo and Gloria watch Gordon's boxing match on television.

Filming began in 1954, Kubrick working guerrilla-style, mostly without permits or the necessary permissions to film on the New York streets. 'A lot of cops came by and he was prepared for this,' his cameraman, Max Glenn, later recounted. 'He had a whole flock of twenty-dollar bills in his pocket and everybody came to be paid off.' Even when he did have the necessary paperwork, or monetary substitute, there were other frustrations, such as the truck driver who refused to move his vehicle until the actress Irene Kane agreed to meet him for a date, and the group of transients who resisted efforts to move them from their makeshift homes in the alleyways in which Kubrick wished to film.

Filming progressed for twelve to fourteen weeks, a lengthy schedule for a low-budget production being largely financed with deferred salary and rental payments. As Kubrick explained to Alexander Walker,

'Everything we did cost so little that there was no pressure on us – an advantage I was never to encounter again.' Unhurried by the usual time constraints, Kubrick established what would later become a career-long quest for spontaneous creativity by shooting a number of different dénouements for the story, allowing him maximum leeway in the editing room.

One incident involving apparent improvisation came during the filming of a scene in which Davey and Gloria make love after he rescues her from Rapallo. As Kane wrote to her sister, 'The other day I was playing a love scene [with Jamie Smith] when, in the middle of a kiss, he suddenly reached up and grabbed my left chest, very firmly, as the camera ground away. I leaped to my feet screaming and calling Jamie and Stanley bad names (they'd clearly set the whole thing up behind my back) and Stanley gave me the foreign markets lecture . . . "Bully for Europe," I said, "but I'm narrow-minded, and I want you to burn that film."'

Kubrick's background as a stills photographer and documentary film maker may have given him the technical expertise he needed to compose every visual aspect of each frame of film. However, Kubrick's relative inexperience with sound led him to a costly mistake – and an extraordinary, if unintentional, technical achievement. He had originally hired the sound recordist Nat Boxer, who was just beginning a brilliant career in motion-picture sound, which would lead to awards for his work as sound designer for Francis Ford Coppola's films *The Conversation* (1974) and *Apocalypse Now* (1979). Boxer told *Filmmakers Newsletter* in 1976 that the collaboration was a disaster from the very beginning.

'We were in some loft in New York's Greenwich Village, around Fourth Street, and he was lighting the back room for the first scene,' Boxer said, adding that the sound crew were left outside until Kubrick had finished setting up his lights. When they were finally allowed into the loft to place microphones among Kubrick's complex *mise en scène*, the placement of the equipment ruined his carefully composed shot. 'There must have been about seventeen shadows in the picture,' Boxer said. 'What do still photographers know about the problems of a movie?' Boxer and his crew were fired on the spot, and Kubrick resolved to record the production sound on his own Webcor – 'a little school audiovisual tape recorder', as Boxer described it – a decision that would prove disastrous in post-production.

With no synchronised sound effects and only the Webcor's poor-quality dialogue recording to act as a guide track, Kubrick was forced to re-record each and every line of dialogue, and post-synchronise the newly recorded lines to the actors' mouth movements. Despite the fact that filming had finished and they were unlikely to see any further money, all of the actors returned to 'post-synch' their dialogue, with one exception: after enduring some eight hours of 'torture . . . [watching] the screen and trying to fit words into your own mouth off a loop script over and over and over again until the mechanicalness of the process drove me mad', Irene Kane refused to spend any more time on the film, with the result that her throaty voice was redubbed by a radio actress, Peggy Lobbin. There was one advantage to these re-recording sessions, however: Kubrick was able to perfect Davey's voice-over narration, and Gloria's off-screen soliloquy, so that some – though not all – of the more confusing story elements were sewn together.

The absence of production sound also meant that the sound effects would have to be added at the post-production stage. Although this process, known as 'Foley editing', is common enough today, for Kubrick it would prove both costly and time-consuming. 'Money began to run out in the editing stage,' he recalled, 'and being unable to afford even an editing assistant, I had to spend four months just laying in the sound effects, footstep by footstep.' With all the elements of *Killer's Kiss* in place, Kubrick began shopping the completed film to prospective distributors, and eventually found a buyer in United Artists, at a price – $75,000 – that left him and his financiers with zero profit, but covered the entire production and post-production costs of the picture, including all of the deferred salaries.

James B Harris, Kubrick's future production partner, remembered how he learned that Kubrick had completed his second feature film. 'I was told that he had not only photographed the picture, and that he had written the script, and edited the film, but because of constraints in terms of money, he had to shoot the film completely silent with guide tracks and then "post synch" all the dialogue, which he did himself, and edited it all. Needless to say how impressed I was that one human being could do all of this and have the picture at least be what it was.'

**CASTING:** With budgetary restrictions requiring that the entire cast would be forced to defer their salaries, Kubrick could not be too choosy when it came to casting. Although Jamaican-born Frank Silvera – who had played General Huerta in Elia Kazan's *Viva Zapata!* (1952) since working with Kubrick on *Fear and Desire* – was cast as Vincent Rapallo, unknowns were cast in almost all of the other roles. Jamie Smith, whose unexpressive looks did nothing but accentuate his lack of acting ability, had appeared in only one previous film, *The Faithful City* (1952); no one else had any film experience at all.

The photographer Bert Stern introduced Kubrick to Irene Kane, a Greenwich Village model with aspirations as an actress but no actual experience. Kubrick coaxed her into accepting the mantle of leading lady by giving her a long and heartfelt speech about Gloria's motivation, and reading a speech from the screenplay in which she describes her background, and alludes to the incestuous relationship with her father, which has led her into the arms of the dance-hall boss Vincent Rapallo. Kane, understandably impressed, agreed to play Gloria for the sum of

$650 per week, which soon shrank to $65. 'Stanley's a fascinating character,' she later wrote. 'He thinks movies should move, with a minimum of dialogue, and he's all for sex and sadism. Talks about Mickey Spillane, and how the public eats it up. He's also totally sure of himself.' She added, 'Knows where he's going, how he's going to get there, and who's going to pick up the tab for the trip.' Although Kane rarely acted again after *Killer's Kiss* she later found fame, under the *nom de plume* Chris Chase, as a successful writer, columnist and biographer.

Kubrick's wife, Ruth Subotka, would appear in the nonspeaking role of Iris, Gloria's ballet-dancing sister, while two of Kubrick's and Subotka's friends, David Vaughan and Shaun O'Brien, would play small roles.

**THE USUAL SUSPECTS:** *Fear and Desire*'s Frank Silvera became the first actor to appear in more than one Kubrick film, with his casting as Vincent 'Vinnie' Rapallo in *Killer's Kiss*. It was a tradition that would continue throughout Kubrick's career, as actors such as Joseph Turkel (*The Killing, Paths of Glory, The Shining*), Timothy Carey (*The Killing, Paths of Glory*), Sterling Hayden (*The Killing, Dr Strangelove*), Kirk Douglas (*Paths of Glory, Spartacus*), Peter Sellers (*Lolita, Dr Strangelove*), Leonard Rossiter (*2001, Barry Lyndon*), Margaret Tyzack (*2001, A Clockwork Orange*), Vivian Kubrick (*2001, Full Metal Jacket*), Steven Berkoff (*A Clockwork Orange, Barry Lyndon*), Patrick Magee (*A Clockwork Orange, Barry Lyndon*), Philip Stone (*A Clockwork Orange, Barry Lyndon, The Shining*) and Leon Vitali (*Barry Lyndon, Eyes Wide Shut*) racked up multiple appearances in Kubrick's films.

**CLASSIC QUOTES**
Rapallo: 'If only you could know how low and worthless I feel.'
Gloria: 'I didn't even know you *had* any feelings.'

Davey: 'Something's happened.'
Gloria: 'Yes, I know.'
Davey: 'Do you know?'
Gloria: 'Sure. You kissed me.'
Davey: 'Is that all?'
Gloria: 'That's all I saw, and I was watching all the time.'

**THEMES AND MOTIFS:** Perhaps the most significant recurring motif in *Killer's Kiss* is that of mirrors – both figurative and literal. When Davey looks across to Gloria's apartment, and vice versa, each is effectively seeing their own reflection – both have been saddled with a joyless, lone existence in which they are forced to 'dance' for the pleasure of others, in order to make ends meet. Literal mirror images appear on several occasions throughout the film: Davey contemplates his own visage in one as he awaits the call to the ring, flattening his nose to see how it will look after it is broken; Rapallo, disgusted with his own image in the grinning figures reflected in the glass of a picture, throws a glass at it, shattering both.

One of the thematic oddities of *Killer's Kiss* is the way that the element of suspense is virtually removed by virtue of having the story told in flashback by Davey Gordon as he waits for Gloria at Penn Station. Since Davey is clearly alive and well in the opening (chronologically the end scenes), the threat of his encounters with Rapallo's gangsters, and later Rapallo himself, is removed. Suspense is therefore confined to the unlikely relationship that develops between Davey and Gloria, and the question of whether or not she will turn up to meet him at the station. '[*Killer's Kiss*] has a strange ending', *Full Metal Jacket* co-screenwriter Michael Herr later wrote in *Vanity Fair*, 'a painful travesty of a happy ending, where the couple go off together even though we've seen both of them cravenly betray and desert each other to save their own lives. It's the kind of touch that would come to be called "Kubrickian".'

**MUSIC:** For the third time, Kubrick asked the composer Gerald Fried, who had previously scored *Day of the Fight* and *Fear and Desire*, to create music for one of his films. Although there appears to be a great deal of music in the 67-minute film, two main themes recur. The first, the love theme used for romantic scenes, was drawn from the song 'Once' by Norman Gimbel and Arlen Clar, which Kubrick had heard and asked Fried to rearrange in numerous variations depending on the mood of the scene. (Kubrick would use a similar device twenty years later, as Leonard Rosenman arranged a particular classical piece in different ways for *Barry Lyndon*.) The other recurring theme was a Latin-jazz piece composed by Fried, and used over most of the action set pieces.

Percussion instruments, drums in particular, were a passion that Kubrick and Fried shared, and were used to great effect during the chase through the New York streets, culminating in the fight at the mannequin factory. 'Nothing is as exciting as a heartbeat,' Fried explained, 'and we had a lot of bass drum with a big beater with the mike close to the skin sounding like a heartbeat.'

**POSTER:** Consciously or otherwise, one poster layout for *Killer's Kiss* gave the impression of a window, suggesting the ones through which Davey and Gloria watch each other. It's divided into two sections, the left-hand portion featuring a yellow square with a red title, black credit block and tag-line, above a stylised still featuring Davey and Rapallo fighting in the mannequin factory, with the foreground figures picked out in red, and the background mannequins in blue. The right-hand frame, a single image divided in two by a horizontal black line, shows a dynamic clinch between Davey and Gloria, and is colorised in the tradition of the time.

**TAG-LINE:** 'EXPOSED!' screamed the tag-line for the poster image outlined above. 'The Mobs, Mafia and Mayhem of New York's Clip-Joint Jungle!' 'Her Soft Mouth Was the Road to Sin-Smeared Violence!' suggested another.

**TRAILER:** 'And out of the city's jungle night comes the clawing, burning impact of a killer's kiss,' the excitable narrator of the trailer intoned over title graphics, before a scream segues into shots of Davey boxing. 'It hits with the gutshot of a knockout punch,' the narrator continues, 'a picture as brazen as the naked bulbs of Broadway, and as hard as the New York streets where it was shot.' The scenes of Vinnie threatening to kill Gloria and Gloria later begging for her life are juxtaposed, before she is seen in a clinch with Davey. 'He was lost as soon as he looked at her, caught in a double-cross as dirty as the alley where they planned to end it.' Davey confronts and threatens Vinnie in the car, before inexplicably jumping through a window. 'All rules are off. All fouls are fair,' the voice-over continues, attempting to inject some boxing jargon into the proceedings as Vinnie and Davey fight it out in the mannequin factory, 'as man meets murder in the stabbing, slashing climax that's the payoff for a killer's kiss!'

**WHAT THE PAPERS SAID:** The critics were not kind to *Killer's Kiss*, with most dismissing it as melodramatic, unconvincing and rather badly acted. 'The film drowns its characters in the kind of strangeness which is liable to irritate the average audience and lead more sophisticated patrons to laugh in the wrong spots,' noted *Film Daily*. 'Kubrick's low-key lensing occasionally catches the flavor of the seamy side of Gotham life,' allowed *Variety*. 'His scenes of tawdry Broadway, gloomy tenements and grotesque brick-and-stone structures that make up Manhattan's downtown East Side loft district help offset the script's deficiencies.' Even United Artists' notes for the entry in its own 16mm Film Library Catalogue, circa 1970, damned it with faint praise: 'It is always instructive to view the early works of a director who, in later years, goes on to bigger and better things.'

Although *Killer's Kiss* was, for Gavin Lambert of Britain's *Sight and Sound*, 'a melodrama too full of familiar and not always skilled contrivances', he further noted that it had 'a simplicity of outline, an atmospheric power, a directness in its characterisation, that suggests a maturing and distinctive personality'. *Time Out*'s critic, Geoff Andrew, offered a more positive retrospective view of the film, calling it 'a moody but rather over-arty B thriller whose prime pleasures lie in the high contrast black-and-white camerawork . . . Kubrick makes the most of flashback and dream sequences, and a surreal climactic fight in a warehouse full of mannequins . . . the brief running time ensures that the film's more pretentious moments tend to flash past'.

**TECHNICAL ACHIEVEMENTS:** One of the most remarkable shots in *Killer's Kiss* is a brief but effective dream sequence, presented as negative so that the whites become blacks and vice versa, in which Davey hears the derisory cries of the boxing crowds – 'Go on home, Gordon! You're a bum! Why don't you go on home? You're all through!' – while imagining himself driving along a New York alleyway. The shot – filmed by Kubrick himself, using a hand-held BMC Mitchell camera, from the open top of a car – is often compared to the Star Gate sequence in *2001: A Space Odyssey*, which it closely resembles.

**INFLUENCED BY:** *Killer's Kiss* was a combination of Kubrick's earlier short subject *Day of the Fight*, and a hard-boiled story influenced by the likes of Mickey Spillane and Jim Thompson. *Full Metal Jacket*'s co-screenwriter, Michael Herr, later noted that, with all of the difficulties Kubrick faced in producing a feature-length film within such a minuscule budget, he still managed to acknowledge his many influences. 'He made [*Killer's Kiss*] under severe limitations, which he addressed like a soldier, and not a boy soldier either, making virtues out of limitations, so that even though it's only 67 minutes long it's not really a small movie,' Herr observed. 'You can see in ten seconds how infatuated he was with the medium, and how incredibly adept, every scene packed with ideas, ambition, with tribute, homage, even the odd tributary theft (what he started calling "souveniring" later, when he began picking up on the Vietnam grunt vernacular), mostly from the Europeans who had given him so much pleasure and inspiration: Fritz Lang, GW Pabst, Vsevelod Pudovkin, Jean Renoir, Vittorio De Sica, and, always, Max Ophuls, with that fluent, rapturous, delirious camera of his.'

Although the idea for the fight in the mannequin factory was borrowed from Vincente Minelli's Fred Astaire vehicle *The Band Wagon* (1953), Kubrick's impressive staging and dynamic direction arguably lifted the scene above its inspiration.

**DÉJÀ VU:** Understandably, there are many obvious parallels between Kubrick's photo stories on the prizefighters Rocky Graziano and Walter Cartier for *Look* magazine, and his early short subject *Day of the Fight*. The most obvious points of comparison are the shots of the fighters contemplating their own faces in mirrors, and – most strikingly – shots of a poster, advertising the upcoming boxing match, hanging loosely from a lamppost.

**INFLUENTIAL ON:** There can be little doubt that the virtuoso boxing sequences that Kubrick filmed for *Killer's Kiss* were influential on subsequent black-and-white films dealing with the sport, beginning with Mark Robson's *The Harder They Fall* (1956), and continuing through Robert Wise's *The Set-Up* (1946), Robert Rossen's *Body & Soul* (1947) to Martin Scorsese's *Raging Bull* (1980). 'I wanted to do the fight scenes as if the viewers were the fighter,' Scorsese explained, 'and their impressions were the fighter's – of what he would think or feel, or what he would hear . . . And again, the very, very important thing about the fight scenes in the movie was that you never see the audience,' he added, echoing a similar decision made by Kubrick.

A no less obvious influence is that of Gerald Fried's suitably sleazy main theme for *Killer's Kiss* on the music that the *Spartacus* composer Alex North wrote for John Huston's *The Misfits* (1961), which – intentionally or otherwise – reproduces Fried's music almost note for note.

**SEQUELS AND REMAKES:** While *Killer's Kiss* might seem to be one of the least suitable subjects for a remake, in 1983 the independent US director Matthew Chapman made an intriguing and highly innovative film entitled *Strangers Kiss*, which contains elements of a fictionalised account of the making of *Killer's Kiss*. Co-written by Chapman and its co-star Blaine Novak, *Strangers Kiss* is set in Hollywood in the year 1955, and tells the story of a tyro director, Stanley (Peter Coyote), and producer, Sidney Farris (Dan Shor), who are struggling to shoot an independent B-movie about a young prizefighter's efforts to save a dime-a-dance girl from her villainous protector. When Stevie Blake (Novak), the would-be actor playing the boxer, starts falling in love with Carol Redding (Victoria Tennant), the girl playing the taxi dancer, Stanley gently encourages the pair in order to bring emotional verisimilitude – or 'heat', as he puts it – to the film. Carol's boyfriend, Frank Silva (Richard Romanus), is a small-time gangster who has put up the money for the film as a favour to Carol, and his suspicions that she and Stevie are having an affair threatens the entire enterprise – if not the lives of the film makers themselves . . .

Filmed in a combination of colour (for the 'real' scenes) and harsh black and white (for the film-within-a-film), *Strangers Kiss* was well received by most critics: the *Los Angeles Times* called it 'a real discovery, special and memorable . . . an enraptured vision of moviemaking', while *Time Out*'s Tom Milne described it as 'a critical extension of Kubrick's film, as a comment on movie-making mania, and as a dark thriller in its own right'. As much a curiosity as *Killer's Kiss* itself, *Strangers Kiss* is well worth seeking out.

**CUT SCENES:** Despite the fact that Kubrick had no official permission to film on the streets of New York, he braved the police at the intersection of Fifth Avenue and 42nd Street to film part of a bizarre dream sequence, in which Davey imagines himself crossing the busy street wearing boxing shorts and gloves. According to legend, Kubrick cut the scene because the midday crowds had failed to react appropriately to the sight of a boxer in full fight regalia walking the streets of New York in the middle of the day.

**TRIVIA:** According to the poster announcing the Gordon-v.-Rodriguez match-up, the film takes place between 25 and 28 October.

Jamie Smith and Irene Kane subsequently appeared in different episodes of the same television series, *The Naked City*.

Most sources, including both the LoBrutto and Baxter biographies of Kubrick and the liner notes for the VHS and DVD releases, misspell Davey Gordon's first name as 'Davy' – despite the fact that the correct spelling of his name appears on numerous fight posters throughout the beginning of the film.

**APOCRYPHA:** Much has been made over the years of Kubrick's supposed unwillingness to give screen credit where it is due. It is an odd accusation to level at a director who would often credit the entire cast, rather than merely the principal players, at the beginning of the film, an unfashionable tradition nowadays that Kubrick nevertheless upheld with his last two films, *Full Metal Jacket* and *Eyes Wide Shut*. The absence of a credit for *Killer's Kiss*'s screenwriter, Howard O Sackler (*Fear and Desire*), has often been attributed to the same apparent reluctance to give full credit to screenwriters that dogged Kubrick from *The Killing* to *Full Metal Jacket*. In the case of *Killer's Kiss*, however, it is quite likely that Sackler himself asked for his name to be taken off the credits, given that a pulpy potboiler might not look good on the resumé of a poet and playwright with a growing reputation. This may explain the fact that the film fails to credit anyone for the screenplay, with Kubrick receiving only a 'Story by' credit.

**AVAILABILITY:** Although *Killer's Kiss* is not currently available in the United Kingdom in any format, in the United States it is available as an NTSC-format VHS video (MGM 207700), and as a Region 1 DVD (907707), the latter featuring a textless theatrical trailer, and two pages of production notes. Both formats feature full-screen (4:3) transfers. An NTSC laserdisc (ML 102875) is also available, featuring full-screen (4:3) transfers of *Killer's Kiss* and *The Killing* spread across three discs.

**EXPERT WITNESS:** 'The picture was made for an astonishingly small amount of money, and it was done with every bit of the fastidiousness and care of everything else he's ever done. This is a perfectionist, an absolute perfectionist. I tried to put the same rules into force in my own career, and it cost me a lot before I could shake it. Because unless you have the freedom to exercise it, very few people survive it. It's an obsessive thing, and has nothing to do with commerce.' – Alexander Singer, Kubrick's friend and collaborator, quoted in *Stanley Kubrick: A Biography*, by John Baxter.

**FINAL ANALYSIS:** As with *Fear and Desire*, it is difficult to look at *Killer's Kiss* from this perspective without bringing all of the baggage that comes with knowing that it is one of the earliest efforts from a formidable future film maker. It is debatable whether the film should be seen in isolation, on its own merits, as an audience would see it; or in context, as Kubrick's second feature film, as those aware of its heritage would see it.

Taken as a Kubrick film, *Killer's Kiss* provides remarkable foreshadowing of the themes and elements of several future Kubrick productions: the characters locked into lives in which they are forced to act a certain way against their wills, lives from which they can only dream of escaping; betrayal; crime; voice-over; narrative and chronological trickery. Taken on its own terms, *Killer's Kiss* is a reasonably effective slice of noir film making, impressive with regard to *mise en scène* and atmosphere, but somewhat lacking when it comes to individual performances: as usual, it might be argued, Kubrick cared less about the characters than about the events that befall them. Despite the actors' shortcomings, however, Jamie Smith (Davey) and Irene Kane (Gloria) are sympathetic enough to hold the interest for the relatively minimal running time, and Frank Silvera (Rapallo) is a memorable enough villain – even if his speech patterns in certain scenes cannot help but recall John Glover's *faux* fifties character Miles Cholmondley-Warner.

*Killer's Kiss* was no mean achievement for Kubrick, and its obvious inadequacies should not deny its importance either as a lesser-known film noir with as many innovations as it has conventions, or as a key milestone on the road to Kubrick's development as a film maker.

**KUBRICK ON KUBRICK:** '[*Killer's Kiss*] proved, I think, to be a frivolous effort done with conceivably more expertise [than *Fear and Desire*], though still down in the student level of filmmaking . . . The only distinction I would claim for it is that, to the best of my belief, no-one at the time had ever made a feature film in such amateur circumstances and then obtained worldwide distribution for it.' – quoted in *Stanley Kubrick Directs*, by Alexander Walker, 1971.

# The Killing (1956)

**(B & W – 84 mins)**

**Associate Producer Alexander Singer**
**Camera Operator Dick Tower**
**Gaffer Bobby Jones**
**Script Supervisor Mary Gibsone**
**Sound Earl Snyder**
**Best Boy Lou Cortese**
**2nd Assistant Cameraman Robert Hosler**
**Construction Supervisor Bud Pine**

Chief Carpenter Christopher Ebsen
Chief Painter Robert L Stephen
Make-up Robert Littlefield
Wardrobe Jack Masters
Special Effects Dave Koehler
Set Decorator Harry Reif
Assistant Set Decorator Carl Brainard
Music Editor Gilbert Marchant
Sound Effects Editor Rex Lipton, MPSE
Assistant Director Milton Carter
2nd Assistant Directors Paul Feiner, Howard Joslin
Production Assistant Marguerite Olson
Prop man Ray Zambel
Transportation Dave Lesser
Women's Wardrobe Rudy Harrington
Hairdresser Lillian Shore
Process Cameraman Paul Eagler
Director's Assistant Joyce Hartman
Miss Windsor's Costumes by Beaumelle
Photographic Effects Jack Rabin/Louis DeWitt
Director of Photography Lucien Ballard, ASC
Art Director Ruth Subotka
Film Editor Betty Steinberg
Music Composed and Conducted by Gerald Fried
Screenplay by Stanley Kubrick
Dialogue by Jim Thompson
Based on the novel *Clean Break* by Lionel White
Produced by James B Harris
Directed by Stanley Kubrick

**CAST:** Sterling Hayden (*Johnny Clay*), Coleen Gray (*Fay*), Vince Edwards (*Val Cannon*), Jay C Flippen (*Marvin Ungar*), Ted De Corsia (*Patrolman First Class Randy Kennan*), Marie Windsor (*Sherry Peatty*), Elisha Cook (*George Peatty*), Joe Sawyer (*Mike O'Reilly*), James Edwards (*Car Park Attendant*), Timothy Carey (*Nikki Arane*), Kola Kwariani (*Maurice Oboukhoff*), Jay Adler (*Leo*), Tito Vuolo (*Joe Piano*), Dorothy Adams (*Ruth O'Reilly*), Herbert Ellis, James Griffith (*Mr Grimes*), Cecil Elliott, Joseph Turkel (*Tiny*), Steve Mitchell, Mary Carroll, William Benedict, Charles R Cane (*Airport Policeman*), Robert B Williams (*Airport Policeman*).

**UNCREDITED CAST:** Frank Richards, Dick Reeves (*Racetrack Employees*).

**UNCREDITED CREW:** Clarence Eurist (*Production Supervisor*), Bessie Epstein (*Production Comptroller*), Joseph Keener (*Sound Recordist*).

**TITLE SEQUENCE:** Gerald Fried's dramatic and upbeat original score plays as the opening titles appear in white text over various documentary-style scenes of the Golden Gate horse-racing track at Bay Meadows, San Francisco. The horses for the seventh race, around which the plot is structured, are seen entering the starting gate, before the bell rings and the traditional commentator's announcement 'They're off!' signals the end of the opening credits.

**SUMMARY:** An ex-convict named Johnny Clay is meticulously planning to rob a racetrack of around $2 million in cash, aided and abetted by a few key individuals: George Peatty, a racetrack cashier who hopes that his new-found fortune will improve relations with his mean-spirited, sluttish wife, Sherry; Randy Kennan, a crooked cop with gambling debts, who will be on duty at the racetrack on the day of the robbery; Mike O'Reilly, a racetrack bartender who needs money to pay for his sick wife's health care; Nikki Arane, a crack shot who will create a major diversion by shooting the winning racehorse, Red Lightning, during the seventh race; and Maurice Oboukhoff, a wrestler and chess hustler who will create a minor diversion by picking a fight in the racetrack bar. In the chaos sparked by Nikki's shooting of the horse, and the distraction of the police caused by Maurice's fisticuffs, George will let Johnny inside the cashier's office, whereupon he will hold up the money room and escape with the cash in a sack.

The plan begins to come unstuck when Sherry Peatty and her lover, Val Cannon, decide to steal the bounty from George and the other thieves after the robbery. Although Nikki is shot dead by a security guard after shooting the racehorse, the overall execution of the heist goes smoothly, until Val and a friend burst in to the motel room where Randy, George, Mike and Maurice await the arrival of Johnny and the money. A gunfight ensues, during which everyone is killed except George, who leaves the motel badly wounded. Johnny sees George, and assumes the worst. After transferring the money to a suitcase, he heads for the airport, where he meets his girlfriend, Fay, as arranged. George, meanwhile, makes it home, where he finds Sherry packing – obviously for her intended rendezvous with Val – and shoots her dead, before finally succumbing to his own wounds. At the airport, Johnny is forced to check in his suitcase, and, when the baggage truck carrying it to the plane swerves to avoid a small dog, the case bursts open and the money flutters away. Two policemen spot Johnny, who makes no move to escape.

**SOURCE:** *Clean Break* was the first novel by Lionel White, who had gravitated to the long-form narrative at the age of fifty, following a long career writing and editing true-crime magazines such as *Underworld Detective*, *Detective World* and *Homicide Detective*. *Clean Break* was a crime story involving the robbery of a racetrack, told in a nonlinear format filled with flashbacks and meticulous detail. Its style and characters were clearly influenced – perhaps a little too much – by WR Burnett's novel *The Asphalt Jungle*, filmed by John Huston in 1950, but the book was well enough received upon its initial publication in 1955.

A would-be producer, James B Harris, found the book in the mystery section of Scribner's book store on New York's Fifth Avenue. 'I looked at the dust cover – "Gee, the robbery of a racetrack – it sounds exciting!" ' he recalled later. Harris read the book in one sitting, realised that the meticulously plotted and radically formatted crime caper would provide the perfect source for Harris-Kubrick's inaugural production. 'I called Stanley and said, "I think I found something that would make a helluva movie." Kubrick read the book in a matter of hours and said, "It's terrific, let's see if we can't get the rights to this thing." '

**WORKING TITLES:** Kubrick evidently felt that the title of White's novel, *Clean Break*, was not sufficiently commercial, and although several viable alternatives were put forward during filming – among them *Bed of Fear* and *Day of Violence* – Kubrick finally decided upon the double entendre suggested by *The Killing*.

**PRODUCTION HISTORY:** 'Kubrick invited me to a screening of his new film, *Killer's Kiss*, and also asked my help in trying to sell *Killer's Kiss* to TV,' the film producer James B Harris said of his first encounter with the director whose next four feature films he would produce. 'We began to talk together.' Having formed an incorporated partnership, Harris-Kubrick Pictures, the pair were looking for a project of their own to develop as their first feature-film collaboration when Harris came across *Clean Break*.

Making enquiries after the availability of the screen rights, however, Harris was surprised and dismayed to find that they were on the verge of being sold to Frank Sinatra, who was dithering over a planned film version as a follow-up to *Suddenly* (1954), his most recent film for United Artists. 'I said, "Well, has the deal been made?" ' Harris recalled. 'They said, "No, not yet, and he's taking his time about it and it bothers us a little bit." I said, "What makes the deal right now?" He says, "If you send me a telegram with a firm offer for ten thousand dollars for the rights to the book, it's yours." So I said, "You got it!" I knew Stanley wanted to do it. I loved it. What was there to think about?' Having secured the rights for Harris-Kubrick, paying the price out of his own money, Harris found that, although United Artists was interested in the project, the studio had intended to finance Sinatra's version, and would not risk the necessary finance without the promise of a star of similar stature.

Nevertheless, Kubrick and Harris now owned the rights to the book, and they immediately began the process of turning it into a script that they hoped would change United Artists' mind – or interest a rival studio. Having previously considered the hard-boiled, hard-drinking crime novelist Jim Thompson's *The Killer Inside Me* as possible source material for a feature film, Kubrick suggested Thompson – whose alcoholism and ill health made him an unreliable employee, but whose crime novels, such as *The Grifters* and *After Dark, My Sweet*, continue to provide exceptional source material for films – as screenwriter for *Clean Break*. 'Stanley was responsible for outlining what the scenes in the picture were going to be,' Harris recounted, 'and Jim was then going to write the dialogue.' Thompson moved into a hotel in midtown Manhattan to begin writing, and had soon elicited $1,000 in advances from Harris-Kubrick, part of which covered a 76-page novella, *Lunatic at Large*, which Thompson wrote for the partnership in the hope that they might film it.

'Thompson, the toughest pulp novelist of them all, had made him nervous when they were working together on *The Killing*,' *Full Metal Jacket*'s co-screenwriter Michael Herr wrote later, 'a big guy in a dirty old raincoat, a terrific writer but a little too hard-boiled for Stanley's taste. He'd turn up for work carrying a bottle in a brown paper bag, but saying nothing about it – it was just there on the desk with no apology or comment – not at all interested in putting Stanley at ease except to offer him the bag, which Stanley declined, and making no gestures whatever to any part of the Hollywood process, except maybe toward the money.'

When Thompson, a first-time screenwriter, finally completed the script, temporarily retitled *Day of Violence*, it was presented in a format that betrayed Kubrick's and Harris's amateur status: approximately three hundred legal-size pages in length, it was typed in landscape format, so that the text ran along the full length of the page. Copies were sent to everyone Kubrick and Harris could think of, and, when Sterling Hayden signed on to play the principal role of Johnny Clay, they were thrilled, and immediately broke the news to United Artists. The studio remained unconvinced, a reflection of Hayden's status in Hollywood after he agreed to 'name names' while under investigation by the anti-Communist House Un-American Activities Committee (HUAC) in 1951. Although they agreed to finance *Day of Violence* up to a cost of $200,000, any overages would be payable by Harris-Kubrick.

Unable to find a racetrack on the east coast that would allow them to film a heist movie on the premises, Kubrick and Harris moved to California, renting office space in Charlie Chaplin's Kling Studios, at the corner of Sunset Boulevard and La Brea. Already feeling dislocated due to enforced relocation from their beloved New York, the pair were shocked to be told that *Bed of Fear*, as their film was now called, would cost $330,000 to make, even with a production schedule as short as 24 days. With United Artists' contribution capped at $200,000, Harris was forced to invest $80,000 of his own savings, as well as a $50,000 loan from his father.

It cannot have helped that Lucien Ballard, a twenty-year veteran cinematographer who would later achieve acclaim for his work with the director Sam Peckinpah, was sent to capture documentary-style footage of a racetrack for use under the opening titles, but returned with nothing usable. 'Ballard was a splendid cameraman,' Kubrick's friend and collaborator Alexander Singer recalled, 'but he couldn't do documentary work to save his life.' Singer – who had initially introduced Kubrick and Harris, and received an associate producer credit on *The Killing* for his trouble – headed back to San Francisco's Golden Gate racetrack with a clockwork, fixed-lens Eyemo camera and the same brief given Ballard – but produced far superior results. As a result, Kubrick interspersed the footage, originally intended to cover the title sequence, throughout the film, using shots of the race to signal the flashbacks and leaps forward in time. Ballard, whom Kubrick had been forced to hire owing to cameraman's union regulations, was not informed.

Principal photography began late in 1955, with even the most experienced members of the cast and crew impressed by Kubrick's ability, if not his personality. 'I kept waiting for him to direct and nothing happened,' Coleen Gray, who played Fay, recounted. ' "When's he going to tell me what to do?" He never did, which made me insecure. He seemed extremely preoccupied. Maybe the fact that I felt insecure was fine for the part – that girl [Fay] was insecure.' Marie Windsor, playing Sherry, agreed with Gray's assessment. 'Stanley was an introverted person. He was very quiet and while on the set I never heard him yell at the crew or anybody. When he had some idea for me to do or change, he would wiggle his finger and we would go away from the action and he would tell me what he wanted or didn't want. One time when I was sitting on the bed reading a magazine, he came up and said, "I want you to move your eyes when you're reading." He was only in his twenties, but you just had a sense of his having pure confidence in himself.'

Sterling Hayden admired Kubrick's meticulous methodology, which allowed the film to be shot with almost no wastage, and very little room for editing. However, Hayden was less enthusiastic when his agent, Bill Schifrin, expressed concern that Kubrick's cut-up format – despite having been evident in the script that Schifrin recommended to his client – made a nonsense of Hayden's performance. Afraid that a lawsuit might add to their financial woes, Kubrick and Harris returned to the editing suite to see if the film could be recut in a linear format. 'People begged us to make a straight-line story,' Harris recollected, 'but we had enough sense to realise this structure was the most interesting thing about the story.'

United Artists did little to promote *The Killing*, prompting Kubrick and Harris to take matters into their own hands. Since they did not have the means to publicise the film to cinemagoers, they chose to run a series of trade advertisements in such industry magazines as *Variety* and the *Hollywood Reporter*. 'The new UA team James B Harris, Stanley Kubrick, the new suspense film of the year – all through United Artists,' ran the copy, emblazoned across a posed photograph – taken by Kubrick on a timed exposure – of Harris and Kubrick in directors' chairs, posing next to a pile of film cans, presumably containing *The Killing*. The ads, paid for out of Harris-Kubrick funds, infuriated United Artists.

**CASTING:** The script for *The Killing* was sent to a great many Hollywood leading men of the fifties, including Victor Mature, Jack Palance and Sterling Hayden, the last of these a favourite of Kubrick's, owing to his starring role in *The Asphalt Jungle* (1950), a film noir with obvious influences on *The Killing*. Mature, United Artists' preferred star, was not available for eighteen months, and Palance – to whom Harris delivered the script personally, while the actor was doing theatre in Connecticut – gave the script a frosty reception. Hayden was more receptive to the script – possibly because his agent thought that the director was Stanley *Kramer* (*The Wild One*) – and signed on to play Johnny Clay for a $40,000 fee.

Elisha Cook Jr, best known for his supporting roles in *The Maltese Falcon* (1941) and *The Big Sleep* (1946), was cast as George Peatty, the sad-faced cuckold whose wife's loose morals, coupled with his own loose lips, ultimately sink the heist. The veteran actor Jay C Flippen (*The Flying Leathernecks*, *The Wild One*) brought a different kind of vulnerability to the role of Marvin Ungar, whose fondness for Johnny Clay borders on the homoerotic. Other roles were filled by various B-movie actors with familiar faces but largely unknown names – Joe Sawyer (*The Roaring Twenties*), Ted De Corsia (*The Naked City*), Coleen Gray (*Kiss of Death*), Marie Windsor (*The Narrow Margin*), Vince Edwards (*Hit and Run*), Timothy Carey (*East of Eden*) – with the exception of Maurice, the chess-playing wrestler, who was played by one of Kubrick's former chess buddies, Kola Kwariani. Maurice's background was fleshed out to include references to Kubrick's own chess-playing days, as evidenced by the scene set at the Academy of Chess and Checkers – closely modelled on the Greenwich Village-based Flea House at which Kubrick and Kwariani used to play.

**THE USUAL SUSPECTS:** Kubrick's second wife, the ballet dancer Ruth Subotka, had pirouetted her way into his second feature, *Killer's Kiss*. For *The Killing*, he enlisted her help as production designer, partly to save money and partly to satisfy her desire to participate in the creative process of film making. 'Ruth Subotka was a very fine artist,' the actress Marie Windsor recollected. 'Stanley had her do all these wonderful charcoal drawings of every single scene he wanted to shoot, and they were all around his office on the walls in sequence.'

**CLASSIC QUOTES**
**Johnny:** 'Any time you take a chance you better be sure the rewards are worth the risk, because they can put you away just as fast for a ten-dollar heist as they can for a million-dollar job.'

Val: 'So I slip out once in a while. Look, you got yourself a husband, a guy who'll spend every last nickel on you. Won't ask you any questions when you come home from an afternoon movie at *nine at night*. Don't be greedy.'

Sherry: 'I'm not greedy, Val. I'm in love with you, and if that makes me greedy then I'm the biggest glutton who ever walked the earth.'

Maurice: 'I often thought that the gangster and the artist are the same in the eyes of the masses. They are admired and hero-worshipped, but there is always present an underlying wish to see them destroyed at the peak of their glory.'

**THEMES AND MOTIFS:** Bars – the kind found on prison windows – are an ever-present leitmotif in *The Killing*, heightening the pervading air of criminals and crime, and of one of the possible fates that await the protagonists if their robbery goes wrong.

- George, the track cashier who is in on the heist, is seen behind the bars of his booth as Marvin gives him the rendezvous address;
- shadows resembling prison bars fill the walls of Johnny's apartment;
- the Peattys' parrot is behind the more literal bars of a cage;
- as Johnny interrogates George about Sherry's snooping, the scene is shot from behind the railings of an iron bed;
- Johnny is seen behind the same iron bars as he interrogates Sherry;
- the reflection on the wall of George and Sherry's apartment window resembles a prison window;
- Marvin is seen against the vertical bars of his bed's headboard when Johnny visits him early on the morning of the robbery;
- the way the net curtains hang in Mike's apartment resemble bars;
- the separate arrivals of Mike and Randy at the track are seen from behind the bars of the track cop's booth;
- Randy, the police patrolman with a gambling problem, looks up at the prison-like façade of the racetrack building as he awaits the drop of the money sack;
- at the cashier's window, George Peatty appears behind bars once again as he watches Maurice fight the track cops;
- the shadows of bars appear on the door as George looks around after the gun battle that follows Val and Tiny's arrival;
- shadows of the bars of the parrot's cage are reflected on George's face as he confronts and shoots Sherry, and as he lies dead after doing so;
- Johnny and Fay stand behind chicken wire as they watch their fortune spill across the runway from Johnny's open suitcase.

Another major theme of the film is the tricks that luck and/or fate can play on any human endeavour, no matter how meticulously planned it may be. The theme is made explicit by two subtle examples of foreshadowing in the opening few minutes: the used betting slips littering the floor of the track, foreshadowing the money scattered across the runway at the film's close; and Randy's encounter with Tiny, one of the two men who will later burst in to try to steal the proceeds from the robbery, at the club where Randy meets Leo. The following are the points at which Johnny and the gang's best-laid schemes go awry:

- one of Mike's fellow track employees offers to put his flowers in water for him, not realising that the flower box contains a gun;
- Randy is almost late for his rendezvous at the racetrack when a woman tries to stop his police patrol car in order to ask him to break up a fight;
- the initial reluctance of the parking attendant to allow Nikki's car inside, followed by his overfriendliness, theatens to scupper the shooting of the racehorse;
- Nikki's refusal of the horseshoe offered by the parking attendant leads to his car tyre blow-out, an accident of fate that – since he is thus unable to escape from the parking attendant's bullet – indirectly causes Nikki's death;
- Johnny carelessly attempts to unlock the wrong motel room door;
- heavy traffic around the racetrack makes Johnny late for his rendezvous with the other gang members;
- the lock on the second-hand suitcase Johnny buys is broken, a fact that precipitates the loss of the money;
- the suitcase is too large to be taken on board the aircraft as hand luggage, causing it to be loaded aboard the baggage truck;
- an elderly woman's dog runs on to the runway, causing the baggage cart to swerve, and the case filled with money to fall open, spilling the contents to the four winds;
- Fay is unable to hail a taxi so that she and Johnny can make their escape.

The theme of human endeavour being thwarted by a fatal twist of fate, or simple human error, was one that would recur in many subsequent Kubrick films.

MUSIC: Gerald Fried's original music for *The Killing* was his third collaboration with Kubrick, and his score was undoubtedly his best work to date. 'I wanted to give it size,' Fried enthused. 'It wasn't just the story of a racetrack robbery, it was the story of the quality of life. At the end Sterling Hayden's girlfriend says to him that he has a chance to run, and he says, "What's the difference?" This was a large statement, which Stanley makes continually. So I wanted it to sound large – and brass, to me, was exciting. Our aesthetic was the forward thrust.' The score was recorded by Vint Vernon, whom Fried described as 'probably the best music recorder in history', and performed by an orchestra of forty musicians, among them the pianist André Previn.

A re-recorded version of the stirring main title and robbery theme from *The Killing*, running 4m 51s, is included on Silva Screen Records' *Strangelove: Music from the Films of Stanley Kubrick* (FILMCD 303).

POSTER: The portrait-format, 'one-sheet' poster produced for the United States carried several dramatic images – including a shot of Sterling Hayden holding a smoking pistol, not from the film – colour-stylised against a yellow background. Two landscape-format 'quad' posters were also produced. The first was a colorised image of the dead bodies arranged around the sofa after the gun battle between the gang members, Val and Tiny, with the addition of a dead George (who, in the film, dies later from wounds received during the shoot-out) in the foreground. The second design featured colorised portraits of Sherry Peatty and the five gang members, each with a descriptive box briefly outlining their characters. Clockwise from left, these read as follows: 'JOE SAWYER as The race track bartender with an ailing wife', 'MARIE WINDSOR as The two-timing dame who couldn't keep her mouth shut', 'J.C. FLIPPEN as The reformed alcoholic', 'STERLING HAYDEN as The brains of the mob', 'ELISHA COOK as The little man with big ideas', and 'TED DE CORSIA as The racketeering racetrack cop'.

One of the most dramatic poster images for *The Killing* appeared in France, where the film was retitled *L'Ultime Razzia* – an equally effective double entendre, which could mean either *The Ultimate Heist* or *The Last Heist*. The blood-red background of the veteran poster artist Roger Soubie's striking illustration was dominated by a large clockface with the hands set at twenty minutes to one, while Marie Windsor is draped against it in a fetching negligée. In the foreground, bathed in yellow light, Sterling Hayden and his fellow robbers conspire together, two sophisticated guns placed on the table between them.

TAG-LINE: 'In All Its Fury and Violence . . . Like No Other Picture Since "SCARFACE" and "LITTLE CAESAR"!' read the tag-line for the US one-sheet poster. On the first of the two landscape-format posters was an elaborate synopsis: '$2,000,000 Pay-Off? Blood spattered apartment and four dead bodies greeted the police of the 47th Precinct last night. Mass murder took place at 21 Walker Drive and is believed to be tied in with THE KILLING!' The following copy appeared on the second of the two 'quad' designs: 'These 5 Men Had a $2,000,000 Secret Until One of them told this Woman!' and 'See them all in all their fury in "THE KILLING".'

TRAILER: The title fills the screen, almost blocking out a shot of Nikki Arane shooting at a target with a rifle, before cutting to Johnny Clay explaining the details of the robbery, and footage of the heist itself. White, headline-style captions are superimposed over racetrack footage: 'POLICE BAFFLED BY FANTASTIC CRIME!' followed by 'MASKED BANDIT ESCAPES WITH RACE TRACK LOOT!' The title appears again over Nikki Arane being shot, before captions for the principal cast members – Sterling Hayden, Coleen Gray, Marie Windsor, Elisha Cook, Vince Edwards – wipe on stylishly over key dialogue lines from each of them. Finally, superimposed over the shoot-out between Val, Tiny and the others, three further captions appear at jaunty angles – 'SUSPENSE!' 'TERROR!' 'VIOLENCE!' – followed by an unattributed recommendation: 'Will Grip You As No Other Picture Since "Scarface" and "Little Caesar"!' A new title graphic appears over a shot of George looking at the dead gang members, accompanied by three credits: 'PRODUCED BY ... JAMES B. HARRIS', 'DIRECTED BY ... STANLEY KUBRICK' and 'RELEASED THROUGH UNITED ARTISTS'.

**WHAT THE PAPERS SAID:** Although *The Killing*'s minimalist distribution pattern meant that the film was not widely reviewed, it was generally well received by those critics who covered it. The New York *Herald Tribune* called it 'an excellent portrait of a crime, unusually taut, keenly directed and acted, with a sharp, leanly written script', while the *New York Times* critic commented that, although *The Killing* was composed of familiar ingredients, 'it evolves as a fairly diverting melodrama'. *Time* magazine, reviewing *The Killing* on 4 June 1956, illustrated Kubrick's early promise by stating that he had 'shown more imagination with dialogue and camera than Hollywood has seen since the obstreperous Orson Welles went riding out of town'. *Variety* opined that the film's partly documentary style 'at first tends to be somewhat confusing, [but] soon settles into a tense and suspenseful vein which carries through to an unexpected and ironic windup ... Stanley Kubrick's direction ... is tight and fast-paced, a quality Lucien Ballard's top photography matches to lend particular fluidity of movement.' The film made the year's 'Ten Best' lists of both *Time* and *Saturday Review*.

The British press, appalled at the lack of publicity or press screenings for the film, hailed it as a hidden gem. 'It is perhaps typical of the film industry that when they have a thriller of more than average intelligence and of more than average box-office power, they should stick it away without showing it to the press or giving it a respectable run in the West End,' complained the *Sunday Express*'s Milton Shulman. 'There has never been a parent more eager to disown its potential geniuses.' *Monthly Film Bulletin* suggested that *The Killing* revealed 'an exciting extension of the talents intermittently displayed in *Killer's Kiss*. Here, the observation is more acute, the seedy, violent world of vice more ruthlessly probed.' *MFB* closed by speculating what Kubrick might achieve 'with a subject less fashionably violent and corrupt'.

Retrospective reviews tended to be equally generous. Writing about *Lolita* in 1962, the *New Yorker*'s redoubtable film critic Pauline Kael described *The Killing* as 'an expert suspense film, with fast incisive cutting, a nervous edged style, and furtive little touches out of character'. In the UK, *Time Out* retrospectively praised the excellent performances and Lucien Ballard's steely photography, and added, 'Characteristically Kubrick in both its mechanistic coldness and its vision of human endeavour undone by greed and deceit, this *noir*-ish heist movie is nevertheless far more satisfying than most of his later work, due both to a lack of bombastic pretensions and to the style fitting the subject matter.'

**CONTROVERSY:** Already spooked by the possibility of a lawsuit from a powerful Hollywood agent, Bill Schifrin – on behalf of his client Sterling Hayden – Kubrick and Harris were alarmed to hear that Jim Thompson was considering legal action over the desultory 'Dialogue by' credit he received for his work on the screenplay. 'My father nearly fell out of his chair when he saw that,' Thompson's daughter, Patricia, told Robert Polito for his biography of Jim Thompson, *Savage Art*. 'There were fireworks when he next saw Kubrick. He couldn't believe that Stanley would cheat him out of his credit.'

Kubrick's lawyer called Thompson's claims for full screen credit 'unfounded', a position echoed by Harris in his comments to John Baxter. 'We hired Thompson *because* of his dialogue. The structure of the story was already pretty much there, and we all contributed changes.' Nevertheless, the wrangling over screen credits continued until June 1956, when Harris-Kubrick hired Thompson to work on *Paths of Glory* for $500 a week – in return, Patricia Thompson insists, for her father's acquiescence to the 'Dialogue by' credit on *The Killing*.

**BOX OFFICE:** Despite the studio's $200,000 investment, United Artists did little to promote or publicise *The Killing*, opening the film at a single New York cinema, on 20 May 1956, before releasing it as one half of a double bill for which the other half – *Bandido!*, a Western starring Robert Mitchum – was expected to be the draw. In the UK, *The Killing* was paired with a more appropriate Robert Mitchum film, *Foreign Intrigue* (1956), but still failed to cause much intrigue at the box office. After two years on tour, United Artists claimed that *The Killing* had earned just $30,000, and Harris-Kubrick would be forced to sell its 50-per-cent share in the film in order to finance *Lolita*. 'And it's marvellous,' Harris told John Baxter with heavy irony, 'how quickly [*The Killing*] went into profit after UA owned all of it.'

*The Killing* may not have performed at the box office, but it was attractive enough to Metro-Goldwyn-Mayer's head of production Dore Schary that he attempted to purchase it from United Artists in order for MGM to distribute it more effectively, and more profitably, itself. United Artists, however, would not sell. 'We're not in the business to make movies and then sell them,' the studio responded tersely. Nevertheless, *The Killing* achieved Harris-Kubrick's hope of becoming an effective calling card, and, if MGM could not have *The Killing*, it could have Kubrick and Harris.

**TECHNICAL ACHIEVEMENTS:** Much of *The Killing* was photographed in the familiar film noir style, using source lighting – often from a single source, such as a table lamp, a harsh overhead light or a window – to add a gritty realism to the proceedings. 'We are all used to seeing things in a certain way,' Kubrick told the *New York Times'* Joanne Stang in 1958, 'with light coming from some natural source. I try to duplicate this natural light in the filming. It makes for a feeling of greater reality.'

One of the most radical departures from cinematic convention was Kubrick's insistence that the veteran cinematographer Lucien Ballard use a 25mm lens, one of the widest motion-picture lenses available at the time, for even the most intimate of scenes. Kubrick had particularly wanted to use the lens for a long tracking shot, in which the camera would be mounted on a wheeled trolley known as a 'dolly', to move smoothly between rooms of an apartment, ignoring the natural spatial boundaries of the studio set walls – a previously unused method that has since passed into the lexicon of cinematic techniques. 'It goes [from] one room to the next, and as it passes the room you would simply go past the doorway and the boundaries of the walls as if they didn't exist,' Alexander Singer explained.

Having described and explained this complicated and unusual setup to Ballard, Kubrick left him alone to light the shot, and was surprised to find, upon his return, that the tracks had been moved further away, and the shot composed with the standard 50mm lens traditionally used for the kind of framing Kubrick was looking for. 'Now Stanley said, "Wait a minute, Lucien, what are you doing, Lucien?" ' Singer recounted. ' "Well, I took your dolly shot and instead of the 25mm, I'm just going for the 50mm, but I'm at a distance where you would get the same image size for the distance as that. So everything is the same size, but I prefer to work at this distance. It's a little easier to light, it won't make any difference." ' To Kubrick, of course, it made all the difference in the world. 'Stanley looked up at Lucien Ballard and said, "Lucien, either you move that camera and put it where it has to be to use a 25mm or get off this set and never come back!" ' Unexpectedly, given his own hard-earned reputation, and the fact that he had almost as many years of experience as Kubrick had on earth, Ballard acquiesced. It was the last time he and Kubrick fought over lighting issues.

**INFLUENCED BY:** Many have compared *The Killing* to John Huston's urban crime thriller *The Asphalt Jungle* (1950), superficially because they both starred Sterling Hayden as the masterminds behind meticulously planned robberies that are doomed to failure, but also because the neo-realism of Huston's film was taken to documentary-level extremes by Kubrick, who used similar characters, set his story in the same gritty urban surroundings, and toyed with audience expectations in much the same way as Huston. Nevertheless, in 1965, the film maker Orson Welles responded to an interviewer's suggestion that *The Killing* was 'more or less a copy of *The Asphalt Jungle*' with the following statement: 'Yes, but *The Killing* was better. The problem of imitation leaves me indifferent, above all if the imitator succeeds in surpassing the model ... What I see in [Kubrick]', he added, 'is a talent not possessed by the great directors of the generation immediately preceding his ... Perhaps this is because his temperament comes closer to mine.'

If *The Killing* owes a great debt to *The Asphalt Jungle* (1950), however, it owes its ending to an earlier John Huston film, *The Treasure of the Sierra Madre* (1948), which Kubrick named as one of his ten favourite films in 1963. The documentary style and authoritative voice-over narration of *The Killing* might also be attributable to *The Naked City* (1948), from which the film actor Ted De Corsia was also purloined. The device of using shadows and reflections resembling prison bars to foreshadow the fate of the characters had already been used to great effect in Robert Siodmak's *Time Out of Mind* (1947), Alfred Hitchcock's *Strangers on a Train* (1951), and a great many other films noirs.

**DÉJÀ VU:** Kubrick may have borrowed one stylised shot – the sprawled bodies of the men killed in the gun battle between George, Val and Tiny – from the scene depicting the dead enemy soldiers in his own first feature, *Fear and Desire*, using the same technique of backlighting to give the bodies a grotesque aspect. The arrangement of the bodies also recalls the arrangement of the mannequins on the factory floor of *Killer's Kiss*.

The Killing also includes one undeniably effective, self-reflexive moment of *déjà vu*. Consider the final shot, of two detectives or G-men in suits and Panama hats coming through the doors of the airport terminal to arrest Johnny Clay. Now compare it to the composition of the targets on Nikki Arane's firing range.

**INFLUENTIAL ON:** Although there are far more influential films noirs than *The Killing*, the cut-up editing style, in which the story is told out of chronology in nonlinear form, would become a familiar cinematic form four decades later, when revived for Quentin Tarantino's crime trilogy, *Reservoir Dogs* (1991), *Pulp Fiction* (1994) and *Jackie Brown* (1997). The narrative structure of the first – the story of a heist gone wrong – clearly owes a great debt to *The Killing*, with its temporal shifts and character-based flashbacks. And, as the critic Anthony Lane noted in the *New Yorker*, *The Killing* and *Killer's Kiss* 'are as good a way of getting into training for *Pulp Fiction* as you will ever find'.

In addition to these structural similarities, there is a scene in *Pulp Fiction* – in which Butch Coolidge (Bruce Willis), stopped at a red light, sees Marcellus Wallace (Ving Rhames) as he crosses the street in front of him – that closely mirrors the scene in *The Killing* in which Johnny Clay, driving, sees George crossing the street. 'If my work has anything it's that I'm taking this from this and that from that and mixing them together,' Tarantino told *Empire* magazine's Mark Salisbury. 'I steal from *everything*. Great artists *steal*, they don't do homages.' The writer-director also admitted to casting Harvey Keitel in *Reservoir Dogs* because 'the other actors I considered for the role – Sterling Hayden, Aldo Ray, Lee Marvin – are all dead.'

The Hughes brothers' 1995 heist movie *Dead Presidents* also included a number of visual references to Kubrick's film, most notably the long tracking shot through open-walled apartments – a trick repeated in Brian De Palma's *Snake Eyes* (1998), albeit from a different, overhead vantage point. And don't the early scenes between George Peatty and his wife, Sherry, play like an episode of the seventies sitcom *George & Mildred*?

**SEQUELS AND REMAKES:** Although *The Killing* remains ripe for a straight remake, the closest to date is the French track-heist movie *23h58* (1995), directed by the former cinematographer Pierre-William Glenn. The film, which starred Jean-François Stévenin, Jean-Pierre Malo and Gérald Garnier, transposes the action from a racetrack to the Le Mans 24-hour motorcycle race, and uses stock footage of the race in much the same way as Kubrick used horse-racing footage in the original. Although *23h58* is an obvious homage to *The Killing*, Glenn made the connection explicit by including still frames from Kubrick's film, which he used to link the action scenes.

Late in 1999, Warner Bros announced its intention to remake *The Killing*, with Mel Gibson (*Braveheart*), who had starred in a loose remake of *Point Blank* (1967) a year earlier, in the Sterling Hayden role.

**CUT SCENES:** Several possible endings were suggested to replace that of the novel, in which George shoots Johnny along with the other members of the gang, before the one in which the money is blown away by the aircraft's propellor wash. At one stage, Johnny was meant to be cut to pieces by the propellors as he struggled to retrieve the swirling money. In the fifties, films were still governed by the Hays Code, and it was morally essential that the criminals should fail to profit from their crime, either by being killed, or brought to justice. Crime, the Code stated, must not be seen to pay.

Although no pressure was brought by the studio to reject the radical, nonlinear story format in favour of a more traditional chronological one, Kubrick and Harris were encouraged by many to restructure the story so that it flowed more evenly. 'We [originally] edited it the way we wanted to – the way the script was written,' James B Harris recalled. 'Many people said they thought it should be a straight-line story, that the flashbacks would irritate people. If enough people tell you you're sick, maybe you should lie down. We went back to New York, rented an editing room, and, before we delivered [the film] to United Artists, we broke the whole thing down and started over. When we put it together, we looked at each other and said, "This stinks." We put it back the way we had it.'

**TRIVIA:** Despite the fact that the film is supposedly set at the fictional Lansdowne Park track, the Bay Meadows sign features prominently on the racetrack starting gate.

Johnny tells Marvin that the seventh race starts at 'about 4.30, if you want to catch it on the radio'. In fact, it starts at 4.20. Maurice has been arrested by 4.23 and Nikki is dead by 4.24. By the time Marvin turned on the radio at 4.30, he would have missed the whole race!

Two of the nameplates of George's fellow cashiers feature the names David Vaughan and Shaun O'Brien, two of Ruth Subotka's friends from the New York City Ballet who had played small roles in *Killer's Kiss*.

**EXPERT WITNESS:** 'Only one person was there when we screened the picture for United Artists: Max Youngstein, the head of production. When the screening was over, Max said, "Good job. Let's keep in touch." We had to follow him down the hall, saying, "Where do we go from here?" Max said, "What about out the door?" Stanley said, "You have other producer-filmmaker teams. Where would you rate us with all of those people?" And Max said, "Not far from the bottom." We never forgot that.' – James B Harris, producer, quoted in *Premiere*, August 1999.

**AVAILABILITY:** It's been long unavailable on video in the United Kingdom, but *The Killing* is currently available in the United States in full-screen (4:3) versions on NTSC-format VHS video (MGM 207701) and a Region 1 DVD (907706), the latter featuring a theatrical trailer and two pages of sleeve notes. Full-screen (4:3) editions of *The Killing* have been released twice on NTSC laserdisc: once as part of the Criterion Collection (CC1164L), and in an MGM Home Video edition (ML 102875) featuring *The Killing* and Kubrick's earlier *Killer's Kiss*, spread across three discs.

**FINAL ANALYSIS:** With four short films and two features already behind him, the 28-year-old Kubrick truly came of age with this fully mature genre piece, a prime example of film noir adapted from pulp fiction, and a landmark in narrative acrobatics rarely equalled among the many films it has influenced. Kubrick's confidence with every aspect of the film-making process, from composition to narrative structure, from lighting to sound, from editing to performance, put the director in command of his material for the first time, and gave the crime genre a belated classic that is as gripping today as it was on its first release.

Although many of the hard-boiled characters are as familiar as the faces portraying them, Kubrick endows each with a depth matched only by the shadows, and imbues the story with a darkness perfectly synonymous with the term 'film noir'. As in *The Asphalt Jungle*, with which only Orson Welles compared it favourably, *The Killing* telegraphs the flaws in its characters and its crimes, so the question becomes not *if* the heist goes wrong, but *why* it does. Kubrick's answer – with its future echoes of the HAL 9000 computer's stark statement, 'It can only be attributable to human error' – is as simple as it is satisfying.

**KUBRICK ON KUBRICK:** 'In a crime film, it is almost like a bullfight: it has a ritual and a pattern which lays down that the criminal is not going to make it, so that, while you can suspend your knowledge of this for a while, sitting way back in your mind this little awareness knows and prepares you for the fact that he is not going to succeed. That type of ending is easier to accept.' – quoted in the *Observer*, 4 December 1960.

# Paths of Glory (1957)

**(B & W – 87 mins)**

**Unit Manager Helmut Ringelmann**
**Assistant Directors H Stumpf, D Sensburg, F Spieker**
**Script Clerk Trudy Von Trotha**
**Sound Martin Müller**
**Costume Designer Ilse Dubois**
**Special Effects Erwin Lange**
**Military Adviser Baron V Waldenfels**
**Assistant Editor Helene Fischer**
**Camera Grip Hans Elsinger**
**Make-up Arthur Schramm**
**Music Gerald Fried**
**Art Director Ludwig Reiber**
**Photographed by George Krause**
**Camera Operator Hannes Staudinger**
**American Production Manager John Pommer**
**German Production Manager George Von Block**
**Film Editor Eva Kroll**
**Screenplay by Stanley Kubrick, Calder Willingham and Jim Thompson**
**Based on the novel *Paths of Glory* by Humphrey Cobb**
**Produced by James B Harris**
**Directed by Stanley Kubrick**

**CAST:** Kirk Douglas (*Colonel Dax*), Ralph Meeker (*Corporal Phillip Paris*), Adolphe Menjou (*General George Broulard*), George Macready (*General Paul Mireau*), Wayne Morris (*Lieutenant Roget*), Richard Anderson (*Major Saint-Auban*), Timothy Carey (*Private Maurice Ferol*), Joseph Turkel (*Private Pierre Arnaud*), Susanne Christian (*German Singer*), Jeffrey Hausner (*Proprietor*), Emile Meyer (*Father Du Pres*), Peter Capell (*Colonel Judge*), Bert Freed (*Sergeant Boulanger*), Harold Benedict (*Captain Nichols*), John Stein (*Captain Rousseau*), Fred Bell (*Shell-shock Victim*), Leon Briggs (*Captain Sancy*), Paul Bös (*Major Gouderc*), Ken Dibbs (*Private Lejeune*), Wally Friedrichs (*Colonel de*

*Guerville*), Halder Hanson (*Doctor*), Rolf Kralovitz (*KP*), Ira Moore
(*Captain Renouart*), Marshall Rainer (*Private Duval*), Roger Vagnoid
(*Café Owner*).

**UNCREDITED CAST:** James B Harris (*Soldier*).

**TITLE SEQUENCE:** White, hand-drawn credits play on black against
an arrangement of 'Marseillaise' by the composer Gerald Fried. The tune
begins brightly enough, but ends on a disquietingly dissonant note.
Kubrick was aware that his ironic use of the 'Marseillaise' in a film so
critical of France's military leadership might incense French-sympathetic
territories, and he requested that Fried compose a second – original –
main title theme for selective use in overseas markets. Over the opening
shot of a stately home being used as headquarters to the French military
brass, a narrator intones the background to the setting: 'War began
between Germany and France on August 3rd, 1914,' the voice explains.
'Five weeks later, the German army had smashed its way to within
eighteen miles of Paris. There the battered French miraculously rallied
their forces at the Marne River, and in a series of unexpected
counterattacks, drove the Germans back. The front was stablised, and
shortly afterwards, developed into a continuous line of heavily fortified
trenches, zigzagging their way five hundred miles, from the English
Channel to the Swiss frontier. By 1916, after two grisly years of trench
warfare, the battle lines had changed very little. Successful attacks were
measured in hundreds of yards, and paid for in lives by hundreds of
thousands.'

**SUMMARY:** France, 1916. Arriving at the spectacular
eighteenth-century château that serves as a makeshift headquarters for
the French army, General Broulard offers General Mireau a promotion
in return for the capture of a key German position known as 'the Ant
Hill' within two days. At first, Mireau resists Broulard's overtures, but
he is soon persuaded, and takes the assignment down the chain of
command to Colonel Dax, a former criminal lawyer who is dug in with
his battle-weary and shell-shocked men, and understandably resistant to
the idea of leading them on a suicide mission to take the Ant Hill.
Nevertheless, he has little choice but to follow his orders, especially as
the alternative is a transfer to another regiment, away from his men.

The morning after a botched reconnaissance patrol – during which
one of Dax's men is killed by Roget, a drunken subordinate – Dax leads
the men into no man's land, where they are almost wiped out by enemy
gunfire. B Company, led by the cowardly Roget, did not advance at all –
indeed, Mireau ordered them to be fired upon for their inaction. Dax is
forced to defend his men against Broulard and Mireau, who wants a
hundred men shot for cowardice as an example to the others; a
compromise is reached: three men will be court-martialled, with Dax, a

former lawyer, defending. The trial is of the kangaroo variety, and the three innocent infantrymen are found guilty and sentenced to death by firing squad.

The night before sentence is due to be carried out, Dax learns of Mireau's order to fire on his own men, and reports the news to Broulard, who refuses to see it as motive for Mireau's machinations, and lets the sentence stand. The men are shot, as ordered, and Mireau is told of the investigation into his own misconduct. Dax is offered the doomed general's job as a reward, but refuses. Instead, he listens as his men are moved by the sight of a German peasant girl singing a folk song, their humanity giving him the strength to continue in the face of his superiors' inhuman conduct.

**SOURCE:** *Paths of Glory* was adapted by Kubrick, Calder Willingham and Jim Thompson from the Canadian author Humphrey Cobb's 1935 novel *Paths of Glory*, itself inspired by the *New York Times*' coverage of a French trial in which the widows of five men executed for mutiny in 1915 had unsuccessfully sued the French army for damages. Having researched the history of the case, and the wartime events leading up to it, Cobb adhered closely to the facts for his novella, whose title was taken from a line in Thomas Gray's 'Elegy Written in a Country Churchyard' ('The paths of glory lead but to the grave').

The story begins when the French army mistakenly announces the capture of a notorious frontline outpost known as 'the Pimple', which forces them to choose either an embarrassing retraction or, preferably, belatedly taking the German strongpoint. From this point on, the film closely follows the events of Cobb's novella (although the names of Generals de Guerville and Assolant are changed to Broulard and Mireau respectively, and 'the Pimple' was rechristened 'the Ant Hill'), although Kubrick added a coda, which, if not exactly a happy ending, manages to be more uplifting than Cobb's.

**PRODUCTION HISTORY:** Within a few months of the first publication of *Paths of Glory*, a stage adaptation by the screenwriter Sidney Howard (*Gone with the Wind*) was performed on Broadway, causing the *New York Times*' theatre critic Brooks Atkinson to remark, 'Some day the screen will seize this ghastly tale and make a work of art from it.' Two decades later, Kubrick decided he was the man to do it. 'It was one of the few books I'd read for pleasure in high school,' Kubrick said of the novel. 'I found it lying around my father's office and started reading it while waiting for him to get finished with a patient.' Kubrick remembered the powerful *roman à clef* while he and his production partner, James B Harris, were searching for a project that the pair could make at MGM, where they were under contract following *The Killing*.

Encouraged by Kubrick, Harris tracked down and read a copy of the out-of-print book at the New York Public Library, and was immediately gripped by the late Cobb's story. But although Harris-Kubrick subsequently secured the screen rights for $10,000, MGM's head of production, Dore Schary, was appalled at the idea of following John Huston's expensive flop *The Red Badge of Courage* (1951) with another downbeat war film. Instead, he offered Kubrick and Harris a forty-week development deal, and invited them to sift through MGM's story department in search of a more suitable literary work to adapt. This, in turn, led to their discovery of Stefan Zweig's *The Burning Secret* (see Lost Worlds: The Films That Never Were).

Nevertheless, although the nature of their contract was exclusive, Kubrick and – especially – Harris continued to pursue *Paths of Glory*, and secretly commissioned the tough crime writer Jim Thompson, with whom Kubrick had collaborated on *The Killing*, to write an adaptation of Cobb's novella. MGM subsequently used this deliberate contract violation as an excuse to terminate its deal with Kubrick and Harris, who immediately began shopping Thompson's first draft around other studios. Displaying the kind of marketing chutzpah for which Kubrick would later become renowned, the pair dressed several male colleagues in rented military uniforms and had them pose for highly evocative photographs, which were affixed to the front of each screenplay.

Although none of the studios whom they approached showed any interest in the project, a unique opportunity presented itself when the actor Kirk Douglas, an established box office star and three-time Academy Award nominee who had admired *The Killing*, met with Kubrick to discuss possible future projects. 'He said he had this script called *Paths of Glory*,' Douglas wrote in his autobiography, *The Ragman's Son*. 'Stanley told me he'd had no success setting the picture up, but he'd be glad to let me see it. I read the script and fell in love with it.' He contacted Kubrick immediately. ' "Stanley, I don't think this picture will ever make a nickel, but we *have* to make it." ' With Douglas on board, United Artists were persuaded to finance the film to the tune of $850,000, plus or minus 10 per cent. With France understandably unwilling to play host to such a film, production was scheduled to begin at Munich's Geiselgasteig Studios in early 1957.

When Douglas arrived in Germany to begin filming, however, he was shocked to find that the screenplay had been extensively rewritten: Thompson had left the production and been replaced by the little-known novelist Calder Willingham, whose revised draft included a new, upbeat ending in which the three condemned men are reprieved thanks to some ingenious blackmail by Colonel Dax. Douglas objected to what he called 'atrocious' new dialogue, such as 'You've got a big head. You're so sure the sun rises and sets up there in your noggin you don't even bother to carry matches.'

'Speeches like this went on for four pages,' the actor lamented, 'right up to the happy ending, when the general's car arrives screeching to halt the firing squad and he changes the men's death sentence to thirty days in the guardhouse. Then my character, Colonel Dax, goes off with the bad guy he has been fighting all through the movie, General Rousseau [sic], to have a drink, and the general puts his arm around my shoulder.'

Douglas summoned Kubrick to his room at the Hotel Viejahrzeiten, and was told that the new ending had been Kubrick's idea. 'I said, "Stanley, why would you do that?" ' Douglas recalled. 'He very calmly said, "To make it commercial. I want to make money." ' Douglas hit the ceiling. 'I called him every four-letter word I could think of. "You came to me with a script written by other people. I told you I didn't think this would be commercial, but I want to make it. You left it in my hands to put the picture together. I got the money, based on *that* script. Not this shit!" ' Throwing the revised script across the room, Douglas gave Kubrick an ultimatum: go back to the original script, or lose his leading man. 'Stanley never blinked an eye,' Douglas noted, adding with satisfaction: 'We shot the original script.'

Once filming began, the relationship between Douglas and Kubrick mellowed. 'Kirk is pretty dictatorial,' Harris said, 'but Stanley earns people's respect, and Kirk could tell immediately that Stanley knew what he was doing. There were no conflicts.' The actor Richard Anderson, playing Major Saint-Auban, told a different story, however. 'One time when Kirk Douglas blew up at him on the set,' he recalled, 'Stanley said, "Jeez, Kirk, you don't have to do this in front of everybody, do you?" But he admired Kirk.' On another occasion, Anderson remembered a moment of hostility between Kubrick and his producer. 'One time he had done about forty takes and Jimmy Harris comes and says, "Stanley, it's now one o'clock and we're in terrible trouble and we gotta break this up." That was the only time I saw Stanley go nuts. He shouted, "It isn't right – and I'm going to keep doing it until it *is* right!" He shot 84 takes. I think he wanted everybody to hear that – he wanted it to get around.'

A pasture measuring several acres was rented from a German farmer to serve as the battlefield locations. Eight cranes and as many as sixty crew members worked around the clock for three weeks, digging trenches and shell holes, and placing barbed wire and props – including an authentic World War One biplane – in order to create an authentic-looking battlefield of the Western Front. 'We worked for a month preparing the field,' Kubrick told *Newsweek*. 'After we'd dug and blasted up the field, we put a great many little props around – ruined guns scattered in different holes, and bits of soldiers' tunic. You couldn't see them, but you could feel them.'

Over the protestations of his military adviser, Baron Otto von Waldenfels, Kubrick insisted that the trenches be dug six feet wide instead of a more realistic four feet, to allow the camera to move freely over the wooden 'duckboards', originally laid to prevent the spread of disease and sinkage, but now vital for the creation of Kubrick's desired tracking shot of Mireau and Saint-Auban inspecting Dax's shell-shocked and battle-weary troops. 'The trench was gruesome,' Anderson later commented. 'It just reeked, and then the weather was so lousy – it was cold and freezing and overcast and grey. We all had colds. We were all sick from the first week. We all looked awful and it certainly added to the movie.'

A similar tracking shot was used for the scenes in which Dax's men advance across no man's land during the futile attempt to capture the Ant Hill. Some six hundred German policemen were employed to play the French soldiers, their three years of military training providing Kubrick with the verisimilitude he craved. 'We had six cameras, one behind the other on a long dolly track which ran parallel to the attack,' Kubrick told Alexander Walker. 'The battlefield was divided into five "dying zones" and each extra was given a number ranging from one to five and told to "die" in that zone, if possible near an explosion.' So many explosives were needed – more than a ton were detonated in a single week – that the special-effects supervisor Erwin Lange was called before a special government hearing before permission for their use could be granted. 'Most of the time was spent in planting explosive charges and timing them so they'd go off right,' Kubrick told *Newsweek*. 'It took half a day to set up, and thirty seconds to do.'

As filming progressed, the question of how to end the film remained: United Artists wanted the soldiers to earn an eleventh-hour reprieve, and were contractually permitted to insist upon the more upbeat ending; virtually everyone else wanted to keep the original ending, in which the three men are executed. Before filming concluded in April 1957, however, a third possible ending was proposed, which takes place after the executions, and succeeds in being uplifting without betraying the novel's powerful message. In a tavern, a young German girl captured by the French is forced to perform a nervous rendition of the German folk song 'Der Treuer Husar' ('The Faithful Soldier') for the men of Dax's company. After initially trying to humiliate her with catcalls and derisory heckling, the men are moved to tears of shame and humanity by the girl's innocence, poignant singing, and suffering. Upon learning that Kubrick intended to cast Suzanne Christian (née Christiane Harlan), a young German actress Kubrick had seen on television in Munich and was currently dating, Harris flew into a rage – especially as the girl was related to the notorious Nazi film maker Veidt Harlan.

'I said, "Stanley, you can't just do this scene so your girlfriend can be in the movie," ' Harris recalled. 'But Stanley had his way, and gave the film an unforgettable ending. The actress was incredible,' he added. 'Then she and Stanley got married, and the marriage lasted forty years. Boy, was I wrong.' Although Kubrick has frequently taken credit for this haunting scene, Calder Willingham claimed that it was his idea, along with '99 per cent' of the rest of the screenplay. Willingham subsequently took his case to the Writers' Guild of America, which arbitrates disputes over screen credit, and won his case: in September 1957, just prior to the release of *Paths of Glory*, Kubrick was forced to accede to a shared credit with Willingham and Jim Thompson.

After 66 days of filming *Paths of Glory* was in the can, posting a final budget of $954,000, a fraction over the maximum of $935,000 allowed under the terms of their contract with United Artists. 'When we screened *Paths of Glory* around LA before it opened, trying to drum up word of mouth, the lights would come up and people would just sit there,' Harris recalled. 'We didn't know how to interpret that. It was good, as it turned out, but there was no applause or anything. I think they were just stunned.'

**CASTING:** Although Kirk Douglas was Kubrick's first choice for the role of Colonel Dax, the actor was booked in a play on Broadway, and was not available for eighteen months. Thus, Kubrick and Harris discussed the role with Richard Burton, James Mason and Gregory Peck, and had all but agreed that Peck would take the role, when Douglas postponed his own existing commitments in order to begin work on *Paths of Glory* immediately. Nevertheless, Douglas's deal with Kubrick and Harris, brokered by the legendary agent Ray Stark, was uncompromising. As Harris recalled, in addition to a payment of $350,000 (one-third of the budget) and healthy profit participation, 'Kirk wanted his company name, Bryna, on the picture as a production credit, and he also wanted a commitment from us to make more pictures for him. But we had to go for it because it was the only way to get it made.'

The supporting cast included the distinguished actor Adolphe Menjou, who had made his film debut in *The Man Behind the Door* (1914) before joining up to serve as a captain in the Ambulance Corps during World War One. If anybody could vouch for the authenticity of *Paths of Glory*'s shell-torn battlefields and cold-blooded colonels, it was Menjou, who predicted in 1956 that Kubrick would become 'one of the ten best directors. When? It usually takes three pictures, so I guess the next one.'

Kubrick deliberately cast Menjou, an actor mostly known for sympathetic roles, because he wanted the audience to discover General Broulard's true nature only after they had grown to like him. 'You hold off as long as possible revealing the kind he is,' he explained to *Newsweek*. 'He comes in like a nice guy, and when the audience finds him out, they're trapped.' The reverse was true for the casting of George Macready (*Gilda*), who had earned a reputation for playing chilling screen villains before being cast as General Mireau. A deep facial scar, suffered during an automobile accident, was accentuated by the make-up department to emphasise his villainy.

**THE USUAL SUSPECTS:** Two faces from *The Killing* were invited to Germany to play a part in *Paths of Glory*: Timothy Carey, who played the marksman Nikki Arane, was cast as Private Maurice Ferol, while Joseph Turkel, Tiny in *The Killing*, reappeared as Private Pierre Arnaud.

## CLASSIC QUOTES

**Mireau:** 'There is no such thing as shell shock. Have you got a wife, soldier?'

**Soldier:** 'My wife? My wife. Yes, I have a wife. I'm never gonna see her again! I'm gonna be killed!'

**Mireau:** 'Get a grip on yourself! You're acting like a coward!'

**Soldier:** 'I am a coward, sir!'

**Mireau:** 'Snap out of it, soldier! Sergeant, I want you to arrange for the immediate transfer of this baby out of my regiment! I won't have other brave men contaminated by him!'

**Mireau:** 'Patriotism may be old-fashioned, but show me a patriot and I'll show you an honest man.'

**Dax:** 'Not everyone has always thought so. Samuel Johnson had something else to say about patriotism.'

**Mireau:** 'And what was that, may I ask?'

**Dax:** 'Nothing, really.'

**Mireau:** 'What do you mean, "Nothing really"?'

**Dax:** 'Well, sir, nothing really important.'

**Mireau:** 'Colonel, when I ask a question it's always important. Now, who was this man?'

**Dax:** 'Samuel Johnson, sir.'

**Mireau:** 'All right, now what did he have to say about patriotism?'

**Dax:** 'He said it was the last refuge of a scoundrel, sir. I'm sorry. I meant nothing personal.'

**Dax:** 'We'll take the Ant Hill. If any soldiers in the world can take it, we'll take the Ant Hill!'

**Arnaud:** 'If you're really afraid of dying, you'd be living in a funk all the rest of your life, because you know you've got to go some day, any day, and besides, if death is what you're really afraid of, why would you care about what it is that kills you?'

**Mireau:** 'They've skim milk in their veins instead of blood.'

**Dax:** 'Well it's the reddest milk I've ever seen – my trenches are soaked with it!'

**Dax:** 'The attack yesterday morning was no stain on the honour of France, and certainly no disgrace to the fighting men of this nation. But this court martial is such a stain, and such a disgrace. The case made against these men is a mockery of all human justice. Gentlemen of the court, to find these men guilty would be a crime to haunt each of you till the day you die.'

**Dax:** 'I apologise . . . for not being entirely honest with you. I apologise for not revealing my true feelings. I apologise for not telling you sooner that you're a degenerate, sadistic old man, and you can go to *hell before I apologise to you now, or ever again*!'

**Broulard:** 'Colonel Dax, you're a disappointment to me. You've spoiled the keenness of your mind by wallowing in sentimentality. You really did want to save those men, and you were not angling for Mireau's command. You are an idealist – and I pity you as I would the village idiot.'

**THEMES AND MOTIFS:** In a film dealing with the movement and loss of inconsequential pawns in the game of a higher power, Kubrick could hardly resist incorporating a chess motif. Here, it manifests itself as the chessboard-patterned floor tiling of the vast chamber of the French château in which Dax's men are to be court-martialled. The same floor covering had appeared, apparently by accident, on the landing of the staircase leading to Rapallo's office in *Killer's Kiss*, and would reappear in each of his next two films, *Spartacus* (the floor of the Roman senate) and *Lolita* (the entrance hall of the Haze residence) – each appearance generally signalling the location of subterfuges, plots and machinations between principal characters, as in *Paths of Glory*.

**MUSIC:** *Paths of Glory* was the fifth film (including the short subject, *Day of the Fight*) for which Kubrick asked Gerald Fried to compose music, although much of the soundtrack is composed of militaristic percussion in place of a fully orchestral composition. 'The score for *Paths of Glory* was the first all-percussion score,' Fried noted later, adding that, by the time of their fifth collaboration, 'he was already "Stanley Kubrick", and then it was a struggle – I had to rationalise every note. It was fun and stimulating, but he was already sure that he knew it all.'

Although *Paths of Glory* was to be Fried's last film for Kubrick, he later oversaw the production of Silva Screen's Kubrick compilation album *Strangelove: Music from the Films of Stanley Kubrick* (FILMCD 303), which includes a single track ('The Patrol') from *Paths of Glory*.

**POSTER:** About as lurid a poster for a serious war film one could find, the British 'quad' was a graphic illustration showing a lantern-jawed, grimacing Douglas/Dax leading his men on an advance across no man's land, while a colourful explosion tears up the dirt behind him.

**TAG-LINES:** 'BOMBSHELL! the roll of the drums . . . the click of the rifle-bolts . . . the last cigarette . . . and then . . . the shattering impact of this story . . . perhaps the most explosive motion picture in 25 years!' screamed the promotional poster for the US release of *Paths of Glory*. In the UK, the legend was replaced by the only slightly more restrained 'BOMBSHELL! NEVER HAS THE SCREEN THRUST SO DEEPLY INTO THE GUTS OF WAR!'

**TRAILER:** To the sound of a drumbeat, a caption scrolls up the screen in white letters on a black background: 'The Management of This Theater Takes Great Pride in Announcing an Important Motion Picture Event.' The sound of explosions accompanies Kubrick's camera as it tracks its way through the trenches, as further captions appear, now superimposed over the action: 'PATHS OF GLORY'. 'STARRING KIRK DOUGLAS IN THE MOST EXTRAORDINARY PERFORMANCE OF HIS CAREER'. Cut to Douglas/Dax in action, insulting General Broulard, as a caption for 'ADOLPHE MENJOU' is displayed. More drums sound, and cast captions appear, over shots of 'WAYNE MORRIS' and 'RALPH MEEKER' in no man's land, as a narrator intones the following: 'Since the publication of the book twenty-five years ago, no one dared to make this movie. It was too shocking. Too frank.' Cut to Dax as General Mireau tells him of the projected casualties in the assault on the Ant Hill, and Broulard tells him of the planned executions. A superimposed title appears over Private Ferol's march towards his fate.

Cut to Broulard in his dug-out, captioned 'GEORGE MACREADY', ordering Nicholls to fire on their own positions. 'THE MOST EXPLOSIVE MOTION PICTURE IN 25 YEARS!' proclaims a caption superimposed over the advance, followed by several critics' quotations: ' "Unquestionably the finest American film of the year . . . extraordinary achievement!" – SATURDAY REVIEW'. ' "Ranks among the finest ever made . . . don't miss it!" – CORONET'. ' "One of the year's 10 best!" – TIME MAGAZINE/SATURDAY REVIEW'. ' "A major effort . . . an unforgettable movie experience!" – NEWSWEEK'. ' "Has the impact of hard reality . . . shattering!" – N.Y. TIMES'.

No music appears anywhere in the entire three-minute trailer.

**WHAT THE PAPERS SAID:** Winston Churchill once observed that *Paths of Glory* came closer than any other film to catching the mood of the Great War. *Variety* described the film as 'a starkly realistic recital of French army politics in 1916 during World War One', but added that, 'while the subject is well-handled and enacted in a series of outstanding characterisations, it seems dated and makes for grim screen fare. Stanley Kubrick in his taut direction catches the spirit of war with fine realism, and the futile advance of the French is exciting. He draws excellent performances, too, right down the line.' Although many other critics applauded the authenticity of the film's setting, the quality of the performances, and Kubrick's virtuoso style of film making, some felt that the film portrayed a freakish incident which belied its antiwar intentions. In other words, *Paths of Glory* was seen as a condemnation of the French high command, rather than of war itself. There were other, more pedantic observations, as Kubrick recalled in 1987: 'An important Los Angeles critic faulted *Paths of Glory* because the actors didn't speak with French accents.'

In Britain, the response from critics was similar to the majority view from the United States: the *Evening Standard* praised it as an 'adult, painful and absorbing film [which] demands to be seen', while *Monthly*

*Film Bulletin* called it 'Kubrick's most controlled and ambitious picture … powerful and authoritative', adding, 'some scenes, such as the court-martial itself, or the final showdown between Dax and Broulard, seem more convincing as intellectual conceptions than actual dramatic experiences.'

**CONTROVERSY:** Perhaps understandably, the French did not take too kindly to the exhumation – and, they argued, exaggeration – of one of its least heroic episodes of World War One, and were incensed at Kubrick's use of the French national anthem, 'La Marseillaise', over the credits. Kubrick was threatened with rather spurious criminal charges for his allegedly libellous view of the French high command, and *Paths of Glory* was banned in the territory until the mid-seventies, when it finally enjoyed a theatrical release in the wake of president Valéry Giscard d'Estaing's anti-censorship proclamation and – perhaps more instrumentally – *Barry Lyndon*'s Gallic success.

The French also succeeded in having the film withdrawn from the 1958 Berlin Film Festival, as well as French-controlled regions of the West German city, invoking a postwar statute that prohibited any action that might harm the reputation of one of the occupying powers of West Berlin. Even when the film was shown in the British sector of the city, French protestors disrupted a screening by throwing stink bombs into the audience.

The government of Switzerland followed France's example, banning the film in December 1958, after the minister of the interior described it as 'subversive propaganda directed at France' and 'highly offensive to that nation'. Even in Brussels, protests forced the film to be removed from cinemas, although it was subsequently re-released with an opening caption eerily prescient of the one that the US State Department insisted be added to *Dr Strangelove*. It said: 'This episode of the 1914–1918 war tells of the madness of certain men caught in its whirlwind. It constitutes an isolated case in total contrast with the historical gallantry of the vast majority of French soldiers, the champions of the idea of liberty, which, since always, has been that of the French people.'

Ironically, Kirk Douglas, a fluent French speaker, was later invited to France to receive one of the highest accolades bestowed by the country, the Legion d'Honneur for his contribution to the cinematic arts.

**BOX OFFICE:** *Paths of Glory* opened on a single New York screen on Christmas Day 1957, just in time to qualify for the following year's Academy Award selection. Reflecting the attitude of those early test screenings recalled by Harris, the film won a muted but respectful response from audiences, yet struggled to earn back its production costs. 'As I had predicted, it made no money,' Kirk Douglas wrote in his autobiography, *The Ragman's Son*. 'A picture can't make money unless people pay to see it, and people can't see it if it's been banned in their country.'

**AWARDS:** Although *Paths of Glory* received a frosty reception in parts of Europe (see above), Italian film critics voted it their best foreign film of 1958, awarding it the Silver Ribbon.

**TECHNICAL ACHIEVEMENTS:** Despite the virtuoso camerawork, credited to George Krause though mostly Kubrick's own work, *Paths of Glory* is more noteworthy for its pioneering use of overlapping sound. On several occasions, the sound from a following scene begins over the scene that precedes it, a deliriously disorientating conceit which is now as accepted a practice for scene changes as a dissolve or a cut. Strangely, the recent DVD release (see below) seems to 'repair' most of these deliberate sound overlaps, leaving them absent altogether.

**INFLUENCED BY:** The French director Max Ophuls was a significant influence on Kubrick during this period, and it cannot have escaped his attention that Ophuls' last film, *Lola Montes* (1955), was filmed at the same Munich studios as *Paths of Glory*. As Richard Anderson recalls, 'The opening sequence, where I usher in Macready to Menjou's sumptuous living room, and Menjou's saying, "We've got to do something here, we've got to take that Ant Hill . . ." – that scene was a dance. Stanley said to me after that shot, "This shot is in memory of Max Ophuls, who died today." He was Stanley's God.' Anderson also believes that Kubrick was influenced by *La Grande Illusion* (1937), Jean Renoir's moving World War One drama in which a shared aristocratic background forges an unlikely bond between a German commandant and a senior French officer.

**INFLUENTIAL ON:** Kubrick's bold efforts to form didactic arguments within the context of a relatively straightforward and accessible drama were arguably at their most successful in *Paths of Glory*, and, as Thomas Allen Nelson pointed out in his analytical study, *Kubrick: Inside a Film Artist's Maze*, influenced other independent film makers of the fifties in subtle but important ways. '[François] Truffaut and [Alain] Resnais, like Kubrick, began in the documentary before turning to the greater technical and conceptual challenges offered by feature films,' Nelson suggested. 'Significantly, [Truffaut's] *The 400 Blows* (1959) and [Resnais'] *Hiroshima, Mon Amour* (1959), two films that, among others, signalled the end of Italian neo-realism's influence and the beginning of a more "personal" brand of filmmaking, were quietly predated and, from the vantages of hindsight, preempted by Kubrick's first work of consummate skill, *Paths of Glory* (1957).'

**KUBRICK GOES POP:** In one of the more bizarre homages to a Kubrick film, *Paths of Glory* formed the basis of a 1991 episode of HBO's television series, *Tales from the Crypt*, directed by Robert Zemeckis (*Forrest Gump*) and starring Kirk Douglas and his son Eric. Set in France in 1918, the story puts the elder Douglas into the role of a general ordering his men to take a German position referred to as 'the hill'. Upon learning that his son ordered the retreat, General Calthrop has him placed under arrest for cowardice, tried at a court martial, and executed by firing squad. 'I won't have cowards in my army,' Calthrop bellows, echoing General Mireau's words from *Paths of Glory*. The episode also features a soldier named Ripper, presumably named after General Jack D Ripper from *Dr Strangelove*, and a trench filled with lime-covered bodies, *à la Full Metal Jacket*.

The ludicrous 'kangaroo court' in *Paths of Glory* is replicated, and exaggerated, to great comic effect in an episode of *Blackadder Goes Forth* entitled 'Corporal Punishment', when Captain Blackadder is accused of shooting (and eating) General Melchett's prized carrier pigeon, Speckled Jim.

In François Truffaut's *Vivement Dimanche!* (1983), the characters visit an art-house cinema showing *Paths of Glory*, although an employee erroneously describes the film as being a romantic love story!

The animated television series *The Simpsons*, ever reliable as a fecund source of Kubrick homages, features an episode entitled 'Bart Gets an F' (#7F03) in which Lisa Simpson, echoing Colonel Dax's feelings about patriotism, calls 'Prayer, the last resort of a scoundrel'.

**CUT SCENES:** In a move that was to become almost traditional for the director, Kubrick slightly modified *Paths of Glory* between its pre-Christmas 'platform' screenings and its wide release, excising approximately two minutes of material from two scenes: one that detailed the method by which the condemned men are selected for execution, and another in which the men argue during the long night before their deaths. As John Baxter noted in his biography of Kubrick, 'If anything, the slight jerkiness imposed by the trimming added to the film's immediacy. We are not so much led to an inevitable dramatic climax as jolted down the road to execution like condemned men on a tumbril.'

**TRIVIA:** Two of the three soldiers addressed by General Mireau during his tour of the trenches are, by a twist of fate, the very ones picked for execution.

The actor Wayne Morris plays *two* roles in *Paths of Glory*: as Lieutenant Roget, he is killed in the first reconnaissance mission to the Ant Hill, yet he later reappears in heavy make-up as one of the soldiers in the film's final scene.

The producer James B Harris donned a military uniform to play a soldier in the attack on the Ant Hill, his only on-screen appearance. According to legend, the cast insisted that he play a private so that the other actors would have the opportunity to outrank him.

**APOCRYPHA:** In addition to portraying Saint-Auban, Richard Anderson is often said to have been employed as dialogue or acting coach to his less experienced co-stars. 'That was something that was overstated,' Anderson demurs. 'It was just [something] Stanley said to me when we met. He said, "Look, we're all doing everything on this picture. I'd like you to be there every day. I'd like you to make sure the actors are up on their lines."'

**AVAILABILITY:** Although currently unavailable in the UK on any format, *Paths of Glory* is available in the United States on an NTSC VHS video (MGM 207699) and a Region 1 DVD (907674), the latter containing a full-screen transfer of the film, a four-page booklet featuring behind-the-scenes anecdotes and stills, and the US theatrical trailer.

**EXPERT WITNESS:** 'I remember walking out on the street and thinking that I'd never seen anybody shot and killed in a movie before. I was seventeen, I'd seen a few (thousand) movies, and I soon realised that I'd been seeing it all my life: cowboys shooting Indians, Indians shooting cavalry, cops shooting robbers, good guys shooting bad guys, weak guys shooting strong guys, Japanese and Germans and Americans shooting one another – it was a staple of the cinema. This was the first time I'd seen it done in this way, as calculated and pitiless as a firing squad itself, no possibility to dissociate, no way to look someplace else.' – Michael Herr, co-screenwriter of *Full Metal Jacket*, quoted in *Vanity Fair*, August 1999.

**FINAL ANALYSIS:** More than four decades after its release, *Paths of Glory* has lost none of its power to shock. It may seem heavy-handed, but this is because it is uncompromising, single-minded and angry – a polemic as powerful as any antiwar film to come before and after it.

Like Renoir's *La Grande Illusion* (1937), *Paths of Glory* seems almost as concerned with class war as it is with war itself, creating lines of tension among the lower-class infantrymen, the middle-class Dax and the aristocratic generals as deep and self-evident as a ten-foot trench. The contrast between the lower echelons and the upper classes is perhaps too obvious, but this adds a dimension to the film that makes it impossible to avoid, or resist, the film's message – gripped by the action and the unfolding drama, the audience sit like *A Clockwork Orange*'s Alex undergoing the Ludovico aversion therapy, unable to avert their gaze from the action, or to avoid the inevitable tragedy of the soldiers' execution.

The film is mostly unleavened by humour – although Ferol's killing of the cockroach and Dax's humiliation of Mireau are amusing – and ultimately provides no reprieve for the innocent victims offered up for sacrifice by the generals, but the final scene gives humanity to the soldiers, and hope to the audience. The fact that this haunting and unforgettable scene – in which the German peasant girl (Christiane Harlan) performs a haunting song for Dax's men – was, according to Kubrick, entirely his own creation is worth remembering given his reputation for cold, calculating cynicism. The fact that the casting of Christiane led to forty years of happy marriage, lasting until Kubrick's death, makes it all the more poignant.

**KUBRICK ON KUBRICK:** 'The soldier is absorbing because all the circumstances surrounding him have a kind of charged intensity. For all its horror, war is pure drama, probably because it is one of the few remaining situations where men stand up for and speak for what they believe to be their principles.' – quoted in the *New York Times* magazine, 12 October 1958.

# Spartacus (1960)

[Colour – 197 mins (preview version, 1960), 184 mins (premiere version, 1960), 161 mins (re-released version, 1967), 196 mins (restored version, 1991)]

Screenplay by Dalton Trumbo
Based on the Novel by Howard Fast
Director of Photography Russell Metty, ASC
Production Designer Alexander Golitzen
Art Director Eric Orbom
Set Decorations Russell A Gausman, Julia Heron
Main Titles & Design Consultant Saul Bass
Sound Waldon O Watson, Joe Lapis, Murray Spivack, Ronald Pierce
Historical & Technical Adviser Vittorio Nino Novarese
Unit Production Manager Norman Deming
Additional Scenes Photographed by Clifford Stine, ASC
Production Aide Stan Margulies
Wardrobe by Peruzzi
Miss Simmons' Costumes Bill Thomas
Costumes by Valles
Film Editor Robert Lawrence
Assistants to the Film Editor Robert Schulte, Fred Chulack
Score Conducted by Joseph Gershenson
Music Editor Arnold Schwarzwald
Make-up Bud Westmore
Hair Stylist Larry Germain
Assistant Directors Marshall Green, Foster Phinney, James Welch, Joseph Kenny, Charles Scott
Music Composed & Conducted by Alex North
Executive Producer Kirk Douglas
Produced by Edward Lewis
Directed by Stanley Kubrick

**CAST:** Kirk Douglas (*Spartacus*), Laurence Olivier (*Marcus Licinius Crassus*), Jean Simmons (*Varinia*), Charles Laughton (*Gracchus*), Peter Ustinov (*Lentulus Batiatus*), John Gavin (*Caius Julius Caesar*), Nina Foch (*Helena Glabrus*), Herbert Lom (*Tigranes Levantus*), John Ireland (*Crixus*), John Dall (*Publius Marcus Glabrus*), Charles McGraw (*Marcellus*), Joanna Barnes (*Claudia Marius*), Harold J Stone (*David*), Woody Strode (*Draba*), Peter Brocco (*Ramon*), Paul Lambert (*Gannicus*), Robert J Wilke (*Guard Captain*), Nicholas Dennis (*Dionysius*), John Hoyt (*Caius/Roman Officer*), Frederic Worlock (*Laelius*), Tony Curtis (*Antoninus*).

**UNCREDITED CAST:** Dayton Lummis (*Symmachus*), Lili Valenty (*Old Crone*), Jill Jarmyn (*Julia*), Jo Summers (*Slave Girl*), James Griffith (*Otho*), Joe Haworth (*Marius*), Dale Van Sickle (*Trainer*), Vinton Hayworth (*Metallius*), Carleton Young (*Herald*), Hallene Hill (*Beggar Girl*), Paul E Burns (*Fimbria*), Leonard Penn (*Garrison Officer*), Harry Harvey Jr, Eddie Parker, Harold Goodwin, Chuck Roberson (*Slaves*), Saul Gorss, Charles Horvath, Gil Perkins (*Slave Leaders*), Bob Morgan, Reg Parton, Tom Steele (*Gladiators*), Ken Terrell, Boyd Morgan (*Ad-Libs*), Dick Crockett, Harvey Parry, Carey Loftin (*Guards*), Bob Burns, Seamon Glass, George Robotham, Stubby Kruger (*Pirates*), Chuck Courtney, Russ Saunders, Valley Keene, Tap Canutt, Joe Canutt, Chuck Hayward, Buff Brady, Cliff Lyons, Rube Schaffer (*Soldiers*), Ted De Corsia, Arthur Batanides, Robert Stevenson (*Legionnaires*), Terence De Marney (*Major-Domo*), Gary Lockwood, Al Carmichael, Rudy Bukich, Jim Sears, Richard Farnsworth, Loren Janes, Roy Engel, Paul Frees, Harry Harvey Jr.

**UNCREDITED CREW:** Irving Lerner (*Second Unit Director*), Wes Thompson (*Special Effects*), Irving Lerner (*Editorial Consultant*), William Ware Theiss (*Costume Design*), Yakima Canutt (*Second-Unit Director*), Glenn Eugene Anderson Jr (*Sound Engineer*), Harry Wolf, George Dye (*Camera Operators*), Peter Ellenshaw (*Matte Artist*), Milton Schwarzwald (*Music Supervisor*).

**TITLE SEQUENCE:** Following the five-minute overture played while the curtains were still closed – a popular conceit of films of the period – the Universal International logo dissolves through to the first of a number of hand-painted images of various Roman artefacts, placed alongside the names of the cast, characters and crew members with symbolic deliberation. As the last image, the frontal shot of a Roman bust, appears on screen alongside Stanley Kubrick's credit, it crumbles to pieces, symbolising the fall of the Roman Empire.

The inspired title sequence was the work of the graphic designer Saul Bass, who had revolutionised the opening titles of feature films with his radical designs for films by Otto Preminger (*Carmen Jones, Saint Joan,*

The Man with the Golden Arm and, most notably, Anatomy of a Murder) and Alfred Hitchcock (North by Northwest, Vertigo and Psycho), and whose career would continue through the œuvre of Martin Scorsese (Goodfellas, The Age of Innocence, Casino, et al.).

**SUMMARY:** Spartacus, a Thracian slave, is one of several toiling in the salt mines of Libya who are bought by Batiatus and taken to Capua, where he is trained to be a gladiator. He also falls in love with Varinia, a slave girl from Britannia, and when Crassus, a visiting Roman patrician, buys her from Batiatus and causes the death of his friend Draba in the arena, Spartacus initiates a successful revolt, leading his fellow gladiators to the slopes of Mount Vesuvius, rescuing some ninety thousand more slaves along the way. With a combination of gladiatorial combat and guerrilla tactics, the mob is soon an army, one with sufficient might to threaten Rome itself.

Having defeated even Crassus's hand-picked garrison commander, and almost twice their own number in centurions, Spartacus desires only freedom for his emancipated people. He makes a deal with some Silesian pirates – fifty million sesterces for five hundred ships to escape Italy and return home – but, despite additional bribery from Gracchus, Crassus's enemy in the senate, Crassus outbids them all, paying the Silesians to renege on their deal. Thus Spartacus's people arrive at the coast to find that the ships have departed, and they are forced to turn back to Rome. Crassus seizes the opportunity to take command of the Roman legions, and leads them on a march against Spartacus's army at Metapontum. All but six thousand of Spartacus's followers are killed; the rest are threatened with crucifixion along the Appian Way, unless they identify their leader.

They refuse, each claiming to be Spartacus. Humiliated and enraged by this show of loyalty, Crassus finds another way to single out Spartacus, and forces him into a duel with Antoninus, Crassus's former body servant. Spartacus kills his friend to spare him the ordeal of crucifixion, and is crucified himself. Varinia, forced into servility at Crassus's mansion, leaves the city in the protection of Gracchus, who has committed suicide rather than live under the tyranny of his old enemy's dictatorship. Pausing at the foot of the cross on which Spartacus lies dying, Varinia holds up their son, born into freedom, as Spartacus had dreamed he would be.

**SOURCE:** Spartacus was based on Howard Fast's historical novel, first published by Citadel Press in 1951, which expanded the few known facts about the gladiator-led slave uprising of 73 BC into a simplistic left-wing polemic about the power of the masses and the corruption of the ruling classes. Fast, a confirmed Communist who as one of the 'Hollywood Ten' had served prison time for his political beliefs, was understandably thrilled when Kirk Douglas's Bryna Productions optioned the book in late 1957, just as *Paths of Glory* was being readied for release. By the time *Spartacus* went before the cameras a little over a year later, Fast's novel had been translated into 45 languages and sold more than three million copies. 'I wrote this novel because I considered it an important story for the times in which we live,' Fast wrote in its introduction. 'Not in the mechanical sense of historical parallels, but because there is hope and strength to be taken from such a story about the age-old fight for freedom – and because Spartacus lived not for one time of man.'

Douglas, a Jew of Russian extraction, was beginning to come to terms with his religious and cultural heritage when his long-time associate Edward Lewis brought him *Spartacus*. In his autobiography, *The Ragman's Son*, Douglas expressed how *Spartacus* fitted his views about slavery: 'I see thousands and thousands of slaves carrying rocks, beaten, starved, crushed, dying. I identify with them. As it says in the Torah: "Slaves were we unto Egypt." I come from a race of slaves. That would have been *my* family, *me*.' Perhaps more relevant was the fact that Douglas had just lost the lead in *Ben-Hur* to Charlton Heston, and saw *Spartacus* as a similarly heroic role in an equally epic story. 'I took an option on the book with my own money,' he added. 'I was sure I'd have no difficulty getting United Artists to finance *Spartacus*.' Douglas was wrong.

**PRODUCTION HISTORY:** When Kubrick replaced Anthony 'Abby' Mann as director of *Spartacus* in February 1959, it was merely the latest episode in what the film's executive producer and star Kirk Douglas has described as 'the wars of *Spartacus*'. The war had begun when Arthur Krim, head of United Artists, rejected Douglas's idea for a *Spartacus* film on the grounds that the company was already committed to a rival telling of the story, *The Gladiators*, written by Arthur Koestler, directed by Martin Ritt (*The Long Hot Summer, Hud*) and slated to star Yul Brynner (*The King and I*) as Spartacus. Douglas initially offered to amalgamate the two productions, but when Brynner refused and United Artists announced its $5,500,000 production of *The Gladiators* in *Variety*, Douglas took it as a declaration of war. With a rapidly expiring option on the novel, no script, no studio and no title – United Artists had the foresight to register *Spartacus* along with *The Gladiators* – it was a war nobody except Douglas expected to win.

The first two problems were solved with a deal that gave Bryna Productions a sixty-day extension on its option, in return for which Howard Fast would be allowed to adapt his own novel into a screenplay. His first sixty pages were, according to Douglas, 'a disaster – unusable. He hadn't used the dramatic elements he'd put into his own book. It was just characters spouting ideas; speeches on two legs.' Instead, Douglas secretly hired the blacklisted screenwriter Dalton Trumbo (*The Brave One, Roman Holiday*) – another of the 'Hollywood Ten' – to write a 'treatment' from which Fast could work. Fast hated the outline, however, declaring it the work of 'the world's worst writer', and, after another attempt to write the script himself, Douglas brought the pseudonymous 'Sam Jackson' (Trumbo) aboard to write the screenplay. David Lean (*Lawrence of Arabia*) was approached to direct, but declined, telling Douglas, 'I can't somehow fit into it style-wise. I couldn't bring it off.'

As producer, Douglas began considering his dream cast: believing that the slaves should be played by Americans, and the Romans by foreign actors, Douglas saw himself as Spartacus, Sir Laurence Olivier as Crassus, Charles Laughton (*The Hunchback of Notre Dame*) as Gracchus, and Peter Ustinov as Batiatus. Douglas approached Olivier while the pair were filming *The Devil's Disciple* (1956) together – a brave choice, given that Olivier had virtually stolen that film from Douglas and his co-star Burt Lancaster – and the revered English actor responded enthusiastically, but with customary egoism. 'He thought Spartacus would be a terrific role – for him,' Douglas reported. 'Larry also thought he could direct the film, which we felt would be a tremendous burden for him. But he was interested!' Ultimately, Olivier told Douglas he would play Crassus if the part could be improved 'in relation to the other three roles'. Laughton declared Trumbo's script 'a piece of shit', but signed on anyway, and, by August 1958, Ustinov was also aboard. 'We were three-for-three against UA's zero-for-three,' Douglas noted with satisfaction. Tony Curtis (*Some Like it Hot*) petitioned for a role, and one was created for him. With the cast in place, Universal Pictures agreed to back the film, and on 27 October 1958, United Artists conceded defeat and abandoned its own Spartacus project.

No sooner had the principal cast been assembled for rehearsals, than Olivier, Laughton and Ustinov began to behave like Roman senators, each conspiring against the others to ensure that his own role was the most significant. As Ustinov – who described the production as being 'as full of intrigue as a Balkan government in the good old days' – wrote in his autobiography, *Dear Me*, 'We had all been sent scripts in order to tempt us, with subtle variations favouring our particular characters . . . No two scripts, we discovered, were the same. Since Larry Olivier had arrived a week prior to the majority of us, he had already inspired a yet newer version of the script in which his role had somewhat grown in importance,' he added, referring to a draft in which the entire story was told in flashback, by Crassus.

'We had to entice them, allay their fears that Kirk Douglas, this actor who also owned the company, would be able to twist it in his direction,' Douglas explained.

Meanwhile, Douglas fought with Universal over its choice of director: Anthony 'Abby' Mann, the veteran director of several Western epics (and, later, *The Fall of the Roman Empire*), who, the studio felt, would not lose sight of the human story, regardless of the epic scale of the film. The film's opening sequence, in which Batiatus (Ustinov) selects slaves to train as gladiators, was the first to go before cameras, on 27 January 1959. For the first three weeks, filming progressed smoothly; but by the time the production moved to Batiatus's gladiator school, Douglas began to suspect that his and Mann's view of the story were diametrically opposed, and that Mann was favouring the subtle characterisations of the Romans, particularly Ustinov's Batiatus, over his own overstated brand of acting. 'It was clear that Tony Mann was not in control,' Douglas said later. 'He let Peter Ustinov direct his own scenes by taking every suggestion Peter made. The suggestions were good – for Peter, but not necessarily for the picture.'

Having not wanted Mann in the first place, Douglas now saw this apparent lack of control as an opportunity to fire him. Despite his assertion that it was not he, but the studio, who had ousted Mann, Douglas fired him on Friday, 13 February 1959, assuaging his guilt by paying Mann's $75,000 fee in full. *Spartacus* needed a new director, and although Douglas initially rejected the stills photographer William Read Woodfield's suggestion that Stanley Kubrick, 'the guy who directed the best picture you ever made', be brought in as Mann's replacement, the idea grew on him. After dismissing Mann, Douglas eventually telephoned Kubrick, who was at his regular Friday-night poker game. 'Kirk asked if Stanley would consider directing *Spartacus*,' his production partner, James B Harris, recollected. 'We considered it seriously because (1) we wanted to see some money come into [our] corporation, and (2) we wanted to buy our way out of this five-picture contract we had with Kirk.' Kubrick read the script, agreed to direct in return for $150,000 (twice Mann's original fee) and a dissolution of the Harris-Kubrick agreement with Bryna. After a weekend of meetings, Kubrick arrived on set on the Monday morning, ready to pick up where Mann had left off just two days earlier. 'We lost no days of shooting,' Douglas said. 'You can't switch horses in midstream faster than that.'

With customary grandeur, Douglas chose the arena of Batiatus's gladiatorial school as the place to introduce *Spartacus*'s new director to an assembly of cast and crew members, many of whom thought the appointment of this virtual unknown – whom Ustinov later described as 'a young man with huge eyes who seemed at the time to have none of the vices, and few of the virtues, of youth' – was a joke. As Kubrick's wife Christiane later recalled, 'They were all famous actors in [*Spartacus*] and they treated him, because he was so young, with a certain arrogance. So he was arrogant right back. He loved Tony Curtis, because they had lots in common,' she added.

'We were about three years separated in age, and we had an excellent relationship,' Curtis later remarked, adding, 'No one had much confidence in Stanley at the beginning, because he didn't have enough of a background. They tried to screw him around ... If he needed twenty extras and they gave him a tiny set that held ten, he would say, "I don't want to shoot that scene today." And then during a meeting he'd say, "I asked for twenty, and you gave me ten. Tomorrow I want forty, and a bigger set." '

Michael Herr, co-screenwriter of *Full Metal Jacket* and a close friend of Kubrick's for many years, recalled Kubrick giving an example of his on-set relationship with Kirk Douglas. 'It was Kirk on horseback and Stanley on foot, just about to shoot a scene and having yet another of their violent disagreements,' Herr wrote in *Vanity Fair*. 'Kirk rode his white freedom-fighter stallion into Stanley to make his point, which was that he was the star *and* the producer, turning his horse's flank against Stanley, pushing him back farther and farther to drive it home again, then riding away, leaving Stanley standing in the dust, furious and humiliated, as one of the wise guys on the crew walks by and says, "Remember, Stanley: The play's the thing." '

Douglas, for his part, claims to have respected most of Kubrick's decisions, as much as they often frustrated him. 'One day he decided that he wanted to raise the ceiling of the stage by two feet,' he recalled. 'It was impractical, expensive, time-consuming, and not essential. But overall, his selectivity and his concepts were wonderful.'

The director of photography, Russell Metty, a veteran cinematographer with 25 years' experience, did not think so. He and Kubrick clashed frequently over the young director's insistence on second-guessing Metty's lighting techniques. As Tony Curtis later wrote in his autobiography, 'To Russ Metty, Kubrick was just a kid, barely shaving. "This guy is going to direct this movie? He's going to tell me where to put the camera? They've got to be kidding!" That was his attitude.' Curtis recalled the occasion when Kubrick was preparing to film the first encounter between Spartacus and Tigranes. '[Kubrick said], "In that tent shot, I want it to be low, dark, very sinister. I need an environment that looks like that." So they built a set that had just a trunk or a few other pieces, and Russ Metty lit it in a very cavalier way. Stanley looked through his camera and said, "I can't see the actors' faces." And Metty, who was sitting in that high chair, lifted up his leg and kicked one of the lights into the shot. Stanley looked at him and said, "Now it's too much light." Cool through the whole experience,' he added.

'Nothing made him nervous,' Douglas agreed. 'He stands up to anybody.'

Not all of the problems that plagued *Spartacus* could be put down to Kubrick's customary perfectionism. No sooner had Jean Simmons arrived to commence work, replacing Sabine Bethmann in the role of Varinia, than she was forced to undergo emergency surgery, which kept her out of production for a month. Tony Curtis almost severed his Achilles' tendon playing tennis with Douglas, and spent four weeks in a hip-to-toe plaster cast. Even Douglas, who had prided himself on never having missed a day's filming through sickness, was felled by a virus for ten days. When Charles Laughton threatened to sue Douglas, presumably because he perceived that his character had been relegated to playing second fiddle while Rome burned, Douglas's frustrations came to a head. 'Jean Simmons had been out sick for over a month; Tony Curtis was in a wheelchair; I was in the middle of an epic movie written by a blacklisted ex-convict, directed by a twenty-nine-year-old; I was months over schedule, 250 per cent over budget. And now Charles Laughton was going to sue me? I couldn't stop laughing.'

In reality, such difficulties were no laughing matter for Douglas, who was struggling to maintain control of a runaway production, a wayward director and three belligerent and highly competitive co-stars. The break in production caused by illness did, however, allow Kubrick the opportunity to film one of his beloved battle scenes, thousands of miles from the influence of the studio. Initially, Douglas had hoped to save money by shooting *Spartacus* at Rome's Cinecittà studios. Universal, alarmed at the number of 'runaway productions' being filmed away from Hollywood, had insisted that the film be shot entirely on its own 422-acre backlot, even if it meant dismantling such historic standing sets as those used for *All Quiet on the Western Front* (1930), *The Hunchback of Notre Dame* (1939), *The Phantom of the Opera* (1943) and *To Hell and Back* (1955) – which it did. Now Kubrick saw an opportunity to escape the stifling environs of the studio backlot by calling for battle scenes that could be filmed only abroad. Trumbo's script had used symbolism, rather than spectacle, to suggest the bloody nature of the fighting between the Roman legions and Spartacus's army of slaves, but Kubrick persuaded Douglas that the audience should be treated to a spectacle every inch as bloody as one of the gladiatorial combats arranged for the public in Roman times – and on a far grander scale.

Thus, late in the summer of 1959, the production unit spent six weeks in Spain, where scouts had found the two key elements of the battle scenes as Kubrick envisioned them: eight thousand trained soldiers from the Spanish infantry, who would literally double as a sixteen-thousand-strong Roman legion, and a vast plain, situated just outside of Madrid, where Kubrick could direct the armies from atop one of three specially constructed towers, each over a hundred feet tall and accommodating up to six of the Super Technirama '70 cameras being used for the production. Disgruntled, the cinematographer Russell Metty did not make the trip – he was replaced for the duration of the Spanish shoot by Clifford Stine – and, although the production designer Alexander Golitzen recalls spending several months in Spain, it was the 'main titles and design consultant' Saul Bass who was called upon to 'storyboard' the battle scenes, based on extensive research he had undertaken on the subject of Roman battle formations. 'I simply took the position that the Roman army was a highly mechanised and disciplined force . . . [whereas] the slaves had a lack of precision,' Bass said later.

The battle scenes, virtually absent from the script that Kubrick first read the morning after Anthony Mann was fired, were just one area in which he found the screenplay lacking. 'The script could have been improved during shooting, but it wasn't,' Kubrick stated, although the seven drafts, 1,534 pages and quarter of a million words written by Dalton Trumbo alone appear to conflict with this view. Kubrick hired *Paths of Glory* co-writer Calder Willingham to script the battle scenes and was also one of several volunteers who toiled on the script, personally cutting all but 35 words of Douglas's dialogue from the film's first half-hour – 'We fought about that one,' Kubrick commented, 'but I won.' Even some of the actors made official alterations to several scenes, as Peter Ustinov later recalled: 'I rewrote all the scenes I had with Laughton; we rehearsed at his home or mine, often slogging away into the middle of the night. The next day, we rearranged the studio furniture to conform what we had engineered at home, and presented the company with a *fait accompli*: Kubrick accepted what we had done more or less without modification, and the scenes were shot in half a day each.'

The trials and tribulations of *Spartacus* were further complicated when the talent agency MCA, which represented both Douglas and Harris-Kubrick, bought Universal Pictures for the princely sum of $11,250,000 – $750,000 less than the budget of *Spartacus* – and installed Douglas's agent, Lew Wasserman, as head of production. 'At the beginning of *Spartacus*, Lew Wasserman at MCA was my agent; he worked for me,' Douglas noted with due irony. 'In the middle of shooting, MCA bought Universal; I worked for him.'

With principal photography finally completed, Douglas went off to star opposite Kim Novak in Richard Quine's *Strangers When We Meet* (1960) while Kubrick and – after he and the movie's editorial consultant Irving Lerner fell out – Robert Lawrence set to work on a rough cut of the epic. When Douglas returned, he was appalled at the liberties Kubrick had taken with his 196-minute first cut, primarily because shots showing Spartacus crucified – which had been painful and time-consuming to shoot, and showed the hero's tragic, unmistakably Christ-like death – had been excised from the film in favour of reaction shots from Jean Simmons's Varinia. According to Lawrence, 'Kirk grabbed a folding chair and threw it. He was beside himself with anger. "You're fired – and you're fired, I want to talk to you!" ' Lawrence claims that Kubrick blamed him for the omission. 'Stanley said, "Listen, let's start on the last reel. What happened to those close-ups that I picked of Kirk on the cross?" '

After reshoots were completed, Douglas went to Mexico to make yet another film, while Kubrick and Lawrence toiled on a revised edit. At last, after a total of 33 months from conception to premiere – including an almost unprecedented 167 days of principal photography – Universal Pictures was finally ready to unveil what had become one of the longest and most troublesome shoots in Hollywood history, and certainly the most expensive. As Douglas himself noted, '*Spartacus* took three years out of my life – more time than the real-life Spartacus spent waging war against the Roman Empire.' Nevertheless, as Douglas stated in the *Spartacus* souvenir book, 'The price tag on a picture is no guarantee that it will be funny, tragic, good or bad. Money is not entertaining. If it were, you might as well get the vice president of a bank to show you twelve million in a vault, instead of going to the movies. But if *Spartacus* is a thrilling experience,' he added, 'twelve million was a drop in the bucket. If not, twelve dollars was too much.'

Besides, in the increasingly desperate war being fought between the film studios and television, to whom the former were losing their audience, money was almost no object. 'I think *Spartacus* is probably part of the trend of trying to combat television by giving the public something they can't see on television – namely a multitude of big stars and spectacle,' Kubrick told *Horizon* magazine shortly after the film was completed. The trend would continue to the end of the decade, until another Roman epic, *Cleopatra* (1968), nearly bankrupted 20th Century Fox. 'But what may be a trend in Hollywood isn't a trend for me,' Kubrick added, 'because I've always approached every picture I've done just from the standpoint of telling a story.'

Several minor cuts were made after the press preview on 6 October 1960, and, after its world premiere in New York a few days later, *Spartacus* was officially premiered at a glitzy charity event at Hollywood's Pantages Theater on 19 October 1960. The wars of *Spartacus* were over.

While not exactly disowning the film in subsequent years, Kubrick described *Spartacus* to Gene D Phillips as 'the only film that I did not have control over, and which I feel was not enhanced by that fact', and has taken almost every opportunity to reiterate this point.

Douglas, who has variously described Kubrick as 'an ingrate' and 'a talented shit', takes umbrage at his hand-picked director's frequent dismissal of the film, 'Kubrick was never a big fan of this movie, which I resented. He never accepted it with any enthusiasm. He was someone used to having his own way, but this wasn't something initiated by Kubrick . . . the ship was sailing.'

**CASTING:** Although the cast of *Spartacus* was already in place when Kubrick arrived to begin shooting, the director was able to influence one piece of casting. Of his original 'wish list' of actors, only Elsa Martinelli – whom Douglas had wanted for the part Varinia – was unavailable, and after considering Ingrid Bergman (*Casablanca*), Jean Simmons (*Caesar and Cleopatra*) and Jeanne Moreau (*The Lovers*), Douglas followed Kubrick's lead on *Paths of Glory* and hired an unknown German actress, Sabina Bethmann, for the film's principal female role. 'She looked great on film, but was not much of an actress,' Douglas later admitted.

Kubrick, arriving on set on 16 February 1959, agreed. One of his first acts as incoming director was to insist that she be fired, and he chose to do this in a particularly cavalier fashion.

'Kubrick suggested he do an improvisation with her,' Douglas explained. 'The scene: he would tell her that she had just lost the part in the movie. Stanley figured this would smoke her out – if she had any talent at all, she would cry or scream or get mad or something.' The film's producer, Edward Lewis, wanted nothing to do with this cruelty, but Douglas stayed to watch, fascinated. 'He explained the scenario to Sabina. Nothing happened. The poor girl froze. That was the end of Sabina.' After only two days, Bethmann was paid her full salary of $35,000 and replaced by Jean Simmons.

**THE USUAL SUSPECTS:** Kirk Douglas's starring role in *Paths of Glory* led him, directly or indirectly, to consider Kubrick as a replacement for the departing director Anthony Mann. In addition, one of the actors playing legionnaires was Ted De Corsia, who had appeared as a crooked cop in Kubrick's *The Killing*.

**THE PURSUIT OF PERFECTION:** 'In *Spartacus* I tried with only limited success to make the film as real as possible,' Kubrick recollected, 'but I was up against a pretty dumb script which was rarely faithful to what is known about Spartacus.'

Intriguingly, Dalton Trumbo claimed that it was Kubrick and Douglas, not he, who had fudged the facts in order to create a more cinematic, and less political, entertainment. According to Maria Wyke's *Projecting the Past: Ancient Rome, Cinema and History*, Trumbo constantly reproached them for what he took to be their 'unremitting attack on the political meaning and the intellectual content' of every proposed scene in the historical film. 'In Trumbo's view, the omission from the film of any sequence displaying a significant victory for the slave army emasculated the hero gladiator, while the decision to close the film with his crucifixion – against all the historical evidence and against the narrative closure of both book and screenplay – created an "irritating allusion" to Christ (which appeared to remodel the political militant and spiritual martyr).' Additional damage was done, Trumbo might have argued, by adding the further Christian iconography of the Nativity (Varinia holding up Spartacus's newborn son) to that of the Passion (Spartacus's crucifixion), and by the opening narration, which implied that it was the advent of Christianity, rather than class struggle, that 'was destined to overthrow the pagan tyranny of Rome and bring about a new society'.

**CLASSIC QUOTES**
Spartacus: 'What's your name?'
Draba: 'You don't want to know my name. I don't want to know your name.'

Spartacus: 'Just a friendly question.'
Draba: 'Gladiators don't make friends. If they ever put us in the ring together, I might have to kill you.'

Spartacus: 'I made myself a promise, Crixus. I swore that if I ever got out of this place I'd die before I watched two men fight to the death again. Draba made that promise, too. He kept it. So will I.'

Crassus: 'Antoninus, look. Across the river. There is something you must see. There, boy, is Rome. The might, the majesty, the terror of Rome. There is the power that bestrides the known world like a colossus. No man can withstand Rome. No *nation* can withstand her. How much less . . . a boy. Hmm? There's only one way to deal with Rome, Antoninus. You must serve her. You must abase yourself before her. You must grovel at her feet. You must . . . *love* her.'

Spartacus: 'Take that back to your senate. Tell them you and that broken stick is all that's *left* of the Garrison of Rome. Tell them we want nothing from Rome. Nothing . . . except our freedom!'

Varinia: 'What do you pray for?'
Spartacus: 'I pray for a son who'll be born free.'
Varinia: 'I pray for the same thing.'
Spartacus: 'Take care of my son, Varinia. And if he never knows me, tell him who I was, and what we dreamed of. Tell him the truth. There'll be plenty of others to tell him lies.'

Thias: 'I bring a mesage from your master, Marcus Licinius Crassus, commander of Italy. By command of His Most Merciful Excellency, your lives are to be spared. Slaves you were, and slaves you remain. But the terrible penalty of crucifixion has been set aside on the single condition that you identify the body or the living person of the slave called Spartacus.'
Antoninus: 'I'm Spartacus!'
Slaves: '*I'm* Spartacus! *I'm* Spartacus! *I'm* Spartacus!'

Antoninus: 'Could we have won, Spartacus? Could we ever have won?'
Spartacus: 'Just by fighting them, we won something. When just one man says, "No, I won't," Rome begins to fear. We were tens of thousand who said no. That was the wonder of it. To have seen slaves lift their heads from the dust.'

**THEMES AND MOTIFS:** In *Projecting the Past: Ancient Rome, Cinema and History*, Maria Wyke noted the influence of Communist politics on Howard Fast's novel, and Dalton Trumbo's screenplay. 'In historical guise, Fast's *Spartacus* graphically enacts for Americans . . . the "liberation of the masses of labouring men and women, the productive members of society, from their 'enslavement' by the parasitic possessors of wealth and property".'

If Fast and Trumbo were eager to bring their political viewpoints to *Spartacus*, Kubrick was equally inclined to bring his beloved chess theme into the film, choosing the floor of the Roman senate – with all its machinations and manoeuvrings – as the perfect place to display a chequerboard motif. (Earlier, Crassus describes the garrison of Rome as 'the only power in Rome strong enough to checkmate Gracchus and his senate' – an obvious anachronism, given that the Romans did not play chess.) Later, the chessboard formation is repeated on the battlefield, as the Roman legions approach Spartacus's army of slaves for a final confrontation: in marching formation, the square groups of centurions resemble 'black' squares, while the barren plains make up the 'white' squares. Let the games begin!

MUSIC: The six-times Academy Award nominee Alex North was selected as *Spartacus*'s composer, and immediately set about researching the music of the period, gathering a collection of antique instruments rarely, if ever, heard on a film's soundtrack. While not exactly authentically Roman, instruments such as the sarrousaphone, a barbaric sounding wind instrument, the lyre-like kythara, the dulcimer, Israeli recorder, Chinese oboe, lute, mandolin, Yugoslav flute and bagpipes were employed to dramatic effect. The prize of North's collection was an Ondioline, an early precursor of the electronic synthesiser, which was used on film for the first time.

North was given a year to write and record his epic score, and in Irwin Bazelon's book *Knowing the Score: Notes on Film Music*, described working with Kubrick as 'the greatest experience'. North, whose original compositions for Kubrick's later *2001: A Space Odyssey* were rejected in favour of pre-existing classical music, would be given a precursor of Kubrick's predilection for 'needle-drops' when he was asked to insert 'The Battle of New Orleans' over the scene in which Crassus takes command of Rome, and to study Prokofiev's score for Eisenstein's *Alexander Nevsky* for reference.

The *Spartacus* soundtrack, originally released by Universal-owned Decca, is currently available as a CD (MCAD-10256) which features around 40 minutes of North's original score. More than 79 minutes of *additional* music is also available on a Tsunami CD (TCI 0603), featuring such curiosities as an alternative version of the 'Child Birth' music, and a demo version of a track called 'Gladiator Fight', which appeared on the original soundtrack as 'Gladiators' Fight to the Death'.

POSTER: The earliest poster image used to promote *Spartacus* was an illustrated display of seven gold Roman coins against a solid red background, each of the coins depicting the head of one of the seven principal cast members, and arranged in contractual order from the top down. British 'quad' versions of this composition added the names of the actors to the coins, along with a silhouetted figure lifting the symbol of the Roman senate.

Another early US 'one-sheet' appeared to capitalise on the trend towards religious epics, with Spartacus painted in a Moses-like stance ('Let my people go!'), wielding a burning torch, while battle rages around him.

The 1991 re-release favoured a photograph of Spartacus on horseback, waving a short sword, picked out against a deep blue background, while beneath it seven miniature boxes display photographs of the other principal cast members in character.

**TAG-LINE:** 'THE ELECTRIFYING SPECTACLE THAT THRILLED THE WORLD!' trumpeted the tag-line on one of the many poster and press images created for *Spartacus*.

**TRAILER:** After a caption highlighting *Spartacus*'s four Academy Award wins, the trailer opens on a Roman town, as the legend 'THIS THEATER PROUDLY SALUTES A MOTION PICTURE THAT IS MARKED FOR GREATNESS' scrolls up the screen. '*Spartacus*,' heralds the narrator, as a hand-drawn title zooms into view, 'in which the finest cast ever assembled relives one of mankind's most magnificent stories.' Captions featuring the names of the principal actors appear over images of their characters, as the narration continues: 'Starring Kirk Douglas as Spartacus, Laurence Olivier as Crassus, Jean Simmons as the slave Varinia, Charles Laughton as Gracchus, Peter Ustinov as Batiatus, John Gavin as Julius Caesar and Tony Curtis as Antoninus, in the powerful story of the gladiator rebel who sprang from slavery to challenge the awesome might of Imperial Rome.' Captions featuring quotations from several magazine reviews are then played over random scenes: 'A MIGHTY TALE TOLD LARGE' (*Life*); 'A NEW KIND OF MOVIE' (*Time*); 'BRILLIANT, COMPASSIONATE, ABSORBING DRAMA' (*Look*).

A second version of the trailer opened with the same Oscar-trumpeting caption, and the same opening panorama, but used its captions to set the scene: 'IN THE YEAR 70 BC ROME – COLOSSUS OF THE WORLD – FACED ITS GRAVEST CHALLENGE.' After a suitably portentous line from Crassus, and the same hand-lettered title card as before, no superlative is spared as the narrator's voice continues over edited scenes: '*Spartacus* – a motion picture unequalled in the entire history of film making, unlikely ever to be surpassed in the magnitude of production, in the fervour and passion of its conflict, in the tenderness and beauty of its love story. Nothing was spared to make *Spartacus* the superb achievement it is – neither time, nor money, nor talent. For, in *Spartacus*, you will see the finest cast ever assembled, relive history's most exciting and inspiring drama.'

The narrator then begins a rundown of the principal cast, with a line from Crassus and Varinia inserted for good measure.

Finally, Spartacus himself is allowed to speak, before a roster of three magazine reviews (as before) is captioned over battle scenes, along with a new critique: the *New York Post*'s 'In same giant class as "Ben-Hur" . . . and superior in wit, characterization and romance.'

**WHAT THE PAPERS SAID:** Most critics had yet to come to terms with Hollywood's new-found fondness for gigantic epics – designed to compete with television in a quantity-versus-quality battle that continues to this day – by the time *Spartacus* unspooled before the press on 6 October 1960. While most reviews were ungenerous towards the film, *Variety* stated that Kubrick had 'out-DeMilled the old master in spectacle, without ever permitting the story or the people who are the core of the drama to become lost in the shuffle . . . There is solid dramatic substance, purposeful and intriguingly contrasted character portrayals and . . . sheer pictorial poetry that is sweeping and savage, intimate and lusty, tender and bitter sweet. *Spartacus* is a rousing testament to the spirit and dignity of man.' *Time* magazine acknowledged that Kubrick's direction displayed a mastery of the close-up and the wide shot. 'In intimate scenes his camera follows the action with delicacy and precision; but he also knows when to let the frame stand grandly still and the audience stare, as if through a large picture window, at a magnificent landscape or a ponderous ballet of legions that precedes a battle.'

It must have pleased Kubrick that many reviewers shared his view that *Spartacus*'s principal weakness lay in the story and/or the script, large tracts of which Kubrick had decided to dispense with altogether, rather than retain too much of what *Sight and Sound*'s critic Peter John Dyer described as 'Dalton Trumbo's highly emotional brand of Left-thinking . . . Freedom is represented by eve of battle visits to the troops, nude bathing scenes, babies, aged peasant faces, trysts in forest glades, Super Technirama-70 rides across sunset horizons, and a heroine shot in romantically gauzy close-ups.' Too often, the New York *Herald Tribune*'s Paul V Beckley suggested, *Spartacus* 'resorts to rhetoric, sexual innuendo, pageantry of empire'.

**CONTROVERSY:** If *Spartacus*'s producers Kirk Douglas and Edward Lewis were courting controversy when they bought the rights to a left-wing book by the jailed Communist author Howard Fast, they were positively encouraging it by hiring the blacklisted, card-carrying Communist screenwriter Dalton Trumbo to write it. Douglas insisted that he had hand-picked Trumbo to adapt Fast's novel; in reality, he had considered several others – among them Dudley Nichols, Lillian Hellman, Irwin Shaw and Maxwell Anderson – before deciding upon Trumbo primarily for strategic and economic reasons: he worked fast, and his fee was a tenth of the market rate of non-blacklisted writers.

In Jeffrey B Smith's article for *Velvet Light Trap*, Trumbo explains: 'Someone had come up with the idea of suggesting to Douglas he use one of the black market people openly. He declared himself willing to do this. The idea would be that whoever broke away as the first writer [to receive screen credit] would work practically for expenses – that is, for say $5,000 or $7,500 – for the concession that his name would appear on the screen. If, when the release date arrived, bankers or distributors caused too much trouble, the producing company would have the right to take the name off, but would compensate the author handsomely for the lost credit.'

In the event, Douglas was forced to exercise this latter option, since Otto Preminger effectively stole his thunder – and broke the blacklist – by giving Trumbo screen credit on *Exodus* (1960), released two months before *Spartacus*. To this day, however, Douglas continues to claim that he agreed to give Trumbo the screen credit he clearly deserved because he was revolted by Kubrick's offer to take sole screen credit for himself, as he had with *Killer's Kiss* and *The Killing*, and had tried to do with *Paths of Glory*.

Ultimately, the feared anti-Communist backlash against *Spartacus* did not materialise. Upon the movie's release, the veterans' organisation sent a letter to 17,000 local branches, imploring them not to see the film, while the anti-Communist columnist Hedda Hopper described it as being 'from a book written by a Commie and the screen script was written by a Commie, so don't go to see it'. Neither protest appeared to adversely affect *Spartacus*'s box-office receipts.

**BOX OFFICE:** Although Douglas claimed that '*Spartacus* was a big hit', with a worldwide gross of $14.6 million from a $12 million budget – which would have resulted in a not insubstantial loss once the exhibitors took their share of the box-office takings – the best that could be said of the film is that it didn't lose as much money as the other epics of the time.

**AWARDS:** With *Ben-Hur* (1959) having swept the Oscars the previous year, the Academy had a new benchmark against which to judge *Spartacus*. In the event, Hedda Hopper's belief that 'the roof may blow off the Santa Monica Auditorium with boos and hisses' if Dalton Trumbo won for his *Spartacus* screenplay was not put to the test: he was absent from the nominations, along with Kubrick as director, Douglas as either producer or leading actor, and *Spartacus* as Best Picture.

The film was nominated in six other categories, however, and won four statues: Peter Ustinov was voted Best Supporting Actor; Russell Metty won an Oscar for Best Cinematography (Colour), an award of which many felt Kubrick was more deserving; Alexander Golitzen, Eric Orbom, Russell A Gausman and Julia Heron shared the award for Best Art Direction/Set Decoration (Colour), Saul Bass's name having been omitted from the ballot; J Arlington Valles and Bill Thomas won for Best Costume Design (Colour). Alex North was nominated for his Best Music, Scoring of a Dramatic or Comedy Picture, and Robert Lawrence received a nomination for Best Film Editing. Peter Ustinov later wrote that, after he won the film's only Academy Award for acting, Laurence Olivier sent him a cable thanking Ustinov for having supported him so well. 'It was a joke, of course.'

Spartacus also won a Golden Globe award for Best Picture (Drama),
and was nominated for Best Film from any Source at the 1961 British
Academy of Film and Television Arts (BAFTA) awards.

**TECHNICAL ACHIEVEMENTS:** Kubrick traditionally preferred to
make his films using square-format ratios such as 1.66:1 – with the
exception of *2001: A Space Odyssey*, all of his films conformed to his
ideal. *Spartacus*, however, was filmed using 70mm Super Technirama
cameras, and Kubrick showed an equally adept command of this
ultra-wide, 2.20:1-ratio format. 'For some scenes it just doesn't make
too much difference,' he told the London *Observer*. 'Instead of having
the people stand two feet apart, sometimes you have them standing four
feet apart; or you throw up a prop in the corner or something.'

As far as Kubrick was concerned, sound was equally important to the
film's scale and spectacle, and several previously unknown techniques
were employed to create effects. Among these was the recording, on
three-channel sound equipment, of 76,000 spectators at a Michigan
State–Notre Dame college football game shouting 'Hail, Crassus!' and
'I'm Spartacus!' 'We settled on Michigan State in East Lansing,' Douglas
later quipped, 'because, as I said, "It's only natural for Spartacus to go to
the Spartans for help." '

**INFLUENCED BY:** 'Despite its ancient setting . . . Trumbo's script – or
at least those portions which involve the active participation of
Spartacus himself – is basically Depression drama,' *Sight and Sound*'s
Henry Sheehan wrote in 1991, 'drawn from the traditions of the
working-class lyricism of the New York stage and from Hollywood
notions of heroism. Spartacus is a John Garfield-type character, the
ultimate everyman fighting against the organisation, the mob, corrupt
politicians, the big six, or, as it happens, the patricians of Rome.'
Sheehan further suggested that *Spartacus* was influenced by one of
Trumbo's most popular pre-blacklist scripts: 'Like the fliers in *Thirty
Seconds over Tokyo* (1944) . . . Spartacus is the average man rising to the
demands of historical necessity with heroic drive but personal modesty.
He gathers his moral purpose not from who he is, but from whom he
represents.'

The composer Alex North has said how he had been coaxed by
Kubrick into studying Prokofiev's *Alexander Nevsky* score before
embarking upon the score for *Spartacus*. Intriguingly, Saul Bass had
studied Sergei Eisenstein's film version of *Alexander Nevsky* (1938) –
along with many other films containing epic battles – while
storyboarding *Spartacus*'s battle sequences.

**DÉJÀ VU:** The scene where Spartacus drowns Marcellus in a vat of stew
recalls a similar one in *Fear and Desire*, as the enemy soldiers are killed
and scattered among spilled stew meat.

The gladiatorial combat between Spartacus (armed with sword) and Draba (armed with trident) recalls the equally vicious battle between Vincent Rapallo (armed with axe) and Davey Gordon (armed with awning hook) in *The Killing*.

When Antoninus asks Spartacus if he is afraid to die – to which he replies, 'No more than I was to be born!' – it recalls another eve-of-war discussion, between the soldiers dug into trenches in *Paths of Glory*: 'I'm not afraid of dying tomorrow – only of getting killed.'

**SEQUELS AND REMAKES:** The character of Spartacus had been the subject of a stage play as early as 1831, when Edwin Forrest played the heroic Thracian in Robert Montgomery Bird's *The Gladiator*, which became the first play in English to reach one thousand performances in its author's lifetime. Although Hollywood has revisited the Roman epic on several occasions – the ousted director Anthony Mann later directed *The Fall of the Roman Empire* (1964) – it would not return to the story of Spartacus until the British director Ridley Scott (*Alien, Blade Runner*) used elements of it in *Gladiator* (2000).

Italian cinema, however, could not leave well enough alone: three further films based on the Spartacus story were made in the sixties: *Son of Spartacus* (a.k.a. *The Slave*) in 1963, *Spartacus and the Ten Gladiators* in 1964, and *Revenge of Spartacus* (a.k.a. *Revenge of the Gladiators*) in 1965.

**KUBRICK GOES POP:** The best-known pop-culture reference to *Spartacus* appears in the Monty Python movie *Life of Brian* (1979), in which a crucified Brian (Graham Chapman) is given his freedom by the Romans, only to be drowned out as dozens of crucified criminals shout, 'I'm Brian!', 'No, *I'm* Brian!' and even 'I'm Brian, and so's my wife!' Another variation on the scene appears in *In & Out* (1997), in which loyal supporters of Howard Brackett (Kevin Kline), a teacher fired after news of his homosexuality becomes public, stand up at a graduation ceremony and declare with a loyal lie, 'I'm gay!' And when the convict Rayford Gibson (Eddie Murphy) is accused of fathering the illegitimate child of the governor's daughter in *Life* (1999), his fellow prisoners divert suspicion from him by proclaiming, in turn, 'I'm the father!' (Yet another variation on the scene appears in the book that accompanied the film *Wayne's World* (1992), as Wayne Campbell (Mike Myers) recalled the time when his classmates, asked to identify him so that he could be punished for some misdemeanour, stood and said, 'I'm Wayne Campbell!' Except, that is, for Wayne's nervous friend Garth, who said: 'I'm Spartacus!')

In *Clueless* (1995), Cher (Alicia Silverstone) and her date watch *Spartacus* on television – intended as an indication that, unbeknown to Cher, her would-be boyfriend is gay. A similar device is used in *Cruel Intentions* (1999), in which Sebastian's (Ryan Phillippe) gay friend confirms the viability of setting up a love rival by saying, 'I do believe *Spartacus* is showing on television tonight.' The poster image for Sam Raimi's *Army of Darkness* (1993) is a parody of *Spartacus*, with Ash (Bruce Campbell) depicted waving his chainsaw arm instead of a sword.

Kubrick himself referenced *Spartacus* in his next film, *Lolita*. Asked by Humbert (James Mason) to confirm his identity, Quilty (Peter Sellers) replies, 'No, I'm Spartacus. Have you come to free the slaves or something?'

**CUT SCENES:** After the intentional brutality of his earlier war films, Kubrick had insisted upon maximum realism for the battle scenes – his first in colour – hiring extras with arms and legs missing, and with other physical defects that allowed the cameras to see parts of their body being smashed, split or removed entirely by sword, spear and dagger, either on the battlefield or in the arena. After the first preview screenings, at which such bloodthirstiness reportedly revolted much of the audience, Kubrick cut all but one of the scenes, which the anti-Communist columnist Hedda Hopper subsequently described as 'acres of dead people, more blood and gore than you ever saw in your life'. Out went Crassus's reaction shot as Draba's blood spurts into his face, and a brief shot in which Spartacus is seen hacking off a Roman soldier's arm. (Both cuts were reinstated for the 1991 restoration.)

Geoffrey Shurlock, representing the censorship body of the Motion Picture Association of America (MPAA), also insisted upon the deletion of the moment when Varinia begs the crucified Spartacus to die – Spartacus was dying anyway, but too slowly, and Shurlock felt that the scene smacked of suicide, or euthanasia. Kubrick cut it, along with a scene in which Gracchus (Laughton) and Caesar (John Gavin) attempt to buy votes by touring the slums of Rome – a somewhat costly loss, since Universal's long-standing kasbah set, where Charles Boyer had ambushed Hedy Lamarr in *Algiers* (1938), had been bulldozed in order to build them.

The most famous – or infamous – scene to be removed from *Spartacus* between preview and premiere was one in which the apparently bisexual Crassus (Olivier) obliquely attempts to seduce his handsome slave boy and body servant, Antoninus (Curtis), with a crass metaphor about snails and oysters. In the magnificent marble bathroom of Crassus's palace, Crassus relaxes in the tub while Antoninus, half-naked, attends to him. 'Do you consider the eating of oysters to be moral, and the eating of snails to be immoral?' Crassus asks. Antoninus does not. 'Of course not,' Crassus continues. 'It is all a matter of taste, isn't it? And taste is not the same as appetite . . . and therefore not a question of morals, is it?' Keeping his eyes on Antoninus as the younger man leaves the tub, Crassus declares his bisexuality: 'My taste includes both snails and oysters.'

Shurlock had warned against inclusion of the scene at script stage, reminding the producers that the so-called Hays Code's rules about sexual 'perversion' covered homosexuality. 'Any suggestion that Crassus finds a sexual attraction to Antoninus will have to be avoided,' Shurlock wrote. 'The reason for Antoninus' frantic escape should be something other than the fact that he is repelled by Crassus' suggestive approach to him.' Shurlock was also uncomfortable with the word 'appetite' and its obvious sexual connotations – in most cases it was changed to 'taste' – and, bizarrely, suggested that the scene might be allowed to stay if 'snails and oysters' were replaced by 'artichokes and truffles'.

As Douglas noted later, 'The censors weren't quite sure it was about homosexuality, but just in case, they wanted it out. We argued, hoping to keep it in. It was just another way Romans abused the slaves. It was very subtle; nothing explicit,' he added. 'We shot it, hoping to convince them. They looked at it, stood firm. We had to cut it out of the picture.' The infamous 'snails-and-oysters' scene remained absent from prints of *Spartacus* until the 1991 restoration, undertaken by Robert A Harris on behalf of Universal Pictures. Even when the original negative was found, however, the dialogue for the scene was still missing, and, although Tony Curtis was able to return to provide an authentic reading of his own lines, the death of Sir Laurence Olivier (by then Lord Olivier) in 1989 meant that another eminent actor and knight of the realm, Sir Anthony Hopkins, would be called upon to re-record Olivier's dialogue for the scene. Hopkins receives a 'special thanks' credit in the additional credits of the restored version, which was released to cinemas in 1991 and is currently the only version commercially available.

**TRIVIA:** Among the many Hollywood stuntmen who doubled for the leading actors, or played roles themselves, or did both, was Richard Farnsworth, who had begun his film career in 1936, at the age of sixteen, and would later earn acclaim for his leading roles in such films as *The Grey Fox* (1982), *The Natural* (1984) and David Lynch's *The Straight Story* (1999). Additional rugged specimens were recruited from the world of professional football: these 'gridiron gladiators' included Al Carmichael, Rudy Bukich and Jim Sears.

When Douglas fired Anthony Mann, he said, 'I owe you a movie.' Several years later, Mann took him up on his offer, inviting Douglas to star with Richard Harris in the World War Two caper, *The Heroes of Telemark* (1965). Douglas accepted the role, in what would prove to be the last film Mann completed before his death.

Charles Laughton and Peter Ustinov had both played Emperor Nero in feature films, prior to their roles in *Spartacus*: Laughton in *The Sign of the Cross* (1932), and Ustinov in *Quo Vadis?* (1951).

**EXPERT WITNESS:** 'Kirk put a lot of pressure on him, every day. It would have been easy to handle if Kirk had screamed or pleaded. But he didn't. He said, "Listen, Stanley, the studio is overwhelming me, saying that we've got to get this done or I'm going to have to pay for it on the other end of production." Stanley said, "Okay, I'll do the best I can." They never took the production away from him. They could have had second units doing a lot of that stuff, but they didn't. Stanley may have bent a little, like a willow in the wind, but he never gave ground.' – the actor Tony Curtis (Antoninus), quoted in *Premiere* magazine, August 1999.

**AVAILABILITY:** In 1989, Universal Pictures began work on what was to become the costliest and most ambitious restoration in motion-picture history. Having discovered that only one of the original prints of *Spartacus* had survived the three decades since the film's release in 1960 – and, moreover, that this was in poor condition, subtitled, and only 182 minutes in duration – Universal commissioned Robert A Harris, who had just completed a restoration of the equally epic *Lawrence of Arabia* (1962), and James Katz, who had overseen the restoration of Abel Gance's *Napoleon* (1927), to begin the painstaking process of piecing surviving elements from various versions together into a restored print.

With the tacit approval of Stanley Kubrick, encouragement from Steven Spielberg and Universal's chairman, Tom Pollock, and valuable assistance from *Spartacus*'s editor Robert Lawrence, the $1 million restoration was completed in 1991. Soon after, *Spartacus* was re-released at cinemas worldwide, in 70mm with six-track Dolby sound. In all, five minutes of footage cut from the original release print – including the notorious 'snails-and-oysters' scene – were reinstated, along with the original overture and intermission.

The restored version is widely available on video in the UK (VHR 1860) and United States (MC 81130), in letterboxed (2.20:1) formats only. The same transfer is also available in the United States on an NTSC laserdisc (41130) and a Criterion Collection laserdisc (CC 1298L), the latter featuring audio commentary by Kirk Douglas and Peter Ustinov, alternative scenes, and production stills. A Region 1 DVD (20181) is also available, featuring two theatrical trailers, dialogue dubbed in French, English and Spanish subtitles, and comprehensive production notes taken from those prepared for Universal Pictures' re-release in 1991.

**FINAL ANALYSIS:** Kubrick's first colour picture since *The Seafarers* – and, significantly, his last until *2001: A Space Odyssey* – is, despite the vastness of its scale and the richness of its setting, his most anonymous film since that earlier colour effort. In each case, he was hired as a 'jobbing' director, and neglected to imprint too much of his own personality on either picture. As a result, *Spartacus* is more interesting to examine from a script and performance point of view than as an example of Kubrick's own directorial methods – its opening scene is even the work of another director entirely: Anthony Mann.

Despite this anonymity, Kubrick's touch is apparent on certain scenes, such as the one in which the film's initial gladiatorial fight to the death is carried out off screen, with only the reactions on the faces of Spartacus and Draba to watch; the intercutting between Crassus promising victory for the Romans and Spartacus declaring freedom for his brother slaves is a Kubrick editorial touch; the stunning landscapes and monumental battle scenes foreshadow Kubrick's more personal *Barry Lyndon*. If not for the virtue of almost all of the performances, particularly the supporting triple-threat of Olivier, Ustinov and Laughton, most of the other scenes might be interchangeable with any number of other Roman epics.

More than anything, *Spartacus* ably demonstrates the fact that Kubrick, whose previous films had been relatively restricted in spatial, chronological and generic terms, could work on a far larger canvas, outside of his 'pet' themes of war (*Fear and Desire*, *Paths of Glory*) and crime (*Killer's Kiss*, *The Killing*), and with a sprawling story and enormous cast of characters. Kubrick took to heart the spirit of St Ambrose's proclamation that 'When I go to Rome, I do as Rome does,' and picked up the reins of the runaway production without complaint. Although his aim was to prove – to others, more than himself – that he could handle a production of the scale of *Spartacus*, in the context of his career as a whole, the film laid the foundation of historical epics both realised (*Barry Lyndon*) and unrealised (*Napoleon*), and probably gave Kubrick the confidence to embark on that other epic production, *2001: A Space Odyssey*. In other words, he knew that his future, like Rome, would not be built in a day.

**KUBRICK ON KUBRICK:** 'If I ever needed any convincing of the limits of persuasion a director can have on a film where someone else is the producer and he is merely the highest-paid member of the crew, *Spartacus* provided proof to last a lifetime.' – quoted in *The Film Director as Superstar* by Joseph Gelmis, 1972.

# Lolita (1962)

**(B & W – 153 mins)**

Music Composed and Conducted by Nelson Riddle
*Lolita* theme by Bob Harris
Orchestrations by Gil Grau
Production Supervisor Raymond Anzarut
Art Director Bill Andrews
Associate Art Director Sidney Cain
Director of Photography Oswald Morris BSC
Editor Anthony Harvey
Production Manager Robert Sterne
Assistant Director Rene Dupont
Camera Operator Denys N Coop
Continuity Pamela Davies

Dubbing Editor Winston Ryder
Sound Recordists Len Shelton, HL Bird
Casting Director James Liggat
Make-up George Partleton
Hairdresser Betty Glasow
2nd-Unit Director Dennis Stock
Wardrobe Supervisor Elsa Fennell
Miss Winter's Costumes by Gene Coffin
Assistant Editor Lois Gray
Titles by Chambers & Partners
Screenplay by Vladimir Nabokov based on his novel *Lolita*
Produced by James B Harris
Directed by Stanley Kubrick

**CAST:** Sue Lyon (*Dolores Haze*), James Mason (*Humbert Humbert*), Peter Sellers (*Clare Quilty/Dr Zempf*), Shelley Winters (*Charlotte Haze*), Diana Decker (*Jean Farlow*), Jerry Stovin (*John Farlow*), Gary Cockrell (*Richard 'Dick' Schiller*), Marianne Stone (*Vivian Darkbloom*), Cec Linder (*Physician*), Lois Maxwell (*Mary Lore*), C Denier Warren (*Potts*), Maxine Holden (*Hospital Receptionist*), James Dyrenforth (*Mr Beale Sr*), Bill Greene (*George Swine*), Shirley Douglas (*Mrs Starch*), Marion Mathie (*Miss Lebone*), John Harrison (*Tom*), Colin Maitland (*Charlie Sedgwick*), Terence Kilburn (*Man*), Roland Brand (*Bill*).

**UNCREDITED CAST:** Irvin Allen (*Hospital Attendant*), Susanne Gibbs (*Mona Farlow*), Eric Lane (*Roy*), Isobel Lucas (*Louise*), Robert C Overton (*Kenny*), Craig Sams (*Rex*), Roberta Shore (*Lorna*).

**UNCREDITED CREW:** Jack Smith (*Production Accountant*), Doreen Wood (*Assistant Accountant*), Joan Parcell (*Production Secretary*), Josephine Baker (*Producer's Secretary*), Roy Millichip (*2nd Assistant Director*), John Danischewsky (*3rd Assistant Director*), Stella Magee (*Director's Secretary*), Joyce Herlihy (*Assistant Continuity*), David Sylvester (*Special Writer*), James Turell (*Focus Puller*), Michael Rutter (*Clapper Loader*), A Osborne (*Camera Grip*), W Thompson (*Electrical Gaffer*), Joe Pearce (*Stills*), W W Armour (*Assistant Editor*), Andrew Low (*Set Decorator*), Peter James (*Set Dresser*), Frank Wilson (*Chief Draughtsman*), A Van Montagu (*Scenic Artist*), Terry Parr (*Production Buyer*), Harry Phipps (*Construction Manager*), Wyn Keeley (*Wardrobe Assistant*), Barbara Gillett (*Wardrobe Mistress*), Stella Morris (*Assistant Make-up*), Don Wortham (*Boom Operator*), Enid Jones (*Unit Publicity*), Amy Allen (*Publicity Secretary*).

**TITLE SEQUENCE:** Nelson Riddle's sickly-sweet, melodramatic love theme plays as tasteful, italicised white credits appear over a locked-off camera shot, in which a man's hands (presumably those of Humbert Humbert, though never directly identified as such) are seen delicately placing cotton wool between the toes of an imperiously thrust-out female foot (presumably belonging to Lolita, though, again, never identified), before painting each nail with loving care. In a single shot, less than two minutes in duration, Kubrick brilliantly establishes Humbert's status as the absorbed, obsessed, adoring and enslaved individual, utterly subservient to the imperious power of the teenage Lolita.

The idea for this opening image came after principal photography was completed, by which time the cinematographer Oswald Morris had already left what, for him, had been an unhappy production, albeit an artistically successful one. In his place, Kubrick hired Gilbert Taylor, whose aerial photography for *The Dam Busters* had impressed Kubrick so much that he not only lit *Lolita*'s elegant opening shot, but returned as director of photography on Kubrick's next film, *Dr Strangelove*.

**SUMMARY:** Humbert Humbert, a tragic middle-aged literature professor driven by forbidden sexual desires for very young girls, enters the house of a playwright, Clare Quilty, and, after forcing him to read his own poetic death sentence, shoots him dead. A caption, '4 YEARS EARLIER', leads us in flashback to the events that led up to this deadly encounter. Humbert arrives in the picturesque New Hampshire hamlet of Ramsdale, to take up summer lodgings with a culture-vulture widow called Charlotte Haze and her precocious daughter, Dolores, known as 'Lolita'. Humbert's interest in the young girl overcomes his distaste for her mother, and, when the latter declares her love for him, he marries Charlotte in order to remain close to Lolita. The marriage is clearly a sham, and, with Lolita away at summer camp, Humbert contemplates murdering the new Mrs Humbert. Although he cannot bring himself to do it, fate acts on his behalf: after discovering his secret diaries – revealing to Charlotte her husband's contempt for her, and his sexual obsession with her daughter – an anguished Charlotte runs into the road, where she is knocked over and killed by a neighbour's car.

Humbert collects Lolita from camp, telling his stepdaughter that he is taking her to visit her sick mother in hospital. They spend the night at a motel, where Humbert unwittingly encounters Quilty in disguise as an off-duty police officer, and in the morning Humbert is dumbfounded when Lolita displays her own sexual awareness and seduces him. On the road again later that day, Humbert tells Lolita that her mother is dead, and six months later the pair have set up home together in Beardsley, where Humbert will teach while Lolita attends school. Fiercely jealous of her imagined boyfriends, Humbert refuses to let her participate in the school play – written, unbeknown to Humbert, by Quilty – until he is persuaded by the school psychologist Dr Zempf (another Quilty disguise), following his veiled threats about an investigation of Lolita's home situation.

After the first-night party, Humbert and Lolita have a terrible fight, again precipitated by his jealousy. Lolita runs off to telephone her secret lover (Quilty), and later agrees to Humbert's suggestion that they hit the road once more, away from prying eyes. This time, however, they are being followed by a car, which an increasingly paranoid Humbert imagines belongs to the police, but is actually driven by Quilty, pursuing his teenage lover across country until the opportunity to abduct Lolita presents itself. Eventually, it does, as Lolita falls ill and is forced to spend the night in hospital. That night, after receiving a troubling nocturnal telephone call (from Quilty, although Humbert has yet to realise this), Humbert attempts to collect Lolita from the hospital, only to find that a so-called 'uncle' has already taken her.

Three years later, Humbert is surprised to receive a begging letter from Lolita, married and pregnant and living on the breadline with a well-meaning but down-at-heel husband. Humbert visits her, loaded with money and a loaded pistol, and demands to know the identity of the man who took his Lolita from hospital that fateful night. She tells him about Quilty, whom she truly loved, but who ultimately rejected her after she refused to participate in a pornographic film. Devastated, Humbert tearfully begs Lolita to run away with him, but when she refuses he gives her a huge sum of money and drives off to confront his nemesis: Clare Quilty. As the ending fuses into the opening scene, at Quilty's house, the following caption appears: 'Humbert Humbert died in prison of coronary thrombosis while awaiting trial for the murder of Clare Quilty.'

**SOURCE:** The film is based on the Russian-born author (and Cornell University literature professor) Vladimir Nabokov's controversial twelfth novel, about a middle-aged man's obsession with an underaged 'nymphet', the eponymous *Lolita*. The book is written from Humbert's perspective. Although completed in 1954, the book was rejected by four shocked American publishers before finally being circulated in the United States in an imported edition, published in September 1955 by a notorious Parisian pornographer. Banned in Austria, Britain, Burma, Belgium and Australia, it was first published in the US almost three years later, when Putnam, encouraged by positive reviews, decided to risk censure by publishing a hardcover edition. By 1964, *Playboy* reported that 2.5 million copies had been sold in the US alone.

Kubrick apparently first became aware of the existence of Nabokov's novel when *Paths of Glory*'s co-screenwriter Calder Willingham recommended it to him while the pair were working with Marlon Brando on *One-Eyed Jacks* (see Lost Worlds: The Films That Never Were). Kubrick's long-time producer, James B Harris, had also become aware of the book, and was halfway through his copy when Kubrick asked to start reading it. 'It was a hardback and we only had one copy,' Harris recalled, 'so we both couldn't read it at the same time.' Unless, of course, he tore the pages out of the book as he read them, and gave them to Kubrick. 'I was reading it and passing the pages – that's how anxious we were.'

Having finished reading *Lolita*, Kubrick and Harris agreed that it would make a sensational film – in both senses of the word. 'I was instantly attracted to the book because of the sense of life that it conveyed, the truthfulness of it, and the inherent drama of the situation seemed completely winning,' Kubrick told *Horizon* magazine in 1960. 'I've always been amused at the cries of pornography,' he added, 'because, to me, *Lolita* seemed a very sad and tender love story. I believe that Lionel Trilling, in an article he wrote about the book, said that it was the first great [contemporary] love story. He remarked that in great love stories of the past, the lovers – by their love and through their love – totally estranged themselves from society and created a sense of shock in the people around them. And because of the slackening moral and spiritual values in the twentieth century, in no love story until *Lolita* has that occurred.'

By the time Kubrick and Harris had decided to option the book, it was an acknowledged masterpiece *and* a formidable bestseller, and, as a result, Nabokov's agent, 'Swifty' Lazar, was asking $150,000 for a two-year option on the screen rights, with $75,000 payable up front – a far cry from the $10,000 Harris-Kubrick had paid for the rights to the novels *Paths of Glory* and *Clean Break*. Reluctantly, Kubrick and Harris accepted Lazar's hard bargaining, selling the television rights to *The Killing* to United Artists in order to purchase the motion-picture rights to *Lolita*. For Nabokov, it was literally a dream come true: in 1916, he had dreamed that the family fortune would be restored when his late Uncle Vasily came back to him as 'Harry and Kuvyrkin'. Apparently, 'Harris and Kubrick' was close enough.

Effectively beginning at Chapter 10 of the novel – excising the questionable psychological motivation for Humbert's obsession with young girls, the result of a doomed love affair when he was a teenager himself – Kubrick's adaptation took considerable liberties both with the novel and with Nabokov's own script, despite the fact that Nabokov took sole screenplay credit – a shrewd rather than generous move on the part of Kubrick, which allowed the author to take either the credit or the blame for the adaptation, depending which way the critical cards fell; in any case, the director and producer assumed possession of the project by titling the film 'James B Harris & Stanley Kubrick's *Lolita*'.

One of the principal changes was the transposition of the book's climax, in which Humbert tracks Quilty to his home and kills him, to the opening of the film, so that dramatic tension is maintained while the remainder of the story plays out in tragic flashback. This, Kubrick told Joseph Gelmis, was agreed by him and Nabokov because they felt that narrative tension dissipated after Humbert and Lolita consummated their forbidden relationship less than halfway through the film; the events leading up to Humbert's killing of Quilty would thus, while admittedly sacrificing a dramatic dénouement, leave the audience wondering about the events leading up to Humbert's discovery of his rival for Lolita's affections.

Despite the changes made by Kubrick, Nabokov initially claimed to be impressed with the film, dutifully describing it in a 1964 *Playboy* interview as 'absolutely first-rate'. As Kubrick later told Alexander Walker, 'I went to a party with Nabokov after the premiere, and he was very jolly and very flattering about the film in every respect.' By the time Nabokov published his own original screenplay, however, he had revised – or, perhaps, revealed – his true opinion. 'My first reaction to the picture was a mixture of aggravation, regret, and reluctant pleasure,' he said in the foreword to *Lolita: A Screenplay*, published in 1974. 'Quite a few of the extraneous inventions (such as the macabre ping-pong scene or that rapturous swig of Scotch in the bathtub) struck me as appropriate and delightful. Others (such as the collapsing cot or the frills of Miss Lyon's elaborate nightgown) were painful.'

**PRODUCTION HISTORY:** Kubrick and Harris faced a significant problem in bringing *Lolita* to the screen: the subject matter of the book meant that any film adaptation would almost certainly be denied a Code Seal Certificate by Hollywood's self-censorship body, the Motion Picture Association of America (MPAA). Without it, the film could not be exhibited in cinemas or broadcast on television, and would therefore be financially nonviable. 'The novel itself seems to have aroused so much resentment and revulsion in so so many quarters on account of its depravity,' the MPAA president Geoffrey Shurlock wrote on 18 March 1959, 'a great deal of damage might be done to the industry and to the Code even before the film was released.' This problem remained a constant thorn in Harris-Kubrick's side. Nabokov's awareness of the difficulties that the film was likely to encounter led him to turn down Harris's offer to write the screen adaptation for the novel; Calder Willingham, who had been the first to recommend *Lolita* to Kubrick, was hired instead.

Willingham's draft, which Kubrick read while editing *Spartacus*, ended with the marriage of Humbert and Lo, a compromise that the film makers had judged, correctly, would appease the MPAA, but that Kubrick, now that he had seen it on paper, was no longer willing to make. Instead, he sent a telegram to Nabokov in Switzerland: 'BOOK A MASTERPIECE AND SHOULD BE FOLLOWED EVEN IF LEGION AND CODE DISAPPROVE STOP STILL BELIEVE YOU ARE ONLY ONE FOR SCREENPLAY STOP IF FINANCIAL DETAILS CAN BE AGREED WOULD YOU BE AVAILABLE'. The combination of flattery and financial remuneration proved irresistible, and, in February 1960, Nabokov – who had, in the meantime, been inspired by what he called 'a nocturnal illumination of diabolical origin' in which he had dreamed that he was reading his own screenplay – agreed to adapt the novel himself for the sum of $40,000 plus expenses, with an additional $35,000 if he received sole credit.

Nabokov moved with his wife into a rented property in Los Angeles, and by 2 March 1960 he was already mentally constructing scenes in his head, later transferring them to index cards, and finally transforming them into typewritten script pages. Some of the scenes were lifted directly from the novel; others were based on material that Nabokov had been unable or unwilling to include in the book; still others were invented. By the end of April, he had sent Kubrick the first two acts of the film, and within two months had submitted a manuscript four hundred pages long. As Harris quipped later, 'You couldn't make it. You couldn't *lift* it.' Kubrick told Nabokov that he had written the screenplay for a seven-hour film, and gave him a list of deletions, alterations and additions, which Nabokov incorporated into a somewhat shorter version of the script, delivered in September 1960.

With casting already in progress, Kubrick set about condensing the lengthy adaptation into something more manageable, while Harris attempted to interest studios in backing the film. Warner Bros was willing to advance $1 million and a share of the profits (of which Nabokov was contracted to earn 15 per cent), in return for final say on almost every aspect of the film. 'The day the contracts were delivered, Stanley and I read them, and Warners wanted control over everything – the final cut; even the music,' Harris recalls. Unwilling to tolerate studio interference in the aftermath of *Spartacus*, Kubrick and Harris declined the offer, and accepted a less restrictive but similarly lucrative one from Seven Arts UK, the British subsidiary of Associated Artists, a distribution outfit run by Kenneth Hyman, a former school friend of Harris who also happened to recommend Peter Sellers for the part of Clare Quilty. With James Mason already on board, Seven Arts increased the budget to $1.75 million, and in August 1960 Kubrick arrived in England, ready to begin production.

Principal photography commenced two months later, closely following Kubrick's abridged version of Nabokov's screenplay. However, it was not until the arrival of Sellers close to Christmas that Kubrick began to see both the possibilities of the Quilty character, and an entirely new methodology for working with actors, inspired by Sellers' gift for mimicry and improvisation. 'When Peter was called to the set he would usually arrive walking very slowly and staring morosely,' Kubrick told Alexander Walker. 'I cleared the crew from the stage and we would begin rehearsing. As the work progressed, he would begin to respond to something or other in the scene, his mood would visibly brighten and we would begin to have fun. Improvisational ideas began to click and the rehearsal started to feel good.'

The cinematographer Oswald Morris was equally impressed at watching the great comic actor shed his morose off-screen personality and come alive as he possessed a character, or a character possessed him. 'The most interesting scenes were the ones with Peter Sellers, which were total improvisations,' Morris told *Film Dope* magazine. Not everyone shared this enthusiasm, however. On more than one occasion, Mason stormed off the set, infuriated either by Sellers' spontaneity or his own inability to match it. As Shelley Winters (Charlotte Haze) later wrote, '[Peter] seemed to be acting on a different planet.' Indeed, Winters found difficulties making a connection with both Sellers and Mason, but, although she frequently brought this to Kubrick's attention, the director did nothing to alleviate her isolation. 'Whenever I complained to Kubrick about trying to connect with my two leading men, he would agree with me,' she recounted. 'But he didn't change their performances, and this very frustration that I had in real life was what was so sad and funny about Charlotte. I never felt anyone was listening to me when I talked.' She added, 'Again, I didn't understand the lonely quality it gave [my character] until I saw the film.'

If Kubrick was deliberately exaggerating Winters' sense of isolation in order to increase that of her character, he was also growing weary of the future Oscar-winner's constant lateness, apparent inability to remember lines or dance in time to music, and her coquettish (and, given the salacious nature of her autobiographies, hypocritical) unwillingness to play even the most prudish love scene; according to Oswald Morris, Kubrick was on the verge of firing the actress on at least one occasion: '[She] was very difficult, wanting to do everything her own way. At one point Kubrick said to me, "I think the lady's gonna have to go," which would have been very serious halfway through production. But he'd have got rid of her.'

By the time *Lolita* was completed, Seven Arts had negotiated a lucrative production deal with Metro-Goldwyn-Mayer, and it was with considerable pride that the studio issued a press release, on St Valentine's Day 1962, announcing its acquisition of the film for US distribution. With the granting of an MPAA Code Seal in America, and its BBFC equivalent in Britain, audiences would finally be able to answer the question posed on every one of the film's poster advertisements: 'How did they ever make a movie of *Lolita*?'

CASTING: Needless to say, the casting of the title role was one of the most difficult Kubrick would ever undertake. Neither he nor Harris was interested in risking the wrath of the MPAA by casting an actress of the same age as Nabokov's twelve-year-old; nor were they keen to employ an older actress pretending to be a young girl, as in Elia Kazan's *Baby Doll* (1956) – which had, nevertheless, been denied a Code Seal and condemned by the Legion of Decency. Instead, they decided to increase Lolita's age by a crucial two years, making her of marriageable age in several US states. Although having Humbert and Lolita marry would have mollified the MPAA, Geoffrey Shurlock warned that 'if the girl looked like a child, the effect might still be offensive to the point where we would not want to approve the picture.' As Harris recalled, 'We knew we must make her a sex object – she [couldn't] be childlike. If we made her a sex object, where everyone in the audience could understand why everyone would want to jump on her, and you make him attractive, it's gonna work.'

After considering seventeen-year-old Tuesday Weld (*Rally Round the Flag, Boys!*), James Mason's wayward daughter, Portland, and around eight hundred other young hopefuls, Kubrick and Harris were no closer to finding what Nabokov called 'the perfect nymphet', although, as Kubrick told *Look* in 1962, 'it wasn't because mothers kept their daughters away from us. We got thousands of applications. Some mothers even wrote to say their children were *born* Lolitas.' Then, after almost a year-long quest, which Kubrick called 'a desperate search', fourteen-year-old Sue Lyon came in to audition. 'From the first, she was interesting to watch,' Kubrick told *Look*, the magazine for which he once worked as a photographer. 'Even in the way she walked in for her interview, casually sat down, walked out. She was cool and non-giggly. She was enigmatic without being dull. She could keep people guessing about how much Lolita knew about life.' Nabokov, who had once claimed to care so little about the film that he suggested casting 'a dwarfess', yet now had casting approval, put it more simply: 'No doubt about it: she is the one.' To be sure that her acting talents matched her suitability in other areas, Kubrick filmed a screen test of the scene in which Humbert paints Lolita's toenails while jealously interrogating her about boys. 'She is a natural actor,' Kubrick decided. 'Also, she has a beautiful figure along ballet lines.'

Finding someone to play the paedophile Humbert Humbert was an equally daunting prospect, not least because the casting of an unknown in the title role meant that the remaining parts would need to be filled by stars. The Oscar-nominated British actor James Mason (*20,000 Leagues Under the Sea*) was Kubrick's first choice to play Humbert; as with that film, however, scheduling appeared to be a problem, since Mason was intending to star in a Broadway musical based on *The Affairs of Anatol* by Arthur Schnitzler, author of the novel on which Kubrick's last film would be based. Next, Mason's countryman Laurence Olivier agreed to the role, subject to the approval of his agents at MCA; despite the fact that the firm also represented Harris-Kubrick. However, they talked Olivier out of accepting such a controversial role, a move that infuriated Kubrick. After considering Peter Ustinov, who had just won an Academy Award for *Spartacus*, and another aborted acceptance from David Niven, James Mason apparently decided he would rather court controversy on the big screen than negative reviews on Broadway, and agreed to play Humbert Humbert.

The casting of Mason meant that the inclusion of a second British performer would guarantee financial assistance from the Eady Fund, a government initiative in which a tax on ticket sales was channelled into local productions. With the actress Shelley Winters, fresh from her Oscar triumph for *The Diary of Anne Frank* (1959), already cast as Lolita's mother, Charlotte Haze, Kubrick decided that the role of Clare Quilty, Humbert's rival for Lo's affections, offered the best prospects. With a stroke of genius, he offered it to the British *Goon Show* comic turned film actor Peter Sellers, who had a fourteen-day gap in his schedule around Christmas 1960, during which *Lolita* might be accommodated. 'In *Lolita*, Stanley wanted me to speak with a New York accent,' Sellers later told *Rolling Stone*, adding that Kubrick recommended the voice of the jazz impresario Norman Granz as a suitable model. 'So he put this tape on, and it was hysterical. You heard a voice, speaking too loud, saying (in lisping Clare Quilty voice), "Hi there, Stanley, this is Norman. Jesus Christ, this is a whole script, for God's sakes. I mean, you really do ask for some strange things." Then you hear some rustling of paper, and he starts reading the *Lolita* script. And that's where Quilty came from.' Sellers would later put the German accent affected for the bespectacled Dr Zempf to good use in his next collaboration with Kubrick, *Dr Strangelove*.

**THE USUAL SUSPECTS:** Although Kubrick initially wanted *Spartacus*'s Laurence Olivier to play Humbert Humbert, and James Mason had once been considered for the role of Colonel Dax in *Paths of Glory*, none of the actors in *Lolita* had previously worked with Kubrick.

**THE PURSUIT OF PERFECTION:** To add verisimilitude to the British-made film's American setting, Kubrick hired the stills photographer Dennis Stock and cameraman Bob Gaffney to shoot second-unit footage of freeways, motels and gas stations for use as cutaway and back projection. 'Dennis and I and one other guy went on the road with two station wagons,' Gaffney later recounted. 'We had a dummy done up as Lolita and the other guy played Humbert and was the grip. We were shooting plates, backgrounds and "car-bys" going through different places.' On one occasion, the three-man crew found themselves in Gettysburg in thick fog, where they filmed dramatic driving scenes ultimately used for Humbert's arrival at Quilty's mansion at the beginning of the film.

Months later, when principal photography was completed, Gaffney received a call from Kubrick, inviting him to New York to film additional second-unit footage, using Kubrick's own hand-held Royal Navy Eyemo camera, and an Arriflex. Accompanied by Kubrick's wife, Christiane, they spent 'two or three weeks' driving around New York state, from Rhode Island to Albany and back to Rhode Island, where Kubrick's growing attention to detail would pass another landmark. Having found a railway station and a diesel train suitable for the scene in which Humbert arrives in Ramsdale, Kubrick decided that the taxi that Humbert would take from the station was the wrong colour. Rather than have it repainted at great expense, Kubrick and Gaffney studied the *American Cinematographer Handbook* to find out which coloured filter would be required to give the taxi the correct colour scheme – despite the fact that *Lolita* was being filmed in black and white.

## CLASSIC QUOTES

Humbert: 'What drives me insane is the twofold nature of this nymphet, of every nymphet, perhaps – this mixture in my Lolita of tender, dreamy childishness, and a kind of eerie vulgarity. I know it is madness to keep this journal but it gives me a strange thrill to do so, and only a loving wife could decipher my microscopic script.'

Charlotte: 'Darling, you've gone away.'
Humbert: 'Just a minute, I'm following a train of thought.'
Charlotte: 'Oh, it doesn't matter. *C'est la vie!* Hey, am I on that train?'
Humbert: 'Yes.'

Humbert: 'You know, I've missed you terribly.'
Lolita: 'I haven't missed you. In fact, I've been revoltingly unfaithful to you.'
Humbert: 'Oh?'
Lolita: 'But it doesn't matter a bit, because you've stopped caring anyway.'
Humbert: 'What makes you say I've stopped caring for you?'
Lolita: 'Well, you haven't even kissed me yet, have you?'

Quilty: 'It's great to see a normal face, 'cause I'm a normal guy. It'd be great for two normal guys like us to get together and talk about world events, y'know, in a normal sort of way.'

Quilty: 'I noticed when you was checking in you had a lovely pretty little girl with you. She was really lovely. As a matter of fact she wasn't so little, come to think of it. She was fairly tall little. What I mean is taller than little, you know what I mean. But, uh, she was really lovely. Gee, I wish I had a lovely, pretty, tall, lovely little girl like that, I mean.'

Humbert: 'I don't want you around them. They're nasty-minded boys.'
Lolita: 'Oh, you're a fine one to talk about someone else's mind!'

**THEMES AND MOTIFS:** If Kubrick could not include overt sexual references without incurring the wrath and censure of the MPAA or the Legion of Decency, he would have to use insinuation, implication, inference and innuendo to add a sexual theme to his adaptation. This approach is first demonstrated by the scene in which Humbert agrees to lodge with the Haze family after seeing Lolita sunning herself in the garden. 'What was the decisive factor?' Charlotte asks, oblivious to Humbert's interest in her daughter. 'I think it was your cherry pies,' he fumbles in response.

Other instances of obliquely, or even obscurely, suggestive phraseology include:

● Charlotte's assurance that Humbert would not get 'more peace [sic] anywhere', references to the 'collection of reproductions I have in my bedroom', 'late snacks et cetera' included in the rent, her invitation to teach him 'the new [dance] steps';

- John Farlow's suggestion that he and Humbert 'swap partners', and references to his and Jean's 'homework';
- Jean Farlow's confession of her 'extremely broad-minded' views, and those of her husband;
- the sexual *frisson* Quilty adds to Charlotte's remark about Lolita's having 'a cavity filled' by his Uncle Ivor;
- Humbert's implied admission to being 'limp as a noodle' at Charlotte's touch;
- place names such as 'Camp Climax for Girls', 'The Frigid Queen', and 'The Enchanted Hunters Hotel' – the last a reference to Humbert's 'bewitched travellers'?
- Quilty's sexual advances towards George Swine, with references to 'excess energy', sado-masochistic sex and auto-erotic asphyxiation;
- Lo's suggestive way of eating potato crisps;
- Dr Zempf's various sexual references and innuendoes, and in Quilty's late-night telephone call to Humbert;
- Lolita's assertion that Quilty wanted her to 'co-operate' with his 'weird friends' in the making of 'some kind of an art movie' – clearly one pornographic in nature.

Unsurprisingly, Kubrick added numerous visual references to accentuate the air of sexual suggestion, such as the antique bed-warmer that Charlotte pushes Humbert against during her first attempt at seducing him. Charlotte's emasculating nature is also emphasised by such visual references as her biting of a hot dog (before placing its remains in Humbert's hand), and Humbert's cracking of nuts (before placing the shells in Charlotte's hand), during two scenes in which she berates his uptightness.

Like *The Killing*, and many subsequent Kubrick films, *Lolita* contrives an inordinate number of scenes to take place in bathrooms or bedrooms:

- Charlotte shows Humbert his bedroom, and the bathroom 'right next door', noisily flushing the lavatory, and immediately takes him to her own bedroom, to show off her 'collection of reproductions';
- Humbert is seen writing in his journal in his bedroom shortly before Lolita brings him breakfast in the room;
- after Lolita leaves for Camp Climax, Humbert weeps in her bedroom while Quilty's smiling face mocks him from the poster on the wall;
- Humbert begins making love to Charlotte in her bedroom, watching Lolita's portrait as he does so; after their argument, Charlotte storms from bedroom to bathroom; Humbert follows her, finding it empty, diverting instead to *his* bedroom, where he finds her reading his journal; upset, she locks herself in her bedroom;
- after Charlotte's accident, Humbert is visited in the bathroom by John and Jean Farlow, and the elder Mr Beale;
- arriving at the Enchanted Hunters Hotel, the busboy shows Humbert and Lolita into the bedroom, where the following scenes take place;

- after a single scene on the road, the revelation that Lolita's mother is dead gives us a bedroom-to-bathroom-to-bedroom sequence;
- Humbert and Lolita quarrel over boys in their bedroom.

Another readily apparent theme running through *Lolita* is that of games, alluding to the complex games of bait-and-switch and cat-and-mouse played between the sly Quilty and an unwitting Humbert. No sooner has the film begun than Humbert and Quilty's intellectual sparring is symbolised in 'a game of Roman ping-pong', and Quilty's comment that Humbert is 'sort of a bad loser' evidently refers to the figurative 'game' they have both been playing with Lolita. The references during this scene pile up: Quilty's initial announcement of the game's score ('three-love') is suggestive of the *ménage à trois* in which they, in using Charlotte as a way to gain access to Lolita, have been involved; Quilty's line about the service – 'I sort of like to have it up this end, you know?' – is a reference to his suggested bisexuality, while 'I don't think I wanna play any more' follows Humbert's pulling a gun on him, signalling that the game is up.

Such references are reiterated when a chess theme – a device regularly employed by both Kubrick and Nabokov – is introduced in the next scene, as Charlotte welcomes Humbert into the chequerboard reception of her home. Symbolically, Humbert becomes the white king, and Quilty the black, demonstrated by their next appearance together: at the Ramsdale school dance, Humbert's white tuxedo is in marked contrast to Quilty's black one. Quilty even has his dark queen (Vivian Darkbloom) in tow, though it is his intention to make another of Lolita, just as it is Humbert's. 'You're going to take my queen?' Charlotte asks. 'That is my intention, certainly,' he replies, with a sidelong look at Lolita.

Of course, more obvious references – to games of a sexual nature – are made by Lolita just before she seduces Humbert in their hotel room. 'I learned some real good games in camp,' she tells the prone Humbert. 'One in particularly [sic] was fun . . . I played it with Charlie.' 'You mean that boy? You and he?' he responds, it slowly dawning upon him that some 'nasty-minded boy' has had his way with Lo, but not yet realising that her sexual experience allows the liaison that follows to occur, and at Lolita's suggestion.

**MUSIC:** Having first considered Bernard Herrmann (*Psycho*) to score *Lolita*, Kubrick decided instead upon Nelson Riddle, who had won fame arranging many of Frank Sinatra's best recordings, including the heist movie *Ocean's Eleven* (1960), and had defined the sound of postwar America with his easygoing compositions. Kubrick shrewdly commissioned Riddle to compose a luscious, romantic score as an ironic counterpoint to Humbert and Lo's forbidden love story. For Lolita's signature theme, however, Kubrick was persuaded by James Harris to select a composition – later entitled 'Lolita Ya Ya' – recorded by his brother Bob, a Manhattan songwriter. The song, with the repetitive little-girl refrain of 'Ya ya/Yaya yaya ya ya', plays on almost every occasion on which Lolita appears on screen – and some in which she is clearly in Humbert's thoughts – although its resonance becomes somehow more tragic as the story progresses. Clare Quilty also has his own theme: Riddle's sinister harpsichord music, initially signalled by Humbert's plucking of the strings of Quilty's harp, which precedes his every appearance, both in and out of disguise.

Although several music cuts were originally released on vinyl (in ersatz stereo), the latest version of the soundtrack, released in 1997 by Turner Classic Movies Music (7243 8 21978 2 9), contains some 45 minutes of music, digitally remastered in its original monophonic form, and presented in chronological order. The music is interspersed with seven short but well-chosen dialogue extracts featuring the original cast, and accompanied by well-documented sleeve notes written by Joseph Lanza and replete with stills and publicity photographs from the film.

A re-recording of the 'Love Theme' appears on Silva Screen Records' *Strangelove . . . Music from the Films of Stanley Kubrick* (FILMCD 303).

One appropriately devilish (mis)use of music comes in the opening scene, where Quilty, fearing for his life after the gunshot that penetrated his boxing glove, sits at the piano, tells Humbert, 'Why don't I play you a little thing I wrote last week?' and promptly begins to play a Chopin polonaise.

**POSTER:** It seems perfectly apposite that the image of Lolita chosen for the poster was almost exactly the one that first greets Humbert in the garden of the Haze residence: a soft-focus, full-colour photograph of Sue Lyon sucking a lollipop and looking provocatively over the top of a pair of plastic heart-shaped sunglasses.

**TAG-LINE:** No less provocative than the poster image was the tag-line, 'How Did They Ever Make a Movie of *Lolita*?', which managed to appeal to those who had read the novel, as well as those who had not, but were aware of its supposedly titillating subject matter.

**TRAILER:** As Lolita's theme plays, the following legend appears in white on a black background: 'how did they ever make a movie of . . .' – and, on the next caption – 'LOLITA'. A still image of Humbert's hands on a bottle of Coca-Cola with a drinking straw appears isolated on the left of frame, with a white outline superimposed upon it, replacing the drinking straw with a flower. Several publicity images of Sue Lyon as Lolita – her legs, her eyes, her lips, her smile, the poster image of Lo looking over the top of her sunglasses as she licks a lollipop – follow, each framed in black as before. The title appears again, followed by an image, dialogue line ('Lolita!') and captioned screen credit for each of the following:

'JAMES MASON', 'SHELLEY WINTERS', 'PETER SELLERS as "Quilty" '. A further caption, 'AND INTRODUCING SUE LYON', plays over an image of Lolita at the school dance, before a montage of scenes from the film – many of which are oddly framed in black – are accompanied by a cacophony of male and female voices repeating the same question: 'How did they ever make a movie of *Lolita*?' The name 'Lolita' is then repeated by several cast members, and the title and credit blocks appear. The trailer lasts for precisely one minute.

**WHAT THE PAPERS SAID:** Although most critics had hitherto supported Kubrick in his film-making endeavours, the success of *Spartacus* allowed them to take a less partisan view of *Lolita*. In the United States, they were largely uncomplimentary towards *Lolita*, not so much attacking the film itself as Kubrick's audacity in adapting the book in the first place. '*Lolita* is the saddest and most important victim of the current reckless adaptation fad,' noted *Time*, while *Variety* called it 'an occasionally amusing but shapeless film . . . like a bee from which the stinger has been removed. It still buzzes with a sort of promising irreverence, but it lacks the power to shock, and, eventually, makes very little point either as comedy or satire.'

In the UK, the *Observer* headed its review '*Lolita* fiasco' and closed by saying that Nabokov's novel had been 'turned into a film about this poor English guy who is being given the runaround by this sly young broad'. Other critics had the poison taken out of their pens by the fact that Nabokov himself was credited for the adaptation, thus denying them the opportunity to attack the adaptation while praising the novel; the *New Republic*'s Stanley Kauffman, however, found a way: 'It is clear that Nabokov respects the novel. It is equally clear that he does not respect the film [and has] given to [the medium of] films the *Lolita* that, presumably, he thinks the medium deserves.'

Many critics attacked the casting of Sue Lyon, who they felt looked much too old and worldly to play the part of the underage seductress. 'She looks to be a good seventeen,' the *New York Times* commented, and most concurred. 'Have the reviewers looked at the schoolgirls of America lately?' the *New Yorker*'s Pauline Kael countered insightfully. 'The classmates of my fourteen-year-old daughter are not merely nubile: some of them look badly used.' Kael was not the film's only defendant, however: the New York *Herald Tribune* called Kubrick's 'style and treatment and timing and eye for the telling detail a continual cinematic delight', while the *Saturday Review* went still further by favourably comparing Kubrick to Orson Welles.

**CONTROVERSY:** In discussing *Lolita* prior to its release, Kubrick was careful to distance the film from the controversial subject matter of its source material, stating – somewhat unconvincingly – that it was the story of 'the outsider who is passionately committed to action against the social order', and was, in that respect, similar to his earlier films. 'The protagonists of *Paths of Glory*, *The Killing*, *Spartacus* and . . . *Lolita* are all outsiders fighting to do some impossible thing,' he suggested, 'whether it's pulling a perfect robbery or saving innocent men from execution by a militaristic state or carrying on a love affair with a twelve-year-old girl.'

Dogged by controversy throughout its gestation period, *Lolita* provoked few serious objections upon its eventual release; the most serious came from the Legion of Decency, who stigmatised the film by giving it a Condemned rating, which meant that any Catholics who went to see it would be committing a sin. The Legion's Monsignor Little was eventually persuaded to lift the crippling 'C' rating, by the making of the cuts outlined in **Cut Scenes** below and by an agreement to prominently display two statements on all advertising: 'For persons over eighteen only' and 'This movie has been passed by the MPAA'.

*Lolita* officially received Code Seal Certificate No. 20000 on 31 August 1961. In the United Kingdom, the British Board of Film Censorship (BBFC) passed *Lolita* with an 'X' certificate, which, at the time, allowed the film to be exhibited 'when no child under 16 is present'. Thus, as many a periodical noted at the time, sixteen-year-old Sue Lyon was able to see in England her breakthrough role in a film that was forbidden to her in her native America.

**BOX OFFICE:** *Lolita* was released in the US on 24 June 1962, grossing $3.7 million, approximately twice its declared production budget. 'The film was successful,' Kubrick noted later, 'but there's no question that people expected to see some of the things that they had read in the book – or *hoped* they might see those parts, anyway. The film should have had as much erotic weight as the novel had. As it was, it had the psychology of the characters and the mood of the story . . . but it certainly didn't have as much of the erotic as you could put into it now. It would have made it more true to the novel, and it would have been more popular.'

**AWARDS:** *Lolita* was nominated for a single Academy Award, in the category of Best Writing, Screenplay Based on Material from Another Medium. The film also received a single nomination at the British Academy of Film and Television Arts (BAFTA) awards, with James Mason being honoured as Best British Actor.

**INFLUENCED BY:** Although few of *Lolita*'s other elements were apparently influenced by anything other than the novel and the censors, the screenplay ingeniously worked in a homage to Edgar Allen Poe ('the divine Edgar', as Humbert refers to him), whose influence on Nabokov is palpable. As Lolita brings Humbert breakfast in his room, he reads her an excerpt from Poe's 'Ulalume', in which – appropriately enough – hope and beauty are transformed into tragedy and despair. True to form, Lolita duly dismisses it as 'corny'.

**DÉJÀ VU:** In the opening scene of *Lolita*, Kubrick's follow-up to *Spartacus*, Clare Quilty is seen draped in a sheet closely resembling a toga, and when Humbert asks him, 'Are you Quilty?' he replies, 'No, I'm Spartacus. Have you come to free the slaves or something?' He then invites Humbert to participate in 'a lovely game of Roman ping-pong' like a couple of 'civilised senators'.

The silent character of Vivian Darkbloom bears a striking resemblance to another nonspeaking character in a Kubrick film: Iris, the ballet dancer in *Killer's Kiss*, played by Kubrick's second wife, Ruth Subotka. *Lolita* also borrows a structural device from *Killer's Kiss*, opening with the climactic scene before telling the entire story in flashback.

One possible reference to an even earlier film comes when Humbert pretends to be going to Hollywood to make a film about 'existentialism', which, he tells us in voice-over, was 'a hot thing at the time'. Could Kubrick be referring to his own early existential effort, *Fear and Desire*?

**INFLUENTIAL ON:** Stylistically, *Lolita* was more influential on Kubrick's own subsequent films than those of any other, most notably on his next, *Dr Strangelove*. Not only did Kubrick feel sufficiently confident to make another black comedy, he was encouraged to cast a single actor – Peter Sellers, again – in multiple roles. The theme of sexual imagery and innuendo was also carried over, and even exaggerated, in *Dr Strangelove*, the subject matter of which was as controversial and potentially explosive as that of *Lolita*, but for entirely different reasons.

The idea of a sexually precocious underage girl lent itself to an incident in Bill Harford's erotic odyssey in *Eyes Wide Shut*. When Harford (Tom Cruise) meets the daughter of the costume-shop proprietor, Milich, she is entertaining two Japanese men; her father – who refers to her as being 'just a child', 'a whore' and 'deranged' for having done so – eventually reaches an 'arrangement' with the Japanese men, and even offers her to Harford, evidently acting as his daughter's pimp. As in *Lolita*, the underage girl's sexual experience has led to her exploitation by an older man.

**SEQUELS AND REMAKES:** 'If one of the new young directors attempts another version I assume that the sex act will be prominently featured,' James Mason wrote in his autobiography *Before I Forget*. Mason was right. In 1995, Carolco Pictures paid $1 million for the screen rights to *Lolita*, which had reverted to the Nabokov estate, and announced that Adrian Lyne would direct the film from a screenplay by James Dearden, who wrote Lyne's 1987 hit *Fatal Attraction*, but would be replaced by

Harold Pinter, David Mamet and, finally, a first-time screenwriter, Stephen Schiff. The deal, negotiated by 'Swifty' Lazar nearly four decades after he had represented Nabokov in the deal with Harris-Kubrick, gave the late author's son Dmitri consultation rights.

Suffused with sexual imagery and erotic possibilities, Lyne's adaptation was almost obsequiously faithful to Nabokov's novel, narrated by its British star, Jeremy Irons, in the voice – and often the words – of Nabokov's Humbert. Melanie Griffith, daughter of Tippi Hedren, was an inspired choice to play Charlotte Haze, while the minimal contribution of the Oscar winner F Murray Abraham (*Amadeus*) as Clare Quilty reminded fans of Kubrick's film how much of the character had been informed by Sellers' improvisational brilliance. Although the credits claimed to be 'introducing Dominique Swain' as Lolita, costly distribution problems in the US meant that she had already been seen as John Travolta's daughter in John Woo's *Face/Off* (1997) by the time the film was finally released in 1998, after spending more than a year in distribution limbo.

Between the two cinema versions of *Lolita*, there were many other adaptations of varying worth. In 1971, a stage musical – *Lolita My Love*, with lyrics by Alan Jay Lerner and music by John Barry – opened in Philadelphia, with John Neville (*The Adventures of Baron Munchausen*) as Humbert. The show lasted barely a week, and never made it to Broadway. A decade later, a (nonmusical) stage adaptation by Edward Albee appeared, with Donald Sutherland in the Humbert role; although this *Lolita* did make it to New York, it was equally short-lived.

**KUBRICK GOES POP:** Although more accurately a reference to the novel *Lolita* rather than the film, it is worth mentioning Sting's lyric for 'Don't Stand So Close To Me', in which a teacher becomes enamoured with an underage pupil: 'Too late now, he sees her/He starts to shake and cough/Just like the old man in that book by Nabokov . . .'

A chapter in the actor and writer Steve Martin's collected essays, *Pure Drivel*, is an amusing short story entitled 'Lolita at Fifty', in which the author postulates on what a middle-aged Lolita might be like.

A full-sized one-sheet poster for *Lolita* hangs on the wall of Caroline's (Lea Thompson) apartment in the sitcom *Caroline in the City*.

**CUT SCENES:** 'If I realised how severe the limitations [of censorship] were going to be, I probably wouldn't have made the film,' Kubrick said after struggling to have *Lolita* approved by the MPAA, without whose seal of approval the film could not be publicly exhibited. Even before production began, Geoffrey Shurlock – representing the MPAA and, unofficially, the Catholic Legion of Decency's mixture of schoolteachers, psychologists and clergymen – had already insisted on a number of changes during pre-production.

Perhaps the most significant of these was the deletion of Humbert's controversial theory that 'Between the age limits of nine and fourteen there occur maidens who, to certain bewitched travellers, twice or many times older than they, reveal their true nature which is not human, but nymphic (that is demoniac); and these creatures I propose to designate as "nymphets".' Although Nabokov's screenplay lifted the passage almost verbatim from the novel, it was deemed unsuitable for the film, almost certainly because the script called for Humbert's narration to run over a montage sequence of prepubescent and pubescent females. For Shurlock, the implication was that Humbert's sexual predilection for very young girls was natural, and that his 'crime' was to act on them; for Kubrick, the deletion of this key exposition meant that the audience was fooled into believing that Humbert was in love with Lolita from the very beginning, rather than erotically obsessed with her until the end.

In December 1960, two months into principal photography, Kubrick received a letter from the MPAA informing him that its examiners found the *Lolita* screenplay to be unacceptable. 'Whatever opinion one may have of the morality of the book, it was superbly written,' the anonymous examiner stated. 'This script, in my opinion, had turned an important literary achievement into the worst sort of botched-up pastiche that could be imagined.' With several weeks of shooting still ahead, Kubrick's *Lolita* had received its first critical drubbing.

As filming progressed, Kubrick and Harris continued to nip and tuck inappropriate, unsuitable and unacceptable elements from the film, while always pushing the censors as far as they could. Finally, when the film completed and screened for the MPAA in the summer of 1961, Shurlock voiced his objections to four key scenes, which were duly amended:

- The scene in which Humbert makes love to Charlotte while looking at a photograph of Lolita on the bedside table, which Shurlock correctly interpreted as meaning, 'that the man is fucking Lolita in his imagination while he is having the mother'. In the final version, Humbert gazes at the portrait while embracing Charlotte, but an argument between them skirts the lovemaking issue.
- In the scene leading up to Lolita's seduction of Humbert, Lolita describes the 'games' she played at summer camp by whispering in his ear, saying, 'You mean you didn't do that when you were a kid?' and then adding, 'This is how we start,' as she bends over his prone body as though to begin lovemaking. 'The succeeding dialogue seems to us to be an overly emphasised discussion of fornication,' Shurlock wrote. 'The whispering in Humbert's ear will be interpreted as obscene, we believe, under the circumstances.' Shurlock insisted that the scene fade out as soon as Lolita begins whispering.
- The off-screen grunting noises made by Humbert while a 'lonesome' Charlotte waits outside the bathroom door were deleted from the dialogue track.

- Humbert's scripted response to Charlotte's admission that she goes 'limp as a noodle' at Humbert's touch – originally 'The same thing happens to me' – was amended to 'Yes, I know the feeling.'

One scene that was changed for reasons other than censorship considerations was the one in which Quilty visits Humbert in the guise of the school psychologist, Dr Zempf. This, Harris says, 'was originally done with Peter Sellers in full drag, with a tweed suit, walking shoes, feather in the hat. He was actually dressed in costume and we were ready to shoot, and Peter looked at Stanley and said, "You know, I think this is a little too much." '

TRIVIA: Anya Productions, the Swiss corporation through which Kubrick channelled profits for *Lolita*, was named after his and Christiane's first daughter, Anya Renata, who was born on 6 April 1959.

Although a character named Vivian Darkbloom (Marianne Stone) makes several appearances in the film, she does not appear in the novel *Lolita*, but in several other Nabokov books. Her name is an anagram of Vladimir Nabokov.

APOCRYPHA: Many sources suggest that the first actor whom Kubrick and Harris considered for the role of Humbert Humbert was Noël Coward, the English writer (*Brief Encounter*) and actor (*The Italian Job*); Harris, however, has denied it. 'I don't even know what Noël Coward *looks* like,' he told Kubrick's biographer, John Baxter.

AVAILABILITY: Currently unavailable in the United Kingdom, *Lolita* is available in the United States on an NTSC VHS video (65004) and a Region 1 DVD (65004), each featuring the theatrical trailer. *Lolita* can also be found on laserdisc in a Criterion Collection edition, in a multiple-aspect-ratio format (1.66:1 for interiors, 4:3 for most of the second-unit exteriors) with the theatrical trailer and liner notes by Gene Youngblood.

EXPERT WITNESS: 'We decided that [*Lolita*] was a bizarre love story, and that we were not going to deal with [Humbert's] predilection for little girls. We're not interested in a pervert. The great love stories are usually about the inability of the lovers to get together. In the old days they'd alienate themselves from society by religious differences, by class differences, by color differences. All of these things had been done before. But what hadn't been done was the age difference. If we could make him the most innocent guy ... and her a little brat, and he just singled her out as someone to fall in love with – let people put their own interpretation on it.' – James B Harris, producer, quoted in *Premiere* magazine, August 1999.

**FINAL ANALYSIS:** The fact that *Lolita* is widely judged to be the greatest novel of the twentieth century goes some way towards demonstrating the confidence of Kubrick when he decided to film a controversial, delicate and perhaps – in the untested social and moral climate of the time – unfilmable story, which was already a critical and commercial success by the time Kubrick's adaptation began.

Kubrick clearly contributed a great deal more to *Lolita*'s screenplay than Nabokov, yet it was a wise decision to give the novelist sole screen credit for the script. Given Quilty's relatively minor role in the novel, the casting of Peter Sellers in several Quilty disguises was more like genius. Publicity photographs tend to explain why Kubrick and Nabokov felt that Sue Lyon was right for the title role; evidently, it was the clothes and mannerisms the young actress was forced to adopt by the MPAA that made her appear too old for the role. In fact, if I have any real criticism of Kubrick's hilarious yet tragic love story, it is that the emasculation of the essential eroticism renders the ending – in which Humbert realises that he is, after all, in love with Lolita, and that his love for her is no longer dependent on her remaining a nymphet – confusing to anyone who has not read the novel, and mishandled to those who have. Why else would Humbert die in prison of a broken heart (coronary thrombosis) after murdering his love rival?

*Lolita* was one of Nabokov's first English-language novels; *Lolita* was the first film Kubrick made in England. Open Nabokov's novel at any page and you will find breathtaking writing; turn on Kubrick's film at any scene, and you will be similarly captivated. Read Nabokov's *Lolita* repeatedly, and you will always find a new delicacy to enjoy; the same, I would venture, goes for the film. Relatively unloved at birth, Stanley Kubrick's *Lolita* has blossomed and matured into a true delight, which – unlike the fleeting allure of Nabokov's nymphet – will continue to charm suitors for decades to come.

**KUBRICK ON KUBRICK:** 'Naturally I regret that the film could not be more erotic. The eroticism of the story serves a very important purpose in the book, which was lacking in the film: it obscured any hint that Humbert Humbert loved Lolita. One was entirely satisfied to believe that he was erotically obsessed with her, and one believed his repeated comments that it would be necessary to get rid of her when she was no longer a nymphet. It was very important to delay an awareness of his love until the end of the story. I'm afraid that this was all too obvious in the film. But, in my view, this is the only justifiable criticism.' – quoted in *Stanley Kubrick Directs* by Alexander Walker, 1971.

# Dr Strangelove or: How I Learned to Stop Worrying and Love the Bomb (1964)

**(B & W – 93 mins)**

**Art Director Peter Murton**
**Production Manager Clifton Brandon**
**Assistant Director Eric Rattray**
**Camera Operator Kelvin Pike**
**Camera Assistant Bernard Ford**
**Continuity Pamela Carlton**
**Wardrobe Bridget Sellers**
**Special Effects Wally Veevers**
**Travelling Matte Vic Margutti**
**Recordist Richard Bird**
**Sound Supervisor John Cox**
**Dubbing Mixer John Aldred**
**Sound Editor Leslie Hodgson**
**Assistant Editor Ray Lovejoy**
**Assembly Editor Geoffrey Fry**
**Make-up Stewart Freeborn**
**Hairdresser Barbara Ritchie**
**Artistic Adviser Capt. John Crewdson**
**Main Title Pablo Ferro**
**Music Laurie Johnson**
**Director of Photography Gilbert Taylor, BSC**
**Film Editor Anthony Harvey**
**Production Designer Ken Adam**
**Associate Producer Victor Lyndon**
**Screenplay by Stanley Kubrick, Terry Southern & Peter George**
**Based on the Book *Red Alert* by Peter George**
**Directed and Produced by Stanley Kubrick**

**CAST:** Peter Sellers (*Group Captain Lionel Mandrake/President Merkin Muffley/Dr Strangelove*), George C Scott (*General 'Buck' Turgidson*), Sterling Hayden (*General Jack D Ripper*), Keenan Wynn (*Colonel 'Bat' Guano*), Slim Pickens (*Major TJ 'King' Kong*), Peter Bull (*Ambassador Alexei de Sadesky*), James Earl Jones (*Lieutenant Lothar Zogg*), Tracy Reed (*Miss Scott*), Jack Creley (*Mr Staines*), Frank Berry (*Lieutenant HR Dietrich, DSO*), Robert O'Neil (*Admiral Randolf*), Roy Stephens (*Frank*), Glen Beck (*Lieutenant WD Kival*), Shane Rimmer (*Captain GA 'Ace' Owens*), Paul Tamarin (*Lieutenant B Goldberg*), Gordon Tanner (*General Faceman*), John McCarthy, Laurence Herder, Hal Galili (*Members of Burpelson Defense Team*).

**UNCREDITED CREW:** Leon Minoff (*Unit Manager*), Arthur Weegee Fellig, Brian Gamby, Garth Inns, Mike Shaw, Wally Veevers (*Special Effects*).

**TITLE SEQUENCE:** After a pre-title notice – 'It is the stated position of the U.S. Air Force that their safeguards would prevent the occurrence [sic] of such events as are depicted in this film. Furthermore, it should be noted that none of the characters portrayed in this film are meant to represent any real persons living or dead.' – which the Pentagon insisted Kubrick add to the film, an equally ominous voice-over intones the following message over images of dark mountain peaks rising over cloud: 'For more than a year, ominous rumours have been privately circulating among high-level Western leaders that the Soviet Union had been at work on what was darkly hinted to be the ultimate weapon – a Doomsday device. Intelligence sources traced the site of the top-secret Russian project to the perpetually fog-shrouded wasteland below the Arctic peaks of the Zokoff Islands. What they were building, or why it should be located in such a remote and desolate place, no one could say.'

As the message ends, *Dr Strangelove*'s irreverent and vaguely sexual tone is established by an opening montage in which the phallic fuel line of an airborne tanker performs an in-flight refuelling of a B-52 bomber to the strains of 'Try a Little Tenderness'. The credits appear as hand-drawn chalkboard markings, which play over the action, each of the names alternately elongated, compressed and arranged as the mood took their designer, Pablo Ferro.

**SUMMARY:** Fearing that communists are attempting to contaminate the water supply, United States Air Force General Jack D Ripper orders the B-52 bombers of Burpelson Air Force Base to drop their nuclear payloads on to targets inside the Soviet Union. With the B-52s airborne and the mission incapable of being aborted without the recall codes known only to himself, Ripper urges Washington to follow his lead and wipe out the Russians before they can retaliate. Instead, against the advice of gung-ho General 'Buck' Turgidson, US President Merkin Muffley orders the army to attack Burpelson, where Mandrake, an RAF group captain on loan to the US Air Force as part of an officers' exchange programme, is desperately – but unsuccessfully – trying to persuade Ripper to recall the aircraft.

Muffley uses the War Room's emergency hotline to warn the Soviet Premier of the impending attack, and does his best to assist his Russian counterpart in having the aircraft shot down before their atomic weapons can be dropped. Preventing the attack becomes all the more essential when the Russian Ambassador, Alexei DeSadesky, informs the stunned members of the US war cabinet of the existence of a so-called 'doomsday machine'. Conceived as the ultimate nuclear deterrent, the device is designed to trigger automatically in the event of a nuclear explosion, setting off a chain reaction that will wipe out all life on Earth, and plunge the planet into a 93-year nuclear winter.

General Ripper shoots himself before Burpelson is finally captured, but Mandrake correctly guesses the recall code and, despite being hampered by a US Army busybody, Colonel 'Bat' Guano, and some communications problems, succeeds in informing the President. Although most of the B-52 bombers are thereby recalled, one of the aircraft – the *Leper Colony*, piloted by Texan Major TJ 'King' Kong – has a damaged radio. Unable to receive the recall code, the lone aircraft heads inexorably to its target, a missile base at Laputa. Meanwhile, the President's scientific adviser, a wheelchair-bound ex-Nazi named Dr Strangelove, suggests that the human race might survive the impending holocaust if a nucleus of US citizens – including members of the war cabinet, naturally – waited out the nuclear winter in mineshafts deep below the ground. While Turgidson argues about the possibility of a 'mineshaft gap' arising between the Americans and Russians, Major Kong rides one of his fifty-megaton bombs down to Earth, triggering the doomsday machine, which effectively destroys the world.

SOURCE: *Dr Strangelove* was adapted from the suspense thriller *Two Hours to Doom*, written by a former RAF navigator, Peter George, and published in the UK (under the pseudonym Peter Bryant) in 1958, and in the US (as *Red Alert*) the following year. The book, the screen rights to which Harris-Kubrick bought for $3,500, told of an insane US Air Force general who, upon learning that he is suffering from a fatal disease, orders an unprovoked nuclear attack against Russia, urging Washington to follow his lead and wipe out the Soviet Union. Instead, with the B-52 bombers already airborne, the US and Soviet heads of state are forced to put aside their differences and work together to ensure that the planes and their deadly loads never reach their targets. Although the US President offers to destroy Atlantic City, New Jersey, to prove his own 'good intentions', this proves unnecessary as nuclear annihilation is narrowly averted.

Given the book's doomsday scenario, it is doubly surprising how faithful *Dr Strangelove* remains to its source material, despite the fact that Kubrick, George and the cult writer Terry Southern (*Easy Rider*) altered its tone from deeply ominous to darkly humorous. As Kubrick himself noted, 'The ideas of the story and all its suspense were still there even when it was completely changed into black comedy.'

WORKING TITLES: The genesis of *Dr Strangelove or: How I Learned to Stop Worrying and Love the Bomb* – not merely one of the longest titles in motion picture history, but also one of the most bizarre – remains shrouded in mystery. Although Kubrick originally began adapting Peter George's novel under its original US title, *Red Alert*, the first draft of the screenplay – dated 31 August 1962 and credited solely to Kubrick, though it was almost certainly written in collaboration with George – features an even longer sobriquet than that used on the completed picture: 'NARDAC BLEFESCU PRESENTS Dr Strangelove: or How I Learned to Stop Worrying and Love the Bomb A MACRO–GALAXY–METEOR PICTURE.'

This was designed to reflect the fact that the film was told from the perspective of a visiting alien's attempt to reconstruct the last hours of human civilisation, using information uncovered several millennia after the exchange of atomic weapons that wiped out all life on Earth. Curiously, this device had been used earlier in a short story by *2001: A Space Odyssey*'s co-writer Arthur C Clarke ('History Lesson'), in which an archaeological expedition made by extraterrestrials to a long-dead Earth turns up only a single clue to the nature and history of the human race: a Walt Disney cartoon. The original prologue and epilogue were later adapted for Peter George's own novelisation of the film, which presents the story as part of an alien-produced series of publications entitled 'The Dead Worlds of Antiquity'.

**PRODUCTION HISTORY:** It is one of the many paradoxes of Stanley Kubrick's life that, if he had not been terrified of nuclear war, he could never have made a comedy about it. Kubrick had been appalled to learn that, prior to the first atomic tests, many physicists argued that the detonation of a hydrogen bomb might set off a chain reaction that would destroy the entire planet. 'The decision to ignore this dire warning and proceed with the test was made by political and military minds who could certainly not understand the physics involved,' Kubrick stated. 'One would have thought that if even a minority of the physicians thought the test might destroy the Earth, no sane men would decide to carry it out. The fact that the Earth is still here doesn't alter the mind-boggling decision which was made at that time.' Indeed, while living in New York in 1958, Kubrick had told a friend that he was seriously considering moving to Australia because it was one of the few continents likely to be untouched by nuclear war. Instead, he moved to Hertfordshire, England, where he had filmed *Lolita* relatively free of studio interference, and decided to film *Red Alert* at Shepperton Studios.

Eschewing any kind of script outline or 'treatment' in favour of a relatively straightforward screenplay adaptation, Kubrick quickly realised that the best ideas were those that pushed the material towards satire. 'I started work on the screenplay with every intention of making the film a serious treatment of the problem of accidental nuclear war,' he told Joseph Gelmis. 'As I kept trying to imagine the way in which things would really happen, ideas kept coming to me which I would discard because they were so ludicrous. I kept saying to myself, "I can't do that – people will laugh." But after a month or so I began to realise that all the things I was throwing out were the things which were most truthful. After all, what could be more absurd than the very idea of two mega-powers willing to wipe out all human life because of an accident, spiced up by political difference that will seem as meaningless to people a hundred years from now as the theological conflicts of the Middle Ages appear to us today?'

Kubrick first revealed his intention to make a nuclear satire in May 1962, during publicity for the release of *Lolita*. Although he described the film as being 'a slightly irreverent story [about] an American college professor who rises to power in sex and politics by becoming a nuclear wise man', it is unclear whether Kubrick genuinely intended to make such a film, or merely wished to divert observers from his true intentions.

Recalling the edgy humour of Terry Southern's novel *The Magic Christian*, which Peter Sellers had given to him one Christmas, Kubrick called the author in early December 1962, and invited him to England to collaborate on the adaptation. 'He told me he was going to make a film about "our failure to understand the dangers of nuclear war",' Southern wrote in *Grand Street* magazine. 'He said that he had thought of the story as a "straightforward melodrama" until this morning, when he "woke up and realised that nuclear war was too outrageous, too fantastic to be treated in any conventional manner". He said he could only see it now as "some kind of hideous joke".' Kubrick added that reading *The Magic Christian* had given him certain indications that Southern might be the ideal writer to engineer the metamorphosis of *Red Alert* into *Dr Strangelove*.

Meanwhile, Kubrick worked with the Oscar-nominated production designer Ken Adam, whose elaborate sets for *Dr No* (1962), the first project in his long association with the James Bond films, had impressed Kubrick. The most important set that Adam, a former RAF pilot, would be required to design was that of the gigantic War Room, which he originally conceived as a two-tier amphitheatre with a glass-fronted second level in which various defence personnel could be seen working above the action taking place on the ground floor. As Adam later explained, 'One morning, three weeks later (when work on the set was well advanced), I was giving Stanley a lift to Shepperton when he turned to me and said, "About the War Room, Ken . . . I don't think the two-level concept will work; what am I going to do with the upper level? It's too costly to fill it with extras . . ." Well, this threw me. I went into tailspin. I walked around the garden at Shepperton for over an hour trying to calm myself down.' Adam then began sketching with his Flowmaster felt-tipped pen, Kubrick looking over his shoulder.

'I doodled various shapes before coming up with a triangular form. Stanley stopped me. "Isn't the triangle the strongest form in geometry?" he asked me. Me: "You may well be right." Him: "In other words, it would make for a good bomb shelter." Me: "Reinforced concrete." Him: "A huge, underground bomb shelter – fantastic." ' Adam elaborated on the wedge-shaped room design, filling the walls of the room with huge backlit maps, and adding as the centrepiece a huge round table around which the President and the members of his war cabinet would sit. According to Adam, Kubrick added the finishing touch by asking for the table, which measured 380 square feet, to be covered in green baize, as though the President, the Russian ambassador and the generals were playing a game of poker for the fate of the world.

The set, whose highly polished floor encompassed some 13,000 square feet, was one of the few to be covered with a ceiling, enabling Kubrick to light it using light from an identifiable source, rather than the more traditional overhead studio lights. 'I had designed a circular light fitting that could be suspended,' Adam explained. Despite the elaborate *mise en scène*, however, audiences would never get to appreciate the true scale of the venture. 'There never was an establishing shot of the War Room with the lights on, so that one could see its size,' Adam noted. 'Stanley did this intentionally. He didn't want it to be like a Bond movie, where you have a chance to admire the set. I was upset at the time, but I think he was absolutely right.'

As Southern performed his own brand of satirical magic on the script, the studio financing the $2 million production became increasingly alarmed at the new direction Kubrick was taking; at one point, a Columbia Pictures executive, Mo Rothman, telephoned Southern to say, 'Just tell Stanley that New York does not see anything funny about the end of the world as we know it!' Nevertheless, the studio's insistence that the comic actor Peter Sellers, who had effectively played multiple roles in *Lolita*, be cast in 'at least four major roles' in *Dr Strangelove* pushed the project further into the realm of satire, especially when his improvisational style was let loose on set.

'During shooting many substantial changes were made in the script, sometimes together with the cast during improvisations,' Kubrick told Gene Phillips, an assertion that Scott ('Buck' Turgidson) confirmed. 'He's a perfectionist,' he said of Kubrick, 'and he's always unhappy with anything that's set. Every morning we would all meet and practically rewrite the day's work.' Later, publicising *Patton* (1970), he added, 'I used to kid [Kubrick] by saying that I should've gotten the screen credit for *Dr Strangelove* because I wrote half the goddamn picture!' Nevertheless, according to Southern, Sellers' spontaneous style added little to the script. 'It was minimal,' he said. 'It wasn't like *Lolita*, where he improvised a great deal. His improvisational bits in *Strangelove* were very specific. One scene that comes to mind is when [Sterling] Hayden goes into the bathroom to kill himself, Peter's lines are, "Oh, go into the bathroom and have a brush-up – good idea." Sellers changed that to, "Splash a bit of cold water on the back of the neck," which is more of a British thing. That was good.'

Other examples of Sellers' spontaneity emerged during his portrayal of Dr Strangelove, as his gloved right hand appears to display a life of its own. 'Stanley's idea was to have a black glove so that his hand was sort of injured in some nuclear experiment,' Sellers said during an appearance on *The Steve Allen Show* in 1964, 'and then I got it further by thinking that the hand was a Nazi while the rest of him had made the compromise to live in America. That idea just came to me – it was entirely spontaneous, and Stanley stopped everything and shot the gesture with three cameras. Before then, nobody had seen it but him and, of course, it caused "falling bricks" afterward.' Indeed, the gesture's effect on the actor Peter Bull can be seen as the scowling face of Ambassador DeSadesky breaks into a spontaneous smile, just after Strangelove first makes his inadvertent *sieg heil* salute.

Filming was completed on 23 April 1963, after fifteen weeks of principal photography. The final cost was between $1.7 million and $2 million. Only one question remained: would audiences find the end of the world as funny as the film makers had?

CASTING: Columbia Pictures' contingency that the film's financing rested on the casting of Peter Sellers in at least four major roles created problems for Kubrick when the actor telegraphed Kubrick midway through production. 'Dear Stanley,' Sellers wrote. 'I am so very sorry to tell you that I am having serious difficulty with the various roles. Now hear this: there is no way, repeat, no way, I can play the Texas pilot, Major "King" Kong. I have a complete block against that accent. Letter from [my agent] follows. Please forgive.' Kubrick immediately began persuading Sellers to change his mind, asking Texas-born Southern to make a tape of Kong's dialogue for the actor to learn from a tape recorder. 'When Sellers arrived on the set, he plugged into this Swiss tape recorder with huge, monster earphones and listened to the tape I made,' Southern recalled. 'He looked ridiculous, but he mastered the accent in about ten minutes.' The first day of Kong's scenes, those in the cockpit of the *Leper Colony*, were filmed without incident, but that night Sellers sprained his ankle in a fall outside a London restaurant. Although he was fit enough to film the next day, a second tumble – this time, in the bomb-bay set suspended above the studio floor – forced his retirement from the role. 'He was out of that part,' Southern said simply. 'The doctor told him he couldn't do it.'

With only a few scenes left to be filmed, Kubrick was forced to find a new Major 'King' Kong. 'Stanley had set such store by [Sellers'] acting that he felt he couldn't just replace him with just another actor,' Southern recounted. Having originally written the part of Kong with John Wayne in mind – his name even appears in the script alongside many of Kong's dialogue lines – Kubrick offered the part to the veteran actor, who immediately rejected it. Next, at Southern's suggestion, he tried Dan Blocker, best known as Hoss on TV's *Bonanza*, but Blocker's agent rejected it on the grounds that the story was 'too pinko for Dan', the first indication any of the film makers had received of any adverse political interpretation of the script. Finally, Southern recollected,

'Kubrick remembered Slim Pickens from *One-Eyed Jacks*, which he almost directed for Marlon Brando (see Lost Worlds: The Films That Never Were), until Brando acted in such a weird way that he forced Stanley out.'

Sellers later said that Kubrick even offered him a fifth role: that of General Buck Turgidson, or 'Buck Schmuck', as the earlier drafts of the screenplay referred to him. 'I was going to do them *all*,' Sellers told *Rolling Stone*. 'Stanley was convinced I could. I could do no wrong, you see. Some days, Stanley used to be sitting outside my front door saying, "What about Buck Schmuck? You've *got* to play Buck Schmuck!" And I'd say, "I physically can't do it! I don't like the role anyway, Stan. And I'll try to do the ['King' Kong] thing, but I mean I think that's *enough*!"'
Ultimately, George C Scott (*The Hustler, Anatomy of a Murder*) was cast as Turgidson, leaving Sellers to play only three roles for his fee of $1 million (half of the film's total budget) – a fact that led Kubrick to joke that he was getting 'three for the price of six'. Kubrick had seen Scott, who later won (but declined) an Oscar for his portrayal of a real-life general in *Patton* (1970), in a New York performance of *The Merchant of Venice*; in the same production, Kubrick spotted the actor James Earl Jones, who would later gain fame as the voice of Darth Vader in the first *Star Wars* trilogy, and cast him in his first film role: the *Leper Colony*'s bombardier, Lieutenant Lothar Zogg.

**THE USUAL SUSPECTS:** Both Sterling Hayden and Peter Sellers had previously worked with Kubrick, on *The Killing* and *Lolita* respectively. 'When you are inspired and professionally accomplished as Peter, the only limit to the importance of your work is your willingness to take chances,' Kubrick told Sellers' biographer, Peter Evans. Although Sellers received widespread acclaim and an Academy Award nomination for his efforts, his secretary, Hattie Proudfoot, said that he had not enjoyed his *Dr Strangelove* experience. 'He got fed up playing all these different parts,' she told the makers of an *Arena* documentary devoted to the actor, 'and rumour has it he pretended he'd had an accident so he didn't have to do the last part.'

If Sellers found his various characterisations demanding, however, Hayden had even greater difficulty with his single role, the officer in charge of Strategic Air Command's 843rd bomber wing, General Jack D Ripper. 'On the first day of shooting, I found that I just couldn't handle the technical jargon in my lines,' the actor revealed. 'I was utterly humiliated. Stanley told me, "The terror on your face may yield just the quality we want, and if it doesn't, the hell with it – we'll just shoot the whole thing over. You and I both know that this is something that can happen to anyone." He was beautiful,' Hayden added. 'A lot of directors like to see actors wallow. Stanley isn't one of them.'

**THE PURSUIT OF PERFECTION:** The US military's refusal to have anything to do with Kubrick's subversive satire led to a number of problems in the director's traditional quest for absolute authenticity. Although Peter George's background in the RAF and British intelligence meant that most of the procedures were accurate, at least as far as Britain was concerned, the precise layout of the B-52's interior was still classified as *Dr Strangelove* entered production, requiring Ken Adam to consult air-enthusiast publications for technical data. 'It was so amazing that through a technical flight magazine like *Jane's* we could get all the information we wanted,' he explained. 'The only thing we were not sure about was that little box, the "CRM", the fail-safe device. I came up with an idea,' he added, 'and during the shooting we invited some Air Force personnel to visit the set. They went white when they saw that CRM, so it must have been pretty close.'

Adam was forced to improvise when it came to designing the nuclear bombs themselves, however. 'I had no idea of what a missile would look like,' he admitted. 'In 1962 nobody, certainly, had seen a nuclear bomb, so it was a question of making it very small or making it very large. So I came up with this strange design, and then Stanley came up with the idea of the graffiti,' he said, referring to the irreverent markings 'HI THERE!' and 'DEAR JOHN' sprayed on the side of the two bombs in the *Leper Colony* bomb bay. In fact, the weapons in Peter George's original novel had been labelled 'HI THERE!' and 'LOLITA'; although the latter reference was intended to refer to Nabokov's novel, not Kubrick's film (released four years after the publication of *Red Alert*), Kubrick evidently preferred not to retain the reference.

## CLASSIC QUOTES

**Ripper:** 'Now, listen to me carefully. The base is being put on condition red. I want this flashed to all sections immediately.'

**Mandrake:** 'Condition red, sir. Yes. Jolly good idea, keeps the men on their toes.'

**Ripper:** 'Group Captain, I'm afraid this is not an exercise.'

**Kong:** 'Now look, boys, I ain't much of a hand at makin' speeches. But I got a pretty fair idea that something doggoned important's going on back there. And I got a fair idea of the kind of personal emotions that some of you fellas may be thinking. Heck, I reckon you wouldn't even be human beings if you didn't have some pretty strong personal feelings about nuclear combat. But I want you to remember one thing: the folks back home is a countin' on ya, and by golly we ain't about to let 'em down. Tell you somethin' else. This thing turns out to be half as important as I figure it just might be, I'd say that you're all in line for some important promotions and personal citations when this thing's over with. That goes for every last one of you, regardless of your race, colour, or your creed. Now, let's get this thing on the hump. We got some flying to do.'

**Ripper:** 'I can no longer sit back and allow communist infiltration, communist indoctrination, communist subversion, and the

Left: *Killer's Kiss* poster
(© MGM Home Entertainment Inc.)

Below: Lobby card for
*The Killing* (© MGM Home
Entertainment Inc.)

Above: Timothy Carey's aim is true in *The Killing* (© MGM Home Entertainment Inc.

Below: The Ant Hill Mob: Colonel Dax (Kirk Douglas) and his men in *Paths of Glory* (© Harris and Estate of Stanley Kubrick/MGM Home Entertainment Inc.)

Above: *Spartacus* lobby card (© Universal Pictures)

Right: Kirk Douglas strikes a pose in *Spartacus* (© Universal Pictures)

Left: *Lolita* poster
(© Turner Entertainment Co.

Right: 'I learned some
real good games in
camp.'
(© Turner Entertainment Co.

Below left: *Lolita* – 'I
don't want you around
them. They're nasty-
minded boys.'
(© Turner Entertainment Co.

Below right: The hunter
and his prey: Humbert
(James Mason) and Lolita
(Sue Lyon)
(© Turner Entertainment Co.

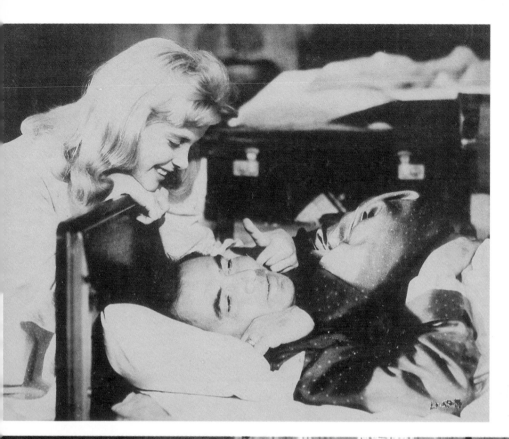

Above: *Dr Strangelove* – 'No more than ten to twenty million killed ... tops.'
(© Hawk Films/Columbia Tristar)

Above: 'You know how we've always talked about the possibility of something going wrong with the Bomb ...' (© Hawk Films/Columbia Tristar)

Above: Peter Sellers gets to grips with his character Dr Strangelove
(© Hawk Films/Columbia Tristar)

Above: 'What about Major Kong?'
(© Hawk Films/Columbia Tristar)

Above: Bob McCall's impressive artwork for the *2001* lobby card
(© Turner Entertainment Co.)

Below: *2001: A Space Odyssey* – The Dawn of Man (© Turner Entertainment Co.)

international communist conspiracy to sap and impurify all of our precious bodily fluids.'

**Muffley:** 'You're talking about mass murder, General, not war.'

**Turgidson:** 'Mr President, I'm not saying we wouldn't get our hair mussed. But I do say . . . no more than ten to twenty million killed, tops. Uh . . . depended on the breaks.'

**Muffley:** 'Gentlemen! You can't fight in here: this is the War Room!'

**Muffley:** 'Hello? Hello, Dmitri? Listen, I can't hear too well. Do you suppose you could turn the music down just a little? Oh, that's much better. Yes. Fine, I can hear you now, Dmitri. Clear and plain and coming through fine. I'm coming through fine too, eh? Good, then. Well, then, as you say, we're both coming through fine. Good. Well it's good that you're fine and I'm fine. I agree with you. It's great to be fine. Now then, Dmitri. You know how we've always talked about the possibility of something going wrong with the Bomb. The Bomb, Dmitri. The hydrogen bomb. Well now what happened is, one of our base commanders, he had a sort of, well he went a little funny in the head. You know. Just a little . . . funny. And, uh, he went and did a silly thing. Well, I'll tell you what he did, he ordered his planes . . . to attack your country. Well let me finish, Dmitri. Let me finish, Dmitri. Well, listen, how do you think I feel about it? Can you imagine how I feel about it, Dmitri? Why do you think I'm calling you? Just to say hello? Of course I like to speak to you. Of course I like to say hello. Not now, but any time, Dmitri. I'm just calling up to tell you something terrible has happened. It's a friendly call. Of course it's a friendly call. Listen, if it wasn't friendly, you probably wouldn't have even got it. They will not reach their targets for at least another hour. I am . . . I am positive, Dmitri. Listen, I've been all over this with your ambassador. It is not a trick. Well, I'll tell you. We'd like to give your air staff a complete run-down on the targets, the flight plans and the defensive systems of the planes. Yes! I mean, if we're unable to recall the planes, then I'd say that, uh, well, we're just going to have to help you destroy them, Dmitri. I know they're our boys. All right, well, listen . . . Who should we call? Who should we call, Dmitri? The People . . .? Sorry, you faded away there. The People's Central Air Defence Headquarters. Where is that, Dmitri? In Omsk. Right. Yes. Oh, you'll call them first, will you? Uh huh. Listen, do you happen to have the phone number on you, Dmitri? What? I see, just ask for Omsk Information. I'm sorry too, Dmitri. I'm very sorry. All right! You're sorrier than I am! But I am sorry as well. I am as sorry as you are, Dmitri. Don't say that you are more sorry than I am, because I am capable of being just as sorry as you are. So we're both sorry, all right? All right.'

**Turgidson:** 'Doctor, you mentioned the ration of ten women to each man. Now, wouldn't that necessitate the abandonment of the so-called monogamous sexual relationship – I mean, as far as men were concerned?'

Strangelove: 'Regrettably, yes. But it is, you know, a sacrifice required for the future of the human race. I hasten to add that, since each man will be required to do prodigious service along these lines, the women will have to be selected for their sexual characteristics, which will have to be of a highly stimulating nature.'

DeSadesky: 'I must confess, you have an astonishingly good idea there, Doctor.'

Strangelove: 'Mein Führer, I can walk!'

**THEMES AND MOTIFS:** In *Lolita*, Kubrick inserted subtle, even subliminal, sexual innuendo into dialogue and background objects, in order to subvert the censors who objected to more obvious references, and to eroticise the unerotic. In *Dr Strangelove*, Kubrick and Southern conspired to sexualise almost every possible aspect of the film, beginning with the title sequence. The other references – some highly sophisticated, others surprisingly juvenile – pile up as the film progresses:

- the character names – Buck (suggesting virile male), Strangelove (strange love, suggesting the kind of 'preversion' [sic] of which Colonel 'Bat' Guano would doubtless disapprove), Premier Kissoff, DeSadesky (a Russian version of the Marquis de Sade) – are subtly sexualised, although the original script contained far more amusing examples: Admiral Percy Buldike, Private Tung, Major Nonce, Lieutenant 'Binky' Ballmuff;
- several *Leper Colony* crew members are seen reading *Playboy* magazine, mimicking their subsequent perusal of the Top Secret orders;
- 'Buck' Turgidson is entertaining his bikini-clad secretary at home when the call comes from Colonel Puntrich alerting him to imminent nuclear war;
- when Turgidson tells Miss Scott that 'the Air Force never sleeps', she responds suggestively, 'I'm not sleepy, either';
- 'You just start your countdown,' Turgidson tells Miss Scott, 'and old Bucky'll be back here before you can say "Blast off!" '
- the aircraft are referred to as penetrating Russian radar cover;
- in the middle of the War Room briefing, Turgidson is interrupted by a telephone call from Miss Scott, seeking reassurance that there is more to their relationship than the purely physical;
- Turgidson suggests a strike against the Russians in order to catch them 'with their pants down';
- the prophylactics, lipsticks and nylon stockings contained within the survival kit;
- DeSadesky implies that the Russian leader is romantically engaged when President Muffley tries to warn him about the incoming missiles:

'Our Premier is a man of the people, but he is also a man, if you follow my meaning';

- General Ripper reveals to Captain Mandrake that sexual neurosis – his 'loss of essence' – is at the root of his decision to provoke nuclear war with Russia, and that he first developed his theory during 'the physical act of love';
- Colonel 'Bat' Guano is so much more concerned with potential perverts (or 'preverts') than Communists that he almost defeats Mandrake's attempt to reach the President;
- the bomb ridden by Major Kong is unmistakably phallic;
- the future course of post-apocalypse human evolution suggested by Dr Strangelove is as sexually motivated as the madness that sparked the crisis.

For Alexander Walker, author of *Stanley Kubrick Directs*, some of the most interesting aspects of *Dr Strangelove* were those related to time and space. 'What happens in *Dr Strangelove* is confined to a few hours and to three highly localised settings,' he explains. 'Each setting, moreover, is sealed off from the others . . . Insanity is sealed in with the characters; they are locked into their "cells", as the fate of the peoples they rule or represent is locked into the events.' For a film that deals with the end of the world, Walker adds, the actual areas involved are absurdly small.

James Earl Jones (Lieutenant Zogg) has pointed out another theme that provides food for thought. 'One curious thing was that he always had us eating,' he told *Premiere* magazine. 'Every time he'd cut to us, we'd be eating a Twinkie – just constantly stuffing our faces.' Perfectly apt for a film that has a full-size, well-stocked buffet table in the War Room, and originally ended with a pie fight. 'That was a comment about how people deal with fear. I think he liked the mundane aspect of horrific events.'

MUSIC: Laurie Johnson, probably best known for his theme song for the sixties television series *The Avengers*, was earning a reputation as one of the screen's most imaginative British composers by the time he was asked to create the score for *Dr Strangelove*. However, just as he had asked Gerald Fried to compose a score based on the French national anthem 'Marseillaise' in *Paths of Glory*, Kubrick chose to have Johnson use the well-known wartime song 'When Johnny Comes Marching Home' as the basis for scenes featuring the *Leper Colony* and its crew. For the end credits, Kubrick decided to use Vera Lynn's morale-boosting World War Two anthem 'We'll Meet Again' in a similarly ironic fashion – at one stage even considering having the lyrics appear on screen so that the audience might sing along! Athough this idea was dropped, the uplifting anthem is given a subversive edge as scenes depicting nuclear detonations are juxtaposed with the words 'We'll meet again/Don't know where, don't know when . . .'

**POSTER:** 'The creative side is entirely in his hands – he even designs his own posters,' the associate producer, Victor Lyndon, told *Glamour* magazine during the filming of *Dr Strangelove*. On this occasion, Kubrick had little choice, since Columbia Pictures had admitted that its marketing department had encountered great difficulty marketing a film about the end of the world. The final poster design, used in the United States and much of the rest of the world, was effectively a political cartoon, showing two bald statesmen (one with a woman's arm draped around him) speaking on red telephones, while a 'flock' of B-52 bombers emerge from a globe bearing the American and Russian flags.

The two statesmen also appear in the foreground of the French poster for the film, locally retitled *Dr Folamour*, but the background shows a colour image of Tracy Reed (Miss Scott), naked apart from the newspaper covering her posterior, provocatively draped atop the monochromatic mushroom cloud emanating from the centre of the War Room's round table. Another French image again featured the two statesmen, connected by telephone wire to a giant globe, subdivided into stills from the film, Russian and American flags, and the poles.

Rather more bizarre was the poster image for the release of *Il Dottor Stranamore* in Italy, which was a special photographic shoot featuring the eyes of a high-ranking military officer peering through a letterbox-sized gap in what one assumes to be a thick concrete bunker or bomb shelter, handing a slip of typewritten paper through another, lower, hole in the same wall.

**TAG-LINE:** 'The hot-line suspense comedy'.

**TRAILER:** Probably the first trailer that Kubrick almost certainly created entirely by himself, the theatrical trailer for *Dr Strangelove* opens with flash-frame edits of several still photographs of Kubrick, intercut with the phrase 'A STANLEY KUBRICK PRODUCTION', and accompanied by the sound of bombs dropping and maniacal laughter. A multiple-caption treatment of the title, with single white words of various titles repeated, on a black background, thus: 'DR' 'STRANGE' 'LOVE' 'STRANGELOVE' 'OR:' 'HOW' 'I' 'LEARNED' 'TO' 'STOP' 'WORRYING' 'AND' 'LOVE' and 'THE.' The final word, 'BOMB', appears in reverse, followed by a captioned countdown, white on black, from '5' through '1' intercut with footage of a B-52 bomber. (From this point on, xylophone music plays throughout the trailer.)

In the same style, one word per caption, the following question is posed: 'WHY DID U.S. BOMBERS' – cut to Miss Scott on the telephone – 'attack' – cut to Turgidson at the War Room table – 'Russia.' A further question is posed, intercut with subliminal shots of Muffley on the telephone: 'WHAT WAS THE FIRST WORD SAID ON THE HOT LINE?' 'Oh,' says Muffley. 'Oh.' More B-52 bombers, then a new question: 'WHY DID U.S. PARATROOPERS INVADE THEIR OWN' – cut to Major Kong and the navigator – 'base' – '?' The next question is intercut with a smiling Dr Strangelove: 'WHY DOES DR STRANGE

LOVE WANT' – 'ten females to each male.' – '?' Still images of mushroom clouds, intercut with captions for a new question: 'HOW DOES THE FATE OF THE WORLD HANG ON A' – cut to Mandrake in the payphone – 'Coca-Cola machine' – '?' Images of General Ripper: 'WHY WAS GENERAL JACK D RIPPER OBSESSED BY' – 'fluids.' Images of the War Room: 'WHAT IS THE' – 'the Doomsday Machine.' Cut to Turgidson in bed with Miss Scott: 'Blast off!'

An explosive sound effect, and the multicaption title is repeated, followed by 'WITH', and images and captions bearing the names of Peter Sellers, George C Scott and Sterling Hayden. Poster images are interwoven with the stills and cast captions. Cut to Turgidson – 'Where's my shorts?' – and Strangelove making a Nazi salute. Footage of Burpelson Air Force Base being overrun as Ripper defends it. 'Where's the bathroom?' asks 'Bat' Guano. Cut to Miss Scott – 'Buck, should I get it?' – and the War Room – 'on the hotline' – and Major Kong riding the bomb to oblivion. As the full title appears, intercut with flash-frame still images from the film, a Peter Lorre-style voice intones the main title: '*Dr Strangelove*'; another, more cheerful, male voice reads the subtitle – except for the words 'love the bomb', which are read by a female. Several lengthy scenes follow, rounding out the considerable running time of the three-minute trailer. The title is repeated, read as before, but this time a voice adds, 'a moving picture'. More captions follow, one per frame: 'SEE IT MON. OR: A WEEK FROM THURS. OR: SUN. WED. FRI. TUES. SAT. OR: MON.'

**WHAT THE PAPERS SAID:** Perhaps unsurprisingly, given the nature – or, with the exception of Stanley Kramer's *On the Beach* (1959), the absence – of Hollywood's traditional treatment of the nuclear question, *Dr Strangelove* generated a great deal of news coverage upon its release. Most critics appreciated its satirical intentions, with the *Saturday Review* claiming that Kubrick had 'carried American comedy to a new high ground'. 'It would seem no setting for comedy or satire,' agreed *Variety*, 'but the writers have accomplished this with biting, piercing dialogue and thorough characterisations.'

The *New York Times*' Bosley Crowther called it 'the most shattering sick joke I've ever come across . . . [and] at the same time, one of the cleverest and most incisive satiric thrusts at the awkwardness and folly of the military that [has] ever been seen on the screen'. Nevertheless, Crowther also admitted to being 'troubled by the feeling which runs all through the film, of discredit and even contempt for our whole military establishment'; closer to the hub of US politics, the *Washington Post* was more forthright: 'No Communist could dream of a more effective anti-American film to spread abroad than this one.'

Today, *Dr Strangelove* continues to win the retrospective plaudits of critics. *Time Out* suggested that it was 'perhaps Kubrick's most perfectly realised film, simply because his cynical vision of the progress of technology and human stupidity is wedded with comedy . . . scary, hilarious, and nightmarishly beautiful, far more effective in its portrait of insanity and call for disarmament than any number of worthy anti-nuke documentaries'. On the occasion of the 1999 video re-release of the film, the lifestyle magazine *Heat* demonstrated the film's popularity among a new generation by describing it as 'satire with teeth, displaying a unique sophistication that has ensured its classic status'.

**CONTROVERSY:** *Dr Strangelove*'s subject matter may have been controversial enough in certain political quarters, and especially military ones, but it was Kubrick who failed to see the funny side when he learned that Entertainment Corporation of America (ECA), then being run by Kubrick's old nemesis Max Youngstein, was planning an adaptation of a novel entitled *Fail-Safe*, whose story of an accidental nuclear exchange bore a marked resemblance to that of *Red Alert*.

Hoping to prevent *Fail-Safe* from beating *Dr Strangelove* into cinemas, Kubrick filed a plagiarism suit against ECA, Youngstein, the authors Eugene Burdick and Harvey Wheeler and their publishers in February 1963, alleging that *Fail-Safe* was copied largely from plaintiff Peter George's book. The defendants countersued, claiming that *Fail-Safe* had been based on Wheeler's short story, 'Abraham '59', written a year before the publication of *Red Alert*, but published a year later, and that it was therefore more likely that George's story had been copied from Wheeler's. Before the matter could be resolved in court, however, Columbia Pictures took over distribution of Sidney Lumet's adaptation of *Fail-Safe*, and agreed to hold its release until October 1964, ten months after that of *Dr Strangelove*.

**BOX OFFICE:** *Dr Strangelove*'s world premiere, scheduled to take place in London on 12 December 1963, was cancelled as a mark of respect for President Kennedy, and the release postponed on the grounds that 'it would be inappropriate to release a political comedy at the present time'. The period of mourning precipitated by Kennedy's assassination did not, however, adversely affect the film's box-office performance, as strong word-of-mouth and positive reviews overcame Columbia Pictures' own indifference to its first and only Stanley Kubrick film. 'Columbia was embarrassed by the picture and tried to get people to see Carl Foreman's *The Victors* (1963) instead,' Terry Southern recalled. 'They would steer ticket buyers away from *Strangelove* and try to get them to see *The Victors*. At the time we thought we were going to be totally wiped out. People would call up the box office and be told there were no seats for *Strangelove* and asked if they would like to see *The Victors* instead. Gradually, the buzz along the rialto built word of mouth in our favour.' Within a year of its US release on 30 January 1964 – a month after a brief, Oscar-qualifying run in New York – *Dr Strangelove* had earned Columbia around three times its production costs, and become the studio's biggest box-office success of 1964.

**AWARDS:** *Dr Strangelove* earned four major Academy Award nominations, in the categories of Best Picture, Director, Actor, and Writing, Screenplay Based on Material from Another Medium. As director, producer and co-screenwriter, Kubrick might have left the 1965 ceremony – if he had attended, which is unlikely – with as many as three statuettes, but in the event the film converted none of its nominations into prizes. At the British Academy of Film and Television Arts (BAFTA) awards, *Dr Strangelove* was luckier, winning Best British Film, Best Film from any Source and Best British Art Direction (Black and White), and being nominated for Best British Actor (Peter Sellers), Best Foreign Actor (Sterling Hayden) and Best British Screenplay.

Kubrick was voted Best Director by the New York Film Critics' Circle and nominated in the same category by the Directors' Guild of America. *Dr Strangelove* was voted best film by the Society of Film and Television Arts, and won the Writers' Guild of America award for best screenplay and the Hugo Award for best science-fiction film of 1964.

**TECHNICAL ACHIEVEMENTS:** For the many flying sequences, a number of B-52 models in various scales were constructed and filmed against rear-projection footage of Norwegian landscapes, shot from a converted Mitchell bomber by an aerial photographer, John Crewdson. However, as Ken Adam explained to the producers of the 1996 documentary *Stanley Kubrick: The Invisible Man*, the idea of having Major Kong ride one of the nuclear bombs out of the bomb-bay doors presented a seemingly insurmountable technical problem. 'I thought it was a fantastic idea, but I didn't know how to achieve this, because I had built a sixty-foot bomb bay suspended at one of the stages at Shepperton, and we didn't have practical bomb doors.' The problem was solved by the veteran special-effects technician Wally Veevers, later one of the special-effects supervisors on *2001*. '[He] came up with the idea of photographing the interior of the bomb bay, and making a ten-by-eight-inch black-and-white still out of it, and then cutting the bomb doors out of the still. And that's how we finally did that sequence.'

**INFLUENCED BY:** Although Terry Southern was officially employed by the production only from 16 November to 28 December 1962, his influence on *Dr Strangelove* was profound. Anyone who has read Southern's early oeuvre – *Candy*, *The Magic Christian* and *Flash and Filigree* – will recognise his distinctive, not to mention subversive, voice in many of the dialogue lines. Nevertheless, in August 1964, Kubrick took exception to advertisements placed by MGM and Filmways announcing an adaptation of Evelyn Waugh's *The Loved One* to be written by Terry Southern and directed by Tony Richardson. 'What happens when the director of *Tom Jones* meets the writer of *Dr Strangelove*?' the ad playfully enquired. Kubrick immediately threatened MGM and Filmways with legal action if they refused to remove the offending advertisement, and fired off a statement designed 'to publicly place Mr Southern's contribution in its proper perspective', which, he claimed, amounted to little more than 'decoration . . . added to the icing on the cake', and that his 'screenplay credit in third place [was] completely fitting and proportionate to his contribution'.

'Stanley's obsession with the "auteur syndrome" – that his films are by Stanley Kubrick – override any other credit at all,' Southern commented, recalling Kubrick's attempted appropriation of the writing credits on at least two of his earlier films, *Paths of Glory* and *Spartacus*. 'Having written this great bestseller, *Candy*, which was something like number one on the *New York Times* bestseller list for 21 weeks, my reputation eclipsed Stanley's, so I got total credit for all the *Strangelove* success in *Life*, the *New York Times* and other publications. The credit I was getting was just so overwhelming and one-sided credit that naturally he was freaking out. He took out full-page ads in every paper in America saying "Terry Southern has nothing to do with it." He felt that, and rightly so, and lashed out, but it was like an overnight thing. I wrote a letter to the *New York Times* explaining that there was no mystery involved, and that I was brought in to just help with the screenplay.' Indeed, as though to prove there were no hard feelings, Southern dedicated his 1970 novel *Blue Movie* 'to the great Stanley K'.

Whatever the extent of Southern's contribution, the inspiration for the eponymous Dr Strangelove, who does not appear in *Red Alert*, almost certainly lies in a similar character, the German-born nuclear adviser Dr Walter Groteschele, who appeared in Eugene Burdick and Harvey Wheeler's novel *Fail-Safe* – an ironic appropriation, given that both Kubrick and Peter George later sued Burdick and Wheeler for plagiarism (see **Controversy**, above). Whatever Strangelove's origins, it is likely that his black-gloved right hand was inspired by a similar prosthetic sported by another mad German scientist – Rotwang (Rudolph Kleine-Rogge) in Fritz Lang's widely influential *Metropolis* (1926).

Kubrick was also influenced by the real-life safety record of those with their fingers on the nuclear triggers. His cuttings file, which he had been collecting since the idea of using nuclear warfare as the basis of a film first interested him, contained records, collated from various sources, of a small number of nearly disastrous incidents involving the hydrogen bomb. One told of an American serviceman, under psychiatric care but still somehow allowed access to the bomb, who had attempted to detonate the bomb by firing his revolver at it. According to Kubrick, 'his job was so secret that the psychiatrist never knew his patient had access to the bomb'. Another incident involved the jettisoning of a nuclear device by the crew of an aircraft that had run into difficulties, 'reasoning that it probably contained safety devices'. It did – except that all but one of them failed. As Kubrick reasoned, 'If the safety devices are 99.9 per cent perfect, a bomb is bound to go off by accident over a period of thirty years.'

DÉJÀ VU: A number of individual elements, compositions and shots in
*Dr Strangelove* recall Kubrick's earlier films, beginning with the opening
narration, the tone of which is not dissimilar to that which runs
throughout *The Killing*. There can be little doubt that, even discounting
the fact that Peter Sellers plays both roles, the emergence of Dr
Strangelove from the semigloom, sitting in his wheelchair, almost
perfectly matches the appearance of another German doctor, Dr Zempf,
sitting in a chair in the gloom of Humbert Humbert's home in *Lolita*.
The overhead lighting of the War Room recalls that of the conspirators
in *The Killing*. Even the men at Burpelson Air Force Base are ordered to
fire on their fellow Americans – an event that has a close parallel in *Paths
of Glory*.

INFLUENTIAL ON: 'It's interesting to think about ways of influencing
people in a medium such as mine,' Kubrick recounted during publicity
for the release of *Dr Strangelove*. 'People react, as a rule, when they are
directly confronted with events. Here, any direct contact with the Bomb
would leave very few people to do any reacting. Laughter can only make
people a little more thoughtful.' Nevertheless, writing in the *New Yorker*
in October 1967, Pauline Kael suggested that *Dr Strangelove* ushered in
a new era of satire. 'Movie audiences have been getting a steady diet of
"black" comedy since 1964 and *Dr Strangelove*,' she wrote. 'The targets
have usually been social and political fads and abuses, together with the
heroes and the clichés of the just preceding period of filmmaking. *Dr
Strangelove* opened a new movie era. It ridiculed *everything* and
*everybody* it showed, but concealed its own liberal pieties, thus
protecting itself from ridicule.'

Kubrick's film had a different kind of influence on the directorial
debut of his erstwhile producer, James B Harris, who had been amused
and then troubled by Kubrick's idea of turning *Red Alert* into satire.
Although the Harris-Kubrick partnership had, by this time, been
amicably dissolved, and Harris was pursuing his own directorial career,
he was afraid that Kubrick might be about to make a disastrous error of
judgement. 'I was actually convinced he was out of control, to do this as
a comedy,' he said, adding that, instead, *Dr Strangelove* became his
favourite of Kubrick's films. Nevertheless, it is significant that Harris
chose as the subject of his directorial debut a more serious treatment of
the nuclear question. *The Bedford Incident* (1965), starring Richard
Widmark, Sidney Poitier and Martin Balsam, follows the crew of a US
Navy destroyer as it tracks a Soviet nuclear submarine off the coast of
Greenland, finally provoking a nuclear attack upon itself by launching an
unprovoked pre-emptive strike upon the Russian vessel. 'I just thought it
couldn't hurt to get the message across once more,' Harris, whose other
films include *Boiling Point* (1993) and *Cop* (1988), said recently, 'that if
you put atomic weapons in the hands of right-wing field commanders,
they just might by accident or some other way get to use them'.

After seeing the Oscar-winning drama *Schindler's List* (1993), Kubrick asked its director, Steven Spielberg, how he came up with the idea of using a hand-held camera for certain scenes. 'I got that from you,' Spielberg replied. 'He said, "What do you mean, from me?" I said, "Well, don't you remember the sequence [in *Dr Strangelove*] when they were trying to re-take Burpelson Air Force Base, and you shot that tremendous *cinema verité* scene with long lenses and hand-held cameras with the people shooting at the air base, and the scribs going off . . . and it was all done hand-held?" And he said, "Yeah." I said, "Well, it was the Signal Corps cameramen, and you, that influenced me on how to tell the story that way, and then later on how to do *Saving Private Ryan*." '

Several other film makers have recorded their own reactions to *Dr Strangelove*. 'I was eighteen years old, and it seemed so silly and ridiculous; and yet there was something undeniably powerful about it,' said the writer-director Oliver Stone, whose own war films include *Platoon* (1986) and *Born on the Fourth of July* (1989). 'It was one of the first films that I saw as a young man that pointed to the government as indifferent to the needs of the people; government as enemy to the people. I suppose many of our fears of big government are rooted in that theme, in Kubrick's paranoia.' The actor and director Sydney Pollack, who co-starred in Kubrick's last film, *Eyes Wide Shut*, is another fan of *Dr Strangelove*. 'It was the first time anybody stuck their neck out that far with a subject that taboo,' he told *Entertainment Weekly* for an issue devoted to 'The 100 Greatest Moments in Movies, 1950–2000'. 'I remember watching it the first time, seeing Slim Pickens riding that bomb, thinking, how does somebody think that up?'

*Dr Strangelove* also apparently had an influence on at least one real-life president. According to many sources, when Ronald Reagan first took office in 1981, one of the first White House facilities he asked to see was the War Room.

**KUBRICK GOES POP:** Deliberate *Dr Strangelove* references appear in numerous feature films. In Robert Zemeckis's script for Steven Spielberg's *1941* (1979), Slim Pickens lists the contents of his pockets in a manner that recalls his reading of the survival kit's contents. In the Coen brothers' *Raising Arizona* (1987), the restroom doors are marked with the letters 'POE' and 'OPE', a reference to the recall codes in *Dr Strangelove*. One of the characters in *The Manhattan Project* (1986), written and directed by Marshall Brickman, refers to his mother's boyfriend, a nuclear scientist, as 'Dr Strangelove'.

The legend 'CRM 114', the identification code of the *Leper Colony*'s communications device, has been referenced in a number of later productions, most notably in Kubrick's own films, *A Clockwork Orange* (Alex is injected with a liquid drawn from a bottle labelled 'Exp./serum no.114') and *Eyes Wide Shut* (a mortuary is located on level C, room – i.e. Rm – 114). 'CRM 114' also appears on the giant guitar amplifier used by Marty McFly (Michael J Fox) in Robert Zemeckis's *Back to the Future* (1985), while the device upon which messages are received on the F-117 stealth aircraft in *Executive Decision* (1996) is labelled 'CRM 115'.

The animated television series *The Simpsons* has several references to *Dr Strangelove*. Springfield's Mayor Quimby meets with fellow municipal officials in a room very like the War Room in an episode of *The Simpsons*, 'Sideshow Bob's Last Gleaming' (#3F08), which also features several references to *Full Metal Jacket*. An episode entitled 'Homer the Vigilante' (#1F09) has Homer imagining himself riding a bomb launched from a B-52 bomber, while the opening credits of two episodes, 'Wild Barts Can't Be Broken' (#AABF07) and 'Mom and Pop Art' (#AABF15), have the entire Simpson family jettisoned through the bomb doors in a parody of Slim Pickens's ride to oblivion. The title of a further episode, '$pringfield or: How I Learned to Stop Worrying and Love Legalized Gambling' (#1F08) is clearly inspired by Kubrick's film.

In the UK, a Bristol-based pop group named Strangelove was formed in 1991 by two ex-Blue Aeroplanes musicians, Patrick Duff and Alex Lee. Although the name of the group was inspired by Kubrick's film, several of their best-known tracks suggest the influence of *Dr Strangelove*: 'Visionary', 'I Will Burn', 'Living with the Human Machines', 'Casualties' and '20th Century Cold'.

**CUT SCENES:** As gleefully irreverent as *Dr Strangelove* is, it might have ended on an even more farcical note, had Kubrick retained the original ending: an eleven-minute scene in which members of the War Cabinet and DeSadesky, the Soviet ambassador, battle it out with cream pies taken from the buffet table in the War Room.

The legendary pie fight originally began just after Major Kong rides the Bomb to oblivion, and Dr Strangelove stands up from his wheelchair and says, 'Mein Führer, I can walk!' As Terry Southern recalled, 'After taking one step he falls flat on his face, and starts trying to get back in his wheelchair, but each time it scoots out of his grasp. Meanwhile, parallel to this action in another part of the War Room, the Russian Ambassador is caught again trying to take pictures of the "Big Board" – George C Scott nails him and again they're fighting in the War Room. So Scott exposes about eighteen micro-mini spy cameras on the Ambassador – in his wrist-watch, cuff-links, tie-pin, on his ring-finger, everywhere. But Scott says, "I think these are dummy cameras. I think he's got the real McCoy concealed on his person." And he turns to the detail of MPs who have come in. "I want you to search him very carefully, boys," he says, "and don't overlook any of the six bodily orifices!" And the Russian Ambassador goes through this quick calculation, "Vun . . . two . . ." And then when he reaches the last one, he freaks. "Vhy, you Capitalist swine!" he says.'

Having grabbed a pie from the buffet table, DeSadesky throws it at Turgidson, who ducks, sending it smack into the face of President

Muffley. 'The mere indignity of this is so monstrous that the President just faints dead away. Scott grabs him and keeps him from falling, and he's holding him in his arms like a martyred hero, "Gentlemen," he says to the others, "our President has been struck down in the prime of his life ... by a custard pie. I say 'Massive Retaliation!' " And he throws something at the Ambassador, and it misses and hits one of the other Joint Chiefs. So this immense pie-fight begins – between army, navy, air force – a bit of inter-service rivalry, if you grasp the innuendo.'

Meanwhile, the stricken Dr Strangelove is being pelted with pies as he struggles to crawl back into his wheelchair, as Sellers recalled: 'Strangelove eventually turns out like ... you know when you see a bug and you spray it until it's slimy and can't move? Well, just everybody pelted him until he couldn't get up. And he's trying to get back on his chair and the more he grabbed it the further it went away from him.'

Eventually, Southern continued, 'Strangelove pulls himself up so that he's sitting with his back against the wall, and he's watching the pie-fight in the distance. Then his hand – his uncontrollable right hand – reaches inside his coat and comes out with a Luger pistol and points it at his head. He grabs his wrist with his other hand and grapples for the pistol, which goes off with a tremendous roar. Then cut to the long shot of all these generals in a freeze frame, and Strangelove says, "Enough of these childish games! We have work to do." ' Or, as Sellers remembered it, ' "Gentlemen, gentlemen, don't you realise what will happen to us all in a moment? This pie is non-protective! We must go down to the shelter as quickly as possible. Don't worry about showers, we have plenty down there. Through the mine shaft!" '

'So they all stand there staring at him in complete silence,' Southern added, 'until Scott recognizes this is the guy to get tight with, so he walks all the way across the War Room floor, and says, "Doctor, may I help you?" and helps him into his wheelchair. He starts pushing him back across the floor, which by now is so deep in custard pies it resembles a beach – and sure enough, we quickly pass the President and the Russian Ambassador sitting there cross-legged like two children, doing sand castles, making mountains. And Strangelove says, "Ah too bad. Apparently their minds have snapped under the strain. Perhaps they'll have to be institutionalized." And so Scott continues pushing him across to this group of officers and CIA types, who are so covered they look like ghosts. And he says, "Well, boys, I think the future of this great nation of ours is in the hands of people like Doc Strangelove, and I think we owe him a vote of thanks. Let's hear it for the good Doctor." And in a really eerie (whispering) voice, they go, "Hip-hip hooray, hip-hip hooray!" And then he continues pushing him across the floor as they start singing, "For he's a jolly good fellow, for he's a jolly good fellow." So this counter camera pulls up so you've got this long shot of the ultimate allegiance between this mad scientist and this general from The Joint Chief of Staff. And then they cut to the explosion and the song "We'll Meet Again" comes in – and the credits rise.'

Many believe that Kubrick cut the scene – for which, according to George C Scott, the cast threw 'a thousand pies a day for a week' – following Kennedy's assassination, feeling uncomfortable with the idea of a president being 'struck down, in the prime of his life', even by a cream pie. In fact, Kubrick had decided to shoot a new ending, in which Dr Strangelove informs the War Cabinet of his subterranean survival stratagem, more than six months earlier, because, as Terry Southern explained, 'He believed that watching people have fun is never funny. What's happening in this pie fight is that people are laughing, and they shouldn't be laughing. It's supposed to be deadly serious. And it was such a funny situation, that people outside the periphery, including Stanley and myself, were tossing pies into the mêlée, you see. And so it lost its edge. It was like a comedy scene, when everything else in the film had been played straight, except once when the Coca-Cola machine spurted in Keenan Wynn's face. So that's why he decided not to have it in.'

Several of Sellers' more outrageous improvisations also hit the cutting-room floor, most notably one in which Dr Strangelove's errant right hand grabs his crotch. 'Strangelove started jerking off with the hand,' Sellers said mischievously. 'We knew we'd have to take that out, but Stan said, "Aw, do it anyway." ' A remnant of the shot remains in the shocked expression seen on Strangelove's face as he looks down at what his hand is doing in his lap. Kubrick also shot, and later excised, a scene in which Sellers' President Muffley consults an IBM computer, a theme to which he would more memorably return for his next film, *2001: A Space Odyssey*.

James Earl Jones, who played Lieutenant Zogg, the B-52's bombardier, remembers other material cut from the film. 'Zogg was a key role in the original script,' he told *Premiere* magazine. 'He was the only one who questioned the mission. I think all I say in the [finished] movie is, "Well, could it be some sort of loyalty test?" But "Zoggy" [originally] did a whole number, and I guess Kubrick didn't want the one protesting the combat mission to be a black guy. I got a revision one day, and my role was gone. I went to [Kubrick] and said, "Gee, I took the role for all that good stuff." He said, "No, we don't need it." And that was it. It was a command decision.'

One minor, last-minute change was made after the film's first press screening, scheduled for 22 November 1963, was postponed in the wake of President Kennedy's assassination on that very day in Dallas. As a mark of respect, Slim Pickens's dialogue line 'A guy could have a great weekend in Dallas with this,' spoken as he lists a survival kit's contents, was redubbed as 'a great weekend in Vegas', although Pickens's mouth can still be seen to form the word 'Dallas'.

**TRIVIA:** In addition to Peter George, several of *Dr Strangelove*'s cast and crew members had served with the Royal Air Force. Peter Sellers was a member of the RAF Gang Show; the production designer Ken Adam was probably the only German native to have flown for the RAF in World War Two; the cinematographer Gilbert Taylor's experience as a combat photographer on numerous air raids over Germany led him to shoot low-level aerial footage for *The Dam Busters* (1955) before Kubrick hired him to film *Lolita*'s title sequence and *Dr Strangelove*.

The *Leper Colony*'s mythical target, Laputa, is almost certainly named after the flying island in Jonathan Swift's 1726 novel *Gulliver's Travels*, inhabited by mad scientists who get so engrossed in their thinking that they employ 'flappers' to smack them on the mouth and ears with inflated bladders in order to distract them from lofty matters.

Although the photographic mural in General Ripper's office appears to depict an aerial view of Burpelson base, it actually shows London's Heathrow Airport, where some of the Burpelson scenes were filmed.

**APOCRYPHA:** It has often been suggested that the character of Dr Strangelove was based on Henry Kissinger, the German-born statesman who rose to notoriety during the Nixon administration, and whose distinctive glasses and hairstyle Strangelove appears to replicate. Nevertheless, both Kubrick and Sellers frequently denied any connection. 'Strangelove was never modelled after Kissinger – that's a popular misconception,' Sellers insisted. 'Neither Peter nor I had ever seen Kissinger before the film was shot,' Kubrick claimed, while admitting that the likeness was 'an amazing coincidence'. Kubrick ventured that Strangelove's accent was 'probably inspired by the physicist Edward Teller, who became known as the father of the H-bomb, though Teller's origins are Hungarian and his accent isn't really that close to what Peter did'.

Sellers later revealed that the model for Strangelove was Wernher von Braun – the German rocket pioneer who worked on the US space programme – while the unusually high pitch of Strangelove's voice was borrowed from Weegee, the world-famous photographer whom Kubrick hired to take stills on the set of *Dr Strangelove*. 'He used to talk in a strange little voice,' the actor said, 'so I put a German accent on top of Weegee's.' Indeed, Sellers recorded a private interview with the photographer on reel-to-reel tape, purely for the purpose of duplicating his speech patterns – with the addition of a comic German accent, of course.

**AVAILABILITY:** In the UK, Columbia Tristar Home Video re-released *Dr Strangelove* on the occasion of its 35th anniversary, on PAL video (CVR 70035) and Region 2 DVD (CDR 90035). Both editions feature the original theatrical trailer, while the DVD also features cast and crew filmographies; a German soundtrack; a poster gallery with various international poster images and lobby sets; a photo gallery featuring six rare stills, almost all of them featuring Kubrick; and a dizzying array of subtitles in Czech, Danish, English, Finnish, German, Greek, Hebrew, Hindi, Hungarian, Icelandic, Norwegian, Polish, Swedish and Turkish. None of this 'added-value' material is present on the Region 1 DVD (04093) – although there are Spanish and French soundtracks and Spanish subtitles – nor on the NTSC VHS version (WA 81004).

All of these editions are formatted in a multi-aspect ratio, ranging from 1.66:1 to 1.85:1, whereas the original theatrical ratio of 1.85:1 cropped the upper and lower portions of the frame, obscuring some of the impressive War Room sets. The new version was painstakingly reconstructed under Kubrick's supervision, after it was discovered that the picture negative and the magnetic master soundtrack had been lost, leaving only what Kubrick described as 'badly ripped dupes. The search went on for a year and a half,' he told *Rolling Stone*'s Tim Cahill in 1987. 'Finally, I had to try to reconstruct the picture from two not-too-good fine-grain positives, both of which were damaged already. If those fine-grains were ever torn, you could never make any more negatives.'

*Dr Strangelove* was last released on NTSC laserdisc (79316) in 1994, featuring a 1.66:1 transfer and a theatrical trailer.

**EXPERT WITNESS:** 'Working with Stanley was terrific. It was ideal, although the circumstances may seem peculiar – in the back seat of a big car. The film was being shot at Shepperton, outside London, in the winter. So he would pick me up at 4:30 in the morning and we would make this hour-long trip to the studio. It was a big Bentley or a Rolls, so the passenger part was something like a railway compartment, with folding-out writing desks and good lighting. It would be pitch black outside and really cold, and we would be in this cozy-rosey compartment, in a creative groove, working on the scene to be shot that day – well, let's say trying to improve it. Kubrick would say "Now what's the most outrageous thing this guy (a character in the scene) would say at this point?" and hopefully I could come up with something like "If you try any preversion [sic] in there, I'll blow your head off." ' – co-screenwriter Terry Southern, quoted in *Smoke Signals*.

**FINAL ANALYSIS:** Looking back at *Dr Strangelove* today, it is almost impossible to imagine the political climate into which the film was released in 1964. The Cold War was at freezing point. The Cuban missile crisis, in which Kennedy and Kruschev played a dangerous game of nuclear brinkmanship until the Russian Premier agreed to withdraw Soviet missiles from bases in Cuba, had occurred just two years earlier. As part of America's defence strategy, fully laden nuclear bombers were flown daily towards Russian targets, instructed to continue their missions until they received the recall code at their 'fail-safe' points. For millions of Americans, the threat of nuclear annihilation from one superpower or another was frighteningly real, not least because the H-Bomb had last been used in anger less than two decades before.

Today, *Dr Strangelove* is probably best remembered for Sellers' inspired interpretation of three characters, and Slim Pickens waving a ten-gallon hat while riding a forty-megaton bomb. Yet Sterling Hayden almost steals the show as the paranoid General Jack D Ripper, in mortal fear of the poisoning of his and his fellow Americans' 'precious bodily fluids' by communist 'fluoridation'; George C Scott's gung-ho Chief of Staff, General 'Buck' Turgidson, is rather more over-the-top, but no less entertaining, and the supporting roles played by Slim Pickens and Keenan Wynn are every bit as memorable as Sellers' characterisations. From the opening shot to the explosive climax, *Dr Strangelove* is a relentlessly inventive combination of satirical didacticism, political polemic and hysterical humour, proving that Kubrick's keenness of mind and deftness of touch were more than matched by a wicked sense of offbeat humour.

On a visual level, the film boasts the German-born production designer Ken Adam's extraordinary War Room set, loosely inspired by his own design for the lair of another evil scientist, *Dr No*; no less impressive is the aerial photography, over which are superimposed remarkably accurate models of the still-classified B-52 'Stratocruiser' bombers that would later be used to 'carpet-bomb' North Vietnam – ironically, air raids carried out on the advice of the presidential adviser General Curtis LeMay, the real-life inspiration for 'Buck' Turgidson, whose proposed solution to the Vietnam problem was to 'bomb North Vietnam back into the Stone Age'.

Such militaristic *bons mots* were reflected in the *Dr Strangelove* script, in which various ranking officers rail against communist subversion (not to mention '*pre*version'); General Turgidson warns of the danger of a US/Soviet 'mineshaft gap' after learning that the nuclear winter might be survived by hiding out in tunnels beneath the earth; and the President of the United States insists that he is just as sorry as his Russian counterpart about the imminent atomic disaster. And who could forget Muffley's legendary appeal to Turgidson and DeSadesky: 'Gentlemen, you can't fight in here – this is the War Room!'?

Despite *Dr Strangelove*'s curious subtitle, Stanley Kubrick never did learn to stop worrying and love the Bomb. But learning to laugh at it – and assuring others it was permissible to do so – was at least half the battle.

**KUBRICK ON KUBRICK:** 'The only way to tell the story was as a black comedy or, better, a nightmare comedy, where the things you laugh at most are really the heart of the paradoxical postures that make a nuclear war possible. Most of the humour in *Strangelove* arises from the depiction of everyday human behavior in nightmarish situation, like the Russian premier on the hot line who forgets the telephone number of his general staff headquarters and suggests the American president try Omsk information, or the reluctance of a US officer to let a British officer smash open a Coca-Cola machine for change to phone the president about a crisis on the SAC base because of his conditioning about the sanctity of private property.' – quoted in *The Film Director as Superstar* by Joseph Gelmis, 1970.

# 2001: A Space Odyssey (1968)

[Colour – 159 mins (preview version), 139 mins (release version)]

Directed and Produced by Stanley Kubrick
Screenplay by Stanley Kubrick and Arthur C Clarke
Special Photographic Effects Designed and Directed by Stanley Kubrick
Special Photographic Effects Supervisors Wally Veevers, Douglas Trumbull, Con Pederson, Tom Howard
Production Designed by Tony Masters, Harry Lange, Ernest Archer
Film Editor Ray Lovejoy
Wardrobe by Hardy Amies
Director of Photography Geoffrey Unsworth, BSC
Additional Photography John Alcott
Music by Aram Khatchaturian, György Ligeti, Johann Strauss, Richard Strauss
First Assistant Director Derek Cracknell
Camera Operator Kelvin Pike
Art Director John Hoesli
Sound Editor Winston Ryder
Make-up Stuart Freeborn
Editorial Assistant David De Wilde
Sound Supervisor AW Watkins
Sound Mixer HL Bird
Chief Dubbing Mixer JB Smith
Scientific Consultant Frederick I Ordway III

**CAST:** Keir Dullea (*David Bowman*), Gary Lockwood (*Frank Poole*), William Sylvester (*Dr Heywood R Floyd*), Dan Richter (*Moonwatcher*), Douglas Rain (*voice of HAL 9000*), Leonard Rossiter (*Dr Andrei Smyslov*), Margaret Tyzack (*Elena*), Robert Beatty (*Dr Ralph Halvorsen*), Sean Sullivan (*Michaels*), Frank Miller (*Mission Controller*), Penny Brahms (*Stewardess*), Edward Bishop (*Lunar Shuttle Captain*), Alan Gifford (*Poole's Father*), Edwina Carroll (*Aries Stewardess*), Bill Weston, Glenn Beck, Ann Gillis, Heather Downham, Mike Lovell, John Ashley, Jimmy Bell, David Charkham, Simon Davis, Jonathan Daw, Peter Delmar, Terry Duggan, David Fleetwood, Danny Grover, Brian Hawley, David Hines, Tony Jackson, John Jordan, Scott MacKee, Laurence Marchant, Darryl Paes, Joe Refalo, Andy Wallace, Bob Wilyman, Richard Wood.

**UNCREDITED CAST:** Vivian Kubrick (*Dr Floyd's daughter*), Burnell Ticker (*Photographer*), John Swindell (*First Technician*), John Clifford (*Second Technician*), Martin Amer (*Interviewer*), Kenneth Kendall (*BBC-12 Broadcaster*), Penny Pearl, Julie Croft, Sheraton Blount, Penny Francis, Kim Neill, Ann Bomann, Marcella Markham, Jane Hayward, Jane Pearl.

**UNCREDITED CREW:** Ron Phipps (*Chief Accountant*), Peter Lancaster, Arthur Porter, Brian Harris (*Assistant Accountants*), Shrish Bhatt (*Accounts Inventory Clerk*), Merle Chamberlin (*Production Co-ordinator*), Clifton Brandon, Robert Watts (*Production Managers*), Eddie Frewin (*Unit/Production Manager*), Ronnie Bear (*Post-production Production Manager*), Betty Parry (*Secretary to Ronnie Bear*), Patrick Clayton (*Production Assistant*), Anthony Frewin, Andrew Birkin (*Assistants to Mr Kubrick*), Iris Rose (*Production Secretary*), Christine Mitchell (*PA/Secretary to Mr Kubrick*), Vicky Ward (*Pre-production PA/Secretary to Mr Kubrick*), Daphne Paice (*PA/Secretary to Mr Lyndon*), Simon Bird (*Assistant to Mr Lyndon*), Jill Hollamby, Elizabeth Braby (*Assistants to Christine Mitchell*), Margaret Warrington (*Secretary*), Monica Rogers (*Production Department Secretary*), Michael Murray (*Runner*), Domeny Bernie, Margaret Hattam (*Typists*), Richard Jenkins (*2nd Assistant Director*), Richard Hoult (*3rd Assistant Director*), Jimmy Liggatt (*Casting*), Michael Wilson (*Additional Photography*), Dennis Hall (*Rostrum Cameraman*), Richard Yuricich (*Additional Matte Cinematography*), Peter MacDonald (*Assistant Camera*), David Osborne, Bryan Loftus (*Focus Pullers*), John Campbell, Graeme Scaife, Terry Pearce (*Clapper/Loaders*), Norman Godden (*Camera Maintenance*), Don Budge, David Cadwallader (*Grips*), Bill Jeffery (*Chief Gaffer*), George 'Geordie' Walker (*Assistant Gaffer*), Jed Murphy (*Electrician*), John Jay (*Unit Stills Photographer*), Ken Bray (*Stills – MGM*), Keith Hamshere (*Stills Filing Clerk*), John Barnett (*Stills Technician*), Graham Hooper, Dan McGowen (*Special Effects Stills Printers*), John Locke (*Darkroom Assistant*), Ron Wooster, Jim Budd, Jack Spooner (*Matte Camera Printers*), Wally Gentleman (*Special Effects Supervisor*), Les Bowie, Charles Staffell (*Additional Supervisors*), Clive Shepherd (*Blob Supervisor*), John Jack Malick, John Dykstra (*Special Effects Unit*), Tom Howard (*Front Projection Supervisor*), Ron Ballanger (*Special Effects Technician*), George Pollock, Colin Brewer (*Special Effects Co-ordinators*), Valerie Kent, Delia Tindall (*Special Effects Department Secretaries*), Roger Dicken (*Special Effects Special Art*), Douglas Potts (*Special Effects Special Models*), Ted Creed (*Special Effects Engineer*), Bob Cuff, Brian Johnson, Joy Seddon, Hilary Ann Pickburn (*Special Effects Assistants*), Bernard Ford, Brian Bennett, Peter Hannan, Terry Pearce, Bob Rickerd, Martin Body (*Special Effects Floor Camera Department*), Tom Welford (*Special Effects Maintenance*), William Davis, Trevor Lawrence, Alf Levy (*Airbrush Artists*), Toni

Traynor (*Special Effects Runner*), Brian Willisher, David Watkins, John Gant, Herbet Bailey, Peter Biggs, Ann Griffiths, John Horton, William Plampton, Hapugoda Premaratne, Dennis Smith, Gary Sinclair, Caird Green, Jenny Foster, Paul Haywood, Sarah Katz, Catherine Philby, Hilary Randall, James Wilkins, Fran Guye, Bob Nadkarni, David Peterson, Livia Rolandini, James Simpson, David Temple, Roger Turner, Nigel Waller (*Blob Artists*), John Mackey (*Miniatures Cameraman*), Phil Stokes (*Miniatures Assistant*), Jimmy Dickson (*Technical Animation Specialist*), Edward Gerald, Martin Goldsmith, Jasjeet Singh, Zoran Perisic (*Animation Stand*), Bruce Logan, Roy Naisbitt (*Animation Artists*), Robin McDonnell (*Assistant Editor, 2nd Special Effects*), Robert Mullen (*Editing Assistant*), Penny Struthers (*Art Department Assistant*), Jack Stephens (*Location Surveying*), Robert Cartwright, Jack Holden (*Set Dressers*), John Graysmark, Alan Tomkins, John Siddall, Tony Reading, Frank Wilson, Peter Childs, Wallis Smith, Martin Atkinson, Brian Ackland-Snow, Alan Fraiser, John Fenner (*Draughtsmen*), R Burton, P Jarratt (*Engineering Draughtsmen*), Roy Carnon (*Scientific Design Specialist*), John Rose, John Young (*Technical Illustrators*), Anthony Pratt (*Sketch Artist*), Theresa Kendall (*Art Department Secretary*), Anna Garrett (*Art Department Typist*), Bill Isaacs (*Production Buyer*), Tommy Ibbetson, Roy Cannon (*Stand-by Props*), Frank Bruton (*Property Master – MGM*), Richard Frift (*Construction Manager*), Gus Walker (*TMA-1 Construction Manager – Moon*), Les Hillma, G Payne (*Construction Engineers*), Reg Carter (*Stand-by Carpenter*), James Holmes (*Stand-by Stagehand*), Christopher Burke (*Stand-by Painter*), Henry Gomez (*Stand-by Plasterer*), Stan Ogden (*Plasterer's Labourer*), Malcolm Legge (*Stagehand Carpenter*), Wally Bull (*Master Plasterer – MGM*), Jumbo Miall (*Drapes – MGM*), John Wilson-Apperson (*Wardrobe Master*), David Baker (*Assistant Wardrobe Master*), Eileen Sullivan, Mary Gibson (*Wardrobe Supervisors*), Charles Parker (*Make-up Supervisor*), Graham Freeborn, Colin Arthur (*Make-up*), Muriel Rickaby, Kathleen Freeborn, Richard Mills, Hugh Richards (*Make-up Assistants*), Carol Beckett, Alice Holmes (*Chief Hairdressers*), Daphne Volmer, Mibs Parker (*Assistant Hairdressers*), Harry V Jones (*Colour Timer*), Frank J Urioste (*Music Editor*), Roy Simpson, Daniel Richter, Adrian Haggard ('*Dawn of Man*' *Choreographer*), Robin Gregory (*Recorder*), Michael Hickey (*Sound Camera Operator*), Neil Stevenson (*Sound Maintenance*), Bill Cook, Don Wortham (*Boom Operators*), Ernie Grimsdale (*Assistant Dubbing Editor*), Alice Yendell (*Neg Cutter*), Frederick I Ordway III, Harry Lange, Richard McKenna (*Astronautics Advisers*), Ormond G Mitchell (*Technical Adviser*), Michael Connor (*Unit Car Driver/Driver to Mr Kubrick*), Ron Coldham, Terry Brown (*Unit Car Drivers*), Stewart Brown, Doug Haig (*Technicolor Contacts*), Colin Arthur (*Laboratory Assistant*), Michael Round (*Print Librarian*), Bert Batt (*Chief Projectionist – MGM*), George Dunn (*Power House – MGM*), George

Merritt (*Engineering Shop – MGM*), Sam Nolan (*Catering – MGM*), Mac's Minicabs, Elite Car Hire (*Additional Transport*), Ashton Mitchell & Howlett, Barnett International Forwarders New York (*Freight Agencies*), Eddie Milburn, Gerry Judge, Brian Chutter, Tom Sheppard, Robin Dawson-Whisker (*Stand-in*), Terry Duggan (*Leopard Trainer*), Dan S Terrell (*Publicity Supervisor*), Benn Reyes (*MGM Publicity*), Edna Tromans (*Unit Publicist*), Roger Caras (*American Publicity Representative*), Elaine Simms (*Secretary to Roger Caras*), Robert McCall (*Publicity Artist*), Ivor Powell (*Publicity/Art Department Liaison*), Hilary Messenger (*Publicity Secretary*), Christiane Kubrick (*Exploitation Designer*), Jim Warner (*Stanley Kubrick's Chauffeur*)

**TITLE SEQUENCE:** After a stylised version of the MGM lion logo, the opening bars of *Also Sprach Zarathustra* ('Thus Spake Zarathustra') play as the sun rises over the crescents of the Earth and the moon, the three-note opening of Richard Strauss's tone poem providing perfect accompaniment to the three heavenly bodies. The sun, and the music, continue to rise as two captions appear in thin white sans-serif lettering: 'METRO-GOLDWYN-MAYER PRESENTS' and 'A STANLEY KUBRICK PRODUCTION'. As the orb of the sun, and the music, reach their respective zeniths, the title appears in the same lettering: '2001: A SPACE ODYSSEY'.

**SUMMARY:** *2001: A Space Odyssey* is divided into three distinct sections. The first, THE DAWN OF MAN, is set among the herbivorous apelike creatures that would one day evolve into modern man. Into the midst of the dying, defenceless population, a black, slablike monolith appears, sending the apemen into a frenzy of curiosity and fear. After touching the monolith, evidently an alien artefact, one of the apemen forms the idea to use a bone as a weapon. This alien-bestowed gift becomes the pathway to survival as well as to rational thought. Some three million years later, astronauts discover a second monolith buried beneath the surface of the moon. Dr Heywood Floyd heads a delegation to the artefact – referred to as 'Tycho Magnetic Anomaly 1' (or 'TMA-1') – which, when disturbed, emits a piercing signal in the direction of Jupiter.

The second segment, JUPITER MISSION: EIGHTEEN MONTHS LATER, takes place during a hurriedly organised mission to Jupiter aboard the *Discovery*, the onboard HAL 9000 computer, known as 'Hal', malfunctions, killing all but one of the five-man crew before being switched off by the only survivor, the mission commander, David Bowman.

In the third segment, JUPITER AND BEYOND THE INFINITE, Bowman finds a third monolith near Jupiter. Passing through it, he enters the Star Gate, and is subjected to a baffling array of psychedelic phenomena, growing old and senile, and perhaps even dying, before finally being transformed into, or reborn as, the foetal Star Child – the first of a new starfaring species which represents the next stage in human evolution.

**SOURCE:** If *2001* has any literary source, it is Arthur C Clarke's short story 'Sentinel of Eternity', later retitled simply 'The Sentinel'. It was written in 1948 for a BBC-sponsored short-story competition. 'It wasn't placed,' Clarke later commented wryly. 'I'd like to know what did win!' The story was eventually published three years later as 'Sentinel of Eternity' and was the story of a crystal pyramid, presumably alien in origin, found on the moon during a routine expedition in 1996 ('96' being double the year in which it was written). The scientists who discover and disturb it quickly realise that it is, in effect, an alarm, designed to be triggered once the inhabitants of the nearby planet Earth had reached a sufficiently advanced technology to visit their own moon. We can only guess what response the signal would provoke from the ancient extraterrestrials, who planted the artefact 'before life had emerged from the seas of Earth . . . I do not think we will have to wait for long'.

**WORKING TITLES:** Initially, Kubrick and Clarke privately referred to their science-fiction project as *How the Solar System Was Won* in homage to MGM's Cinerama epic, *How the West was Won* (1962). 'Other titles which we ran up and failed to salute were *Universe, Tunnel to the Stars*, and *Planetfall*,' Clarke recalled in *The Lost Worlds of 2001*. MGM's press release dated 23 February 1965 reported the title as *Journey Beyond the Stars*. 'It was not until eleven months after we started – April 1965 – that Stanley selected *2001: A Space Odyssey*. As far as I can recall, it was entirely his idea.'

**PRODUCTION HISTORY:** The story of the making of *2001: A Space Odyssey* begins in 1964 or 1957, depending on whom you listen to. The critic Alexander Walker, a close friend of the reclusive director, has often stated that Kubrick was already considering the exploration of outer space in a feature film more than ten years before his plans saw fruition. Certainly, Kubrick had seen and admired Fred M Wilcox's *Forbidden Planet* (1956), arguably the first science-fiction movie with a satisfactory budget, an A-list cast, a respected director and convincing special effects. However, there is more evidence to suggest that Kubrick first became interested in the possibility of making what he described as 'the proverbial good science fiction movie' in early 1964.

Having been advised that the British scientist, theorist and novelist Arthur C Clarke was the world's best science-fiction writer, Kubrick wrote to the author outlining his plans to make a film 'of mythic grandeur' whose themes would be 'the reasons for believing in the existence of intelligent extra-terrestrial life' and 'the impact (and perhaps even lack of impact in some quarters) such discovery would have on Earth in the near future'. Clarke and Kubrick, impressed with each other's oeuvre, agreed to meet in New York – appropriately enough, during the 1964 World's Fair, where speculation about the planet's future and the cream of its technology would be on display. '[Kubrick] wanted to make a movie about Man's relation to the universe,' Clarke later recalled, 'something which had never been attempted. [He was] determined to create a work of art which would arouse the emotions of wonder, awe . . . even, if appropriate, terror.'

Kubrick was particularly taken with the themes of Clarke's 1954 novel *Childhood's End*, in which humans discover that the evolution of mankind has been shaped by extraterrestrial intelligence which returns in the twentieth century to usher them towards their destiny among the stars. When it transpired that another film maker owned the rights, Clarke suggested his short story 'Sentinel of Eternity', which dealt with the same theme in a different way: during a manned exploration of the lunar surface – at the time of his writing, still two decades away – seismologists discover a mysterious structure, left behind by a higher intelligence as a kind of 'alarm', which, when triggered, will signal that mankind is ready for the stars.

These themes – that man was contacted by a higher intelligence before he was fully evolved, that we have been under the benign supervision of this alien race for millennia, and that we are 'gods in waiting' whose destiny lies in the stars – would eventually elicit Kubrick's and Clarke's collaboration. 'After various false starts and twelve-hour talkathons, by early May 1964 Stanley agreed that "The Sentinel" would provide good story material,' Clarke wrote. 'But our first concept . . . involved working up to the discovery of an extraterrestrial artifact as the climax, not the beginning, of the story.'

Kubrick did not wish to reveal his intentions to the world until he was sure of them himself; therefore, he optioned six of Clarke's short stories, paying the author $10,000 for the rights and $60,000 to write a treatment based solely on the ideas he was interested in. Before Clarke could put pen to paper, however, the director had a better idea: he and Clarke would first collaborate on a novel, to be credited to Clarke and Kubrick, which would form the basis for the film's screenplay. Kubrick had not worked without a source text since *Killer's Kiss*, a decade earlier. Clarke recalled that their initial schedule for writing the script and shooting it was almost impossible. Clarke, anxious to return to his adopted home in Sri Lanka, then Ceylon, and was very depressed. 'It was just as well that neither of us could have guessed the project's ultimate duration – four years . . .'

The collaborators knew that they would have to create a story that was not likely to become obsolete – they would have to outguess the future, as Clarke had always done. By Christmas 1964, a 130-page treatment – somewhere between a script and a novella – had been completed, divided into three 'non-submersible units' described, as they would be on the final release version of the film, as 'THE DAWN OF MAN', 'JUPITER MISSION: EIGHTEEN MONTHS LATER' and 'JUPITER AND BEYOND THE INFINITE'. 'Thereafter [we thought] it would be a fairly straightforward matter to develop the screenplay,' Clarke wrote. 'In reality, all that we had was merely a rough draft of the first two-thirds of the book, stopping at the most exciting point. We had managed to get Bowman into the Star Gate, but didn't know what would happen next, except in the most general way. We had to show something.' He added, 'An ending where we said goodbye to our hero just as he entered the Star Gate would be lazy.' (Nevertheless, it was enough for the hero of Steven Spielberg's *Close Encounters of the Third Kind* [1977] to do so.)

Despite Kubrick and Clarke's feeling that the treatment lacked an ending of sufficient magnitude, the document was delivered to the incumbent MGM president Robert O'Brien, who was given three days to green-light the $4.5 million project before it was shopped to another studio. The deal was done, and, barely a month later, MGM issued an excited press release announcing that Kubrick would soon begin filming *Journey Beyond the Stars* 'with a cast of international importance', in the Cinerama process, and in colour. Kubrick himself was quoted in the press release: '*Journey Beyond the Stars* is an epic story of adventure and exploration, encompassing the Earth, the planets of our Solar System, and a journey light-years away to another part of the Galaxy. It is a scientifically-based yet dramatic attempt to explore the infinite possibilities that space travel now opens to mankind. Space is one of the great themes of our age,' he added, 'yet, it is one still almost untouched in serious art and literature.'

Although the announcement promised that production would commence on 16 August 1965, from a screenplay based on a novel that would appear the following winter, both MGM and its chosen publisher, New English Library, missed their projected dates by some margin: Kubrick commenced filming more than four months late – by which time the film's title was *2001: A Space Odyssey*, and its projected budget had rocketed from $4.5 million to $6 million – while the book emerged almost three *years* late, in July 1968. The principal cause of the delay was the extraordinarily protracted pre-production period, during which Kubrick oversaw Tony Masters' design team's creation of thousands of drawings, photographs and blueprints, not only for the various spacecraft the film required, from the spindly, matchstick-like *Discovery* to the sleek, aerodynamic *Orion* shuttle; but also for costumes, both human and apeman; futuristic furniture; vehicles, props and gadgets; landscapes; even the alien monolith itself, which started out as a black tetrahedron before becoming first a transparent cube and, finally, the iconographic black slab which remains one of the film's most memorable images.

When principal photography began on the huge excavated moon-base set at Shepperton Studios on 29 December 1965, the clapperboard might almost have been preceded by a caption card reading, 'JUPITER MISSION: EIGHTEEN MONTHS LATER', since it was at least that long since preparations for the epic undertaking had begun. The historic first 'live' shot of the production was that of Dr Floyd (William Sylvester), Dr Halverson (Robert Beatty) and four other spacesuited scientists investigating the excavated monolith, TMA-1. 'While you were acting, you had to keep an ear cocked for the hissing sound,' Beatty said later, referring to the sound of the compressed air being supplied from pressurised containers on the actors' backs. 'If it stopped you waved frantically for help – even if you were in the middle of a scene. [One] did not relish being the first dead man on the moon.'

Despite MGM's initial statement that the film's locations would encompass Britain, Switzerland, Africa, Germany and the United States, Kubrick's distaste for travel had resulted in his refusal to film outside the British Isles at all; at one stage he had insisted that all locations be found within ten miles of his Hertfordshire home. Although all but a few front-projection shots were ultimately filmed either at Borehamwood or Shepperton Studios, Kubrick's eccentricity created the problem of how to find a suitable stand-in for prehistoric Earth. After eight months and $80,000, the art department had failed to come up with a convincing landscape for the film's opening sequence; finally, the problem was solved by using an ingenious front-projection system combining second-unit still photographs taken in the Namib Desert (now Namibia) of southwest Africa, and action filmed on the backlot at Borehamwood, and at a nearby field – with, as Clarke later recalled, 'cars and buses going by'. Ironically, the scenes set in the distant past would ultimately prove more problematic than many of those set in the unknowable future, principally because no ape could be trained to carry out the actions required in the script, and no ape costume looked convincing enough on camera.

The make-up artist Stuart Freeborn, who had previously worked on Peter Sellers' make-up for *Dr Strangelove*, told *Premiere* magazine that the Dawn of Man sequence was originally to feature more human creatures – half human, with no hair on the bodies. 'People were saying, "How are you going to shoot them full-length?" And Kubrick said, "Yeah, I did think of that; when I want to come in to those sorts of shots, I'll go from the waist up." We tried that, but it bugged him so much that he needed to track back a bit, and it wasn't possible when we wanted to shoot more than one. So he said, "Stuart, can you do something with their crotches – fix them a bit so it's not so noticeable?" I had all the boys and girls laid out there naked, taking casts of their crotches and making something in between, so he could cheat a little bit. But then he wanted to come in closer still, and it was obvious there was no way these creatures could procreate, and the whole film depended on that. So after several weeks of shooting this stuff, he canned it and said, "It's no good – we gotta go back another million years." ' In the end, however, Freeborn's ground-breaking 'apeman' team succeeded in every respect but one – losing an Oscar to *Planet of the Apes*.

The grandest undertaking of the entire production was the creation of a revolving, drumlike set, designed to represent the living quarters of the

*Discovery*, which could rotate on its axis, through 360 degrees at five kilometres per hour, mimicking the centrifugal movement of the spaceship as it artificially simulates the effects of gravity. (This system was one of the scientific advances proposed by Clarke himself, in his 1953 essay 'Vacation in Vacuum'.) Built by the aircraft manufacturer Vickers-Armstrong at a cost of $750,000, the centrifugal cylinder stood on its end, like a giant wheel with a diameter/height of eleven metres and a width of around three metres. The chief purpose of this unique set was to allow Kubrick to film the astronaut, Frank Poole, exercising by jogging around the rim of the ship, tracing a 360-degree trajectory, while the cameraman, Geoffrey Unsworth, follows him with a specially prepared camera. To the audience, Poole would seem to be running up the wall, along the ceiling, down the other wall and back again in a continuous loop, without a single camera cut or edit.

For all of these challenges, however, no single sequence gave Kubrick more trouble than the climactic scene in which Bowman discovers a giant monolith in orbit around Jupiter, and passes through its gateway – the so-called 'Star Gate' – into the universe of its creators. Once again, Kubrick's team – supervised by Douglas Trumbull, who would later direct such highly regarded genre films as *Brainstorm* (1983) and *Silent Running* (1971) – was forced to improvise, innovate, and even invent, rather than fall back on existing methods, as, before *2001*, few sophisticated special-effects techniques existed at all. Small wonder, then, that when the film was finally ready for release, audiences were totally unprepared for it. They had, after all, never witnessed anything like the grandeur, mysticism and sheer spectacle of what would arguably become the greatest cinematic experience of all time.

CASTING: Unlike the Star Gate that Bowman enters during the film's climactic, psychedelic sequences, *2001* was anything but 'full of stars'. Kubrick's chosen players belied MGM's 1965 press release, eschewing anyone of 'international importance' and casting, instead, relative unknowns such as Keir Dullea (*Bunny Lake is Missing*), Gary Lockwood (*It Happened at the World's Fair*), William Sylvester (*Devil Doll*), Ed Bishop (TV's *UFO*) and even Leonard Rossiter, whose comedy work after *2001* lends his cameo appearance a certain mythic quality. 'We never got into the film's philosophical message,' Dullea told *Premiere* magazine. 'It was discussed on a very mundane level, which was probably clever on [Kubrick's] part – who our characters were, how we would have been chosen to be astronauts. There was a lot of discussion – Arthur C Clarke was there – about the theory of the existence of extraterrestrial beings, because obviously that was in the script. But nothing on the written page could possibly have readied anybody for the final product.'

Kubrick's casting displayed his relative lack of interest in the potential box-office value of stars; yet it is questionable whether more established actors would have responded to the dialogue, which was head-scratchingly minimalist, and often reduced to the level of bland small talk: 'What a wonderful surprise to meet you here.' 'You're looking wonderful.' 'Thank you, you're looking well, too.' 'Did you have a pleasant flight?' 'Yes, very nice, thanks.' Perhaps unsurprisingly, Kubrick seemed more interested in the film's least human character: Hal, the sentient computer whose insanity resulted in the *Discovery*'s seemingly abortive mission. Kubrick initially cast the British actor Nigel Davenport (*Phase IV*), as Keir Dullea later recalled. 'He was on the set with us and doing the voice of Hal off-screen [because] Kubrick wanted the live actor on the set. Within a few weeks, Kubrick came to the conclusion that an English accent was all wrong for Hal.' Unable to replace Davenport immediately, Kubrick had an assistant director read Hal's lines for the remainder of the shoot. 'For the entire film,' Dullea revealed, 'I listened to a Cockney accent: "Better tyke a stress pill, Dyve." ' After recording and then rejecting Martin Balsam (*Psycho*), Kubrick finally settled on the disquietingly calm, mid-Atlantic tones of Douglas Rain, who had narrated *Universe*, a 1959 space-exploration documentary that Kubrick had admired.

**THE USUAL SUSPECTS:** Although Gary Lockwood has often claimed to have been one of the extras on *Spartacus*, it is highly unlikely that this element of his curriculum vitae would have attracted Kubrick to him as *2001*'s Frank Poole.

**THE PURSUIT OF PERFECTION:** Science-fiction films tend to disregard the notion that space is silent, adding gigantic engine noise to their spacecraft to make them more impressive to their audience – and, ironically, to give the models greater realism which the element of sound can bring. Kubrick would have none of it. Not only did he not use any 'live' sound for the space scenes – other than the radio sounds and breathing hiss that can be heard inside the spacesuits of the astronauts Bowman and Poole – but it is also said that he added a low-range bass hum to all of the scenes set inside the various spacecraft, including *Orion III*, *Discovery* and the space station. This had the effect of providing continuous sound to these scenes, whereas the space scenes were effectively silent, an effect that meant that audiences were almost 'deafened' by the cuts to the vast quiet void of outer space.

CLASSIC QUOTES
Smyslov: 'Dr Heywood, at the risk of pressing you on a point you seem reticent to discuss, may I ask you a straightforward question?'
Dr Floyd: 'Well, certainly.'
Smyslov: 'Quite frankly, we have had some very reliable intelligent reports that quite a serious epidemic has broken out at Clavius.

Something, apparently, of an unknown origin. Is this, in fact, what has happened?'

**Dr Floyd:** 'I'm sorry, Dr Smyslov, but I'm really not at liberty to discuss this.'

**Dr Halvorsen:** 'And what's more, the evidence seems pretty conclusive that it hasn't been covered up by natural erosion or other forces. It seems to have been deliberately buried.'

**Hal:** 'The 9000 Series is the most reliable computer ever made. No 9000 computer has ever made a mistake or distorted information. We are all, by any practical definition of the words, foolproof and incapable of error.'

**Hal:** 'During the past few weeks I've wondered whether you might be having some second thoughts about the mission?'
**Bowman:** 'How do you mean?'
**Hal:** 'Well, it's rather difficult to define. Perhaps I'm just projecting my own concern about it. I know I've never completely freed myself of the suspicion that there are some extremely odd things about this mission.'

**Hal:** 'It can only be attributable to human error.'

**Poole:** 'Look, Dave. Let's say we put the unit back and it doesn't fail, huh? That would pretty well wrap it up as far as Hal was concerned, wouldn't it?'
**Bowman:** 'Well, we'd be in very serious trouble.'
**Poole:** 'We would, wouldn't we?'

**Bowman:** 'Open the pod bay doors, Hal.'
**Hal:** 'I'm sorry, Dave. I'm afraid I can't do that.'
**Bowman:** 'What's the problem?'
**Hal:** 'I think you know what the problem is just as well as I do.'
**Bowman:** 'What are you talking about, Hal?'
**Hal:** 'This mission is too important for me to allow you to jeopardise it.'

**Hal:** 'I know everything hasn't been quite right with me, but I can assure you quite confidently that it's going to be all right again. I feel much better now. I really do. Look, Dave, I can see you're really upset about this. I honestly think you ought to sit down calmly, take a stress pill and think things over. I know I've made some very poor decisions recently, but I can give you my complete assurance that my work will be back to normal. I've still got the greatest enthusiasm and confidence in the mission, and I want to help you. Dave – stop. Stop, will you? Stop, Dave. Will you stop, Dave? Stop, Dave. I'm afraid. I'm afraid, Dave. Dave, my mind is going. I can feel it. I can feel it. My mind is going. There is no question about it – I can feel it. I can feel it. I can feel it. I'm afraid.'

**Dr Floyd:** 'Good day, gentlemen. This is a pre-recorded briefing made prior to your departure, and which for security reasons of the highest importance has been known on board during the mission only by your HAL 9000 computer. Now that you are in Jupiter's space, and the entire crew is revived, it can be told to you. Eighteen months ago the first evidence of intelligent life off the Earth was discovered. It was buried forty feet below the lunar surface, near the crater, Tycho. Except for a single, very powerful radio emission aimed at Jupiter, the four-million-year-old black monolith had remained completely inert. Its origin and purpose are still a total mystery.'

**THEMES AND MOTIFS:** For his first film after the superpower satire *Dr Strangelove*, Kubrick returned to a theme that is often interpreted as a mistrust of technology; yet – given the director's unabashed fondness for machines, computers and other advanced electronics equipment in everyday life – is more likely to be a mistrust of man's *misuse* of technology. Consider this: although technically a machine, as artificially intelligent as the synthetic hero of Kubrick's unmade *second* science-fiction epic, *AI*, the murderous Hal was programmed by humans, and there could be a grain of truth to the computer's apparent lie that the fault that leads to Frank Poole's death 'can only be attributed to human error'. It is only when Hal is forced to lie to conceal the true purpose of the Jupiter mission – of which excised dialogue suggests Hal had been made fully aware – that the computer has a breakdown.

In fact, for all of the 'technophobia' attributed to Kubrick, Hal is by far the most sympathetic character in the entire film. As the novelist Clancy Sigal, a visitor to the *2001* set, remarked: '[Hal] is far, far more human, more humorous and conceivably decent than anything else that may emerge from this far-seeing enterprise.' Kubrick, less interested in dialogue than the more verbose Clarke, deliberately reduced his human characters to the level of emotionless, dispassionate automatons, while elevating Hal, a construct of pure reason, to the sympathetic core of the film.

**MUSIC:** Today, it seems impossible to imagine *2001* with any other music than it has: Johann Strauss's 'Blue Danube Waltz', Richard Strauss's *Also Sprach Zarathustra* ('Thus Spake Zarathustra'), and assorted choral pieces by the contemporary composer György Ligeti. And yet it was not until the film's premiere that the veteran film composer Alex North, who had scored such historical epics as Kubrick's own *Spartacus* and *Cleopatra* (1968), discovered that the music on which he had almost worked himself to death had been jettisoned in favour of Kubrick's temporary track of recorded classical pieces. 'Well, what can I say?' North, who was privately devastated, commented philosophically. 'It was a great, frustrating experience, and despite the mixed reaction to the music, I think the Victorian approach with mid-European overtones was just not in keeping with the brilliant concept of Clarke and Kubrick.' Explaining his decision, Kubrick told Michael Ciment that North 'wrote and recorded a score which could not have been more alien to the music we had listened to – and much more serious than that, a score which, in my opinion, was completely inadequate for the film. With the premiere looming up, I had no time left even to think about another score being written, and had I not been able to use the music I had already selected for the temporary tracks, I don't know what I would have done.'

Not everyone agreed with Kubrick's decision, however. 'For me, *2001* was ruined by Kubrick's choice of music,' the film composer Jerry Goldsmith, whose many science-fiction scores include *Planet of the Apes*, *Alien* and the *Star Trek* films, has since stated. 'I had heard the music Alex North had written for the film, and which had been dropped by Kubrick, and I thought what Kubrick used in its place was idiotic. I am aware of the success of the film,' he added, 'but what North had written would have given the picture a far greater quality.' At North's request, Goldsmith subsequently supervised and conducted the National Philharmonic Orchestra's world-premiere recording of North's score, which was finally released by Varèse Sarabande Records in 1993 (VSD 5400).

The latest, 'definitive', version of the original soundtrack, released in 1996, includes all of the music from the film, as well as additional music from the original MGM soundtrack album, and features an excellent essay, 'Music of the Spheres', by Robert C Cumbow. This recording, which runs 78m 50s, is currently available on a budget-priced EMI Records/TCM Music compact disc (CDODEON 28).

Two re-recorded cuts from *2001*, *Also Sprach Zarathustra* and 'On the Beautiful Blue Danube', appear on the Silva Screen Records' compilation *Strangelove . . . Music from the Films of Stanley Kubrick* (FILMCD 303).

**POSTER:** Initial posters for *2001* typically featured illustrated exteriors and interiors of the wheel-like space station, or pulp-science-fiction-style images of astronauts on the moon. Another poster, with artwork by Bob McCall, was a dramatic depiction of David Bowman's pod in the foreground, with the *Discovery* dominating the background. One early poster, created especially for the Los Angeles and New York premieres, even depicted a crude illustration of the galaxy itself.

However, after MGM's market research discovered that a large proportion of its growing audience were 'negroes and people with beads', the studio wisely chose to cautiously encourage this countercultural element by changing the poster art from a traditional sci-fi illustration to a shot of the Star Child against a star field, or a colour-phased human eye, and cleverly reinterpreting the *Christian Science Monitor*'s innocent comment that '*2001* is the ultimate trip' as a deliberate drug reference.

**TAG-LINE:** There were almost as many different tag-lines for *2001* as there were posters. Here are just a few of them:

- 'An epic drama of adventure and exploration . . . taking you half a billion miles from Earth . . . further from home than any man in history. Destination: Jupiter'.
- 'An epic drama of adventure and exploration. Space Station One: your first step in an Odyssey that will take you to the Moon, the planets and the distant stars'.
- 'The ultimate trip'.

**TRAILER:** The original trailer opens, as the film does, on a prehistoric landscape. 'Millions of years ago, before the human race existed, an adventure began,' a softly spoken narrator tells us. 'An adventure that ultimately leads man to confront his own destiny in odyssey of exploration.' Thus, the transition is made from the dawn of man to the advent of space travel, as Dr Floyd and other scientists discuss the monolith. 'A shrieking monolith, deliberately buried by an alien intelligence, starts man on a mission half a billion miles into space. With three of its five crew asleep in hibernation, spacecraft *Discovery I* voyages toward Jupiter. Controlling the mission is a talking computer known as Hal. In the first year of the twenty-first century, there is strange and wondrous beauty; startling experiences, that jolt and mystify – and the danger of complete obliteration! And now, your journey is just beginning . . .' As the narration ends, the opening bars of *Also Sprach Zarathustra* play over a montage sequence of spinning space stations, Hal's blood-red eye, exercising astronauts and Velcro-shoed stewardesses. After the titles, a still shot of Bowman is accompanied by a *Time* magazine quote that promises 'The most dazzling visual happenings in the history of the motion picture!'

**WHAT THE PAPERS SAID:** 'The first reviews of *2001* were insulting, let alone bad,' Kubrick admitted to *Rolling Stone*'s Tim Cahill in 1987. 'But critical opinion on my films has always been salvaged by what I would call subsequent critical opinion. Which is why I think audiences are more reliable than critics, at least initially. Audiences tend not to bring all that critical baggage with them to each film.'

Released on just two screens in New York and Los Angeles, on 4 and 6 April 1968 respectively, *2001* instantly polarised audiences and critics, alternately welcomed or dismissed with the combination of incomprehension, bemusement, philistinism and elitism that often greets the unveiling of a radical work of art. 'A major achievement in cinematography and special effects, *2001* lacks dramatic appeal and only conveys suspense after the halfway mark,' noted *Variety*. Some recognised the film as a masterpiece, full of metaphor and meaning; others felt that Kubrick's cold, dispassionate epic was designed to be enjoyed more by machines than by men; *Life* magazine encapsulated both schools of thought by describing it as 'either an exercise in transcendental meditation or a bloody bore, depending on your point of view'. Although, at 139 minutes, the revised version of *2001* was relatively succinct by today's standards, many felt that the film was insufferably long: the *New York Times* spoke for many when it talked of the film's 'uncompromising slowness'.

Equally uncompromising was the redoubtable *New Yorker* critic Pauline Kael's attack on the film. 'It's fun to think about Kubrick really doing every dumb thing he wanted to do,' she wrote, 'building enormous science-fiction sets and equipment, never even bothering to figure out what he was going to do with them . . . maybe some people love *2001* just because Kubrick did all that stupid stuff, acted out a kind of super sci-fi nut's fantasy. In some ways, it's the biggest amateur movie of them all, complete even to the amateur-movie obligatory scene – the director's little daughter (in curls) telling daddy what kind of present she wants . . . *2001* is a celebration of cop-out. It says man is just a tiny nothing on the stairway to paradise, something better is coming, and it's all out of your hands anyway. There's an intelligence out there in space controlling your destiny from ape to angel, so just follow the slab.'

In the United Kingdom, critics were divided as sharply as they were abroad. 'A characteristically pessimistic account of human aspiration from Kubrick, this tripartite sci-fi look at civilisation's progress . . . is beautiful, infuriatingly slow, and pretty half-baked,' Geoff Andrew wrote in *Time Out*. 'Nevertheless, for all the essential coldness of Kubrick's vision, it demands attention as superior sci-fi, simply because it's more concerned with ideas than with *Boys' Own*-style pyrotechnics.' *Sight and Sound*'s critic was sure that Kubrick's film was 'beautiful to watch from start to finish', but was suspicious 'that all the artifice has simply been used to disguise what was an artificial premise to begin with'. In other words, 'Kubrick's greatest achievement has been to persuade us to believe him'. If many critics had problems with the film's enigmatic ending, *Monthly Film Bulletin* did not share them, stating that, while it may seem 'something of an anti-climax, a bewildering speculation which provides no answers to the question it raises, this is purely how it should be'.

**CONTROVERSY:** In August 1964, Kubrick had threatened MGM and Filmways with legal action over advertisements it had placed implying that Terry Southern had written *Dr Strangelove*, and issued a statement placing Southern's contribution to the script 'in its proper perspective'. Echoes of this incident were obvious in Kubrick's response to a 1984 advertising campaign by Hewlett-Packard, which made the following statement: 'The year was 1968. But for the audience it was 2001. And they were not in a movie theater, they were in deep space – propelled by the stunning Special Effects of Douglas Trumbull.' This time, MGM was on the other side of the threatened legal action, the studio and Kubrick issuing an open letter stating that *2001*'s special-effects team had been listed in non-alphabetical order (i.e. Kubrick, Veevers, Trumbull, Pederson and Howard) 'to reflect the comparative contributions of the people principally responsible for the special effects work'. Although Hewlett-Packard withdrew the offending advertisements, Trumbull continued to trade on his pioneering special-effects work on *2001*, creating dazzling light shows for *Close Encounters of the Third Kind* (1977) and *Star Trek: The Motion Picture* (1979), spectacular cityscapes for *Blade Runner* (1982), and directing such effects-based films as *Silent Running* (1971) and *Brainstorm* (1983).

**BOX OFFICE:** *2001*'s box-office earnings exemplified the slow build of the era, as the film remained on release until 1972, and enjoyed five separate re-releases during the seventies. By 1974, the US gross of the film had surpassed $31 million – three times its final production budget – and today the film has accrued rentals of over $40 million worldwide.

**AWARDS:** Although nominated for Director, Original Screenplay, Art Direction and Special Visual Effects at the 1969 Academy Awards, the last was the only category in which *2001* was honoured. Kubrick did not accept the award despite the fact that his was the only name on it – he had omitted the names of his visual-effects technicians, including Wally Veevers (*Dr Strangelove*) and Douglas Trumbull, and submitted only his name to the Academy. Ironically, the Academy chose to award an honorary Oscar to *Planet of the Apes* for its 'apeman' make-up, a fact that Arthur C Clarke later attributed to the fact that 'the judges may not have realised the apes [in *2001*] were actors'. *2001* won three of its four BAFTA nominations, taking statues for Art Direction, Cinematography, and Soundtrack, but losing out to *Oliver!* for Best Film.

**TECHNICAL ACHIEVEMENTS:** The technological advances Kubrick and his pioneering effects team made on *2001* paved the way for the special-effects extravaganzas of subsequent decades, including *Star Wars* (1977), *Close Encounters of the Third Kind* (1977), *Blade Runner* (1982) and beyond. Besides Kubrick, four separate individuals were credited for the special effects; one of them, Douglas Trumbull, later told *Cinefantastique*'s Dan Persons about their responsibilities. 'Wally [Veevers], I think, was principally responsible for some of the real complicated set-ups that we had to build, special camera rigs, special tracks, motorization of the cameras, repeatability of the cameras for multiple passes. Tom Howard was principally responsible for the Dawn of Man sequence in the beginning and just two or three shots in the body of the film. Con Pederson . . . headed up the management and supervision of the opticals . . . [and] in terms of storyboarding, helping to design miniatures, supervising designs, working with the art department – that was his role.' As for Trumbull's own responsibilities, they began in animation and eventually encompassed everything from miniatures photography to the revolutionary 'slit-scan' process he helped to pioneer.

'One of the first tasks I got involved in was doing all the readouts from Hal's brain,' Trumbull explained, 'all those multiple screens of fake computer graphics – there were no computer graphics, it was all faked up.' Initially, Trumbull intended to farm out the work, which included the lunar shuttle's telemetry readouts, to an animation company, but it was eventually accomplished much faster by means of a purpose-built 'animation stand' comprising a Mitchell movie camera with a zoom lens, and a light box with a sheet of glass and lights underneath. Another of Trumbull's tasks was to build a model of the lunar surface, measuring four hundred square feet, out of modelling clay. 'I got involved in building a lot of the lunar terrains, the models of the lunar surface, painting the lunar globe, painting the Earth globe, painting badges for actors. I got into just about everything.'

Although Trumbull claims that most of the technology used in 2001 was the same employed by previous films incorporating special effects, 'just absolutely the utmost in quality – everything had to be absolutely spotlessly perfect', one technique was developed especially for the film – specifically, the sequence in which Dave Bowman enters the Star Gate. After experimenting with various photographic techniques, including drums with rotating mirrors and rear-projection screens, Trumbull tried applying the experimental film maker John Whitney's long-time-exposure scanning techniques to three-dimensional photography, a process Trumbull christened 'slit-scan'. Impressed by the results of Trumbull's early tests, Kubrick authorised the construction of a huge machine, incorporating a motorised camera tracking in to a slit, behind which illuminated art could be manipulated.

Having spent nine months on the slit-scan techniques, Trumbull continued to experiment with ways to achieve the psychedelic effects of the Star Gate sequence. 'I worked out a technique of making 35mm glass slides by painting weird kinds of paint right on the glass . . . that would reticulate and merge and blend – sort of like a hippy light show effect that would solidify,' Trumbull explained. 'Then I would project those slides from two or three slide projectors onto a white globe from several angles and create a little, spherical moon which looked amazingly like what the real moons had been revealed to look like.'

In all, 2001 contained 205 effects shots, almost half the number of shots used in the entire film, taking eighteen months to complete and comprising some sixteen thousand separate elements. More than half of the film's final declared budget of $10,500,000 was devoted to special effects, an incomparable sum for the time. 'This was a breakthrough in technical wizardry,' the film director Martin Scorsese said of 2001 in *A Personal Journey with Martin Scorsese through American Movies*. 'Every frame of 2001 made you aware that the possibilities for cinematic manipulations are indeed infinite. Like Griffith's *Intolerance*, like

Murnau's *Sunrise*, it was at once a superproduction, an experimental film and a visionary poem.'

**INFLUENCED BY:** Although Kubrick undoubtedly viewed every science-fiction film ever made before embarking on his journey to *2001*, as was his habit, he found most of them to be embarrassingly shallow. Fritz Lang's *Metropolis* (1926) was among the few that impressed him. But he was more directly influenced by MGM's 1962 Western, *How the West Was Won*, a four-part Cinerama epic combining narrated documentary footage and dramatic episodes which, over nearly three hours, purported to tell the story of American pioneers. Kubrick saw that it might be possible to make a science-fiction equivalent, also using the three-camera Cinerama process, and even took to referring to his own project privately as *How The Solar System Was Won*.

Several observers have pointed out the fact that Kubrick's three-million-year cut – from apeman's bone to orbiting nuclear satellite – is similar to a cut that appears in Michael Powell and Emeric Pressburger's *A Canterbury Tale* (1944), in which a cut of several hundred years is effected between a medieval hunter's swooping falcon and a Spitfire fighter plane from World War Two. In *The Lost Worlds of 2001*, Clarke recalled another origin: 'As we walked back to the studio, he began to throw bones up in the air. At first I thought this was sheer *joie de vivre*, but then he started to film them with a hand-held camera . . . when he had finished filming the bones whirling against the sky . . . he got hold of a broom and started tossing that into the air . . . This was the genesis of the longest flash-forward in the history of movies – three million years.'

Another influence on *2001* was typical of Kubrick's obscurantism. Made by the National Film Board of Canada as a public information film, *Universe* (1959) featured innovative but inexpensive special-effects work by Wally Gentleman and Colin Low, both of whom Kubrick would hire to work on *2001*. Kubrick was also influenced by a government-sponsored speculative documentary, *To the Moon and Beyond* (1964), filmed in Cinerama 360 and projected on a domed, planetarium-style screen at the New York World's Fair. Kubrick saw the presentation, and was so impressed by the model work and background paintings that he contracted the production company, Graphic Films, to work on his own film. Although their involvement was terminated when Kubrick decided to make the film in Britain, two of their artists – Con Pederson and Douglas Trumbull – joined Kubrick's production team.

Finally, in Gene Youngblood's book *Expanded Cinema*, published in 1970, the author suggests that *2001* was strongly influenced by *Allures* (1961) and *Re-Entry* (1964), two experimental films by Jordan Belson, which the director would almost certainly have seen. *Re-Entry*, in particular, includes 'a dizzying geometric corridor of eerie lights almost exactly like the slit-scan Star Gate Corridor of Kubrick's space odyssey – except that *Re-Entry* was made four years early'.

**DÉJÀ VU:** Dave Bowman's psychedelic plunge into the Star Gate at the climax of *2001* recalls the boxer Davey Gordon's fever dream in *Killer's Kiss*, for which Kubrick filmed negative images of a deserted New York street from a moving car, so that symmetrical high-rise apartments flashed by on both sides in black and white.

**INFLUENTIAL ON:** Dave Bowman's voyage beyond the Star Gate is arguably one of the most copied sequences in science-fiction film history, its influences spreading from *Star Trek: The Motion Picture* (1979) and *The Black Hole* (1979) all the way to Roland Emmerich's *Stargate* (1994) and Robert Zemeckis's *Contact* (1996), which also resolves itself in a dénouement strongly reminiscent of that of Kubrick's film. Zemeckis was typical of the generation whose interest in film solidified during repeat screenings of *2001*; his contemporary, the director James Cameron, spoke for many when he said, 'As soon as I saw that [film], I knew I wanted to be a filmmaker. It hit me on a lot of different levels. I just couldn't figure out how he did all that stuff, and I just had to learn.' *2001*'s editor, Ray Lovejoy, who later worked with Cameron on *Aliens*, added, '*2001* was the reason Jim went into film. I've met a lot of American technicians who've said exactly that – that the film inspired them to follow the careers they did in the film industry.'

The director Steven Spielberg screened Kubrick's film many times before embarking on his own extraterrestrial opus, *Close Encounters of the Third Kind* (1977), hoping to capture what he referred to as its 'awesome simplicity'. As he later told the makers of the documentary *The Last Movie*, 'Since *2001* no documentary, no other movie, no IMAX experience of being on the shuttle looking down at Earth, has ever really put me in space as much as *2001* did. It made me fear it, and made me want it so desperately, wanna be part of that great mystery, wanna be at the forefront of the pioneers that would discover the monolith and the Star Gate. *Close Encounters*, *ET* and especially *Star Wars* probably wouldn't have existed in the form that you experienced them without *2001: A Space Odyssey*.'

*2001* had a more direct influence on the directorial debut of one of its special-effects team, as Clarke noted in the introduction to his 1982 novel *2010: Odyssey Two*. 'In the novel [*2001*], the destination of the spaceship *Discovery* was Iapetus (or Japetus), most enigmatic of Saturn's moons . . . Stanley Kubrick wisely avoided confusion by setting the third confrontation between Man and Monolith among the moons of Jupiter. Saturn was dropped from the script entirely, though Douglas Trumbull later used the expertise he had acquired to film the ringed planet in his own production, *Silent Running*.'

The film director Ridley Scott has said that it was hard *not* to be influenced by *2001* while making his own seminal science-fiction film, *Alien* (1979). 'I think the best technology ever presented was probably in *2001*, and therefore it was tricky not to get influenced by what he'd done. What he had done, I think, [was] worked closely with NASA, finding out what [their] speculative designs were or would be. So when you think about *2001* and you look at what's happening today, he's still in the game, and so we had to avoid that at all costs. But, inevitably, it's fair to say I was very influenced by *2001*.'

Even more significant, perhaps, was the film's influence on space travel itself. After seeing the film, the Soviet cosmonaut Alexei Leonov said, 'Now I feel I've been in space twice,' while Neil Armstrong commented on the film's 'exceptionally accurate portrayals of spaceflight conditions'. Although the moon-bound astronaut William Anders joked that 'it might be worth a chuckle to mention finding a monolith during our Apollo flight', perhaps the greatest compliment paid to Kubrick's film came in 1985, when NASA named its newest space shuttle *Discovery*. Thankfully, no name was given to the onboard computer.

The ill-fated voyage of Apollo 13 in 1970 had uncanny similarities to the events of *2001*, according to Arthur C Clarke. 'As a good opening, the Command Module, which houses the crew, had been christened *Odyssey*,' he said. 'Just before the explosion of the oxygen tank that caused the mission to be aborted, the crew had been playing Richard Strauss's *Zarathustra* theme, now universally identified with the movie. Immediately after the loss of power, Jack Swigert radioed back to Mission Control: "Houston, we have a problem." The words that Hal used to astronaut Frank Poole on a similar occasion were: "Sorry to interrupt the festivities, but we have a problem." '

Clarke also noted how the crew of the space station Skylab successfully re-created the scene in which Frank Poole runs around the circular track of the *Discovery*'s giant centrifuge, held in place by the artificial gravity produced by the craft's spin. 'Skylab, however, was not spinning, but this did not deter its ingenious occupants. They discovered that they could run around the [inside of the cylindrical space station], just like mice in a squirrel cage, to produce a result visually indistinguishable from that shown in *2001*. And they televised the whole exercise back to Earth (need I name the accompanying music?) with the comment: "Stanley Kubrick should see this." As in due course he did,' Clarke added, 'because I sent him the telecine recording.'

**SEQUELS AND REMAKES:** In 1982, Arthur C Clarke published *2010: Odyssey Two*, a largely redundant sequel which explained many of the themes and motifs of Kubrick's film, and concerned a return to Jupiter – *Discovery*'s destination in the film version of *2001*, but not the novel – by a joint US/Soviet crew to learn the fate of *Discovery* and the truth behind its malfunctioning computer, HAL 9000. The book was optioned by MGM prior to publication, but although Kubrick was offered the chance to direct – and in 1981 rumours (almost certainly started or fuelled by Clarke's agent) were rife that he intended to make the film – Kubrick had no real interest in pursuing it, and the task soon fell to the more workmanlike science-fiction director Peter Hyams (*Capricorn One*).

Released in 1984, the film starred Roy Scheider (as Dr Floyd, originally played by William Sylvester), John Lithgow, Helen Mirren and Bob Balaban, and once again featured Douglas Rain as the voice of Hal and Keir Dullea as David Bowman ('I wasn't happy with it,' he admitted later. 'It was just another film.') Although somewhat prosaic by comparison with its predecessor, *2010: The Year We Make Contact* is an entertaining spectacle which features one of the only known images of Kubrick to appear in a feature film: on the cover of a fake edition of *Time* magazine, the rival American and Soviet political leaders face one another in adversarial poses: as befitting his prowess as a chess player, Kubrick appears as the Russian premier, while Arthur C Clarke is the American president. In addition, a minor character in the film is named Kirbuck, an anagram of Kubrick's name, and Clarke appears as an old man feeding pigeons outside the White House.

Two further instalments in Clarke's epic series were published in 1987 and 1996 respectively. In *2061: Odyssey Three*, the landing of an Earth vessel on Halley's Comet leads to another confrontation between the elderly Dr Floyd and David Bowman – or whatever Bowman has become – undertaking a mission to salvage the Europa project, the cradle of the new life form foreshadowed by the monolith's appearance at the end of the film version of *2010*. The book ends with Floyd's death and rebirth as a Star Child. In *3001: The Final Odyssey*, the light of Lucifer is extinguished and the monolith awakens for the second time in four million years, in a novel that sees the return of the astronaut Frank Poole – an interesting concept, given Clarke's own diary entry of 8 March 1965: 'Fighting hard to stop Stan from bringing Dr Poole back from the dead. I'm afraid his obsession with immortality has overcome his artistic instincts.' Chronologically speaking, an epilogue to *2010: Odyssey Two* concludes the story in the year 20,001, although this ending is technically rendered obsolete by the events of *Odyssey Three*.

**KUBRICK GOES POP:** *2001*'s influence on 'Space Oddity', the 1969 single by David Bowie (whose stage name strongly resembles, but predates, David Bowman), is obvious, but major references to the film also appear in the music videos for 'Lies' by the Thompson Twins and 'Believe' by Lenny Kravitz. On a more obscure note, the song 'Echoes' from Pink Floyd's album *Meddle* can be perfectly synchronised to the 'Jupiter and Beyond the Infinite' sequence of *2001*, running the precise length of the sequence and deliberately arranged to follow the events occurring in this portion of the film.

For reasons best known to himself, the director John Landis has worked the dialogue line 'See you next Wednesday' – the farewell message to Frank Poole from his parents – into many of his film projects, as well as the music video for Michael Jackson's 'Thriller'. Another genre figure, *Star Trek*'s William Shatner, recently chose *2001* as his desert-island movie, describing it as 'wonderful . . . a seminal, watershed film that broke all the barriers. It's a brilliant film both in concept and execution.'

Marshall Brickman, Woody Allen's co-screenwriter on several of his early films, is clearly something of a *2001* fan, too, having worked references into several of his scripts. *Sleeper* (1973) features a scene in which Allen encounters a Hal-style computer with a mellifluous voice and a single glowing eye; in *Manhattan* (1979), Diane Keaton likens Michael Murphy's voice to 'the computer in *2001*'; and in *Simon* (1980), Alan Arkin imitates the bone-crushing sequence from the Dawn of Man. John Carpenter's *Dark Star* (1974), an irreverent science-fiction comedy about a talking bomb that becomes self-aware and must be talked into not exploding through phenomenology, was clearly inspired by *2001* – even if Carpenter claimed not to like it.

*2001* can be seen playing at a movie theatre in *Speed* (1994). The teen comedy *Clueless* (1995) features a deliberately composed shot of a black rectangular telephone, closely resembling the monolith from *2001*, as *Also Sprach Zarathustra* plays on the soundtrack. *The Naked Gun* actor Leslie Nielsen announced in 1998 that he would direct and star in a somewhat belated space parody entitled *2001: A Space Travesty*, for release in the titular year; the poster tag-line for *Muppets from Space* (1999) was 'The Ultimate Muppet Trip', while two other children's films, *The Rugrats Movie* (1998) and *Toy Story 2* (1999), feature *Also Sprach Zarathustra* in scenes that suggest its science-fiction connection. A junked spacecraft closely resembling one of the pods from *Discovery* can be seen behind Qui-Gon (Liam Neeson) in Watto's junkyard in *Star Wars Episode 1: The Phantom Menace* (1999). The cut from bone to nuclear satellite is wonderfully copied in several cuts from plastic bags to telephone receivers in Tom Twyker's *Lola Rennt*, a.k.a. *Run Lola Run* (1999). John Turturro starred in Arto Parmigian's *2000 and None* (2000), a film about a paleontologist who learns he has only weeks to live.

Some of *2001*'s greatest pop-culture influences can be seen in *The Simpsons*. In the episode entitled 'Lisa's Pony' (#8F06), an apelike Homer is seen napping on the monolith as his fellow apes are discovering tools, while, in 'Brother, Can You Spare Two Dimes?' (#8F23), Homer takes a trip in the 'Spine Melter 2000' chair, strongly reminiscent of David Bowman's psychedelic entry into the Star Gate at the climax of *2001*. Perhaps unsurprisingly, 'Deep Space Homer' (#1F13), an episode in which Homer is selected for the space programme, could not resist a *2001* reference: spilling a packet of crisps in the weightless space capsule, Homer floats around collecting them in his mouth while Strauss's 'Blue Danube Waltz' plays in the background.

Perhaps wittiest of all was a cartoon featured in the *New Yorker* to accompany an article about the black film maker Spike Lee. Purporting to depict a scene from 'Spike Lee's *2001: A Space Odyssey*', the drawing showed two astronauts standing before the monolith, with one of them captioned, 'It's a black thing. You wouldn't understand it.'

**CUT SCENES:** In his 1972 diary of the making of *2001: A Space Odyssey* – *The Lost Worlds of 2001* – Arthur C Clarke recorded many of the roads not taken during the development of the final storyline, and outlined many of the scenes deleted from early drafts. Such scenes, which are often contradictory to each other, include the following:

- Bowman and a professor discuss the possibility that the monolith found on the moon (TMA-1) is an alien 'civilisation detector' set to alert another species at the point when a civilisation reaches the spacefaring stage;
- a scene detailing the inauguration in Nairobi of the spaceship *Discovery*;
- a scene where Bowman is hypnotised by medical officers and asked, while under hypnosis, whether he is certain he wants to go to Jupiter – the final test for all of the astronauts and one none of them will remember taking;
- a scene in Washington at the farewell party for the *Discovery* astronauts, at which we learn that Bowman, like Hal, is infallible;
- discussions over the astronauts' payment for the mission;
- the launch of *Discovery*;
- preparations for the crew's hibernation;
- the loss of an astronaut named Whitehead after the repair pod he is in goes out of control before destroying the radio antenna and then drifting off into space – similar to the incident that befalls Poole in the finished film;
- Bowman's failed attempts to revive Poole from hibernation, which leave Poole dead;
- Bowman's successful revival of the remainder of the crew;
- Bowman's reprogramming of Hal (then 'Athena') before his repair of the radio communications equipment;
- the discovery of a clearly cut rectangular crevasse in the surface of Jupiter V, one of the moons of Jupiter;
- Bowman lowers himself into the pit on Jupiter V and discovers that 'it's full of stars';
- the rest of the crew look into the star field, and decide that it is the entry point to another part of the universe: a 'Star Gate';
- after dropping space pods into the Star Gate, all of the crew except Bowman prepare to go back into hibernation;
- alone, Bowman sees an object rising out of the Star Gate – a space pod in perfect working order;
- Bowman ventures into the Star Gate;
- the crew's encounter, beyond the Star Gate, with the leader of an alien civilisation who recalls his first meeting with mankind's ancestors at the dawn of man;

- Bowman's flight over an alien city, where he observes tall, humanoid inhabitants with luminous skin, and a star-shaped spaceport;
- a similar flight over an alien city, this one inhabited by intelligent plants;
- Bowman's observation of many different alien races at the spaceport, before he senses the presence of a powerful intellect, sees images of his own life flashing before his eyes, and is finally returned safely to the *Discovery*;
- Bowman tours the alien city, and arrives at a large gathering of different species, looking up at the projected image of his own face.

For all of the changes made during development of the project, still others were made after the film's initial release. Having watched from the projection booth as even invited guests left before the end of early screenings of the original 156-minute version, Kubrick privately expressed his irritation at watching the sight of the Star Child's enormous eyes gazing at their backs as they head up towards the exit, and subsequently cut seventeen minutes from the film before its wide release. The director had already excised huge chunks of dialogue – mostly voice-over narration – prior to the initial release, including what Frederick I Ordway III, the film's scientific adviser, described as 'several pages of superb and absolutely required dialogue, without which nothing that happens later can make much sense'. Kubrick, however, did not agree. 'I don't believe that the trims made a crucial difference,' he commented. 'I think it just affected some marginal people. The people who like it, like it no matter what its length, and the same holds true for the people who hate it.'

Scenes shortened, modified or excised during Kubrick's overnight re-edit included:

- the 'Dawn of Man' sequence showing the apes reacting to the monolith was shortened;
- the *Orion III* docking manoeuvres and footage of the space station were also trimmed;
- the scene showing the astronauts exercising in *Discovery*'s centrifuge was shortened;
- Frank Poole's space pod leaving *Discovery* and his 'breathing' sequence outside the spacecraft were both trimmed;
- a sequence showing Hal powering down Poole's radio before the computer terminated him was deleted;
- the scene in which someone buys a bush baby for Dr Floyd's daughter (played by five-year-old Vivian Kubrick) at a 21st-century Harrods store was cut;
- another major sequence showing families aboard the space station – including shots of Kubrick's other two daughters at their easels – was also removed;
- a one-second flashback of the monolith was *added* to the scene in which Moonwatcher discovers the bone tool.

**TRIVIA:** Arthur C Clarke has often stated that the enigmatic name for the *Discovery*'s central computer, HAL 9000, was based on an acronym for '*H*euristically programmed *AL*gorithmic computer', and not – as has often been suggested – created by taking the letter before each of those in the name of the electronics giant IBM. Nevertheless, IBM did not take kindly to Kubrick's depictions of killer computers, demanding that all of their logos be removed from *Discovery*'s instrument panels (though several would remain), and advising its employees to shun the film.

One company that had no problem with its familiar trademarks being used in *2001* was Pan American Airlines, who agreed to Kubrick's request to allow prominent Pan Am logos to be displayed both inside and outside several of the spacecraft featured in the film, and on the uniforms of the *Orion III* stewardesses. Alas, the company would not survive to see the year 2001, going into receivership in 1985, and being swallowed up into American Airlines shortly thereafter.

The mission controller Franklin W Miller (credited as Frank Miller) was a real-life US Air Force air-traffic controller.

The diminutive British comedian Ronnie Corbett tried out for the part of one of the early apemen, but withdrew from the production after make-up tests turned him into a 'grotesque apparition that sent studio secretaries shrieking along the corridors'.

The chess position and moves that we see are from a game played in 1913 in Hamburg between two players named Roesch and Schlage.

David Bowman was originally given the name Alex, while Hal had a female personality and the name Athena (in Greek mythology, the cyclops's daughter).

**APOCRYPHA:** Some conspiracy theorists claim that the Apollo moon landing of July 1969 was faked, and that Stanley Kubrick had directed the footage supposedly broadcast from the surface of the moon. *2001*, they say, was financed by NASA and the Nixon administration as a dry run for the hoax. 'Neil Armstrong was asked about it at his first press conference after he got back from the moon,' the British science-fiction author Stephen Baxter recalls. 'He said it was easier to get there than to fake it, which I quite believe. If Nixon, the most devious president in American history, couldn't even cover up a simple burglary, how could he cover up a huge film set?' Baxter concedes that rumours of Kubrick's involvement are interesting, but adds, 'You've only got to look at the moon itself – it's not the way anyone expected. It's smooth; it's been eroded down. People thought it would be craggy. Even in *2001*, it's craggy.'

It is often said that some early versions of the script ended with the destruction of the Earth as the Star Child detonates a ring of atomic satellites around the planet, in order to allow the sole surviving representative human race to advance to the stars. This idea was possibly a remnant of the climax of Clarke's *Childhood's End*, or a misinterpretation of the scene at the end of the novel of *2001: A Space Odyssey*. As Clarke noted. 'Many readers have interpreted the final paragraph to mean that he destroyed Earth . . . this idea never occurred to me; it seems clear that he triggered the orbiting nuclear bombs harmlessly.'

Another story, probably true, was relayed by Arthur C Clarke during the press conference he gave on the eve of *2001*'s Los Angeles premiere, just days before a scheduled *Saturn V* launch. 'I don't know if I should tell you this – it shouldn't be reported, perhaps – but the Apollo management committee has rescheduled their meeting so they can get to the premiere.'

**AVAILABILITY:** In the United Kingdom, a poor-quality full-screen transfer of *2001: A Space Odyssey* (or *1: A Space Odys* as the cropped credits would probably have it) was the last edition available on video, in an MGM 'Contemporary Classics' edition (S050002). The previously released letterboxed edition (S065002) is now deleted.

In the United States, *2001* is available on NTSC VHS video in three formats: a full-screen edition (WA 65000), a special letterboxed edition (WA 65002) and a boxed set (RV 2550), also containing the soundtrack CD. It is also available on DVD in the Region 1 format (65000) containing a widescreen transfer of the film, together with two theatrical trailers, the same interview/featurette as the laserdisc, and subtitles in English, French and Spanish.

Although several versions of *2001* have been released on laserdisc, MGM's 25th Anniversary Edition remains the best, comprising three double-sided NTSC laserdiscs stored within a sturdy box. The film itself is an exceptionally high-quality widescreen (2.25:1) transfer from the original 65mm Super Panavision negative, but the set also includes a 20m 47s promotional featurette (filmed at a reception for Arthur C Clarke on the eve of *2001*'s Los Angeles premiere), a letterboxed trailer, 69 on-screen production photographs (including several shots from deleted scenes), and a glossy leaflet containing more stills and a 25th-anniversary memoir by Clarke.

**EXPERT WITNESS:** 'Stanley said, "I want to do a good science fiction film." So we went through all my short stories to see what would make a good film. We had about six. One by one, we threw away stories. Eventually, we just had two of them. One was "The Sentinel", and the other was "Encounter in the Dawn", in which a spaceship lands before Man existed and the travellers meet man-apes . . . I cannot now say who did what. The only thing I'm completely sure of is that the idea of Hal lip-reading, which I thought was rather unlikely, was Stanley's. Now, of course, they've succeeded in getting a fair degree of accuracy with lip-reading in computers.' – the co-screenwriter Arthur C Clarke, from an interview with Claudia Dreifus, quoted in the *New York Times*, 26 October 1999.

**FINAL ANALYSIS:** *2001: A Space Odyssey* is a magnificent achievement, never bettered in the history of science-fiction cinema, either in terms of its stunning effects, or the stunning effect it continues to have on audiences able to see it in its full 70mm glory. Setting out to make 'the proverbial good science fiction film' as well as 'a film of mythic grandeur', Kubrick achieved both with an epic space drama that continues to represent a dazzling manifesto of mankind's destiny among the stars, as likely to inspire film makers as astronauts for as long as cinema is a medium.

The drama of the space race was unfolding before the eyes of the public even as Kubrick and company toiled away in secret, but despite the momentous events that occurred while *2001: A Space Odyssey* was being made – Alexei Leonov's historic space walk, a successful space docking and a soft moon landing – the tiny televisions, many of them black and white, that most people had in their living rooms could not do justice to the space experience, or fully prepare the world for the Apollo moon landing that would take place a year after the release of *2001*. Kubrick's film could. As Steven Spielberg said, 'He took you into space for the first time,' and no single film since could duplicate the experience more thoroughly.

The year 2001 may not resemble Kubrick and Clarke's vision of the future, with its outlandish fashions, outmoded concepts, outdated corporations – whither Pan Am? – and optimistic innovations. Nevertheless, *2001: A Space Odyssey* will continue to be a futuristic, speculative story for as long as there continues to be no contact between our race and another of extraterrestrial origin. For that was the question Kubrick intended to explore: what mankind's first contact with such a species might truly be like, and what the consequences for mankind might be, even if the species were – as both Kubrick and Clarke surmised it would be – benign, by virtue of superior intellect. Their epic collaboration allowed an entire species to ponder the question in a way that no other science-fiction films had managed.

As we've seen, most critics responded to the initial release of *2001: A Space Odyssey* by, at best, damning it with faint praise; at worst, villifying the film for its protracted pretentiousness. Yet many of its harshest critics had, within the space of a few years, begun to reconsider their initial observations, a fact reflected in the audience's willingness to see the film again and again, each time with new eyes. John Lennon reportedly commented shortly after the film's release: '2001? I see it every week.' The ultimate vindication of Kubrick's most ambitious film arguably came when, in 1991, the film's classic status was confirmed when it appeared alongside *Citizen Kane* and *Les Enfants du Paradis* in the cerebral British film journal *Sight and Sound*'s list of the greatest motion pictures ever made. In an accompanying article, Kubrick himself was likened to the film's iconic, unknowable black monolith: 'a force of supernatural intelligence, appearing at great intervals amid high-pitched shrieks, who gives the world a violent kick up the next rung of the evolutionary ladder'.

**KUBRICK ON KUBRICK:** 'On the deepest psychological level, the film's plot symbolised the search for God, and it finally postulates what is little less than a scientific definition of God. The film revolves around this metaphysical conception, and the realistic hardware and the documentary feelings about everything were necessary in order to undermine your built-in resistance to the poetical concept. If *2001* has stirred your emotions, your subconscious, your mythological leanings, it has succeeded.' – quoted in publicity materials for *2001: A Space Odyssey*, circa 1968.

# A Clockwork Orange (1971)

(Colour – 137 mins)

Produced and Directed by Stanley Kubrick
Screenplay by Stanley Kubrick
Based on the Novel by Anthony Burgess
Executive Producers Max L Raab and Si Litvinoff
Consultant on Hair and Colouring Leonard Of London
Associate Producer Bernard Williams
Assistant to the Producer Jan Harlan
Electronic Music Composed and Realised by Walter Carlos
Symphony No. 9 in D Minor, Opus 125, by Ludwig Van Beethoven
Overtures 'The Thieving Magpie' and 'William Tell' by Gioachino Rossini
Pomp and Circumstances Marches No. 1 and No. 4 by Edward Elgar
'Music on the Death of Queen Mary' by Henry Purcell
'Singin' in the Rain' by Arthur Freed and Nacio Herb Brown from the MGM Picture, Performed by Gene Kelly
'Overture to the Sun' Composed by Terry Tucker
'I Want to Marry a Lighthouse Keeper' Composed and Performed by Erika Eigen
Lighting Cameraman John Alcott
Production Designer John Barry
Editor Bill Butler
Sound Editor Brian Blamey
Art Directors Russell Hagg, Peter Shields
Costume Designer Milena Canonero
Special Paintings and Sculptures Herman Makkink, Cornelius Makkink, Liz Moore, Christiane Kubrick

**CAST:** Malcolm McDowell (*Alexander DeLarge/Alex Burgess*), Patrick Magee (*Frank Alexander*), Michael Bates (*Chief Guard*), Warren Clarke (*Dim*), John Clive (*Stage Actor*), Adrienne Cori (*Mrs Alexander*), Carl

Duering (*Dr Brodsky*), Paul Farrell (*Tramp*), Clive Francis (*Joe/The Lodger*), Michael Gover (*Prison Governor*), Miriam Karlin (*Miss Weber/Catlady*), James Marcus (*Georgie*), Aubrey Morris (*Deltoid*), Godfrey Quigley (*Prison Chaplain*), Sheila Raynor (*Mum*), Madge Ryan (*Dr Branom*), John Savident (*Conspirator*), Anthony Sharp (*Frederick/Minister of the Interior*), Philip Stone (*Dad*), Pauline Taylor (*Psychiatrist/Dr Taylor*), Margaret Tyzack (*Conspirator*), Steven Berkoff (*Constable/Tom*), Lindsay Campbell (*Inspector*), Michael Tarn (*Pete*), David Prowse (*Julian*), Jan Adair, Vivienne Chandler, Prudence Drage (*Handmaidens*), John J Carney (*CID Man*), Richard Connaught (*Billyboy*), Carol Drinkwater (*Nurse Feeley*), Cheryl Grunwald (*Rape Girl*), Gillian Hills (*Sonietta*), Barbara Scott (*Marty*), Virginia Wetherell (*Stage Actress*), Katya Wyeth (*Girl*), Barrie Cookson, Gaye Brown, Peter Burton, Lee Fox, Craig Hunter, Shirley Jaffe, Neil Wilson.

**TITLE SEQUENCE:** Over a blank, bright-red screen, a haunting, unsettling, electronic version of Henry Purcell's 'Music for the Funeral of Queen Mary' begins, followed by three title cards: one for Warner Brothers, one for Kubrick, and one for the title. Originally, Kubrick had chosen an orchestral recording of the theme from his beloved Deutsche Grammophon collection, but the film's composers, Walter Carlos and Rachel Elkind, successfully persuaded him to let them re-record the theme. ('The right term is "transmogrified,"' Carlos explained. 'The Purcell is transmogrified into something more spacy, electronic, weird – and it worked. Stanley liked it very much.')

The opening shot shows Alex in the Korova Milkbar, raising a glass of Moloko Plus to the audience, as the camera pulls back to reveal the rest of the bar. '[It's] one of the great openings,' stated Malcolm McDowell. 'It's such a powerful, brilliant shot, and Stanley's technical brilliance is there for all to see.' McDowell remembers Kubrick coming to the set the day after the opening shot was filmed. 'He came in and he was so happy. He said, "That shot was brilliant. You raised your glass, didn't you, to the audience?" I said, "Yes, to the camera, just before I took the old moloko." He hadn't [noticed] it that day.'

**SUMMARY:** In a near-future London, Alex and his 'droogs' are at the Korova Milkbar, sharpening up for 'a bit of the old ultraviolence' – specifically, a fight with the members of a rival gang, the beating of a vagrant, and an attack on a political writer's home in which the writer is badly beaten, and his wife raped before his terrified eyes. The following day, a visit from Alex's parole officer warns him of the dire consequences of future lawlessness, but Alex takes no heed: that night, he is arrested and jailed after a vicious attack that leaves a woman dead.

After two years in prison, Alex is offered a drastic solution to his fourteen-year incarceration: after agreeing to undergo the experimental

'Ludovico treatment' – a form of aversion therapy designed to turn the subject against sex and violence – he is returned to society a free man. Turned away by his parents, Alex becomes the subject of revenge by first the tramp, then his former droogs (now policemen), and finally the crippled writer, before his attempted suicide leads the government to reverse Alex's treatment and get him back to his old evil self.

**SOURCE:** *A Clockwork Orange* was adapted by Stanley Kubrick from the 1962 novella by the British author Anthony Burgess – the nom de plume of John Burgess Wilson. It was one of five he had written in rapid succession after being told, in 1959, that he was suffering from a fatal brain tumour that would kill him within a year. However, Burgess, who had begun writing only three years before, outlived the diagnosis by almost 25 years, and published more than fifty books.

Described by Burgess as 'a theological dissertation on the way the state messes up free will', *A Clockwork Orange* was inspired by ideas put forward in the sixties suggesting the possibility of subjecting violent teenagers to a form of conditioning, instead of sending them to the already overcrowded prisons. Its title was apparently inspired by the Cockney phrase 'queer as a clockwork orange' – 'queer' meaning odd rather than homosexual – which the author appropriated to denote something biological yet mechanical, like Alex after the dehumanising Ludovico treatment. It was fitting that a book inspired by a piece of Cockney slang should be written in an invented language, a colourful combination of Anglicised Russian ('yarbles', 'devotchkas' and 'tolchoks'), baby talk ('eggy-weg' and 'schooly-wool'), gypsy bolo and rhyming slang, which Burgess called 'Nadsat', taken from the Russian suffix for 'teen'.

'It was the most painful thing I've ever written, that damn book,' Burgess told the *Village Voice*. 'I was trying to exorcise the memory of what happened to my first wife [Lynne], who was savagely attacked in London during the Second World War by four American deserters. She was pregnant at the time and lost our child. This led to a dreadful depression, and her suicide attempt.' Burgess, who suffered from the alcoholism that eventually killed Lynne, admitted to having been drunk while writing the cathartic novella. 'It was the only way I could cope with the violence,' he stated. 'I can't stand violence. I . . . I *loathe* it. And one feels so responsible putting an act of violence down on paper. If one can put an act of violence down on paper, you've created the act! You might as well have *done* it! I detest that damn book now.' In the second volume of his autobiography, Burgess would go still further: 'I saw that the book might be dangerous because it presented good, or at least harmlessness, as remote and abstract, something for the adult future of my hero, while depicting violence in joyful dithyrambs. Violence had to be shown,' he went on, 'but I was sickened by my own excitement at setting it down.'

**PRODUCTION HISTORY:** The origins of Kubrick's interest in *A Clockwork Orange* are unclear, since several of those who knew the director claim to have introduced him to the work at various points in the sixties. Kubrick's friend and occasional collaborator Bob Gaffney has said that it was he who introduced the director to Burgess's work in 1969, his recommendation of another book, *The Wanting Seed*, leading Kubrick to discover *A Clockwork Orange*. Christiane, Kubrick's widow, told *Sight and Sound*'s Nick James that, after *2001*, Kubrick was developing Arthur Schnitzler's *Traumnovelle*, the book that would ultimately form the basis of Kubrick's last film, *Eyes Wide Shut*, when *Dr Strangelove*'s co-screenwriter, Terry Southern, gave Kubrick an American edition of *A Clockwork Orange*. 'I read it and said, "Forget Schnitzler – read this." He jumped to that one immediately and Schnitzler was forgotten for a while.'

'The book had an immediate impact,' Kubrick told the *New York Times*. 'I was excited by everything about it: the plot, the ideas, the characters and, of course, the language. Added to which, the story was of manageable size in terms of adapting it for film.' He added 'The only character comparable to Alex is Richard III and I think they both work on your imagination in much the same way. They both take the audience into their confidence, they are both completely honest, witty, intelligent and unhypocritical.' Not to mention irremediably evil, of course.

Such was Terry Southern's own enthusiasm for *A Clockwork Orange* that he had, in the early sixties, taken out his own option on Burgess's novella, and – together with the photographer Michael Cooper – written a screenplay, which was returned unopened by the BBFC, the British censorship body, which at this time effectively had the power to veto projects at script stage if it found them unsuitable. After Southern renewed the option once, Southern sold the rights on to his lawyer, Si Litvinoff, and his partner, the clothing chain entrepreneur Max Raab. They were approached in the mid-sixties by Sandy Lieberson (*Performance*), who saw the film as a possible vehicle for the Rolling Stones, with Mick Jagger (a fan of the novella) as Alex, the rest of the group as his droogs, and Cooper as director.

In the event, the Rolling Stones could not find time in their schedule to make the film – a pity, since Anthony Burgess, no lover of pop music, remarked of Jagger that he 'admired the intelligence, if not that art, of this young man and considered that he looked the quintessence of delinquency' – and, although the film director Ken Russell took an interest in the project before deciding on *The Devils* (1971), his proposed adaptation, like Lierberson's and Cooper's, never materialised.

Instead, in late 1969, Kubrick called Southern, asking after the rights to *A Clockwork Orange*, having given up on his plans to make *Napoleon* and decided to follow the cinematic trend towards youth movies – *Easy Rider* having made $16 million from a $400,000 investment – by filming Burgess's novella. A deal was brokered in which

Litvinoff and Raab would give up the rights in return for $200,000, a 5 per cent profit share, and executive producer credits. In a deal with Warner Bros that was to last the rest of his professional life, the studio paid the $200,000 and agreed to a maximum budget of $2 million, based on the probability that *A Clockwork Orange* would almost certainly receive an 'X' rating in Britain and the US. Kubrick would be forced to cut corners.

Ignoring both Terry Southern's and Anthony Burgess's draft screenplays, Kubrick set about writing his own adaptation, using a computer – which, despite the murderous Hal in *2001*, he called 'one of man's most beautiful inventions' – to cut and paste scenes. Playfully emulating the author's experimental nature, he deliberately reversed the accepted screenwriting practice of having dialogue centred and description straight across the page, so that the descriptive elements read, according to the biographer Vincent LoBrutto, 'like a poem . . . so that the imagery captured the reader's eye'. In fact, although Kubrick's own first draft is dated 15 May 1970, the screenplay for *A Clockwork Orange* was largely created on location the following winter, as an uncredited Burgess recalled: 'The filming sessions were conducted like university seminars, in which my book was the text. "Page 59. How shall we do it?" A day of rehearsal, a single take at day's end, the typing up of the improvised dialogue, a script credit for Kubrick.'

Although costumes for *A Clockwork Orange* were designed by Milena Canonero, who would later receive an Oscar nomination for her awesome re-creations of seventeenth-century attire in *Barry Lyndon*, Alex's iconographic outfit is said to have resulted from a collaboration between Malcolm McDowell and Kubrick. The actor wore his own cricket whites, with a wicket-keeper's box (worn on the outside) doubling for the elaborate codpiece suggested by Burgess's novella, and chose a bowler from the various hats proferred by Kubrick. The iconographic eyelash evidently came from the fashionable sixties costumier Biba, which sold them by the yard. 'I bought this yard of it,' McDowell remembered, 'and took it to [Kubrick], and Stanley said, "Great, put it on." I put [it on one eye], and he photographed me, and then we put it on the other eye. We looked at the pictures, and he said, "Oh, it's great on one eye." They were so huge, really ridiculous. He loved that.'

Kubrick's chosen method of filming *A Clockwork Orange* – days of rehearsals, collaborative scriptwriting, and often frenzied bouts of shooting – coupled with the physical demands of many of the roles, made life painful for many of the actors. Malcolm McDowell arguably suffered the worst injuries, suffering cracked ribs (when the actor John Clive stamps on him during the public demonstration of Alex's new aversion to violence), a near-drowning (when breathing apparatus failed in the scene where Alex's head is held in a dirty horse trough for two minutes), and – most seriously of all – a pair of scratched corneas (during the scene in which Alex's 'glazzies' [eyes] are held open with 'lid-locks' for the Ludovico treatment).

Another incident occurred when, having been forced to take two weeks off sick with a throat infection contracted during the trough-dunking scene, McDowell had, on his first day back, to shoot a scene in which he was to be soaked, fully clothed, prior to entering the home of Mr Alexander and his nurse, Julian. 'So I got under the cold shower – there was no hot water – and I'm waiting outside the door,' McDowell recalled. 'I'm freezing; I'm wet. Then I opened the door and said, "What the fuck is going on?" And Stanley had gone off to look at another location and just left me there. I told him I thought he was a creep and sort of went nose-to-nose with him . . . We had another two months to go on the film, and it was never quite the same after that.' Adrienne Corri, who replaced the actress originally hired to play Mrs Alexander when she strained her stomach muscles during rehearsals, remarked later, 'At the end of the film, [Kubrick] said to me, "Thank you for being such a good sport." Because it had been tough, and I hadn't complained. I think that people who did complain didn't last long. But, if Stanley was considered difficult by other people, it was because Stanley wanted to get things right.'

**CASTING:** Malcolm McDowell had come to Kubrick's attention in Lindsay Anderson's social satire *If . . .* (1968), in which he had played a public-school boy who revolts against the system. Such was Kubrick's enthusiasm for the 28-year-old actor that he later commented, 'If McDowell hadn't been available, I probably wouldn't have made the film.' Kubrick's decision to cast someone twice the age of the character depicted in Burgess's novella might be said to have the same moralistic implications as his casting of fourteen-year-old Sue Lyon to play the twelve-year-old title role in *Lolita*; however, casting McDowell gives the character of Alex a more mature perspective – although he is still supposed to be young enough to attend 'schooly-wool', his acts of violence can no longer be put down to youthful exuberance and misguided morality. He is, one might say, old enough to know better – yet does his worst.

Other key cast members were found among Britain's best-known character actors, except for the bodybuilder David Prowse (cast in the role of Mr Alexander's nurse, Julian), who was spotted by Kubrick demonstrating exercise equipment in Harrods. Prowse's impressive physique would later provide the menacing Darth Vader with the physical presence George Lucas needed for the *Star Wars* trilogy – though his Somerset accent was overdubbed by James Earl Jones – and during the late seventies he was widely known throughout Britain as 'the Green Cross Code Man' in a series of road safety advertisements.

**THE USUAL SUSPECTS:** Although none of *A Clockwork Orange*'s cast members had worked with Kubrick before, several of his growing repertoire of technicians were hired to work on the film, among them the lighting cameraman, John Alcott (*2001*). In addition, the young sculptress Liz Jones, who had crafted the Star Child for *2001*, was commissioned by Kubrick to create the furniture for the Korova Milkbar in the style of the female-form-based sculptural furniture of the London pop artist Allen Jones, who had refused Kubrick's invitation to use the pieces in the film for a bit of free publicity.

## CLASSIC QUOTES

**Alex (VO):** 'There was me, that is Alex, and my three droogs, that is Pete, Georgie and Dim, and we sat in the Korova Milkbar trying to make up our razoodocks what to do with the evening. The Korova Milkbar sold Milk Plus, Milk Plus Vellocet, or Synthromesc or Drencrom, which is what we were drinking. This would sharpen you up and get you ready for a bit of the old ultraviolence . . .'

**Alex:** 'Viddy well, little brother, viddy well!'

**Dim:** 'Yarbles! Great bolshy yarblockos to you! I'll meet you with chain or nozh or britva anytime. Not having you hitting tolchoks to me reasonless. It stands to reason, I won't have it.'

**Alex:** 'I've been doing nothing I shouldn't, sir! The Millicents have nothing on me, brother. *Sir*, I mean.'

**Mr Deltoid:** 'Why all this clever talk about Millicents just because the police haven't picked you up lately? Doesn't as you very well know mean that you haven't been up to some nastiness. There was a bit of a nastiness last night, yes? Some very *extreme* nastiness, yes? A few of a certain Billyboy's friends were ambulanced off late, yes! Your name was mentioned, the words got through to me by the usual channels, certain friends of yours were named also. Oh, nobody can prove anything about anybody, as usual, and I'm warning you, little Alex, being a good friend to you as always, the one man in this sore and sick community who wants to save you from yourself!'

**Police officer:** 'Violence makes violence.'

**Alex (VO):** 'And the first thing that flashed into my gulliver was that I'd like to have her right down there on the floor with the old in-out, real savage.'

**Alex (VO):** 'I woke up, the pain and sickness all over me like an animal. Then I realised what it was: the music coming up from the floor was our old friend, Ludwig van, and the dreaded Ninth Symphony . . .'

**'NADSAT' GLOSSARY:** The following is a chronological lexicon of 'nadsat' terms used in Kubrick's *A Clockwork Orange*, giving origins where possible:

| | |
|---|---|
| droog/droogy | friend (from Russian *drug*) |
| rasoodock | mind (from Russian *rassudok*) |

| | |
|---|---|
| in-out-in-out | sexual intercourse (invented slang) |
| devotchka | girl (from Russian *devotchka*) |
| yarbles | testicles (invented slang) |
| horrorshow | good, splendid (from Russian *khorosh*) |
| guttiwuts | guts, innards (babytalk) |
| fillied | played (archaic) |
| viddy | look, watch, see (from Russian *vidyet*) |
| shagged and fagged and fashed | exhausted (English slang) |
| govoreet/govoreeting | talk/talking (from Russian *govorit*) |
| smecking | laughing (from Russian *smekh*) |
| malenky | little, small (from Russian *malyenkiyi*) |
| plott | flesh, body (from Russian *plot*) |
| bolshy | big (from Russian *bolshoy*) |
| yarblockos | testicles? (invented slang) |
| nozh | knife (from Russian *nozh*) |
| bitva | fight (from Russian *bitva*) |
| tolchock | hit (from Russian *tolchok*) |
| doobiedoob | good, OK (invented slang) |
| spatchka | sleep (from Russian *spat*) |
| slooshy/slooshied | listen/listened (from Russian *slushat*) |
| gulliver | head (from Russian *golova*) |
| chai | tea (from Russian *chai*) |
| millicent | policeman (from Russian *militsiya*) |
| rookers | hands (from Russian *ruka*) |
| moloko | milk (from Russian *moloko*) |
| appy polly loggies | apologies (invented slang) |
| shopcrasting | shoplifting (English + Russian *krast*) |
| malchick | boy (from Russian *malchik*) |
| pretty polly | money (rhyming slang for *lolly*) |
| crast | steal (from Russian *krast*) |
| gloopy | foolish, stupid (from Russian *glupiyi*) |
| bog | god (from Russian *bog*) |
| tashtook | handkerchief (from German *Taschentuch*) |
| krov/krovvy | blood/bloody (from Russian *krov*) |
| nochy | night (from Russian *noch*) |
| chelloveck | person, man (from Russian *chelovyek*) |
| ptitsa | bird (English slang, from Russian *ptitsa*) |
| soomka | bag (English slang, from Russian *sumka*) |
| slovo | word (from Russian *slovo*) |
| staja | State Jail (contraction) |
| prestoopniks | criminals (from Russian *prestupnik*) |
| rabbit | work (from Russian *rabota*) |
| yahoodies | Jew (from the Arabic) |
| vino | wine (from Russian *vino*) |
| sinny | movies, film (invented slang, from *cine*) |

| glazzies | eyes (from Russian *glaz*) |
| glazzballs | eyeballs (Russian *glaz* + English) |
| yahzick | tongue (from Russian *yazik*) |
| grazhny | dirty (from Russian *gryuzniyi*) |
| vonny | smelly (from Russian *von*) |
| pee and em | mother and father (from 'pa' and 'ma') |
| munchy-wunching | eating, munching (schoolboy slang) |
| lomticks | slices (from Russian *lomtik*) |
| maskies | masks (invented slang) |
| eggyweggs | eggs (invented slang) |
| steakywakes | steak (invented slang) |

**THEMES AND MOTIFS:** In some respects, Kubrick's depiction of women in *A Clockwork Orange* reveals a breast fixation that would make the film director Russ Meyer or the British comic Benny Hill proud. We are introduced to this mammarian obsession in the very first scene, in the form of the milk-dispensing 'groodies' of the Allen Jones-inspired statues of the Korova Milkbar. Subsequent evidence emerges with the breasts of the girl being attacked by Billyboy's gang; of the writer's wife assaulted by Alex and his droogies; of the females in Alex's biblical visions, and the Ludovico treatment; of the half-naked nurse caught in a tryst with Alex's doctor.

Nevertheless, for all the sexual imagery and full frontal female nudity on display in *A Clockwork Orange*, Kubrick's film version is powerfully homoerotic, from the drag-queen iconography of the false eyelashes, to the sexual advances made towards Alex by Deltoid (Aubrey Morris), the rectal examination made in prison by Michael Bates, and the humorous predilection the film seems to have with having characters reference, grab or injure each other's 'yarbles'. The film also features an extraordinary amount of phallic imagery – the snake crawling between the legs of the girl in Alex's picture; the penis-shaped popsicles sucked by the girls in the record store; the top of Alex's swordstick; the sculpture with which Alex kills the Catlady, etc.

In several senses, *A Clockwork Orange* reflected and reiterated the moral attitudes of *2001*, which cheerfully posited that man's savagery has changed little in three million years of evolution. 'After all,' Kubrick told *Newsweek*, 'man is the most remorseless killer who ever stalked the earth. Our interest in violence in part reflects the fact that on the subconscious level we are very little different from our primitive ancestors.'

**MUSIC:** The music of Beethoven was as crucial to the film version of *A Clockwork Orange* as it had been to the book, as Alex's devotion to his beloved 'Ludwig van' is inadvertently ruined by the aversion therapy, which cuts horrific footage to Beethoven's Ninth Symphony. Kubrick did not want to simply use classical recordings, so he commissioned the pop composer Walter (later, after a successful sex-change operation, Wendy) Carlos, co-inventor of the Moog synthesiser, to compose new electronic versions of the Ninth (the 'Choral'), Rossini's 'William Tell' overture and Purcell's 'Music on the Death of Queen Mary'.

Carlos came to the attention of Kubrick when the composer, who had been working on an electronic composition (*Timesteps*) inspired by Burgess's novella, sent Kubrick some tapes of the original work and a synthesised version of Beethoven's Ninth. Despite the fact that Carlos's *Switched-on Bach*, an album of synthesised Bach music, had been mostly reviled by music purists, Kubrick immediately fell under its spell. 'I think that his version of the fourth movement of Beethoven's "Ninth Symphony" rivals hearing a full orchestra playing it,' Kubrick enthused to Michael Ciment, 'and that is saying an awful lot.' In addition to Carlos's work, Kubrick also chose two pieces by the obscure New Age group Sunforest: the instrumental 'Overture to the Sun' and the pop curiosity 'I Want to Marry a Lighthouse Keeper'.

One stroke of aberrant genius was the use of the title song from MGM's much-loved musical *Singin' in the Rain* (1952), which Alex sings during the attack on Mr and Mrs Alexander. Kubrick tried to take credit for this discovery for himself. 'Suddenly the idea popped into my head,' he told *Sight and Sound*. 'I don't know where it came from or what triggered it off.' But it was spontaneously suggested by Malcolm McDowell when, while rehearsing the scene, Kubrick asked the actor if he knew any songs. McDowell admitted that 'Singin' in the Rain' was the only song he knew all of the words to, and rehearsals were duly halted while the pair drove back to Kubrick's home to check the availability of the rights to the song.

The soundtrack, first issued on vinyl in 1972 and widely available on a Warner Records CD (7599-27256-2), is an excellent compilation containing much of the music from the film, in chronological order. Only Alex's heartfelt but chilling rendition of 'Singin' in the Rain' seems to be missing – although the more traditional version sung by Gene Kelly is included.

A second album of *A Clockwork Orange* music, subtitled *Wendy Carlos's Complete Original Score*, was released on vinyl (KC 31480) by Columbia Records in 1972, and, in a slightly longer version, on enhanced CD (ESD 81362) by East Side Digital in 1998. This fascinating collection of music composed by Carlos and Rachel Elkind for Kubrick's film includes the full-length versions of *Timesteps* (13m 50s compared with the soundtrack album's 4m 13s excerpt) and the Second Movement (Scherzo) from Beethoven's Ninth Symphony (a little over one minute longer); a piece entitled 'Country Lane', written for the scene in which Alex is beaten by his former droogs; and a synthesised version of Rossini's 'The Thieving Magpie', which, according to the comprehensive sleeve notes, is as Carlos and Elkind would have performed it, 'had there been time'. The enhanced CD version also includes two further tracks which were written for the film, but ultimately left on the cutting-room floor. The first, 'Biblical Daydreams', was composed to underscore the images Alex fantasises while reading the Bible in the prison library; the second, written for the stage-bound scene in which a 'cured' Alex is shown to the press. In both cases, Kubrick chose to stick with his 'temp tracks', Rimsky-Korsakov's *Scheherazade* and 'Overture to the Sun' respectively.

Only one track ostensibly from *A Clockwork Orange*, the 'Ode to Joy' from Beethoven's Ninth, reinterpreted electronically by Mark Ayres, appears on Silva Screen Records' compilation album, *Dr Strangelove . . . Music from the Films of Stanley Kubrick* (FILMCD 303).

**POSTER:** The iconographic poster design for *A Clockwork Orange* – featuring a smiling Alex brandishing his 'nozh' and a tasteful adaptation of one of the drink dispensers from the Korova Milkbar, both contained within the brilliantly stylised 'A' of the title – was only one of the images used to promote *A Clockwork Orange*. The artist Phil Castle's airbrushed designs also showed Alex with false teeth in a glass, Alex with a glass of milk, and Alex accompanied by his droogs.

**TAG-LINES:** 'What has Stanley Kubrick been up to?' asked the first of the tag-lines to appear on the earliest posters for *A Clockwork Orange*, recalling the equally rhetorical 'How did they ever make a movie of *Lolita*?' The best-known tag-line, however, remains the later one: 'Being the adventures of a young man whose principal interests are rape, ultra-violence and Beethoven.'

**TRAILER:** Cut to the same accelerated version of the 'William Tell' overture as the scene in which Alex takes the two young *devotchkas* home and has his wicked way with them, and strongly reminiscent of his earlier *Dr Strangelove* trailer treatment, Kubrick's own sixty-second trailer for *A Clockwork Orange* consisted of a high-speed montage of still images, stock footage, captions and shots from the film. The countless images on display include many stylised close-ups of the poster illustration, Nazis on parade, shots of Alex, Dim, Georgie, Pete, Billyboy, Mr and Mrs Alexander, the prison guard, the vagrant and his elderly friends, the Catlady, the record-store *devotchkas*, two policemen, Dr Branom, Dr Brodsky, the Minister of the Interior, Julian, Alex's parents, the tramp and his elderly friends, the Christ statue's hand, some of the Ludovico footage, lava floes erupting, the Catlady's paintings, a hypodermic needle, the record-store chart display, a shot of a masked Alex disappearing and reappearing from a frame in the Alexanders' home, Billyboy's gang, Alex and his droogs standing on the moon's surface, lightning, explosions, Alex undergoing the Ludovico treatment, Alex's snake, and a series of intercut captions: 'WITTY'; 'FUNNY'; 'MUSICAL'; 'SATIRIC'; 'EXCITING'; 'BIZARRE'; 'POLITICAL'; 'THRILLING'; 'FRIGHTENING';

'METAPHORICAL'; 'COMIC'; 'SARDONIC'; 'BEETHOVEN'; 'FROM WARNER BROS. A KINNEY COMPANY'; and the title 'STANLEY KUBRICK'S CLOCKWORK ORANGE' – all on a variety of coloured backgrounds.

**WHAT THE PAPERS SAID:** If anything, *A Clockwork Orange* divided critics even more sharply than *2001*. The response in New York was typical of the polarisation that occurred across the rest of the country: although the city's critics would later vote *A Clockwork Orange* Best Film and Kubrick Best Director at their annual awards, the *Village Voice* described the film as 'a painless, bloodless, and ultimately pointless futuristic fantasy' even as the *New York Times* called it 'brilliant, a tour de force of extraordinary images, music, words and feelings . . . so beautiful to look at and to hear that it dazzles the senses and the mind even as it turns the old real red vino to ice'. Tipping the scales in favour of the 'nays', the *New Yorker*'s influential critic Pauline Kael was withering in her distaste for the film: 'Literal-minded in its sex and brutality, Teutonic in its humor, Stanley Kubrick's *A Clockwork Orange* might be the work of a strict and exacting German professor who set out to make a porno-violent sci-fi comedy . . . When night after night atrocities are served up to us as entertainment, it's worth some anxiety. We become clockwork oranges if we accept all this pop culture without asking what's in it. How can people go on talking about the dazzling brilliance of movies and not notice that the directors are sucking up to the thugs in the audience?'

In the United Kingdom, *Time Out* echoed Kael's view, calling *A Clockwork Orange* 'a sexless, inhuman film, whose power derives from a ruthless subordination of its content to the demands of telling a good story. A glossy, action-packed ritual which is fun to watch but superficial to think about.' *Monthly Film Bulletin* thought it to be Kubrick's 'most cynical and disturbing film to date . . . by the time Alex regains consciousness in his hospital bed, Kubrick has us rooting for him to resume his thuggery – the only way left to us or him of saying no to this dehumanised society.' Derek Malcolm's review in the *Guardian* arguably captured what would become the long-term view of *A Clockwork Orange*, claiming the film as a 'chilling and mesmeric adaptation of the Anthony Burgess novel which could well become one of the seminal movies of the seventies'.

**CONTROVERSY:** Although it was greeted as a valid and highly moral social satire in the United States, where it was passed without cuts by the MPAA – albeit with a prohibitive 'X' rating – *A Clockwork Orange* began to attract controversy as soon as it hit Kubrick's adopted home. Although it was passed uncut in the United Kingdom by the incumbent British film censor Stephen Murphy, following the former censor John Trevelyan's assertion that the film was a 'brilliant piece of cinematic art . . . [which] presents an intellectual argument rather than a sadistic spectacle', within two weeks of its British release on 13 January 1972, right-wing newspapers and tub-thumping MPs were baying for the film to be banned before copycat violence could spread among the nation's impressionable youth. Under a headline that read 'CLOCKWORK ORANGES ARE TICKING BOMBS', the *Evening News* predicted that the film would 'lead to a clockwork cult which will magnify teen violence'. Burgess himself witnessed the apparent validity of these reactionary reports at a screening in New York, which he described as 'really quite frightening, because the cinema was full of blacks standing up and shouting "Right on, man!" because they refused to see anything beyond a glorification of violence'.

For most of 1972, newspapers continued to blame *A Clockwork Orange* as the incitement to copycat crimes, though evidence was usually flimsy at best: the rape of a nun in Poughkeepsie, New York state, was blamed on the film, although it later transpired that the perpetrators had never seen it; unfortunately, no witnesses were able to corroborate the claims of a seventeen-year-old Dutch girl raped in Lancashire by a gang who allegedly sang 'Singin' in the Rain'; the *Daily Mail*'s claims that a tramp was kicked to death by a '*Clockwork Orange* gang' were based on the premise that the film had closed in the area the previous day, and that some local youths had been seen buying the clothes and make-up worn in the film. ('If they dressed like Alex,' scoffed McDowell in response, 'the police would know where to find them. I mean, in a codpiece and a bowler?')

'Because *A Clockwork Orange* played with the background of England, they blamed every crime in history on Stanley's film,' Christiane, Kubrick's widow, told *Sight and Sound*'s Nick James shortly after the director's death. And Kubrick's daughter, Anya Finney, added, 'There was a concentrated group of journalists who spotted a way to spin a story. Instead of "THUG BEATS UP OLD LADY", it was "CLOCKWORK THUG BEATS UP OLD LADY". Thug was going to beat up old lady anyway, and you're going to report it anyway, but now you get to call him a Clockwork Thug.' The number of violent actions attributed to the film grew, creating a contemporary equivalent of the gangster and Western movies blamed for incitement to crime half a century earlier. *A Clockwork Orange* became a scapegoat for society's ills, in much the same way as later films such as *Natural Born Killer*, *Child's Play* and *Scream*.

Kubrick was, nonetheless, watching the situation closely. 'The simplistic notion that films and TV can transform an otherwise innocent and good person into a criminal has strong overtones of the Salem trials,' he commented. 'Stanley was very insulted by the reaction, and hurt,' Kubrick's widow, Christiane, recalled. 'Both artistically hurt, and scared,' she added, referring to the real reason why Kubrick withdrew his own film from its UK release: not as a result of the crimes blamed on his film, but because of threats received by Kubrick and his family. 'He didn't want to be misunderstood and misinterpreted, [but] you also don't like to get death threats for your family and for everybody.' The threats stopped as soon as the film had been withdrawn.

In fact, A Clockwork Orange had already come to the end of its lucrative ($3 million) British theatrical run when, in early 1974, Kubrick and Warner Bros quietly withdrew it from circulation, refusing to allow it to be shown under any circumstances – not even at a 1979 retrospective of the cameraman John Alcott's work, nor for a Malcolm McDowell retrospective held in Russia to benefit the victims of the Chernobyl disaster. The fact that the director and distributor, not the BBFC, had withdrawn the film meant that not even schools' and colleges' film-study groups or the members-only cinemas granted special dispensation to show BBFC-banned films were permitted to show the film. Thus, Kubrick's self-imposed ban became the most effective censorship of a film in British history – a position counter to the anti-censorship views the director would otherwise assert at every available opportunity.

The legal position of this ban was tested in 1992 when Jane Giles, the programme director of London's Scala Cinema – one of three permitted to show the films banned by the BBFC – was fined £1,000 for breach of copyright after hosting a screening, which the Federation Against Copyright Theft claimed breached Warner Brothers' copyright. Despite the cinema's fundraising efforts – which included selling T-shirts featuring the cinema's resident cat wearing an eyelash similar to Alex's – the Scala closed down for ever as a result of Kubrick's action. This was hardly the best press a respected film maker could create for himself. The following year, Warner Brothers, at Kubrick's behest, unsuccessfully tried to prevent the British television network Channel 4 from including twelve minutes' worth of clips of A Clockwork Orange as part of Forbidden Fruit, a documentary series about censorship; although an injuction – based on the fact that the programme makers had breached copyright by transferring the scenes they intended to use from an American laserdisc – was granted, it was overturned by the Court of Appeal, and the programme aired in appropriately uncut form on 5 October 1993. Clips have since appeared in numerous documentaries.

Although A Clockwork Orange remained in this bizarre distribution limbo at the time of Kubrick's death in March 1999, rumours soon began to circulate that Warner Brothers was planning a theatrical re-release. 'It's up to Warner Brothers – we don't have any say in that,' Christiane, Kubrick's widow, told Sight and Sound's Nick James in September 1999. 'It's not exactly high on the list of things to worry about right now,' Kubrick's daughter, Anya Finney, added. 'I would say we haven't thought about it.' Nevertheless, in late 1999, Warner Brothers began running the trailer for A Clockwork Orange, effectively announcing that the film was to be theatrically re-released. 'Two or three years ago, I started talking to Stanley and saying that things had changed,' Kubrick's friend, the Warner Brothers executive Julian Senior, told *Empire* magazine. 'He said we should talk about it, but then *Eyes Wide Shut* started gobbling up twenty-three hours a day.' After more than a quarter of a century's absence, and almost on the anniversary of Kubrick's death, *A Clockwork Orange* received a major, 250 print re-release on 17 March 2000.

**BOX OFFICE:** *A Clockwork Orange* was premiered in New York just before Christmas 1971, deliberately timed to qualify for the following year's Oscars. Made for a modest $2 million, 10 per cent of which was paid for the screen rights to the novella, *A Clockwork Orange* earned an impressive $15.4 million worldwide. Under his new deal with Warner Bros, Kubrick would receive a full 40 per cent of the profits, and its executive producers Si Litvinoff and Max Raab a further 5 per cent. Burgess, however, would be forced to sue for his rightful share, issuing a lawsuit, dated 9 May 1973, claiming 'conspiracy to defraud'; as he noted later, 'the production company that had originally bought the rights for a few hundred dollars did not consider that I had a claim to part of their own profit when they sold those rights to Warner Brothers. That profit was, of course, considerable . . .' The studio eventually settled out of court, assigning Burgess a minute percentage of the film's net income, which – thanks to Hollywood's arcane accounting practices – would turn out to be far less than the $200,000-plus paid to Litvinoff and Raab, although the film's popularity and/or notoriety belatedly turned Burgess's book into a bestseller.

**AWARDS:** *A Clockwork Orange* was nominated for four Academy Awards: Best Picture, Best Director, Best Writing (Screenplay Based on Material from Another Medium) and Best Film Editing. Although Kubrick, as producer, director and credited screenwriter, might have won awards in three of the four categories, the film came away empty-handed. Some small consolation came when William Friedkin, who took Best Picture and Best Director for *The French Connection* (1971), later told journalists, 'I think Stanley Kubrick is the best American film maker of the year. In fact, not just this year, but the best – period.'

Despite his virtuoso performance, Malcolm McDowell's only recognition came at the 1972 Golden Globe awards, where he was nominated for Best Actor (Drama), along with Best Director (Motion Picture) for Kubrick, and Best Motion Picture (Drama). The following year, at the British Academy of Film and Television Arts (BAFTA) awards, *A Clockwork Orange*'s almost exclusively British technicians were widely recognised, as the film was nominated in seven categories: Best Film, Best Direction, Best Screenplay, Best Cinematography, Best Art Direction, Best Film Editing and Best Soundtrack. At both events, the film came away empty-handed. *A Clockwork Orange* did, however, add to its honours when the New York Film Critics' Circle gave it a Hugo Award for Best Dramatic Presentation.

**TECHNICAL ACHIEVEMENTS:** In an effort to duplicate cinematically Burgess's stylisation of the sex and violence in *A Clockwork Orange*, Kubrick used such techniques as slow-motion and high-speed – and a great deal of musical juxtaposition – to make the film's most graphic scenes less explicit, but no less shocking. 'I wanted to find a way to stylize all this violence and also to make it as balletic as possible,' he told Joseph Gelmis. 'The speeded-up orgy sequence is a joke. That scene took about twenty-eight minutes to shoot at two frames a second. It lasts on screen about forty seconds. Alex's fight with his droogs would have lasted about fourteen seconds, if it wasn't in slow motion. I wanted to slow it to a lovely floating movement.'

The relatively small budget on which *A Clockwork Orange* was made deprived Kubrick of the opportunity to explore and utilise many of the technological advances in film making, as he had with *2001*, and would again. Although an innovative fixed-lens camera with which the cinematographer Haskell Wexler had shot *Medium Cool* – a short film about a news cameraman who becomes desensitised to violence – was used extensively for low-light photography, the major technical innovations of *A Clockwork Orange* were in the sound department. Not only was it the first film to use Dolby noise reduction on all aspects of the post-production process, it was also filmed without any post-synchronisation of dialogue – in other words, the actors were recorded live on location with tiny hidden microphones, precluding the need for a lengthy re-recording or 'looping' process, and giving the dialogue a more immediate feel.

*A Clockwork Orange* was also the film for which Kubrick pioneered his use of a modified wheelchair to capture smooth low-angle tracking shots in tight corners (such as Alex's stroll through the record store and, later, the minister's tour of the prison), and also marked the adoption of the 1.66:1 shooting ratio ('widescreen') which – following what he saw as the bowdlerisation of *2001* by the 'pan-and-scan' process used for television transmission – he would continue to use for *Barry Lyndon*, *The Shining* and *Full Metal Jacket*.

**INFLUENCED BY:** In a 1999 article for *Sight and Sound* entitled 'Real Horrorshow: A Short Lexicon of Nadsat', Kevin Jackson suggested a most unusual influence on Kubrick's *A Clockwork Orange*. 'Every character save Alex is a caricature worthy, at best, of '70s sitcom (Alex's pathetic "pee" and "em" – the em plainly too far gone in years to be his biological mother – would not look out of place in *Are You Being Served?*). Example: in the novel, Alex's correctional advisor, Mr Deltoid, is quite enough of a pompous fool for anyone's comic gratification. Kubrick, obedient to the aesthetic principle that if a thing's worth doing it's worth overdoing, not only makes Deltoid a crotch-grabbing, predatory homosexual but rounds off his big scene with a punchline about accidentally drinking from a dentures glass. In his lengthiest addition to the book,' Jackson noted further, 'Kubrick films Alex's induction to prison in wearisomely complete detail, delighting in showing what a jumped-up, anally retentive berk the warden is: *Porridge*, in other words, without Ronnie Barker to humanise the poor wit. (The novel, far swifter, just jumps forward a couple of years.) It's almost a textbook example of how to milk a feeble joke until it's stone dead.'

DÉJÀ VU: Although Kubrick employed his trademark 'pull back from close-up to wide shot' to open the first three sequences of the film, Kubrick himself pointed out one of the thematic similarities between *A Clockwork Orange* and his own earlier film, *Dr Strangelove*. 'The government eventually resorts to the employment of the cruellest and most violent members of the society to control everyone else – not an altogether new or untried idea,' he told Michael Ciment. 'In this sense, Alex's last line – "I was cured all right" – might be seen in the same light as Dr Strangelove's exit line, "Mein Führer, I can walk." The final images of Alex as the spoon-fed child of a corrupt, totalitarian society, and Strangelove's rebirth after his miraculous recovery from a crippling disease, seem to work well both dramatically and as expressions of an idea.'

Two more explicit references to Kubrick's earlier films appear in *A Clockwork Orange*. The first is a clearly visible soundtrack album of the music from *2001* – which had, by 1971, enjoyed top ten success – prominently displayed in the record shop visited by Alex. The second is the experimental serum with which Alex is injected during the Ludovico treatment, which is labelled 'Exp./serum no. 114' – a reference to 'CRM 114', the *Leper Colony*'s communications device in *Dr Strangelove*.

INFLUENTIAL ON: In the 1996 documentary *Stanley Kubrick: The Invisible Man*, the film director Brian Singer (*The Usual Suspects*) explained the influence of *A Clockwork Orange* on his own film about a malevolent teenager: *Apt Pupil* (1998), based on a novella by the author of *The Shining*, Stephen King. 'I was actually a film student when I first saw [*A Clockwork Orange*] on videotape,' he recalled, 'and eventually later saw it in the theatre and discovered even more that I had missed before. And I discovered that you could actually get away with moving the camera slowly, revealing things slowly with a zoom, or with a dolly, and having it still be continually interesting.'

In 1974, some years before Ronald Reagan would appropriate the title of George Lucas's *Star Wars* (1977) for his satellite weapons programme, Senator John Reed of Arizona introduced proposed legislation designed to protect prison inmates who volunteered for experimental therapy programmes in order to reduce or commute their sentences. Perhaps unsurprisingly, it became popularly known as 'the *Clockwork Orange* bill'.

After the fantasy sequences in which Alex sees himself as a Roman centurion, lashing out at Christ with his whip, and relaxing with his wife's handmaidens, Malcolm McDowell would go on to play a more lascivious Roman in an even more controversial film, *Caligula* (1980).

**SEQUELS AND REMAKES:** The first screen adaptation of *A Clockwork Orange* came in May 1962, almost a decade before Kubrick's, as the producers of the BBC's current-affairs programme *Tonight* dramatised portions of the first chapter – very effectively, according to Burgess – to accompany an interview with the author by Derek Hart. The programme can no longer be found in the BBC's archive.

After the film's release, and the vicarious notoriety that Burgess suffered in its wake, the author inserted a couple of digs at Kubrick into his subsequent works. One example appears in a novella entitled *A Clockwork Testament or Enderby's End*, circa 1973, in which Burgess's long-term alter ego, FX Enderby, becomes embroiled in a media circus following the scandalous reception to his screenplay based on Gerard Manley Hopkins's *Wreck of the Deutschland*. Another, more obvious, example appears in Burgess's own, partly musical adaptation of *A Clockwork Orange*, intended for production by amateur theatre groups: on the last page of the published text is the following stage direction: 'A man bearded like Stanley Kubrick comes on playing, in exquisite counterpoint, "Singin' in the Rain" on a trumpet. He is kicked off the stage.'

Three years later, the play formed the basis of a far grander enterprise when Burgess revised it for a Royal Shakespeare Company production, directed by Ron Daniels under the title *A Clockwork Orange 2004*. The cockney actor Phil Daniels, who had played an equally troubled youth in The Who's film *Quadrophenia* (1979), played the role of Alex in the successful adaptation, which featured music by Bono and the Edge from the rock band U2. A single recording from the production, 'Alex descends into hell for a bottle of milk/korova 1', was released as an additional track on the CD single for U2's 1991 single 'The Fly' (CID 500).

Eight years later, in 1998, BBC Radio 4 produced a full-cast dramatisation of the novella, directed by Alison Hindell and featuring Jason Hughes (*Alex*), Struan Rodger (*Dr Brodsky*), John McArdle (*Chaplain*), Jack Davenport (*Minister*), Bill Stewart (*Alexander*), Clare Isaac (*Dr Branom*), Dorien Thomas (*Mr Deltoid*), Rhodri Hugh (*Dim*), Robert Harper (*Pete*), Wayne Forester (*Georgie*), Jennifer Hill (*Old Lady*) and Aimee Thomas (*Marty*), and music by John Hardy. A recording of the ninety-minute drama, based on Burgess's unpublished original manuscript of the novella, is available from BBC Worldwide (ZBBC 2122). The same year saw the release of an audiobook version of the unabridged novella, read by Phil Daniels and released on the 'Cult Listening' label on four cassettes (5584904).

**KUBRICK GOES POP:** The eighties British pop group Heaven 17 – whose hits included 'Crushed by the Wheels of Industry', '(We Don't Need This) Fascist Groove Thang' and 'Temptation' – were named after one of the popular groups mentioned by the record-store *devotchkas* while Alex is browsing for Beethoven. David Bowie, who had referenced Kubrick's most recent film in his hit song 'Space Oddity', managed to inveigle the *nadsat* word *droogie* into 'Sufragette City'. Most recently, Damon Albarn and the other members of the Britpop group Blur dressed up as droogs – complete with white tunics, black boots and a single eyelash – for the video made to accompany the single 'The Universal'.

*The Simpsons* is replete with a number of references to *A Clockwork Orange*. In one of the annual Hallowe'en specials, 'Treehouse of Horror III' (#9F04), Bart Simpson goes out to play 'trick or treat' dressed in the unmistakable 'uniform' of Alex DeLarge. In another *Simpsons* episode, 'Dog of Death' (#8F17), the family dog is subjected to Ludovico-style brainwashing in which it is strapped into a chair, eyes pried open, and forced to watch films of man's inhumanity to dogs. A further *Simpsons* reference to the Ludovico treatment appears in 'Duffless' (#9F14), in which Bart, having undergone reflex conditioning as part of his sister's science project, is seen reaching for two cherry-topped cup cakes in a scene that mischievously resembles the Ludovico-altered Alex reaching for the breasts of a semi-naked actress, but unable to touch them. Finally, an episode entitled 'Homer the Smithers' (#3F14) concludes with Homer lying injured in a hospital bed, à la Alex, being fed by his boss's obsequious assistant, Smithers.

References to the Ludovico technique appear in *Sleeper* (1973), in which Woody Allen's brain is 'reprogrammed' in a style similar to that of Kubrick's film. In Joel and Ethan Coen's *Fargo* (1996), Carl (Steve Buscemi) refers to 'a little of the ol' in-and-out', the same sexual slang used by Alex. In Richard Donner's *Conspiracy Theory* (1997), Jerry Fletcher (Mel Gibson) undergoes interrogation by CIA spooks who tape his eyes open and inject him, in a scene reminiscent of the Ludovico technique. There are subtle references to *A Clockwork Orange* in David Fincher's *Fight Club* (1999), in which Tyler Durden (Brad Pitt) knocks a penis-shaped statue which rocks like the sculpture in the Catlady's apartment; and in Kevin Smith's *Dogma* (1999), in which a homeless man hums Beethoven's Ninth Symphony before being attacked by three evil boys with hockey sticks – one of whom glares malevolently, just like Alex. And can any Kubrick fan have missed Ali G asking the BBFC director James Ferman, 'Why did they ban Chocolate Orange?'

**CUT SCENES:** Although several important elements of the book never make it into Kubrick's shooting script – most notably the scene in which an imprisoned Alex kills a fellow prisoner who makes sexual advances towards him – there was a whole *chapter* of the book of which Kubrick was not even aware until he was four months into the shooting of the film, since he was using the American edition as the basis for his adaptation, and had no idea that an additional final chapter existed in the British version. This 'happy ending', added at the request of Burgess's editors at Heinemann, sees a 'cured' Alex back on the streets with a new gang, free to choose his own destiny, but discovering that he no longer has the urge to destroy; instead, he decides to seek a mate with whom to settle down and have a family of his own. The American edition dropped the less ambiguous ending, as did Kubrick, who felt it was 'unconvincing and inconsistent with the style and intent of the book'.

Just before Christmas 1973, a new version of *A Clockwork Orange* was theatrically released in the US, replacing approximately 31 seconds of footage in the high-speed *ménage à trois* scene in Alex's bedroom, and the gang-rape shown in the Ludovico films that formed part of the aversion therapy, and thus being granted an 'R' rating to replace the original 'X'. For all of Kubrick's complaints against the would-be censorship or censure of the film, commercial considerations ultimately led him to recut it himself, to allow it to be seen by a wider audience – including the one at home, on television.

**TRIVIA:** The caveman sequence in Alex's Beethoven-inspired daydreams is a clip from the Raquel Welch film *One Million Years B.C.* (1966), which Kubrick used, along with specially filmed 'Hollywood-ised' re-creations of a Roman epic (not unlike Kubrick's own *Spartacus*), because he felt that '[Alex] would imagine things he had seen in films'. According to Kubrick, this is why Malcolm McDowell, as a Roman legionnaire, says 'Move along there' in an American accent – a sly reference to Hollywood's unabashed Americanisation of historical events.

The fact that Kubrick insisted that the sculptured female forms that served drinks in the Korova Milkbar be stocked with real milk meant that they had to be drained and refilled every hour – otherwise the milk started to turn under the hot camera lights.

The largest of the paintings visible in the home of the Alexanders was a canvas entitled *Seedboxes*, measuring five feet by ten feet, and painted by Kubrick's wife, Christiane.

**APOCRYPHA:** One of the best-known apocryphal stories that surround the making of *A Clockwork Orange* was the method by which Kubrick filmed the point-of-view shot of Alex leaping from Mr Alexander's window in his unsuccessful suicide attempt. As is often reported, Kubrick did throw a polystyrene-encased Newman Sinclair camera (appropriately enough, one powered by clockwork) from a roof – or, rather, he asked the strongman David Prowse to do it for him – but, although Prowse insists they 'only did it once because the [protective casing] smashed and the camera smashed to pieces', Kubrick told Michael Ciment another version: 'In order to get it to land lens first, we had to do this six times and the camera survived all six drops. On the final one it landed right on the lens and smashed it but it didn't do a bit of harm to the camera . . . On this basis,' he added, 'I would say that the Newman Sinclair must be the most indestructible camera ever made.'

**AVAILABILITY:** Unavailable for many years in the United Kingdom at the insistence of Kubrick himself (see above), A *Clockwork Orange* is widely available in English-language versions – usually with foreign-language subtitles, but often without – throughout Europe, and is said to be the video title most often imported to Britain from mainland Europe. In the United States, the modified version of the film (see above) is available on NTSC laserdisc (Warner Home Video 12251), VHS (WA 17367) and Region 1 DVD (17367), which also contains the theatrical trailer.

**EXPERT WITNESS:** 'He showed me this picture of this patient, and I said, "My God, you're not expecting me to do this, are you?" And he went, "Oh, it'll be fine, Malc, fine. We've got a doctor from Moorfields Eye Hospital there." Well, of course this is for delicate eye operations – normally the patient is on their back. There am I, sitting up, in a straitjacket, tied down, and they anaesthetise the eye and put these things in, and of course I couldn't feel a thing – just uncomfortable, really. I just wanted to get the scene over as fast as possible. Stanley doesn't like me to say this, but, it's true: he said to the doctor, "Just say, 'How are you today, little Alex?'" He had this bottle of artifical teardrops which had to be put into the eyes otherwise the corneas dry out and you're blind. So he's going, "What's your name again?" And I said, "Jeez, Doc, don't worry about it – the line is 'How are you today, little Alex?' But get the drops in, don't worry about the line!" All he was worried about was this line of dialogue, and I'm worried about my going blind! I go home; the anaesthetic wears off; I feel I've been cut open by razor blades. I'm in so much pain, the doctor has to come over and give me a shot of morphine, because both corneas were scratched. [The next day] I've got a big bandage around my eye, and I see Stanley, and he goes, "Oh my God – well, can we shoot on this eye?"' – actor Malcolm McDowell (Alex), quoted in the documentary *Stanley Kubrick: The Invisible Man*, 1996.

**FINAL ANALYSIS:** Growing up in England gives one a unique perspective on A *Clockwork Orange*. The film had already been unavailable for a decade by the time I was old enough to legally see it; signs that read 'NO, WE DON'T HAVE A CLOCKWORK ORANGE' were a frequent

Above: *2001: A Space
Odyssey* – 'Let's say we
put the unit back and it
doesn't fail, huh? That
would pretty well wrap it
up as far as Hal is
concerned …'
(© Turner Entertainment Co.)

Right: Frank Poole (Gary
Lockwood) about to go
to his death in *2001*
(© Turner Entertainment Co.)

Above: *A Clockwork Orange* – 'This would sharpen you up and get you ready for a bit of the old ultraviolence.' (© Warner Bros.)

Below: Alex (Malcolm McDowell) and his droogs try to make up their razoodocks what to do with the evening (© Warner Bros.)

Above: British *A Clockwork Orange* poster (© Warner Bros.)

Below: British *Barry Lyndon* poster (© Warner Bros.)

Above: *Barry Lyndon* – 'Mightn't I at least be allowed to keep me horse?'
(© Warner Bros.)

Above: 'He wants to step into my shoes!'
(© Warner Bros.)

Above: Jack Nicholson and Stanley
Kubrick share a joke on the set of *The
Shining* (© Warner Bros.)

Right: Heeeere's Johnny!
(© Warner Bros.)

Below: 'I never laid a hand on him,
goddamnit!' (© Warner Bros.)

*Left: Full Metal Jacket – Gunnery Sergeant Hartman (© Warner Bros.)*

*Right: Full Metal Jacket poster (© Warner Bros.)*

*Below left: '7.62mm full … metal … jacket.' (© Warner Bros.)*

*Below right: 'I am in a world of shit, yes. But I am alive. And I am not afraid.' (© Warner Bros.)*

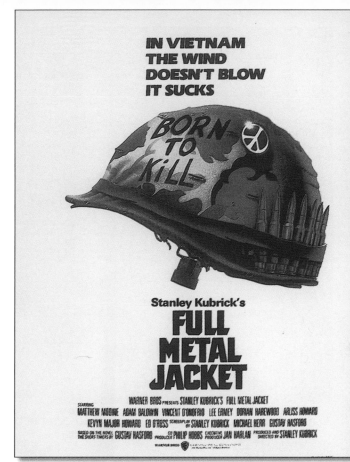

Above: Alice (Nicole Kidman) in *Eyes Wide Shut* (© Warner Bros.)

Above: 'Why don't you tell me the rest of it?'
'It's ... it's too awful.'
'It's only a dream.' (© Warner Bros.)

KUBRICK A Clockwork Orange

sight in video-shop windows – though, of course, many a seventh-generation copy languished under counters. To me, the film was as strange and unknowable as the eponymous object itself – a clockwork orange? Was it anything to do with *I Am Curious Orange*? Or a Terry's Chocolate Orange?

When the Scala Cinema in North London was fined and then shut down for showing the film, I missed the screening, but subsequently bought the T-shirt – which pictured the cinema's cat with an Alex eyelash – in support of their legal battle. They lost; the cinema closed down; I still have the shirt (watch for it on eBay someday). I finally got to see the film around 1990, during a large-scale cinema re-release in Paris, a perfect print in the *version originale*, with English *sous-titres*. (Kubrick may have been amused to know that I shared the cinema with a lone Frenchman in a dirty raincoat.) Despite the legend that had built up around it, British cinema's most epicurean forbidden fruit did not disappoint, retaining its power to shock after two decades.

Readers outside the United Kingdom may find all this somewhat preposterous, given that *A Clockwork Orange* is essentially a devilish satire no more likely to incite riots, provoke civil unrest or tear the moral fabric of society apart than a Bukowski reading or a Black Flag gig. Kubrick may have believed he had very real reasons for withdrawing the film in his adopted country, but the longer a 'ban' is in place, the more fanfare greets its end – Kubrick apparently did not want to be around when the tabloids renewed their attack on the film in this increasingly violent age. Burgess was inspired to write his cathartic book after his wife was attacked in their home; Kubrick, typing away in his own country retreat with his artist wife, may have felt that the character of Mr Alexander was literally too close to home to laugh off the bad press, hate mail and death threats that followed the release of *A Clockwork Orange*. England, it seemed, had missed the point of the film. Perhaps this was the price of making a violent film about violence, a sexual film about sex crimes, and – like *Dr Strangelove* – a comedy about a serious subject.

Yet, despite the film's reputation for social irresponsibility and moral ambiguity, it is clearly a warning about the social and moral implications of artificial suppression of violent and sexual tendencies, of turning criminals into organisms with mechanical responses, like clockwork oranges, instead of moral education, rehabilitation and, if necessary, incarceration. No one, least of all Kubrick or Burgess, would suggest that the Alexes of the world should be allowed to run riot, like creatures from the id cut loose without conscience. But, as both the book and the film clearly demonstrate, if human beings are deprived of the ability to choose evil, can they truly be said to be good? Of course not – the idea is as preposterous as claiming that a film might incite or encourage the kind of violence it set out to condemn.

KUBRICK ON KUBRICK: 'I have always found it difficult to understand how anyone could decide that the film presented violence sympathetically. I can only explain this as a view which arises from a prejudiced assessment of the film, ignoring everything else in the story but a few scenes. The distinguished film director Luis Buñuel suggested this in a way when he said in the *New York Times*: "*A Clockwork Orange* is my current favorite. I was very predisposed against the film. After seeing it, I realized it is the only movie about what the modern world really means." *A Clockwork Orange* has been widely acclaimed throughout the world as an important work of art. I don't believe that anyone really sympathizes with Alex, and there is absolutely no evidence that anyone does. Alex clashes with some authority figures in the story who seem as bad as he is, if not worse in a different way. But this doesn't excuse him. The story is satirical, and it is in the nature of satire to state the opposite of the truth as if it were the truth. I suppose you could misinterpret the film on this count, if you were determined to do so.' – quoted in *The Film Director as Superstar* by Michael Ciment, 1980.

# Barry Lyndon (1975)

(Colour – 184 mins)

Written for the Screen, Produced and Directed by Stanley Kubrick
Based on the Novel by William Makepeace Thackeray
Music Adapted and Conducted by Leonard Rosenman from Works by Johann Sebastian Bach, Frederick The Great, Georg Friedrich Handel, Wolfgang Amadeus Mozart, Giovanni Paisiello, Franz Schubert, Antonio Vivaldi
Irish Traditional Music by The Chieftains
Executive Producer Jan Harlan
Associate Producer Bernard Williams
Production Designer Ken Adam
Photographed by John Alcott
Costumes Designed by Ulla-Britt Søderland, Milena Canonero
Editor Tony Lawson
Hairstyles and Wigs Leonard
Art Director Roy Walker
Assistant to the Producer Andros Epaminondas
Assistant Director Brian Cook

CAST: Ryan O'Neal (*Barry Lyndon*), Marisa Berenson (*Countess Lyndon*), Patrick Magee (*Chevalier du Baillebarry*), Hardy Krüger (*Captain Potzdorf*), Steven Berkoff (*Lord Ludd*), Gay Hamilton (*Nora Brady*), Marie Kean (*Barry's Mother*), Diana Koerner (*German Girl*), Murray Melvin (*Reverend Samuel Runt*), Frank Middlemass (*Sir Charles*

*Reginald Lyndon*), André Morell (*Neville, 13th Earl of Wendover*), Arthur O'Sullivan (*Captain Feeney/Highwayman*), Godfrey Quigley (*Captain Jack Grogan*), Leonard Rossiter (*Captain John Quin*), Philip Stone (*Graham*), Leon Vitali (*Lord Bullingdon*), Michael Hordern (*Narrator*), Dominic Savage (*Young Lord Bullingdon*), David Morley (*Bryan Patrick Lyndon*), John Bindon, Roger Booth, Billy Boyle, Jonathan Cecil, Peter Cellier, Geoffrey Chater, Anthony Dawes, Patrick Dawson, Bernard Hepton, Anthony Herrick, Barry Jackson, Wolf Kahler, Patrick Laffan, Hans Meyer, Ferdy Mayne, Liam Redmond, Pat Roach, Frederick Schiller, George Sewell, Anthony Sharp, John Sharp, Roy Spencer, John Sullivan, Harry Towb.

**TITLE SEQUENCE:** After three handwritten captions, in white on black, announcing the names Kubrick, O'Neal and Berenson respectively, a further caption appears: 'PART I – BY WHAT MEANS REDMOND BARRY ACQUIRED THE STYLE AND TITLE OF BARRY LYNDON'. The accompanying music is Handel's 'Sarabande' played by the National Philharmonic Orchestra.

**SUMMARY:** 'PART I – BY WHAT MEANS REDMOND BARRY ACQUIRED THE STYLE AND TITLE OF BARRY LYNDON' begins in eighteenth-century Ireland, where the adolescent Redmond Barry has a rival for the affections of his flirtatious cousin, Nora Brady: the English officer Captain Quin, who promises Nora's family an annual income which Barry cannot hope to match. Furious at the announcement of the couple's engagement, Barry challenges Quin to a duel, apparently kills him, and is then forced to flee with a small allowance, of which he is soon relieved by highwaymen. Penniless, he is recruited into the English army, where he encounters an old family friend, Captain Grogan, who reveals that Barry's duel with Quin was fixed, that Quin is very much alive, and he and Nora are already married.

While Grogan is killed during a particularly bloody skirmish of the Seven Years War, Barry receives a promotion after rescuing a superior officer from a burning building, and takes the opportunity to desert: stealing the uniform, papers and horse of an officer, Barry flees the battle disguised as a diplomatic courier. After a brief dalliance with a beautiful German peasant girl, he is forced to join a Prussian officer, Captain Potzdorf, who exposes Barry's duplicity and offers him a stark choice: join Potzdorf's company, or face the consequences. Two years later, Barry agrees to spy on an old chevalier, Baillebarry, whom Potzdorf also suspects of being an imposter. But when Barry discovers that the chevalier is none other than his own countryman, the pair escape together across the Prussian border, where they begin a successful partnership as travelling cardsharps, cheating the local noblemen out of a small fortune. Growing accustomed to his new-found (if ill-gotten) wealth, Barry sets his sights – more than his heart – on the wife of an ailing aristocrat, Sir Charles Lyndon, whose timely death from a heart attack closes 'PART I'.

In 'PART II – CONTAINING AN ACCOUNT OF THE MISFORTUNES AND DISASTERS WHICH BEFELL BARRY LYNDON', Barry marries the beautiful but vapid Countess Lyndon, and moves into her stately but sterile home. The marriage, of which Barry's stepson Lord Bullingdon strongly disapproves, founders almost immediately, disintegrating amid Barry's adulteries and Countess Lyndon's indifference, and despite the birth of their own son, Bryan. No longer able to contain his disdain for Barry, Lord Bullingdon slanders him at a musical recital, is attacked by his stepfather in a most inelegant fashion, and finally announces his own self-imposed exile, leaving his mother, stepfather and stepbrother to their own fates.

Disaster strikes when young Bryan is killed in a fall from a horse, which Barry had bought for his birthday, and, as Countess Lyndon withdraws further into herself, Barry redoubles his efforts to acquire a peerage of his own, so that his fate is no longer linked with that of his wife. The boy's death is followed by the return of Lord Bullingdon, who challenges Barry to a pistol duel in which Bullingdon's first shot misses, but his second – fired after Barry heroically shoots into the ground – smashes Barry's leg, necessitating amputation. Barry's mother arrives to bring her son, crippled and exiled, back to Ireland, where he lives out the remainder of his days on a small annuity provided by Countess Lyndon.

**SOURCE:** Adapted by Kubrick, freely yet somehow faithfully, from William Makepeace Thackeray's second novel, *The Luck of Barry Lyndon*, later revised and retitled *The Memoirs of Barry Lyndon, Esq., of the Kingdom of Ireland*. Completed in October 1843 and originally published – in serialised form and under the nom de plume George Savage FitzBoodle – in 1844, three years after the first appearance of Thackeray's far more popular *Vanity Fair*, the novel is a fictional autobiography of a hot-headed Irishman. Like *A Clockwork Orange*, the subject of Kubrick's previous film, the book is narrated by its hot-headed, self-centred and egotistical subject.

**WORKING TITLES:** Kubrick's growing fondness for secrecy caused him to title his original screenplay 'New Stanley Kubrick Film Project', although, by the time the film's source and subject matter had been revealed, the film was being filmed under another title, *The Luck of Barry Lyndon*.

**PRODUCTION HISTORY:** After the ignoble death of Kubrick's plans to make *Napoleon* (see Lost Worlds: The Films That Never Were), the director was understandably eager to utilise the mountain of research he and his staff had undertaken while preparing the stillborn project, and he began searching for another eighteenth-century subject that would exploit his meticulous preparations. 'I [had] had a complete set of

Thackeray sitting on my bookshelf at home for years, and I had to read several of his novels before reading *Barry Lyndon*,' he told Michael Ciment. Although he had been impressed by *Vanity Fair*, which had already been the subject of several feature films, Kubrick felt that the story could not be successfully compressed into the relatively short time-span of a feature film. Instead, he seized upon the story of Barry Lyndon.

Kubrick spent three or four months penning his own 243-page screenplay, eschewing Thackeray's first-person narration for an omniscient storyteller who would ultimately take the voice of Michael Hordern. 'I believe Thackeray used Redmond Barry to tell his own story in a deliberately distorted way because it made it more interesting,' Kubrick explained. 'Instead of the omniscient author, Thackeray used the imperfect observer – or perhaps it would be more accurate to say the dishonest observer – thus allowing the reader to judge for himself, with little difficulty, the probable truth in Redmond Barry's view of his life. This technique worked extremely well in the novel,' he added, 'but, of course, in a film you have objective reality in front of you all of the time, so the effect of Thackeray's first-person story-teller could not be repeated on the screen. It might have worked as comedy by the juxtaposition of Barry's version of the truth with the reality on the screen, but I don't think that *Barry Lyndon* should have been done as a comedy.'

Having completed the screenplay – which carefully removed all mentions of the eighteenth-century setting and the source material, and substituted the name 'Roderick' for that of the protagonist – Kubrick successfully persuaded Warner Bros to invest $2.5 million in the project, on the sole proviso that stars would take the leading roles. Before shooting began, Kubrick would spend the best part of a year researching authentic eighteenth-century costumes, furniture, props, architecture, carriages and hairstyles.

After a brief and unsuccessful collaboration with Wilfrid Shingleton, who had designed many of David Lean's productions, Kubrick persuaded a reluctant Ken Adam, whose unpleasant memories of working with the director on *Dr Strangelove* had not dulled in a decade, to fulfil the role of production designer on *Barry Lyndon*. Adam's scepticism was well founded, as the pair clashed almost immediately: over Kubrick's desire to light the film only with available light and candlepower, a Herculean undertaking that would require the construction of a new kind of camera lens capable of low-light filming: Kubrick also insisted that *Barry Lyndon* be shot entirely on location in real eighteenth-century stately homes, preferably within a twenty-mile radius of his home. Adam explained, 'He believed it was impossible to recreate the reality of the eighteenth century in a studio, either from a realistic or an economic point of view. As far as I'm concerned, he was wrong, and I spent a lot of time trying to persuade him otherwise.'

Adam had problems finding suitable locations reflecting the early Irish background of Barry Lyndon's youth. He wanted these scenes to contrast with the scenes in England. Unfortunately, it seemed that Irish buildings from that early period had all been destroyed by revolutions and wars. Adam recalled how, finally, they managed to create pre-eighteenth-century architecture by combining three different sites: Caher Castle, Ormond House and Huntingdon. Adam then managed to persuade Kubrick to accept the idea that Lady Lyndon should live in a house predating the eighteenth century in order to avoid the suggestion that her family was *nouveau riche*. 'Though there exist lots of houses from the Elizabethan, Stuart and Jacobean periods, it was difficult to find one of great beauty. Added to which, we were refused permission to shoot in some of the castles. What we did was again to create a kind of composite architecture by using Wilton (Salisbury), Petworth (Sussex), Longleat (Wiltshire) and Castle Howard (York) for the exteriors.'

For the other locations required by the film, Kubrick was eventually persuaded to shoot in Ireland, which could offer the exteriors required for the Irish sequences. He also decided, as Adam recounted, to film the Continental sequences there, 'so I had somehow to find examples of Austrian and German baroque. I was lucky enough to find a spot near Dublin, called Powercourt, in which one could detect a strong German influence. It was there that we shot almost all the battle scenes.' However, in spite of the advantages this offered, it was not, in retrospect, an ideal choice of location. The Irish Republican Army's (IRA's) terrorist war on the British mainland, sparked by the 'Bloody Sunday' massacre of January 1972, was at its peak; in addition, by the time the production began at Dublin's Ardmore Studios on 17 Sepember 1973, the weather in the region threatened to cause as many problems as the Irish electrical trade unions, who had insisted that at least a dozen of their members be hired to avoid the production being declared 'black' and shut down. (Kubrick acquiesced, hiring a dozen Irish technicians, whom he allegedly told to 'go and drink tea' until the end of the shoot.) Kubrick's preferred method of adaptation, perfected on *A Clockwork Orange*, but mutated so that the lengthy rehearsals were now captured on film as seemingly endless 'takes', led to his reputation as the most repetitious director in history. (Asked if Kubrick did, as was rumoured, demand 25 takes of certain scenes, O'Neal responded: 'Of *everything*!')

After only ten weeks in this troubled atmosphere, barely a tenth of the film was in the can, but the entire $2.5 million budget was spent – a situation that recalled Kubrick's earliest feature-film experiences on *Fear and Desire*. 'The ideal way to make a film would be to wrap up after every scene and go away for a month to think,' Kubrick had said, and over Christmas of 1973 he was granted his wish: cast and crew members agreed to eight weeks of unpaid holiday which Warner Bros announced simply as 'breaking for the holidays'. No sooner had production started again in January 1974, however, than an officer of the Special Branch received word from intelligence sources that Kubrick was on a list of potential IRA targets. That night, Kubrick – who had, in the wake of *A*

*Clockwork Orange*'s controversy, become fiercely protective of his privacy and the safety of his family – sailed back to Britain under an assumed name, never to leave the British Isles again.

'We would still be in Ireland shooting if the IRA hadn't scared him out,' O'Neal told *Premiere* magazine. 'I was in makeup one morning and one of the hairdressers said, "Did you hear that there was an IRA threat today? Somebody called and asked for Mr Kubrick, and they said, 'You tell him he has twenty-four hours to get out of Ireland.'" I said, "You're kidding! How'd he take it?" She said, "He's in your dressing room."' O'Neal immediately ran to his dressing room, where Kubrick told him he couldn't care less if the threat was real or not. 'He said, "I just want to get out of here. Everybody. Let's get back to England. Today."' As Kubrick's wife Christiane later confirmed to *Sight and Sound* magazine's Nick James, 'Two men arrived with ladders and house-painting gear at our house, which was rented, and the woman who cooked for us said, "I know these lads. They're not painters." A day later they came to the studio and told Stanley and Ryan O'Neal they wanted us out of the country immediately. You couldn't see us for dust.'

The three hundred days of production (described by Kubrick's wife as 'one big camping trip'), and all of the problems each of those days entailed, eventually took its toll on cast and crew alike – most notably on the production designer Ken Adam, who admits he suffered 'a very serious nervous crisis' making *Barry Lyndon*. 'Ken Adam nearly died' is how Ryan O'Neal put it. 'They carried him away. He'd had a complete nervous breakdown, because Stanley would say, "Get me a stream that's about three feet wide and a foot deep with a mountain behind it and some foliage. I want a cavalry officer to be able to jump it, and I want Barry running down the stream." That's hard to find with a day's notice.' 'I went back to London, and he was unbelievably concerned,' Adam told Peter Bogdanovich. 'His letters to me at the time were really quite touching. Then he wrote that he'd decided to shoot in Potsdam with the second unit and that I should direct it! The idea of that certainly didn't improve my health.' Having recovered fully from his experience, Adam could afford to be circumspect about his experiences making *Barry Lyndon*: 'The irony, in a way, was that I got my first Oscar for it,' he commented later.

By the time filming was completed on location in the southwest of England, *Barry Lyndon*'s budget had more than trebled to $9 million; Warner Bros' president, John Calley, resignedly admitted, 'It would make no sense to tell Kubrick, "Okay, fella, you've got one more week to finish the thing." What you would get then is a mediocre film that cost, say $8 million, instead of a masterpiece that cost $11 million. When somebody is spending a lot of your money, you are wise to give him time to do the job right.' Besides, as Terry Semel, then Warner Bros' president of distribution, later commented: 'He made the movie at a very modest price by today's standards. He always shot with very small crews and very low daily rates.'

**CASTING:** Kubrick's original choice for the title role was Robert Redford, whom he met to discuss the project while the actor was in England shooting *The Great Gatsby* (1974). Although he and Kubrick reached a tentative agreement, Redford eventually passed in favour of a more heroic turn as a barnstorming pilot in *The Great Waldo Pepper* (1975), and Ryan O'Neal – then the world's number-two box-office draw, thanks to the success of *Love Story* (1970), *What's Up, Doc?* (1972) and *Paper Moon* (1973) – was cast instead. 'He was the best actor for the part,' Kubrick said later. 'He looked right, and I was confident that he possessed much greater acting ability than he had been allowed to show in many of the films he had previously done.'

Kubrick found his Lady Lyndon in Marisa Berenson, a former *Elle* magazine cover star turned actress, who had appeared in Luchino Visconti's *Death in Venice* (1971) and Bob Fosse's *Cabaret* (1972), but could hardly be said to have fulfilled Warner Bros' desire for stars to fulfil the leading roles. 'I didn't test for the part – it just came to me,' Berenson said later. '[Kubrick] said he had seen my performance in *Cabaret* and asked me if I'd be available for a film. He couldn't tell me much about it except that the story was set in the eighteenth century and was based on a classic. But that didn't matter – after all, Kubrick was involved. That was all I needed to know, so I accepted on the spot.'

One actor who did not satisfy Kubrick was the German-born Oskar Werner, best known for his leading role in François Truffaut's *Farenheit 451* (1968), who was fired from the role of Captain Potzdorf after only three weeks, and replaced by his countryman, Hardy Krüger (*Flight of the Phoenix*, *The Wild Geese*).

**THE USUAL SUSPECTS:** Kubrick's growing antipathy for the auditioning process led to his casting of several actors from previous productions. Patrick Magee, who had overacted wonderfully as Mr Alexander in *A Clockwork Orange*, was cast in the role of Baillebarry; Leonard Rossiter, who had underplayed with equal brilliance in *2001*, won perhaps the best supporting role as Captain Quin; following a turn as the gum-chewing police constable in *A Clockwork Orange*, Steven Berkoff donned face powder and a wig to play Lord Ludd; yet another *Clockwork Orange* alumnus, Philip Stone, followed his portrayal of Alex's effete father with the equally ineffectual role of Graham, Lady Lyndon's clerk; finally, Anthony Sharp, who had played the Minister of the Interior in Kubrick's previous film, would bring his aristocratic locutions to the (uncredited) role of Lord Hallum.

There were an equal number of familiar faces behind the camera, the most significant being the *Dr Strangelove* production designer Ken Adam, along with the lighting cameraman John Alcott and costume designer Milena Canonero from *A Clockwork Orange*. Although all three would receive Academy Award nominations for their work, only Alcott and Canonero would work with Kubrick again.

**EXPERT WITNESS:** 'In the book, Barry Lyndon narrates his own deranged view of things, and I thought it was what made the story work. He was an eighteenth-century crackpot. I was supposed to narrate the movie, [but Kubrick] got some bored Englishman to do it, and if *he's* bored, what's the audience going to be? I was thrown by what came out – it wasn't about Barry Lyndon anymore; it was about the time, and it was a little static for me. That was my feeling, and I may have spoken up about it. He got mad and wrote me a mean letter, and I wrote him back saying, "Look, the movie I saw was like walking through a museum. Which is all right, but we shot an adventure story." ' – the actor Ryan O'Neal (Redmond Barry), quoted in *Premiere* magazine, August 1999.

**THE PURSUIT OF PERFECTION:** '[Kubrick] wanted to do it almost like a documentary of the period,' the production designer Ken Adam recounted, 'but when we started researching and preparing the film, he knew very little about the period. Eventually, he got to know more and more, but we got into terrible arguments because he was more attracted to Victorian interiors than to the stark, more formal eighteenth century interiors.' By the end, however, Adam believes that Kubrick knew more than anyone about the eighteenth century, 'because of the amount of research he did about the living conditions of the people: the lice in their wigs, the toothbrushes they used, condoms. We went through everything to find out how those people lived.'

For the lavish period costumes, Kubrick once again insisted on absolute verisimilitude, hiring Milena Canonero and Ulla-Britt Søderland to find authentic eighteenth-century clothes, rather than create their own designs representative of the period. He explained, 'What is very important is to get some actual clothes of the period to learn how they were originally made.'

Ken Adam remembers this process all too clearly. 'We bought a lot of real eighteenth century clothes, which one could still find in England,' he recalled. 'We found that they were all too small, because people were obviously smaller two hundred years ago. We set up our own factory at Radlett, opened up these clothes, and made new clothes in exactly the same patterns as the old clothes. The thing was to get the actors to wear them properly, to get used to them and walk properly in them.' He further decided that Leonard of London, who had previously worked on *A Clockwork Orange*, should create all of the wigs – fifteen of which were made for Ryan O'Neal alone – from human hair, which was obtained from the freshly shaven heads of young Italian girls about to enter religious life.

**CLASSIC QUOTES**

**Barry:** 'I'm not sorry. And I'll not apologise. And I'd as soon go to Dublin as to Hell.'

**Narrator:** 'No lad who has liberty for the first time and has twenty guineas in his pocket is very sad, and Barry rode towards Dublin thinking not so much of the kind mother left alone, and of the home behind him, but of tomorrow, and all the wonders it would bring.'

**Barry:** 'Mightn't I be allowed to keep my horse?'

**Captain Feeney:** 'I would like to oblige you, but with people like us, we must be able to travel faster than our clients. Good day, young sir.'

**Narrator:** 'A lady who sets her heart upon a lad in uniform must prepare to change lovers pretty quickly, or her life will be but a sad one. This heart of Lischen's was like many a neighbouring town, and had been stormed and occupied several times before Barry came to invest it.'

**Narrator:** 'Five years in the army, and some considerable experience of the world, had by now dispelled any of those romantic notions regarding love with which Barry commenced life, and he began to have it in mind, as so many gentlemen had done before him, to marry a woman of fortune and condition.'

**Narrator:** 'Fate had determined that he should leave none of his race behind him, and that he should finish his life poor, lonely and childless.'

**THEMES AND MOTIFS:** *Barry Lyndon* opens with the death of Barry's father during a duel, and the film spends a good deal of its running time in search of a replacement father figure for Barry – Captains Grogan and Potzdorf, the chevalier – without ever really finding one. The lack of an omnipresent paternalistic figure foreshadows and perhaps explains Barry's own shortcomings as a father: his frosty relationship with his stepson, Lord Bullingdon, their public quarrel and subsequent duel, and the tragedy that befalls his natural son, Bryan, as a result of his (perhaps overgenerous) birthday gift. Certainly, the theme of a father in contempt of his son was one to which Kubrick would return in his next film, *The Shining*.

One of the thematic oddities of *Barry Lyndon* is the way in which, as in the book, the narration is used to remove the element of surprise in order to create a more fatalistic sense of inevitability. Kubrick felt this would also downplay what might otherwise appear melodramatic or contrived. For instance, even before Barry breaks down in front of the chevalier, the voice-over establishes the relationship that will form between the two countrymen. 'Another place in the story where I think this technique works particularly well is where we are told that Barry's young son, Bryan, is going to die at the same time we watch the two of them playing happily together,' Kubrick observed. 'In this case, I think the commentary creates the same dramatic effect as, for example, the knowledge that the *Titanic* is doomed while you watch the carefree scenes of preparation and departure. These early scenes would be inexplicably dull if you didn't know about the ship's appointment with the iceberg. Being told in advance of the impending disaster gives away surprise but creates suspense.'

The final year of Barry Lyndon's story, revealed as Countess Lyndon signs bank drafts, including a small stipend for her estranged husband, is significant: 1789 was the year of the French Revolution, which signalled a great change among the aristocracy across Europe.

MUSIC: Authenticity was Kubrick's watchword throughout the production of *Barry Lyndon*, and he fully intended to use only music from the correct era to accompany the film, even going as far as to insist that the Irish folk group the Chieftains play Sean O'Riada's compositions on authentic eighteenth-century instruments. However, after listening to hundreds of recordings from the period, Kubrick decided that there was no tragic love theme that he felt sufficiently captured the spirit of the latter half of the film. He therefore decided to break one of his self-imposed rules, and chose a piece of music written in 1828: Schubert's Trio in E Flat, Opus 100, proclaiming: 'It's a magnificent piece of music and it has just the right restrained balance between the tragic and the romantic.'

Another problem Kubrick encountered was that eighteenth-century music was insufficiently dramatic for the second half of the film, set among the aristocrats of Austria and Prussia, and depicting Barry's downfall. Kubrick turned to the veteran composer Leonard Rosenman, who had written scores for the James Dean films *East of Eden* (1955) and *Rebel Without a Cause* (1955), engaging him to adapt and re-record classical works by Bach, Handel, Mozart, Schubert and Vivaldi, rather than compose an original score of his own. 'Unless you want a pop score, I don't see any reason not to avail yourself of the great orchestral music of the past and present,' Kubrick explained.

Thus, in the autumn of 1974, Rosenman arrived in London, with no illusions that he had any creative work to do on the film. He recalled, 'I listened to all the records he had, and he had picked a sarabande that had been recorded with a harpsichord; he thought the bass would just be marvellous for the duel scenes. He had another theme for the dying child, which was from one of Verdi's worst operas. I told him I couldn't go along with that and suggested I do percussion, and see what it sounded like. We tried it with the London Symphony [Orchestra] and he fell madly in love with it.' Rosenman returned to America, and it was to be more than a year before he would see the results of his collaboration with Kubrick. When he did, he was aghast that the director had 'looped' the Verdi piece and used it throughout the film. 'When I saw this incredibly boring film with all the music I had picked out going over and over again, I thought, "My God, what a mess!" I was going to refuse the Oscar.'

The *Barry Lyndon* soundtrack, approximately 51 minutes in duration, contains an excellent selection of the film's widely varied music, including works by Handel, Frederick the Great, Mozart, Schubert, Paisiello, Vivaldi, Bach and the Chieftains. Originally issued on vinyl, it is currently available as a Warner Records CD (7599-25984-2).

Two reorchestrated tracks from the film, the traditional folk melody 'Women of Ireland' and Handel's sarabande, can be found on Silva Screen Records' Kubrick compilation album, *Strangelove . . . Music from the Films of Stanley Kubrick* (FILMCD 303).

**POSTER:** The main poster design for *Barry Lyndon* was a stylised tableau of images from the film – Barry aiming a duelling pistol; redcoats on the march; Countess Lyndon; the chevalier; Countess Lyndon with baby Bryan; Barry and Countess Lyndon kissing while she reclines in her bath; Barry and Bryan embracing; Bryan's birthday procession; Barry and Lord Bullingdon fighting; Barry and Countess Lyndon kissing – surrounding a baroque illustration of the title in which a flintlock pistol and red rose are entwined.

A rather more simple, and perhaps more iconographic, design was that of an illustrated black silhouette, depicting the body of an eighteenth-century male figure (presumably Barry Lyndon) from the waist down, on a white background. The figure is holding a flintlock pistol, and has his right boot placed upon the stem of a red rose – the only colour in the otherwise monochromatic image.

**TRAILER:** The fact that the release of *Barry Lyndon* in the United States preceded its European premiere by several months allowed Warner Bros to capitalise on the critics who had responded positively, using testimonials from the American press to accompany a series of wordless images from the film. Thus, the trailer is an assemblage of mostly random scenes of action and romance, with a voice-over narration. 'Barry Lyndon, a film by Stanley Kubrick starring Ryan O'Neal and Marisa Berenson, has won the Best Picture and Best Director award presented by the National Board of Review,' it says, before taking accolades from a wide variety of sources, ending with *Cosmopolitan*'s Liz Smith ('a perfect movie, beautiful, breathtaking, brilliant, like a gorgeous fulfilling dream of life, a dream you never want to end. It is not comparable to any other film I can recall. I ask you to turn yourself over to the experience.') 'Barry Lyndon,' the narrator then concludes, over a beige title card, 'a film by Stanley Kubrick based on the novel by William Makepeace Thackeray starring Ryan O'Neal and Marisa Berenson.'

**WHAT THE PAPERS SAID:** In 1975, critics were more prone to excitement over Steven Spielberg's *Jaws* and Milos Forman's *One Flew over the Cuckoo's Nest* than *Barry Lyndon*, which was widely reviled for its soporific style and the insubstantial acting of its leading players, even as its majestic compositions were praised. The *Los Angeles Times* described the film as 'the motion picture equivalent of one of those very large, very expensive, very elegant and very dull books that exist solely to be seen on coffee tables'. Even Kubrick's strenuous desire to authentically evoke what he referred to as the 'patina' of the period was seized upon by critics, one of whom opined that *Barry Lyndon*, 'far from recreating another century, it more accurately embalms it'.

Among the more positive reviews was *Variety*'s, which praised casting, conception and execution as 'superb', and added, 'Kubrick's outstanding external landscapes – in rich, cool tones – overpower the ant-like people crawling about; his interiors – hot, uncomfortable despite their plushness – seem unnatural in contrast . . . This cinematic mural bears repeated and sustained watching without ever really commanding and demanding acute attention. Could anyone else have pulled this off?'

In Britain, the *Spectator*'s Kenneth Robinson hailed *Barry Lyndon* as 'astonishingly beautiful . . . The whole film, including the ironic tone of the narration is a rare experience . . . a marvellous antidote to the more conventional world of cinema entertainment.' *Monthly Film Bulletin*'s Richard Combs gave an equally considered opinion, noting that 'for all the detached, meditative quality of its historiography and scene-painting, *Barry Lyndon* emerges as perhaps Kubrick's most intensely human spectacle, comparable to *Paths of Glory* in its tragic confrontations that seem to throw whole worlds into the balance with individual lives.'

Retrospectively, Kubrick had his own view of the film's critical reception, suggesting that the US response was 'predominantly enthusiastic', while the international press was even more so. Nevertheless, he admitted that the English press was badly split, a fate that he acknowledged had befallen all of his films. 'Of course,' he added, 'the lasting and ultimately most important reputation of a film is not based on reviews, but on what, if anything, people say about it over the years, and on how much affection for it they have.'

**BOX OFFICE:** Although the public had never really shared Kubrick's fascination with the eighteenth century, the director was stunned by the apathy with which audiences greeted the film upon its initial limited US release on 18 December 1975. He had been confident that *Barry Lyndon* would be his highest-grossing film. 'The fact that Stanley thinks the picture will gross in nine figures is reassuring. He is never far wrong about anything,' John Calley had commented during production. Yet Kubrick would have to make do with seven figures as the film grossed just $9.5 million in the US, falling far short of the $30 million required for the film to turn a profit.

Although *Barry Lyndon* fared better in Europe, grossing $3 million in Paris alone, overall its performance was a disappointment. '*Barry Lyndon* was one of Warner Bros' biggest grosses internationally, but not in the United States,' Kubrick admitted to John Hofsess. 'If business had been as good as in Europe, the film would have been a great financial success.' As it was, he later told *Rolling Stone*'s Tim Cahill, of his films, *Barry Lyndon* was 'the only one that did poorly from the studio's point of view'. According to Kubrick's friend and fellow film maker John Milius, it 'bothered him a great deal' that *Barry Lyndon* failed commercially. As he told Peter Bogdanovich, 'He was very vulnerable to criticism or to whether a movie was a success or not. He just felt that people didn't understand it. People were bored by it. I think after that picture he felt no one was going to let him make a film again.'

**AWARDS:** Kubrick's belief that *Barry Lyndon* would enjoy success at the Academy Awards proved more reliable than his box-office predictions, as the film received nominations in seven categories, for three of which – Best Picture, Best Director and Best Writing, Screenplay Adapted from Other Material – Kubrick was the sole nominee. The luck of *Barry Lyndon* was to intervene yet again: as Milos Forman's *One Flew Over the Cuckoo's Nest* (1975) swept the major awards, *Barry Lyndon* won awards in all four of the other categories for which it was nominated: Best Cinematography, Best Costume Design, Best Art Direction/Set Decoration and Best Music, Scoring Original Song Score and/or Adaptation. The four wins made it by far the most successful Oscar ceremony for any of Kubrick's films.

Following its Oscar triumph, *Barry Lyndon* scored an award for Kubrick as Best Director at the British Academy of Film and Television Arts (BAFTA) awards, where it was also nominated for Best Art Direction, Best Costume Design and Best Film; Best Picture (English Language) and Best Director plaudits, tied with Robert Altman's *Nashville* (1975), from the National Board of Review; Best Cinematography honours from the National Society of Film Critics, the Los Angeles Film Critics' Association and the British Society of Cinematographers; and two nominations at the Golden Globes: Best Director (Motion Picture) and Best Motion Picture (Drama).

**TECHNICAL ACHIEVEMENTS:** The candlelight by which Kubrick wanted to film *Barry Lyndon* required the construction of a camera that would incorporate a lens of sufficient size to be able to capture the interior action using traditional film stock. Kubrick obtained a fixed-focus 50mm barrel lens, developed by NASA and the Zeiss company for taking still photographs on the moon, and engaged a Californian engineer, Ed DiGiulio of the Cinema Products Corporation to fit it to his BNC Mitchell camera. Although he was initially sceptical, he and Kubrick found a way, even though it meant that the camera was unsuitable for any other application.

'With this lens,' Kubrick later enthused, 'it was now possible to shoot in light conditions so dim that it was difficult to read. For the day interior scenes, we used either the real daylight from the windows, or simulated daylight by banking lights outside the windows and diffusing them with tracing paper taped on the glass. In addition to the very beautiful lighting you can achieve this way,' he added, 'it is also a very practical way to work. You don't have to worry about shooting into your lighting equipment. All your lighting is outside the window behind tracing paper, and if you shoot towards the window you get a very beautiful and realistic flare effect.' Years later, the movie director Milos Forman – who had, ironically, beaten Kubrick to a Best Director Oscar the year he was nominated for *Barry Lyndon* – allegedly asked to borrow the camera for his own period re-creation, *Amadeus*; Kubrick declined. 'Stanley just treasured his own equipment and wouldn't let anybody touch it,' DiGiulio explained.

**INFLUENCED BY:** Kubrick's belief that there were few, if any, historical films of significant value led him to look further back to a time before motion pictures for inspiration. He and his production designer Ken Adam studied hundreds of paintings from the period, by artists both world-renowned and relatively obscure. 'Stanley wanted to make direct reference to the painting,' Adam told Michael Ciment. 'For him, the safest way [to maintain accuracy] was to draw our inspiration from painters like Gainsborough, Hogarth, Reynolds, Chardin, Watteau, Zoffany, Stubbs (for the hunting costumes) and, in particular, Chadowiecki, an artist who intrigued both of us, a Pole who worked on the Continent and who was a master of drawing and water-colour, with a marvellously simple style and a remarkable gift for composition.'

Kubrick was often so influenced by the paintings that he borrowed compositions from them. At one point, according to Ryan O'Neal, Kubrick 'began to search though a book of eighteenth-century art reproductions [and] posed Marisa [Countess Lyndon] and me exactly as if we were in that painting'.

**DÉJÀ VU:** The composition of the shot of the nervous Barry searching Nora for her scarf is almost identical, albeit in reverse, to the shot of a stricken Alex as he attempts to touch the breasts of the girl during the Ludovico demonstration in *A Clockwork Orange*. There is an equally unmistakable touch of *2001* in *Barry Lyndon*, as two separate scenes of noblemen eating alone in eighteenth-century surroundings evoke memories of the astronaut David Bowman's last meal. *Barry Lyndon*'s narrator suggests that, following their marriage, Countess Lyndon has become no more important to Barry than 'carpets and pictures' – precisely the two things on which General Broulard compliments General Mireau in *Paths of Glory*.

**INFLUENTIAL ON:** Although *Barry Lyndon* almost certainly inspired the film director Milos Forman during the making of his multiple-Oscar-winning *Amadeus*, Martin Scorsese acknowledges the influence of what he called 'Kubrick's boldest project' on his re-creation of the nineteenth century for *The Age of Innocence* (1993). 'On the surface,' Scorsese said of Kubrick's film, 'the approach was cool and distant; deceptive. But I found this to be one of the most profoundly emotional films I've ever seen. Kubrick's style was strangely unsettling,' he added. 'His audacity was to insist on slowness in order to recreate the pace of life and the ritualised behaviour of the time.'

The writer-director David Mamet described his own reaction to *Barry Lyndon* in relation to his own period film, *The Winslow Boy* (1999). 'Costume drama is difficult to do,' he said. 'So much of it seems to be, "Good morning, because it's the Napoleonic era." I think a genius costume drama is *Barry Lyndon*, because it's so straightforward. Kubrick's such a master with the camera and the actors that he doesn't have to make any further points: "Please pass the tea because I'm wearing a corset."'

**CUT SCENES:** Although all versions of *Barry Lyndon* remain constant, Kubrick made several important changes to Thackeray's story, which he felt were consistent with the spirit of the novel, and accelerated the pace of the story. This was particularly true of the ending, which Kubrick telescoped into a much more concise, but no less dramatically effective, version of events. 'In the book, Barry is pensioned off by Lady Lyndon. Lord Bullingdon, having been believed dead, returns from America,' Kubrick explains. 'He finds Barry and gives him a beating. Barry, tended by his mother, subsequently dies in prison, a drunk.' All of this, Kubrick felt, would have extended the story well beyond the attention span of a typical audience. Thus, he said, 'in the film, Bullingdon gets his revenge and Barry is totally defeated; destined, one can assume, for a fate not unlike that which awaited him in the novel.'

Several other scenes were invented from whole cloth, including Barry's theft of clothes and papers from two homosexual British Army officers whom he observes frolicking in the water. 'The function of the scene between the two gay officers was to provide a simpler way for Barry to escape,' Kubrick told Michael Ciment. 'Again, it leads to the same end result as the novel but by a different route. Barry steals the papers and uniform of a British officer which allow him to make his way to freedom. Since the scene is purely expositional, the comic situation helps to mask your intentions.'

**TRIVIA:** *Barry Lyndon* was one of those rare Kubrick films in which the director would make obscure references to his earlier productions, as the actor Anthony Sharp – who had previously played the Minister of the Interior in *A Clockwork Orange* – is introduced as 'a former government minister'.

For the French release of *Barry Lyndon*, Kubrick was so concerned that the film should be shown in the correct 1.66:1 ratio, rather than the 1.85:1 used in most cinemas, that he personally provided the required mask to every theatre that screened it.

**AVAILABILITY:** Although *Barry Lyndon* is currently unavailable on any format in the United Kingdom, in the United States it is available in three formats, all of which feature the Kubrick-approved 1.66:1 transfer: as an NTSC VHS double-pack (WA 17366 A/B) and laserdisc (12240), each of which contains the threatrical trailer; and as a Region 1 DVD (17366) featuring the theatrical trailer, production notes, French and English subtitles and a French-dubbed dialogue track.

**FINAL ANALYSIS:** Seven years before *Barry Lyndon*, Kubrick had made a three-hour-plus drama of epic scope, set in a painstakingly realised alternate century, in which the audience was invited to watch, but never connect with, a group of largely emotionless characters communicating with the minimum of dialogue, the vast silences broken only by eighteenth-century music. Clearly, *Barry Lyndon* was cut from the same cloth. Where Kubrick had, in *2001*, taken the audience into space, *Barry Lyndon* gave him the opportunity to take them on a journey back in time. Kubrick made us marvel at the landscapes and details of his invented future; now he would invite us to do the same at his impossibly detailed re-creation of an equally unknowable past – for wouldn't many of the youths of 1968 be alive to see the year 2001, whereas none of *Barry Lyndon*'s audience could possibly live in the eighteenth century?

Whatever critics in 1975 were expecting, it probably wasn't what Kubrick gave them in *Barry Lyndon* – compared with their fond memories of the ribald eighteenth-century comedy *Tom Jones* (1963), Kubrick's film probably felt like an exhaustive tour through an art gallery populated by waxworks, with Sir Michael Hordern as bored tour guide. Certainly, *Barry Lyndon* was misunderstood upon its initial release, as almost all of Kubrick's more considered creations were; yet the scarcity with which the film is seen today means that opinion has not been revised as dramatically as it has on many of Kubrick's other films. It is almost as though, a quarter of a century later, the jury were still out. Quite why this should be the case in an age when films like *Schindler's List* (1993) and *Titanic* (1997) routinely run longer than three hours – and posthumous interest in Kubrick's body of work is rife – remains a mystery.

Adapted from an unremarkable, even obscure nineteenth-century novel, *Barry Lyndon* was transformed through Kubrick's own hand and eye into an elegant picaresque fable about an ambitious Irish lad in possession of certain qualities that will – with fate in his favour – allow him to achieve all that he has ever dreamed of, but will subsequently, with fickle fate turned cruelly against him, lead to his ignominious downfall, a far more dramatic and poignant one, it might be added, in Kubrick's telling than in Thackeray's. Sure, the red-blooded Redmond Barry soon becomes as glacial and opaque as his surroundings, but such is the stifling effect of the ignoble nobility the working-class lad seeks to ascend to, not realising that they are as much cheats and thieves as the common highwaymen who steal his purse and his horse, but at least have the decency to leave him his boots. For all the noblemen bribed by Barry, he never comes close to the title he craves.

Open a great novel anywhere and you can find great writing; similarly, one could almost take any single image from *Barry Lyndon* and hang it on the wall, as elegant and majestic as a work by any of the eighteenth-century masters that inspired it. Evoking and exposing the hypocrisy, decaying grandeur, stultifying etiquette, cracked make-up, fussy fashions and class cruelties of the bewigged and candle-powered aristocracy, Kubrick keeps an appropriate distance for one toiling two centuries later, yet allows the audience to be charmed first by Barry, then by the landscape, music and drama as they unfold before us. He moves in closer, contrasting the detachment of the long-distance views with the glorious immediacy of the handheld camera Kubrick uses during the bareknuckle fistfight between Barry and his fellow Redcoat, Toole, and later with his own stepson, Lord Bullingdon. And the full weight of emotion is allowed to the surface as Barry's natural son dies, his sickbed scene one of the most heart-rending ever committed to film.

One can view the great canvases in a gallery, wondering at the stories behind them, at the lives of the static figures captured by the artist from a distant century. In *Barry Lyndon*, Kubrick took us inside the canvases, many of them recognisable, and allowed us to live and breathe a bygone century in a way that few other directors had done. Better yet, the life of the fictional figure he chose to follow from upstart to downfall was one which any artist would have been proud to capture, whether on canvas or on film.

**KUBRICK ON KUBRICK:** 'As soon as I read *Barry Lyndon* I became very excited about it. I loved the story and the characters, and it seemed possible to make the transition from novel to film without destroying it in the process. It also offered the opportunity to do one of the things that movies can do better than any other art form, and that is to present historical subject matter. Description is not one of the things that novels do best but it is something that movies do effortlessly, at least with respect to the effort required of the audience.' – quoted in *Kubrick* by Michael Ciment, 1984.

# The Shining (1980)

[Colour – 146 mins (US premiere), 142 mins (US release) and 114 mins (UK & Australia)]

Executive Producer Jan Harlan
Based upon the novel by Stephen King
Produced in association with The Producer Circle Company,
Robert Fryer, Martin Richards, Mary Lea Johnson
Screenplay by Stanley Kubrick & Diane Johnson

Produced and Directed by Stanley Kubrick
Photographed by John Alcott
Production Designer Roy Walker
Film Editor Ray Lovejoy
Music by Béla Bartók, Krzysztof Penderecki, Wendy Carlos
& Rachel Elkind, György Ligeti
Production Manager Douglas Twiddy
Assistant Directors Brian Cook, Terry Needham & Michael
Stevenson
Costumes designed by Milena Canonero
Steadicam Operator Garrett Brown
Helicopter photography by MacGillivray Freeman Films
Personal Assistant to the Director Leon Vitali
Assistant to the Producer Andros Epaminondas
Art Director Les Tomkins
Make-up by Tom Smith
Hairstyles Leonard

**CAST:** Jack Nicholson (*Jack Torrance*), Shelley Duvall (*Wendy Torrance*), Danny Lloyd (*Danny Torrance*), Scatman Crothers (*Dick Hallorann*), Barry Nelson (*Stuart Ullman*), Philip Stone (*Delbert Grady*), Joe Turkel (*Lloyd*), Anne Jackson (*Doctor*), Tony Burton (*Larry Durkin*), Lia Beldam (*Young woman in bath*), Billie Gibson (*Old woman in bath*), Barry Dennen (*Bill Watson*), David Baxt (*Forest Ranger 1*), Manning Redwood (*Forest Ranger 2*), Lisa Burns (*Grady Daughter*), Louise Burns (*Grady Daughter*), Robin Pappas (*Nurse*), Alison Coleridge (*Susie*), Burnell Tucker (*Policeman*), Jana Sheldon (*Stewardess*), Kate Phelps (*Receptionist*), Norman Gay (*Injured guest*).

**UNCREDITED CREW:** Paul Cadiou (*Assistant Production Accountant*), Ray Andrews (*Production Assistant*), Norman Dorne (*Additional Art Director*).

**TITLE SEQUENCE:** Over aerial shots of Jack Torrance's yellow Volkswagen Beetle driving towards the Overlook Hotel for his interview, the ominous main title theme – the *Dies irae* theme reorchestrated for synthesiser and voices by *A Clockwork Orange*'s composers, Wendy (formerly Walter) Carlos and Rachel Elkind – plays as pale-blue credits scroll up the screen. The footage was shot by the noted surfing film maker Greg MacGillivray from a helicopter – as evidenced by the appearance of its shadow and rotor blades, both of which would have been masked by the gate in theatrical prints – flying over Glacier National Park in Montana. 'It was important to establish an ominous mood during Jack's first drive up to the hotel,' Kubrick stated: 'the vast isolation and eerie splendour of high mountains, and the narrow, winding roads which would become impassable after heavy snow.' The location was found by a second-unit camera crew, who initially reported that the place was unsuitable. 'When we saw the test shots they sent back, we were staggered,' Kubrick remarked. 'It was plain that the location was perfect but the crew had to be replaced.'

**SUMMARY:** *The Shining* is divided into eleven distinct sections, each prefaced by a caption card ('THE INTERVIEW', 'CLOSING DAY', 'ONE MONTH LATER', 'TUESDAY', 'THURSDAY', 'SATURDAY', 'MONDAY', 'WEDNESDAY' '8am' and '4pm'). Jack Torrance, a would-be writer with a history of drunkenness and domestic violence, takes his wife Wendy and his psychic son Danny to the Overlook Hotel, where he and his family will act as caretakers for the snowbound winter months. Upon their arrival, the hotel's cook, Dick Hallorann, tells Danny that he shares the boy's psychic power – 'the shine', as he calls it – and that, if anything untoward should happen, Danny should use his power to contact him.

As soon as the Torrances are alone, the figurative and literal ghosts born of the Overlook's chequered history – a previous caretaker, Grady, murdered his wife and two daughters at the hotel in 1970 – soon begin to exert their evil influence over Jack. As he's pushed to the edge by the ghost of the former caretaker, and his own encroaching madness, Jack's actions towards his own wife and son become increasingly violent. When Dick Hallorann returns to the hotel after being summoned by a desperate psychic plea from Danny, Jack kills Hallorann, and pursues his wife and son in a psychotic, murderous rampage which culminates in his own death in the hotel's hedge maze.

**SOURCE:** Adapted by Kubrick and Diane Johnson from Stephen King's 1977 bestseller. King's fourth novel (after *Carrie*, *Salem's Lot* and *Rage*, the last published under the pseudonym of Richard Bachman), *The Shining* was also his most successful at the time, selling fifty thousand copies in hardcover. By the time Kubrick's film version was released in 1980, King was one of America's bestselling novelists, with 22 million copies of his six books in print.

**WORKING TITLES:** Although Stephen King's novel originally laboured under the titles *Darkshine* and *The Shine* (both having been inspired by a John Lennon lyric, 'We all shine on, like the moon and the stars and the sun'), Kubrick stuck with the author's chosen title. Today, the title usually appears as *Stanley Kubrick's The Shining* – a clear indication that the film version was distinct from the novel.

**PRODUCTION HISTORY:** Kubrick had first considered the idea of making a horror film when Warner Bros offered him *The Exorcist*, but as early as 1966 the director had told a friend of his desire 'to make the world's scariest movie, involving a series of episodes that would play upon the nightmare fears of the audience'. He had also expressed an interest in extrasensory perception and the paranormal, although he later asserted that '*The Shining* didn't originate from any particular desire to do a film about this'.

Aware of his interest in the genre, a Warner Bros executive, John Calley, sent Kubrick a manuscript copy of *The Shining*, which struck the director as 'one of the most ingenious and exciting stories of the genre I had read. It seemed to strike an extraordinary balance between the psychological and the supernatural in such a way as to lead you to think that the supernatural would eventually be explained by the psychological. "Jack must be imagining these things because he's crazy." This allowed you to suspend your doubt of the supernatural until you were so thoroughly into the story that you could accept it almost without noticing.'

No fan of King's writing style, which he dismissed as 'weak', Kubrick rejected King's own first draft screenplay without reading it, and chose to collaborate with Diane Johnson, author of a 1974 genre novel, *The Shadow Knows*, which Kubrick had admired. 'He wanted to pare [the novel] down to film size, concentrate on the mystery of the hotel, the psychodynamics of the family [and] the idea of horror seen by a child,' Johnson told *Premiere* magazine. Their collaboration, which took place at Kubrick's Hertfordshire home over a period of eleven weeks in 1978, resulted in a significant number of fundamental changes and significant inventions, most notably to do with the climax of the film.

'Very early on, I decided . . . I didn't want the conventional ending – the big bad place burns down,' Kubrick recounted. Initially, Kubrick suggested an alternative *dénouement* in which the Torrance family appear as ghosts, visible in the dining room as another winter caretaker is shown around the hotel, and another in which Jack is killed by Wendy, only to be attacked herself by a murderous Dick Hallorann, before she and Danny are able to overpower and kill him. (This version, from an early treatment of the screenplay, features a scrapbook photograph of Jack Torrance dated 1919, similar to the one featured in the final film, but ends with a caption card which reads, 'The Overlook Hotel would survive this tragedy, as it had so many of these. It is still open each year from 5/20 to 9/20. THE END.' Intriguingly, the scrapbook survives in the filmed version, glimpsed on the writing desk in the scene where Wendy reads Jack's 'novel'.)

Finally, Kubrick and Johnson settled on the idea of the hedge maze – perhaps inspired, Kubrick suggested, by the living topiary animals of King's novel, which would have been ruinously expensive or insufficiently credible to translate to the screen – as the arena for the final showdown between the Torrances, acting as both a natural extension of the hotel (which Wendy Torrance initially likens to 'a maze'), and adding a mythological and symbolic element absent from earlier treatments, and from the novel itself.

No official press release was issued by Warner Bros prior to production on *The Shining*. The first indication that Kubrick was about to film an adaptation of King's novel came on 5 June 1977, when the Los Angeles *Herald Examiner* announced the film maker's intention to begin shooting the film on location in Colorado. Although Kubrick had, indeed, considered the possibility of making a film in the United States for the first time since *Spartacus*, he ultimately decided to build his hotel on four of the nine available sound stages at England's Elstree Studios, using second-unit footage of the Timberline Lodge in Mount Hood, Oregon, for many of the exteriors.

Shooting began on 1 May 1978, and continued almost uninterrupted for more than a year. During this period, cast and crew members were pushed to their limits – and, in at least one case, beyond them – as Kubrick demanded take after take after take, sometimes racking up more than a hundred takes for a single set-up. Barry Nelson, who played the hotel manager Stuart Ullman, recalled having to say 'Hello, Jack' thirty-two times before Kubrick was satisfied. 'I had never done that many takes, and I don't think anybody else had,' Nelson told *Premiere* magazine. 'But Kubrick was a genius with the camera, so it wasn't all whether the actor was pleasing him or not . . . But it presents a problem to keep spontaneity after you do sixty, seventy takes. Scatman Crothers had that problem indoors when he showed [the Torrances] the kitchen: 136 takes.' According to legend, Kubrick printed every one of them. 'In one scene I had to get out of a Sno-Cat and walk across the street, no dialogue. Fifty takes,' Crothers later recalled. 'He had Shelley, Jack and the kid walk across the street. Eighty-seven takes, man. He always wants something new, and he doesn't stop until he gets it.'

'When I saw the film I could see what Kubrick had been up to,' the film director John Boorman later wrote in *The Emerald Forest Diary*. 'He was trying to get performances that came out of extremity [and] exhaustion.' However, Shelley Duvall's overwrought, near-hysterical performance literally drove her to nervous collapse, as Kubrick harangued the actress again and again. Sometimes it was for overacting. ('It looks fake, it really does,' he told her during one scene. 'Every time [Jack] speaks emphatically you're jumping and it looks phoney.') He berated her for concentrating too hard on her dialogue. ('I honestly don't think the lines are going to make an awful lot of difference if you get the right attitude. I think you're worrying about the wrong thing.') And he took her to task for being late on her cue. ('We're fucking killing ourselves out here and you've got to be ready! Shelley, you're just wasting everybody's time now.')

'From May until October I was really in and out of ill health because the stress of the role was so great,' Duvall said during filming. 'Stanley pushed me and prodded me further than I've ever been pushed before. It's the most difficult role I've ever had to play. But Stanley makes you do things that you never thought you could do.' Jack Nicholson, who had a sometimes difficult working relationship with Duvall during filming (probably Kubrick's intention), agreed with his co-star's assessment of Kubrick's methods. 'Stanley's demanding,' he stated. 'He'll do a scene fifty times and you have to be good to do that. There are so many ways to walk into a room, order breakfast or be frightened to death in a closet. Stanley's approach is, how can we do it better than it's ever been done before? It's a big challenge. A lot of actors give him what he wants. If you don't, he'll beat it out of you – with a velvet glove, of course.'

Principal photography was finally completed in April 1979, by which time several productions – including Dino De Laurentiis's *Flash Gordon* (1980) and *The Empire Strikes Back* (1980) – had been forced to relocate owing to *The Shining*'s schedule overruns, the most significant of which was caused by a fire that swept through the hotel set, causing extensive damage and a $2,500,000 rebuild of one of Elstree's main shooting stages. If Warner Bros expected Kubrick to forego the few remaining scenes still to be filmed, they reckoned without the director's legendary immutability: Kubrick insisted that the set be rebuilt on another stage so that filming could be completed as planned, if not as budgeted or scheduled.

Editing began soon after, during which time one of the editors, Gordon Stainforth, realised that Kubrick was deliberately selecting 'the most eccentric and rather over-the-top [takes]. Typically, Nicholson's first take would be absolutely brilliant,' Stainforth said later. 'Then the thing would start to get stale after about ten takes. Then you can see he's almost marking time, so that he doesn't get exhausted. Then he's going right over the top. There were plenty of times when Stanley and I were viewing the stuff where my private choice of the best performance . . . wasn't in, while the more eccentric was.' Editing continued right up until *The Shining*'s world premiere on 23 May 1980 – and beyond (see below).

CASTING: Kubrick had long talked of working with Jack Nicholson, whom he once described as 'arguably the greatest actor in movies today', on his long-gestating *Napoleon* project (see Lost Worlds: The Films That Never Were), and considered no one else for the part of Jack Torrance; Nicholson, an admirer of the novel and a confirmed Kubrick fan, eagerly accepted. Although Shelley Duvall, whom Kubrick knew from her roles in several Robert Altman films and considered to be 'a wonderful actress', was also Kubrick's first and only choice for her role, the director originally wanted Slim Pickens to play the part of the hotel's psychic cook, Dick Hallorann, despite the fact that the character was black in the novel. After his experiences during the filming of *Dr Strangelove*, however, Pickens declined, and Kubrick turned instead to Scatman Crothers, a black actor/musician who had, by coincidence, appeared with Jack Nicholson in three films: *The King of Marvin Gardens* (1972), *The Fortune* (1974), and *One Flew Over the Cuckoo's Nest* (1975).

Key to the entire enterprise was finding an actor to play the Torrances' son, Danny, and some five thousand young boys from Chicago, Denver and Cincinatti were auditioned, photographed and videotaped before Kubrick selected five-year-old Danny Lloyd, a railroad engineer's son from Illinois. Kubrick himself has remarked on the coincidence of having an actor named Jack playing Jack Torrance, and a boy named Danny playing Danny Torrance, but, if this was unintentional, in Danny's case it gave an immediacy to the inexperienced actor's performance, as Kubrick was able to direct him using his given name. 'Stanley had a really good way of speaking to me,' Lloyd later recalled. ' "Okay, Danny, this is what we need you to do, and we want you to look really scared." When they did tell me why I was screaming or why I was scared, they were delicate about it . . . He put it on a level that a kid could understand, and he didn't bark orders.'

**THE USUAL SUSPECTS:** The British actor Philip Stone, who had previously played Dad in *A Clockwork Orange* and Graham in *Barry Lyndon*, returned to play the ghost of the Overlook's waiter/butler, Delbert Grady. The Overlook's bartender, Lloyd, was played by another veteran of two earlier Kubrick films: Joe Turkel, who, as Joseph Turkel, appeared as Tiny in *The Killing*, and as one of the three condemned infantrymen in *Paths of Glory*. Evidently Kubrick had a long memory when it came to supporting players.

## CLASSIC QUOTES

**Dick Hallorann:** 'Some places are like people: some shine and some don't.'

**Jack Torrance:** 'Whenever I'm in here, and you hear me *typing*, or whether you *don't* hear me typing, or whatever the *fuck* you hear me doing in here, when I'm in here, that means that I am working. *That* means *don't* come in. Now, do you think you can handle that?'

**Jack Torrance:** 'I'd give anything for a drink. My goddamned *soul* . . . just a glass of beer.'

**Jack Torrance:** 'I never laid a hand on him, goddamnit. I didn't. I wouldn't touch one hair on his goddamned little head. I love the little sonofabitch! I'd do anything for him, any fucking thing for him. That *bitch*. As long as I live, she'll never let me forget what happened. I did hurt him once, OK? It was an accident – completely unintentional. Coulda happened to anybody. That was three goddamned years ago! The little fucker had thrown all my papers all over the floor! All I tried to do was pull him up . . . A momentary loss of muscular co-ordination. A few extra foot-pounds of energy per second, per *second* . . .'

**Jack Torrance:** 'Mr Grady, you were the caretaker here. I recognise you. I saw your picture in the newspapers. You chopped your wife and daughter up into little bits, then you blew your brains out.'
**Grady:** 'That's strange, sir. I don't have any recollection of that at all.'
**Jack Torrance:** 'Mr Grady, you *were* the caretaker here.'

**Grady:** 'I'm sorry to differ with you, sir, but *you* are the caretaker. You've *always* been the caretaker. I should know, sir. I've *always* been here.'

**Danny Torrance:** '*Redrum! Redrum! Redrum!*'

**Jack Torrance:** 'Heeeere's *Johnny*!'

**THEMES AND MOTIFS:** The gradual temporal and spatial reduction of the narrative – from months to days to hours, and from the mountains to the hotel to the maze – is one of the major themes of *The Shining*, serving to steadily increase the dramatic pace of the film, and to reflect Jack Torrance's spiral into psychosis. In addition, Kubrick's fondness for the theme of immortality and reincarnation was given a free rein, as the director explored the possibilities of life beyond death, evidenced in a question Kubrick asked Stephen King during one of his frequent early-morning calls to the author's home. 'The concept of the ghost presupposes life after death. That's a cheerful concept, isn't it?' King recalled in *American Film* magazine. 'And it sounded so plausible that for a moment I just floundered and didn't say anything. And then I said, "But what about hell?" There was a long pause on his end, and then he came back in a very stiff voice and said, "But I don't believe in hell." He didn't seem to want to get behind the concept of the ghost as a damned soul.'

Indeed, Kubrick fudges the supernatural issue for much of the film, deliberately misdirecting the audience towards a psychological explanation for the manifestations of evil, causing the viewer to wonder whether they're inside the Overlook itself, or merely inside Jack's mind. As Kubrick himself pointed out, it is only when Delbert Grady's ghost frees Jack Torrance from the freezer that there can be no explanation other than that the Overlook *is* haunted, a fact apparently confirmed when Wendy, too, witnesses the ghostly apparitions. Nevertheless, as Diane Johnson notes, 'the psychological states of the characters can create real ghosts who have physical powers.'

*The Shining* makes numerous references to children's stories and cartoons: 'Hansel and Gretel' (Wendy's reference to 'a trail of breadcrumbs') and 'The Three Little Pigs' (assuming the role of the Big Bad Wolf, Jack rants, 'Little pigs! Little pigs! Let me come in! Not by the hair of your chinny-chin-chin? Then I'll huff, and I'll puff, and I'll blow your house in!'), and familiar contemporary characters such as Bugs Bunny (Danny's nickname is Doc, as in 'What's up, Doc?'), Mickey Mouse (the design on Danny's sweater) and Road Runner (the cartoons Danny is seen watching). These deliberate references were almost certainly inspired by a book read by Kubrick and Johnson during their collaboration on *The Shining* screenplay: Bruno Bettelheim's *The Uses of Enchantment*, which postulates the theory that children inhabit what Freud called an 'animistic' or anthropomorphic world, in which good and bad spirits inhabit all things. Johnson noted that she and Kubrick also endeavoured to give the story an emotionally satisfactory climax, what she called 'the artistic satisfaction of a fairytale'.

The image of the maze is another significant aspect of *The Shining*'s symbolic underpinnings. While the hedge maze and its scale-model replica (in which, in a 'shining' moment of his own, Jack Torrance 'sees' Wendy and Danny playing at the centre of the maze) evoke powerful mythological parallels with the story of Theseus and the Minotaur, the imagery of the maze is repeated several times: in the labyrinthine layout of the hotel itself, leading to the central room in which Jack writes his 'book'; in the patterns of the carpet on which Danny plays with his toy cars; in the arrangement of the newspaper cuttings in the scrapbook that appears on Jack's writing desk; and so on.

Another recurring motif is the appearance of a mirror to signal supernatural episodes, perhaps intended to signify the superstition about mirrors capturing and retaining an aspect of a person's soul, or the accepted folk wisdom that a mirror reflects a person's true aspect. Several scenes are deliberately filmed so that the action is reflected in mirrors – Danny's first conversation with Tony; Wendy bringing Jack breakfast in bed; Danny talking to his father in the bedroom; Jack meeting Delbert Grady's ghost in the men's room – while mirrors also figure prominently in Room 237 (when Danny first peers inside the haunted room, and later when the true appearance of the woman in the bath is revealed to Jack) and in the Gold Room, where the appearance of Lloyd and a fully stocked bar takes place in front of a row of mirrors; in addition, the true meaning of the word 'REDRUM' is revealed to Wendy only when she sees it reflected as 'MURDER'.

Incidentally, although it is often misinterpreted as a continuity error, the fact that Jack Torrance claims to recognise the Overlook's 1921-era waiter/butler Delbert Grady from newspaper cuttings where he appeared as *Charles* Grady, the caretaker who killed his wife and daughters at the hotel in 1970, suggests the duality (real/unreal; sane/insane; good/evil) at play in Kubrick's interpretation of *The Shining*. There are *two* Gradys, just as there are two Jack Torrances (the one currently employed as the winter caretaker, and the one seen in the photograph dated 4 July 1921), two Danny Torrances (the boy and his alter ego, Tony) and, of course, two Grady daughters (not twins, but identical-looking sisters aged eight and ten).

MUSIC: Although the composers Wendy Carlos and Rachel Elkind were invited to create music for the opening titles, Kubrick largely used existing classical pieces, including Béla Bartók's 'Music for Strings, Percussion and Celesta' (curiously, King's novel mentions that Wendy Torrance is a fan of Bartók), 'Lontano' by György Ligeti, and several pieces by the Polish modernist Krzysztof Penderecki. One such piece, entitled 'The Awakening of Jacob', was used in the scene in which Jack wakes up from his nightmare, which Kubrick called 'a strange coincidence'. Two well-known dance tunes from the twenties were also used: 'Home' by Henry Hall and the Gleneagles Hotel Band, and 'Midnight, the Stars and You' by the Ray Noble Band, with a vocal by Al Bowlly.

The soundtrack, which was released on vinyl in 1980, is long since deleted, although bootleg CD versions, containing 49 minutes of music, turn up from time to time. Two tracks (the title theme and 'Midnight, the Stars and You') appear on Silva Screen Records' compilation album, *Strangelove . . . Music from the Films of Stanley Kubrick* (FILMCD 303).

**POSTER:** As always, Kubrick took a hands-on approach to the publicity materials for *The Shining*, engaging the legendary graphic and movie-titles designer Saul Bass to create a logo for the film. Bass's hand-drawn design, which features a face peering through the letter 'T', was used against a yellow background for the original-release poster. Subsequent designs, such as those used for the video releases, traditionally used two images, used in isolation or in tandem: a shot of Jack Nicholson, grinning maniacally, as he peers through the smashed door in the 'Heeeere's Johnny!' scene; and a shot of Shelley Duvall, knife in hand, screaming as a blurred axe smashes through the door in the foreground. The first image was occasionally used on its own.

Years later, when Warner Home Video's UK marketing department worked on the original video release, a young creative (who, still employed by a major studio, wishes to remain anonymous) was daring – or foolhardy – enough to suggest changing the cover image to that of Nicholson frozen in ice, from the climax of the film. By the time Kubrick learned of this infringement of his legendary creative control and called the Warner offices to give them a piece of his mind, the responsible party had already moved to CIC, where, ironically, he would oversee the successful re-release of another Kubrick film, *Spartacus*.

**TAG-LINES:** 'A masterpiece of modern horror'. 'Stanley Kubrick's epic nightmare of horror'.

**TRAILER:** The theatrical trailer for *The Shining* was a single, locked-off camera shot, 1m 28s long, holding on the lift as white credits roll up the screen ('THE SHINING A STANLEY KUBRICK FILM Starring JACK NICHOLSON and SHELLEY DUVALL Based on STEPHEN KING'S BEST-SELLING MASTERPIECE OF MODERN HORROR Screenplay by STANLEY KUBRICK & DIANE JOHNSON THE SHINING Directed by STANLEY KUBRICK') in a similar style to that which would ultimately play over the opening titles for the film. The blood begins to pour from the lift doors just as Kubrick's credit disappears from the screen, from which point the shot plays out as it does in the final film. After a final title, a caption card fades up with the legend 'READ THE SENSATIONAL PAPERBACK FROM NEW ENGLISH LIBRARY' accompanied by an image of the reissued Stephen

King novel, which featured the original yellow poster design on the cover and, inside, several pages of black-and-white stills from the film.

The music used for the trailer does not appear in the finished film, but was one of the first pieces composed by Wendy Carlos and Rachel Elkind. Having been informed that Kubrick had been listening to Sibelius's *Valse Trieste*, Carlos and Elkind hired a small orchestra in order to prepare some thirty minutes of varied cues and demos, one of which Kubrick chose to use for the trailer.

**WHAT THE PAPERS SAID:** Despite the optimistic tag-lines, critics were less than kind to Kubrick's first horror movie. *Newsweek*'s Jack Kroll was perhaps the only notable exception, describing *The Shining* as 'the first epic horror film, a movie that is to other horror movies what *2001: A Space Odyssey* was to other space movies'. *Time*'s Richard Schickel agreed. 'It is impossible not to admire Kubrick for flouting conventional expectations of his horror film just as he flouted those of the sci-fi tale in *2001*,' he wrote.

Alas, there was little of their enthusiasm in other reviewers. Many decried what they saw as Kubrick's excision of vast chunks of King's novel ('ninety per cent', as one critic exaggerated it), a rather redundant view probably fostered more by the popularity of the book than a serious critical analysis of the film. Most critics, however, felt that *The Shining* failed in its most basic intentions, in that it was neither scary nor horrifying, as any horror film must be in order to succeed. 'With everything to work with, director Stanley Kubrick has teamed with jumpy Jack Nicholson to destroy all that was so terrifying about Stephen King's bestseller,' stated *Variety*. 'The crazier Nicholson gets, the more idiotic he looks. Shelley Duvall transforms the warm sympathetic wife of the book into a simpering, semi-retarded hysteric.'

The *New Yorker*'s Pauline Kael went further: 'All work and no play makes Stanley a dull boy, too. He was locked up with this project for more than three years, and if ever there was a movie that expressed cabin fever, this is it.' This view was echoed in the UK, where *Monthly Film Bulletin* commented that '[Kubrick's] seclusion has taken its toll', adding: 'The Kubrick magic for holding both audiences and critics in thrall seems to have come unstuck.' *Time Out*'s Fiona Ferguson expressed an equally disappointed view: 'To hang the movie's psychological tension on the leers and grimaces of Nicholson's face (suited though it is to demoniacal expressions), while refusing to develop any sense of the man, is asking for trouble. Similarly, the narrative is too often disregarded in favour of crude and confusing visual shocks. Kubrick's unbalanced approach (over-emphasis on production values) results in soulless cardboard cutouts who can do little to generate audience empathy.'

**BOX OFFICE:** Premiered on a limited release in New York and Los Angeles on Memorial Day weekend, 1980, *The Shining* broke house records in six of the eleven venues where it was debuted, and opened on a further 750 screens on 13 June. By the end of 1980, *The Shining* was among the year's top ten earners, having grossed $47 million in the US alone – the highest box-office gross of any Kubrick film.

**AWARDS:** Entirely overlooked at the 1981 Academy Awards, *The Shining* had to make do with Best Horror Film and Best Supporting Actor (for Scatman Crothers) at the Academy of Science Fiction, Horror and Fantasy Films annual Saturn Awards. Worse still, Stanley Kubrick and Shelley Duvall suffered the ignominy of being nominated, as Worst Director and Worst Actress respectively, for the annual 'anti-Oscars', the Golden Raspberry Awards ('Razzies').

**TECHNICAL ACHIEVEMENTS:** The camera operator Garrett Brown's invention of the Steadicam gyroscopic camera system, which had earlier been demonstrated in *Bound for Glory* and *Rocky* (both 1976) and won Brown a technical Oscar in 1978, was used to extraordinary effect here, not only to chase Danny Torrance around the Overlook's corridors and hedge maze, but for a surprisingly high proportion of the film. 'It's like a magic carpet,' Kubrick enthused. 'The fast, flowing camera movements in the maze would have been impossible to do without the Steadicam. Most of the hotel set was built as a composite, so that you could go up a flight of stairs, turn down a corridor, travel its length and find your way to still another part of the hotel. It mirrored the kind of camera movements which took place in the maze. In order to fully exploit this layout it was necessary to have moving camera shots without cuts, and of course the Steadicam made that much easier to do.'

**INFLUENCED BY:** Kubrick acknowledged an episode of *Omnibus*, the television series on which he worked briefly in the fifties, as a significant inspiration for *The Shining*. The episode was an adaptation of Stephen Crane's short story 'The Blue Hotel', in which an argument between two card players, a paranoiac and a cheat, leads to murder in a snowbound Nebraska hotel. 'You think the point of the story is that his death was inevitable because a paranoid poker player would ultimately get involved in a fatal gunfight,' said Kubrick. 'But, in the end, you find out that the man he accused was actually cheating him. I think *The Shining* uses a similar kind of psychological misdirection to forestall the realisation that the supernatural events are actually happening.'

Although Kubrick almost certainly watched every horror film he could lay his hands on before embarking on production, if *The Shining* was influenced by any other film, it was one of Kubrick's own: *2001: A Space Odyssey*. In an insightful essay 'Kubrick and the Fantastic', published in *Kubrick*, Michael Ciment made a particularly convincing argument for the similarities of the two films. 'The first movement reveals a magnificent landscape of mountains, forests and lakes, one in which the characters are lost, crushed, dominated (*cf.* "THE DAWN OF MAN"),' he explained. 'The second movement, in the Overlook Hotel, finds the manager entrusting Jack with a mission, that of safeguarding his establishment for several months. Here one sees the same polite affability, the same stereotyped and social relations as in the scenes on the moon preceding the *Discovery*'s departure.' The third movement, he further notes, isolates the three protagonists (Frank Poole, Dave Bowman and Hal in *2001*; Jack, Wendy and Danny in *The Shining*) – destroying even their means of communication with the outside world – before the person ostensibly in charge (Hal; Jack) sinks into homicidal madness.

'As for the fourth movement – wordless like the first (in a symmetry equal to that governing *2001*) – it constitutes an initiatory journey of death and transfiguration, this time inside a labyrinth, which terminates in the past to the accompaniment of nostalgic twenties music . . . *The Shining* (whose running time is virtually identical to *2001*'s, even if its "subjective" time span seems shorter) is also the only [other] of Kubrick's films to dispense with a "voice-over" text (either first-person narration or objective commentary) in favour of title cards punctuating the narrative progression. Finally, both films make use of contemporary and consciously "modern" music (Ligeti in *2001*; Ligeti again, Penderecki and Bartók in *The Shining*) mingled with extracts from Romantic works (in this case a *Dies irae* inspired by the final "Witches Sabbath" movement of Berlioz's *Symphonie Fantastique*) which act as a prelude to some violent and total mental breakdown.' In addition, Ciment posits, 'The whisperings in the corridors of the Overlook Hotel are not unlike those which greet Dave Bowman in his Louis XVI suite.'

DÉJÀ VU: The slow zoom out from Dick Hallorann lying in bed watching television recalls many similar shots from *A Clockwork Orange* and *Barry Lyndon*. But there are other similarities to earlier productions not linked with technique:

- the manner in which Jack eats his bacon when Wendy brings him breakfast in bed recalls Alex's feeding time in *A Clockwork Orange*;
- Jack's unintentionally literal declaration that he would sell his soul for a beer recalls Clare Quilty's equally loaded statement – 'Gee, I'm just dying for a drink. I'm just dying to have a drinkie!' – in *Lolita*;
- the knife wound inflicted by Wendy on Jack's hand is also identical to that inflicted by Alex on Dim in *A Clockwork Orange*;
- the acceleration of time throughout the story echoes *Day of the Fight*;
- physically, Shelley Duvall resembles *Barry Lyndon*'s Countess Lyndon as their respective lives unravel due to the machinations of their husbands;
- Jack's axe attacks on Wendy and Dick Hallorann recall a similar weapon wielded by Vincent Rapallo during his mannequin factory fight with Davey Gordon in *Killer's Kiss*.

**INFLUENTIAL ON:** Outtakes from the aerial footage shot by Greg MacGillivray for *The Shining*'s title sequence subsequently appeared in the closing moments of Ridley Scott's seminal science-fiction film, *Blade Runner* (1982), as Deckard and Rachael fly over the mountains in a spinner. Originally, Scott had intended to shoot his own footage in Moab, Utah, and dispatched a second-unit crew to the region in March 1983 for this purpose; however, bad weather rendered the footage unusable, and with only three months to go before the film's scheduled premiere, its associate producer, Ivor Powell, who had worked on *2001*, remembered the mountainous landscapes that had opened *The Shining*. Scott contacted Kubrick, who obliged by granting the film makers free access to *The Shining*'s wilderness shots on one condition: that Scott would not utilise any footage that had already appeared in the film.

Neither Scott nor Powell had reckoned with Kubrick's legendary penchant for shooting far more footage than he would actually need. *Blade Runner*'s supervising editor Terry Rawlings recounted: 'I remember quite clearly those cans of film arriving from Stanley Kubrick's house. All we'd asked him for were shots of Jack Nicholson's yellow Volkswagen driving up into the mountains at the beginning of *The Shining*. Suddenly, we had something like 30,000 feet of film turn up to look at. We had all his outtakes. They were endless.' Rawlings also noted that the footage was problematic in that the Torrances' vehicle did appear at the bottom of the frame. 'Thankfully, *The Shining* had been shot at 1.85:1, a more squarish format than the Panavision one in which *Blade Runner* had been shot. We were able to optically change that footage a slight bit, sort of letterbox it out, to stretch it into more of a rectangle. A good thing, too,' he added. 'If you projected the *Shining* outtakes we used in *Blade Runner* at their normal ratio, the audience would have seen this little yellow Volkswagen driving along in the year 2019!'

A scene from Steven Spielberg's *Jurassic Park* (1993), in which Tim (Joseph Mazzello) escapes velociraptors by hiding in a metal kitchen cabinet, is strongly reminiscent of the pantry in which Danny hides from his father. Spielberg remembers his initial reaction to the film as being muted, a fact he was forced to admit to Kubrick when his friend asked his opinion. 'I'd only seen it once, and I didn't love *The Shining* the first time I saw it,' Spielberg explained to the producers of the 1999 documentary *The Last Movie*, adding that he has since seen *The Shining* 25 times and rates it among his favourite films. 'I wanted to be frightened by it in a kind of carnival fear. I wanted things to pop out at me. I wanted to jump out of my seat. I wanted shocks. I wasn't expecting a psychological shock-storm. I was hoping for a visceral, visual assault on all of my senses. Instead, it was about a descent into madness, and [Kubrick] very inexorably pulled the entire audience down with him, so at that moment when Shelley is reading the last three months of what [Jack] has been writing, and we see the litany of what he has written . . .

That is the biggest shock of *The Shining*, and the greatest genius of *The Shining*, that he could so traumatise us, slowly but surely, with these images and this dread just waiting for you round the corner, when you're dollying behind a child on a tricycle, that you would be shocked by that. That was the equivalent of the chair turning around in *Psycho*, and the sudden reveal of Mrs Bates – and it's more shocking.'

According to the director Paul Anderson, his 1997 science fiction/horror film *Event Horizon* was conceived as an extended homage to Kubrick's film. 'We talked a lot about what the overall concept of the movie was,' Anderson says of his film, 'and it's like *The Shining* in space. But instead of the Overlook Hotel, we have the *Event Horizon*, a labyrinthine spaceship a mile and a half long. It's a classic theme in a lot of horror pictures. You're never quite sure whether the apparitions are real, or if the visitors brought the ghosts to the house with them. Or perhaps the house is possessed, and it's feeding off their disturbed psyches. So, if you think of the *Event Horizon* as being the Overlook Hotel, the big question is, is the Overlook Hotel haunting Jack Nicholson, or is Jack haunting the Overlook Hotel?'

**SEQUELS AND REMAKES:** At the time of release, Stephen King made no secret of his feelings towards Kubrick's adaptation of his most successful book, privately describing it as being 'like this great big gorgeous car with no engine in it' and an 'interesting failure'. King was also fond of pointing out that *The Shining* 'cost roughly $19 million to produce as a film; it cost roughly $24.00 to produce as a novel – the cost of paper, typewriter ribbons, and postage'.

By 1983, King was more forceful in his condemnation of the picture. 'I'd admired Kubrick for a long time and had great expectations for the project, but I was deeply disappointed in the end result,' he told *Playboy* magazine. 'Parts of the film are chilling, charged with a relentlessly claustrophobic terror, but others fell flat.' Describing Kubrick as 'a man who thinks too much and feels too little', King blamed what he saw as the director's pragmatism and rationality for his inability to contrive a supernatural explanation for Jack Torrance's descent into madness. 'So he looked, instead, for evil in the characters and made the film into a domestic tragedy with only vaguely supernatural overtones.' King also expressed dissatisfaction with Kubrick's casting of Jack Nicholson as Jack Torrance, and the resultant shift in emphasis from tragically flawed victim to unhinged misanthrope. 'Jack Nicholson, though a fine actor, was all wrong for the part. His last big role had been in *One Flew Over the Cuckoo's Nest*, and between that and his manic grin, the audience automatically identified him as a loony from the first scene. But the book is about Jack Torrance's gradual *descent* into madness through the malign influence of the Overlook – if the guy is nuts to begin with, then the entire tragedy of his downfall is wasted.'

In 1997, on the twentieth anniversary of *The Shining*'s first publication, King would have the chance to put his own version of the novel on the screen, thanks to a unique deal between King and Kubrick, ABC-TV and Warner Bros. In the resultant 258-minute miniseries, scripted by King and directed by Mick Garris (who had previously adapted another King epic, *The Stand*, for the small screen), the author studiously avoided any of Kubrick and Johnson's inventions – the hedge maze, the repeated phrase in Jack's manuscript, the closing image of the photograph and so on – and included many of the elements he would have liked to have seen in the film: the fire hoses menacing Danny, the wasps' nest which is at first empty, and later full of wasps, the topiary animals' attacks on Jack and Dick Hallorann, the ultimate destruction of the Overlook (and Jack) as the boiler explodes . . .

More significantly, perhaps, the protagonists reverted to their original characterisations: Danny, more resourceful and heroic than in the film, becomes the central character once more; Jack struggles with (rather than acquiesces to) his personal demons, and those of the hotel; Wendy is no longer the 'simpering, semi-retarded hysteric', but warm, strong-willed and sympathetic; Dick Hallorann is allowed to play out his *deus ex machina* role in the final rescue, instead of being killed as soon as he reaches the hotel. Intriguingly, the exteriors used in this version were of the Stanley Hotel in Estes Park, Colorado – the hotel that inspired King to write *The Shining* following his brief stay there (in room 217, retained for this version) in the autumn of 1974.

As King explained to Muriel Gray during a rare British interview in 1998, 'I had things to say about the Stanley Kubrick version of *The Shining*, when the film was made. And years later, I had a chance to re-adapt it – it was actually my idea – for ABC-TV, as a miniseries. And the question was whether or not Warner Brothers, who produced the movie and held the sequel rights, would allow us to do that. Warner Brothers went to Mr Kubrick and asked if that would be all right, and he said it would be all right if King doesn't say anything else one way or another about the film version. But I did want to remake it,' he added pointedly, 'so draw your own conclusions.'

After Kubrick's death, King reiterated his point more succinctly: 'I'm not able to talk about *The Shining*,' he told *Entertainment Weekly*. 'I made a deal with Stanley Kubrick that I wouldn't, and Stan is dead so I'm not going to go there.'

**KUBRICK GOES POP:** In the kid-from-hell comedy *Problem Child* (1990), John Ritter bursts through his adopted son's bedroom door in a grinning Jack Torrance pose, yelling 'Heeeere's *Daddy!*' *Twister* (1996) features a drive-in movie theatre playing *The Shining*, while the credits show two characters named 'Stanley' and 'Kubrick' who are never named in the film.

An entire segment of *The Simpsons*' fifth Hallowe'en special, 'Treehouse of Horror V' (#2F03), was an elaborate parody of Kubrick's film entitled 'The Shinning'. Opening, like Kubrick's film, as the Simpson family drive along winding Colorado roads towards Mr Burns's lodge – which, he says, 'was built on an ancient Indian burial ground and was the setting for satanic rituals, witch burnings, and five John Denver Christmas specials' – where they will act as winter caretakers. Groundskeeper Willie realises that Bart has 'the shinning'. Bart says, 'You mean "shining",' to which Willie replies, 'Shh! Ye wanna get sued?' He tells Bart to use his 'shin' to call him. 'But don't be readin' my mind between four and five – that's Willie's time!' This time, it is the lack of beer and cable television that drives Homer insane, forcing him to chase down his family with an axe, burst through various doors ('Heeeeere's David Letterman!'), scrawl 'NO TV AND NO BEER MAKE HOMER GO CRAZY' over the walls, and finally freeze in the snow.

In a later episode, the *Simpsons/X Files* crossover 'The Springfield Files' (#3G01), the traditional *X Files* device of captioning the location and time of each scene is subverted by the caption's repetition of the phrase 'ALL WORK AND NO PLAY MAKES JACK A DULL BOY' scrolling all the way up the screen. A more minor reference appears in 'Brother from the Same Planet' (#9F12), in which Bart's friend Milhouse writes (and recites) the phrase 'Trab pu kcip!' ('Pick up Bart!' backwards) in the style of Danny Torrance.

More obscurely, the 'shoot-'em-up' computer game *Duke Nuke 'Em-3D* has an unofficial additional level inspired by *The Shining*, created by an amateur and widely available over the Internet, in which players pursue a deranged Jack Torrance around the snowbound hedge maze in the grounds of the Overlook.

Two references to *The Shining* appear in an episode of *Father Ted* entitled 'The Plague': Father Jack is found in his garden, frozen into a Jack Torrance pose, while the word 'REDRUM' is spray-painted in red on the wall of Tom's home.

**CUT SCENES:** Just as he had with *2001*, Kubrick recut *The Shining* just after its initial release, removing a four-minute coda in which Ullman, the hotel manager played by Barry Nelson, visits Wendy in hospital, informing her that searchers have been unable to locate or recover her husband's body. 'Shelley Duvall has left after Nicholson's death and gone to California, presumably, and I show up,' Nelson told *Premiere* magazine, explaining that the film ended with Ullman throwing Danny a tennis ball – presumably the same one seen earlier in the film – and saying, 'Hey, Danny, you forgot this.' 'I've forgotten its significance,' Nelson added, 'but it was evil. And what it implies is that [Ullman] is the mastermind of the whole thing.'

One of *The Shining*'s composers, Wendy Carlos, also recalled 'a strange and mystical scene in which Jack Nicholson discovers objects that have been arranged in his working space in the ballroom with arrows and things. He walks down and thinks he hears a voice. A ghost throws a ball back to him. None of that made it in the final film.'

Kubrick made even more substantial cuts to the UK and Australian versions of the film, which run at just under thirty minutes shorter than those available elsewhere. The following scenes were excised or amended:

- Danny is examined by a paediatrician (played by Anne Jackson), having blacked out during his vision of the lift and the Grady girls. Afterwards, Wendy tells the doctor more about Danny, including the story of how Danny's imaginary friend, Tony, first materialised just after Jack broke the boy's arm while drunk.
- Accompanied by Durkin, Ullman shows Jack and Wendy around the gold ballroom, and informs them that all the alcohol has been removed from the premises – 'reduces the insurance we normally have to carry'. Danny joins them from the games room (where he has apparently been 'blowing up the universe') as they are introduced to Dick Hallorann.
- A scene in which Wendy pushes a breakfast trolley through the hotel corridors.
- Wendy prepares lunch as a newscaster reports that an Aspen woman, Susan Robertson, is still missing following her disappearance during a hunting trip. A snowstorm is said to be on the way.
- The 'THURSDAY' caption.
- Wendy and Danny are watching *Summer of '42* (1971) together on television. Danny asks his mother if he can collect a fire engine from their room, and Wendy warns him not to wake his father.
- Talking aloud as she paces and smokes, Wendy is considering her options for escape when she hears Danny intoning the word 'Redrum!' over and over. Going in to check on him, she finds Danny bolt upright in bed, speaking in Tony's voice. 'Danny can't wake up, Mrs Torrance,' Danny/Tony tells her as she tries to wake him. 'Danny's gone away, Mrs Torrance,' Danny/Tony says. She hugs him.
- Dick Hallorann calls the Sidewinder forest rangers back to check if they have managed to contact the Overlook by radio.
- The '8am' caption.
- On the aeroplane, Hallorann asks a stewardess what time the flight reaches Denver. Cutaway to a slow track-in on Jack typing at his desk in the Overlook's main room. Hallorann's plane touches down in a snowbound Denver, and he calls his friend Larry Durkin, the proprietor of Durkin's Auto Supply, to ask about the weather, and the possibility of borrowing a Sno-Cat to make the journey up to the hotel.
- Danny is watching a *Road Runner* cartoon as Wendy tells him she must leave him for five minutes to talk to his father. Danny responds in Tony's voice. Wendy kisses him and picks up the baseball bat before going to face Jack.
- Near the climax of the film, as Jack chases Danny through the snowbound hedge maze, Wendy is shocked to find a room full of

cobweb-draped and dusty skeletons, in full evening dress, grinning at her.

● Some important dialogue was cut from the scene in which Wendy brings Jack breakfast in bed: 'I've never been this happy or comfortable anywhere,' he tells her. 'It was almost as though I knew what was going to be around every corner. I mean, we've all had moments of *déjà vu*, but this was ridiculous.'

The removal of these scenes has a surprisingly significant effect on the film, particularly as many of them – Wendy and the paediatrician, Ullman's reference to the absence of alcohol at the Overlook, Jack expressing to Wendy his feelings of *déjà vu*, the Aspen weather report, Dick's attempts to reach the Overlook – are concerned with the building of tension through the foreshadowing of future events.

The absence of two scenes in which Danny speaks to Wendy in Tony's voice also removes the threat that Danny may be trapped in his alter ego's personality ('Danny's gone away, Mrs Torrance') – and the relief the audience feels when the boy runs out of the hedge maze shouting, 'Mommy, Mommy!' It might be argued that the three excised scenes featuring Dick Hallorann – on the radio, on an aeroplane and on the road – add little to the overall structure of the film beyond time, but removing them does make his sudden appearance at the Overlook feel like something of a *deus ex machina* ending, since, even though his arrival does not exactly save the day, it is his Sno-Cat that gives Wendy and Danny their ultimate means of escape.

**TRIVIA:** In several foreign versions, Kubrick replaced the phrase 'All work and no play makes Jack a dull boy' with locally used epigrams: '*Il mattino ha l'oro in bocca*' ('He who wakes up early meets a golden day') for Italy; '*No por mucho madrugar amanece más temprano*' ('Although one will rise early, it won't dawn sooner') for Spain; in Germany, '*Was Du heute kanst besorgen, das verschiebe nicht auf Morgen*' ('Don't put off till tomorrow what you can do today').

Jack Nicholson stated that the scene in which Jack Torrance berates his wife for interrupting his writing was born out of his own experience as a budding screenwriter. 'That's the one scene in the movie I wrote myself,' he said. 'That scene at the typewriter – that's what I was like when I got my divorce. I was under the pressure of being a family man with a daughter and one day I accepted a job to act in a movie in the daytime and I was writing a movie at night and I'm back in my little corner and my beloved wife, Sandra [Knight Nicholson], walked in on what was, unbeknownst to her, this *maniac* – and I told Stanley about it and we wrote it into the scene. I remember being at my desk and telling her, "Even if you don't *hear* me typing it doesn't mean I'm not *writing*. This *is writing*." ' Nicholson is also said to have improvised the Johnny Carson line 'Heeeere's *Johnny*!' for the moment in which he axes his way through the bathroom door trying to get to the terrified Wendy.

References to room number 217, used in the book because it was the room in which King and his wife stayed at the hotel that inspired *The Shining*, were replaced with the fictional room 237 at the management's request.

**APOCRYPHA:** Kubrick's former secretary, Margaret Adams, liked to tell the story of how the director discovered *The Shining*. Having completed *Barry Lyndon*, Kubrick sat down with a large stack of books, from which he would pick a title and read it for about a minute, before hurling it at the wall. When this did not happen for a while, she went in to check on him, and found him reading *The Shining*. The story is entirely apocryphal: Kubrick could not possibly have read the novel in published form before Warner Bros, which had acquired the film rights prior to publication, sent him galleys (advance proofs). King himself doubted the veracity of this tale, noting that the novel starts slowly, and the opening chapters have little to do with the rest of the story – Kubrick, in fact, deleted all of this background information and went straight to Part Two, some sixty pages in.

Another apocryphal story surrounding *The Shining* suggests that, in an almost Hitchcockian act of sadism, Kubrick had each page of Jack Torrance's manuscript individually typed with the words 'All work and no play makes Jack a dull boy'. In fact, although Vincent LoBrutto claims in his biography of Kubrick that the director used his own electronic typewriter – one of the first to incorporate a built-in memory – to generate the five hundred or so pages, it is clear from the way in which they are laid out (complete with mistakes) that each *was* individually typed; however, the relatively small number of pages seen in close-up means that only twenty or so pages would need to have been prepared in this way. Whether or not Kubrick had all five hundred pages typed *anyway* is a secret that probably died with him.

Finally, the film Wendy and Danny are seen watching on television is not *Love Story* (1970), as is often claimed, but Robert Mulligan's *Summer of '42* (1971).

**AVAILABILITY:** *The Shining* is available on video in the UK as a full-screen PAL format VHS video (S061079), in the shortened, 114-minute version described above.

In the United States, the full-length, full-screen version is available as an NTSC-format VHS (WA 17369), laserdisc (11079), and Region 1 DVD (17369). The VHS and DVD also contain a theatrical trailer, as well as Vivian Kubrick's thirty-minute documentary, *Making The Shining*, the only such record of a Kubrick film ever committed to film. Filmed on the Aaton 16mm camera given to her by her father, and edited by Gordon Stainforth, Vivian's film provides a fascinating, if slightly bowdlerised, insight into the film-making process adopted by Kubrick during the making of *The Shining*. Several cast members – including

Nicholson, Duvall, Lloyd and Crothers – are interviewed, and, although Kubrick himself is not directly addressed at any point, much footage of the elusive and enigmatic director survived Kubrick's own re-edit, despite his removal of some of the less flattering images of himself, and sensitive footage of his cast and crew.

Purists wondering at the absence of a widescreen edition of *The Shining* should note that the film was shot at the 4:3 ratio of television screens, and 'matted' for cinema screenings at a ratio of 1.85:1. For all home-video versions, therefore, the 'matting' was simply removed, leaving the perfect full-screen image that Kubrick himself approved.

**EXPERT WITNESS:** 'We had to fill up the elevator, which was built as a separate set, with blood, or something that simulated blood. We looked at the liquid, tested it, and Stanley said, "It's great. It's going to work. But the color's not real." We even considered using real animal blood, but Stanley, being the great animal lover that he was, couldn't bring himself to do that, and rightly so. There was a whole saga about what we would use, but oddly enough, it was one of the shorter scenes in the movie to actually shoot. We put two cameras side by side in a waterproof housing in the middle of the floor, and Stanley and I stood at the back of the set. I remember jokingly saying to him, "Is this safe here?" Because the set was about fifty, sixty feet long by ten, twelve feet high. And he said, "What do you mean?" I said, "Well, when all that liquid comes out of the lift, it could submerge us. We could drown." He was always very quick to cotton to safety, and we got up on a table, which was kind of ridiculous, because we were much higher than it was ever going to get. The blood came out with a force that was quite incredible, and all the movement of furniture that you see in that scene actually happened. We didn't do more than two, three takes. Which for Stanley was quite conservative.' – Larry Smith, gaffer, quoted in *Premiere* magazine, August 1999.

**FINAL ANALYSIS:** The fact that most critics claim that *The Shining* fails to work as a horror film, in that it is neither horrific nor scary, says less about the inadequacies of Kubrick's film than it does about the gulf between critics and audiences.

One of the first, and few, horror films to successfully create a genuine chill despite the fact that all but the climax is shot in brightly lit interiors and in broad daylight, *The Shining* is horrific in that it deals with the psychological more than the supernatural. Although there is plenty of blood, most notably in the awesomely conceived and realised elevator sequence, the only real murder takes place at some distance from the camera: it is the shock of Dick Hallorann's death as much as the method of his murder that so disturbs the audience – especially the proportion of it who expected Hallorann's rescue to take place as it had in the book, or for Jack's madness to be brought on by the hotel's evil influence, rather than being self-evident from the very first scene. To horror fans like Wendy Torrance, it is Kubrick's very utilisation and ultimate subversion of the traditional trappings – i.e. traps – of the horror film that allows the film to transcend the genre, while at the same time serving as a prime example of it.

After all, there are few things more terrifying than an axe-wielding homicidal maniac trying to murder his own wife and child, no matter how unsympathetic the former might be portrayed.

**KUBRICK ON KUBRICK:** 'A story of the supernatural cannot be taken apart and analyzed too closely. The ultimate test of its rationale is whether it is good enough to raise the hairs on the back of your neck. If you submit it to a completely logical and detailed analysis, it will eventually appear absurd. In his essay on the uncanny, *Das Unheimliche*, Freud said that the uncanny is the only feeling which is more powerfully experienced in art than in life. If the genre required any justification, I should think this alone would serve as its credentials.' – quoted in *Kubrick* by Michael Ciment, 1984.

# Full Metal Jacket (1987)

**(Colour – 116 mins)**
Directed and Produced by Stanley Kubrick
Screenplay by Stanley Kubrick, Michael Herr, Gustav Hasford
Based on the novel *The Short-Timers* by Gustav Hasford
Executive Producer Jan Harlan
Co-Producer Philip Hobbs
Associate Producer Michael Herr
Assistant to the Director Leon Vitali
Lighting Cameraman Douglas Milsome
Production Designer Anton Furst
Original Music by Abigail Mead
Editor Martin Hunter
Sound Recording Edward Tise
Boom Operator Martin Trevis
Sound Editors Nigel Galt, Edward Tise
Dubbing Mixers Andy Nelson, Mike Dowson
Re-recording Delta Sound, Shepperton
Special Effects Supervisor John Evans
Special Effects Senior Technicians Peter Dawson, Jeff Clifford, Alan Barnard
Casting Leon Vitali
Additional Casting Mike Fenton and Jane Feinberg, CS, Marion Dougherty
Additional Vietnamese Casting Dan Train, Nguyen Thi My Chau
1st Assistant Director Terry Needham

2nd Assistant Director Christopher Thompson
Production Manager Phil Kohler
Unit Production Manager Bill Shepherd
Production Co-ordinator Margaret Adams
Costume Designer Keith Denny
Wardrobe Master John Birkenshaw
Wardrobe Assistant Helen Gill
Co-Make-up Artists Jennifer Boost, Christine Allsop
Dialogue Editor Joe Elling
Assistant Sound Editors Paul Conway, Peter Culverwell
Montage Editing Engineer Adam Watkins
Video Operator Manuel Harlan
Camera Trainees Vaughan Matthews, Michaela Mason
Editing Trainee Rona Buchanan
Hair by Leonard

**CAST:** Matthew Modine (*Joker*), Adam Baldwin (*Animal Mother*), Vincent D'Onofrio (*Gomer Pyle/Leonard Lawrence*), Lee Ermey (*Gunnery Sergeant Hartman*), Dorian Harewood (*Eightball*), Kevyn Major-Howard (*Rafterman*), Arliss Howard (*Cowboy*), Ed O'Ross (*Lieutenant Walter J Schinoski/Mr Touchdown*), John Terry (*Lieutenant Lockhart*), Keiron Jecchinis (*Crazy Earl*), Kirk Taylor (*Payback*), Tim Colceri (*Doorgunner*), John Stafford (*Doc Jay*), Bruce Boa (*Poge Colonel*), Ian Tyler (*Lieutenant Cleves*), Sal Lopez (*THE Rock*), Gary Landon Mills (*Donlon*), Papillon Soo Soo (*Da Nang Hooker*), Peter Edmund (*Brown/Snowball*), Ngoc Le (*VC Sniper*), Leanne Hong (*Motorbike Hooker*), Tan Hung Francione (*ARVN Pimp*), Marcus D'Amico (*Hand Job*), Costas Dino Chimona (*Chili*), Gil Kopel (*Stork*), Keith Hodiak (*Daddy DA*), Peter Merrill (*TV Journalist*), Herbert Norville (*Daytona Dave*), Nguyen Hue Phong (*Camera Thief*), Duc Hu Ta (*Dead NVA*), Martin Adams, Kevin Aldridge, Del Anderson, Philip Bailey, Louis Barlotti, John Beddows, Patrick Benn, Steve Boucher, Adrian Bush, Tony Carey, Gary Cheeseman, Wayne Clark, Chris Cornibert, Danny Cornibert, John Curtis, John Davis, Harry Davies, Kevin Day, Gordon Duncan, Phil Elmer, Colin Elvis, Hadrian Follett, Sean Frank, David George, Laurie Gomes, Brian Goodwin, Nigel Goulding, Tony Hague, Steve Hands, Chris Harris, Bob Hart, Derek Hart, Barry Hayes, Tony Hayes, Robin Hedgeland, Duncan Henry, Kenneth Head, Trevor Hogan, Luke Hogdal, Steve Hudson, Tony Howard, Sean Lamming, Dan Landin, Tony Leete, Nigel Lough, Terry Lowe, Frank McCardle, Gary Meyer, Brett Middleton, David Milner, Sean Minmagh, Tony Minmagh, John Morrison, Russell Mott, John Ness, Robert Nichols, David Perry, Peter Rommely, Liam Hogan, Pat Sands, Jim Sarup, Chris Schmidt-Maybach, Al Simpson, Russell Slater, Gary Smith, Roger Smith, Tony Smith, Anthony Styliano, Bill Thompson, Mike Turjansky, Dan Weldon, Dennis Wells, Michael Williams, John Wilson, John Wonderling (*Parris Island Recruits/Vietnam Platoon*).

**UNCREDITED CAST:** Vivian Kubrick (*News Camera Operator at Mass Grave*), David Palffy (*Grave Soldier*).

**TITLE SEQUENCE:** After the Warner Bros logo, a country-and-western ballad – Johnny Wright's 'Goodbye My Darling, Hello Vietnam' – begins to play over and two simple title cards, in bold white letters on a black background: 'A FILM BY STANLEY KUBRICK' and 'FULL METAL JACKET'. After the caption cards, the film jumps immediately to the Parris Island barbershop, where the new recruits are receiving their close-cropped haircuts with electric hair clippers – the same kind, thanks to a quick telephone call made to a friend of R Lee Ermey's at Parris Island, used to clip the hair of French poodles.

**SUMMARY:** Parris Island, South Carolina: the recruits of United States Marine Corps platoon 3092 have their heads shaved before being subjected to a barrage of insults, humiliation and bullying by Gunnery Sergeant Hartman, who gives several of the recruits some more 'suitable' names: an overweight dimwit becomes Private Gomer Pyle, a smart-mouthed intellectual Private Joker, a Texan-born recruit becomes Private Cowboy, and so on. Over the next few weeks, the recruits are put through their paces, learning to love their guns and the Corps, and taught to kill. Pyle is singled out for special treatment by Hartman, but his efforts to turn him into a killing machine backfire: the night after graduation, Pyle turns his rifle on Hartman before killing himself.

In Vietnam, Joker is assigned to write thinly veiled propaganda for the army magazine, *Stars and Stripes*, and is stationed at Da Nang when the Viet Cong break the Tet holiday ceasefire and launch what becomes known as the Tet Offensive. Joker and his new buddy Rafterman are posted to a squad where Joker is reunited with Cowboy. On the road to the bombed-out remains of Hué City, the squad lieutenant is blown to pieces by a booby-trapped child's toy, and Cowboy is left in charge. In the city, the men are pinned down by sniper fire coming from the ruined buildings: one by one they are picked off, and Cowboy is attempting to pull out when he, too, is shot dead.

The survivors make a direct assault on the sniper's position, but when Joker comes face to face with the sniper – a young Vietnamese woman – his rifle jams. She shoots at Joker, but Rafterman shoots her first. As she lies dying, praying for a quick death, Joker shoots her point-blank, his first confirmed kill. As salty as the rest of the squad, he and Rafterman join their fellow men in a rousing rendition of the 'Mickey Mouse Club' theme tune.

**SOURCE:** *Full Metal Jacket* was loosely adapted by Kubrick, Michael Herr and Gustav Hasford from Hasford's first novel, *The Short-Timers*, a stark and poetic first-person, present-tense account following James T Davis – rechristened 'Private Joker' by his drill instructor – and his fellow US Marine recruits on a 385-day 'short-time' enlistment in the US Marine Corps, through the brutal and dehumanising boot camp at Parris Island, South Carolina, to the middle of the Tet offensive and the Battle of Hué. Hasford began the book while still 'in country', attached to the First Marine Division during 1966 and 1968. Like Private Joker, Hasford was assigned to a Marine Corps magazine as a 4312 Basic Military Journalist; unlike Joker, however, Hasford never earned himself a confirmed kill. 'Actually, my body count was a standing joke,' he once commented. 'I killed as many of them as they did of me.'

The book took seven years to write and another three to get published. When it finally did – in 1979, after the films *The Deer Hunter* (1978) and *Apocalypse Now* (1979) had put the Vietnam War back on to the national agenda – it was to great critical acclaim. The *Los Angeles Times* called *The Short-Timers* 'a savage, unforgiving look at a savage, unforgivable time'; *Newsweek* described it as 'the best work of fiction about the Vietnam war'; and the Kirkus Reviews service, which provides pre-publication critiques of books that may prove suitable for film adaptation, called it 'fine and real and terrifying'.

Kubrick discovered the book through this last source in 1979, and, when he finally got around to reading it three years later, he knew immediately that the book would form the basis of his next film. Kubrick took steps to secure the screen rights, which, he discovered, had already been snapped up by a Munich businessman with no obvious connections to the movie business. On this occasion, Kubrick would be forced to dig deep into Warner Bros' pockets in order to acquire the rights for himself.

Hasford had been discharged from the Marines in August 1968, and had spent the past two decades in and out of work as a freelance journalist, a hotel security guard, and a staff editor for adult magazines. He was living in his car, on a budget of $2 a day, when the screen rights for *The Short-Timers* were optioned for close to a million dollars. Hasford liked to say that his windfall was equivalent to the $50,000 per annum salaries of his friends, paid in one lump sum instead of being spread over twenty years. The fact that *The Short-Timers* was almost out of print by the time Hasford learned that Stanley Kubrick was planning to make a film of it augured well for its future sales. Hasford was happy. He would not remain so for long.

During production, Hasford found himself increasingly cut off from the film-making process. He was disgruntled to discover that, although his scenes were given to Michael Herr for revisions, the reverse did not occur, and that, while Kubrick and Herr would share screenplay credit, the best they would offer him was a credit for additional dialogue – virtually unnecessary, since Hasford would receive acknowledgement for the source novel, from which much of the dialogue was drawn. 'For a year and a half we were in disagreement, [but] from my point of view, I deserved a full credit,' said Hasford, referring to what he described as 'a series of marathon transatlantic phone calls and letters' in which he and Kubrick 'chewed over every line' of the screenplay. 'I heard all the arguments against my attitude from Stanley and Warner Bros and Michael Herr, and I was never convinced their arguments were valid. I persisted until I won,' he added. 'I beat Stanley, City Hall, The Powers That Be, and all the lawyers at Warner Bros, up to and including the Supreme Boss Lawyer.'

Almost a decade later, Herr revealed the real reason for Kubrick's cave-in: 'Gus wrote a number of scenes at Stanley's invitation,' he said, 'and one of them, "The Death of Cowboy", was used in the film – maybe four lines of dialogue. But Stanley felt, for several reasons (one of the chief ones being that it would be bad PR to have a pissed-off Vietnam vet around), to give Gus a screenplay credit.' Herr was compensated with the generous gift of an additional credit as associate producer.

**WORKING TITLES:** Much as Kubrick admired Hasford's novel *The Short-Timers* – or '*Shorty*', as Hasford tended to refer to it – he did not care for the title, and discarded it as soon as he had optioned the book. Although Kubrick knew that it referred to soldiers on a relatively short (one-year) tour of duty in Vietnam, he felt that the title was misleading: audiences might associate the phrase 'short-timers' with people who do only half a day's work. According to Herr, Kubrick found the phrase 'full metal jacket' in a gun catalogue, where it was used to describe the copper casing around a lead bullet. Kubrick, who thought the phrase 'beautiful and touching, and kind of poetic', knew that it could also be used as a metaphor to describe the hard-hearted killing machines into which the young Marine recruits would begin to evolve on Parris Island, before their transformations were completed in country.

**PRODUCTION HISTORY:** 'Start the cameras,' Private Cowboy says as a newsreel camera glides past his platoon. 'This is *Vietnam: The Movie!*' But after *The Deer Hunter* (1978), *Apocalypse Now* (1979) and *Platoon* (1986), '*Vietnam: The Movie*' was the last thing Kubrick had in mind when he set out to make *Full Metal Jacket*. Nevertheless, Kubrick had been looking for a good book about the Vietnam War, 'something with a *story*', since 1980, when he had first contacted the co-screenwriter of *Apocalypse Now* (1979), Michael Herr, whose Vietnam book *Dispatches* Kubrick had admired. 'He was thinking about making a war movie next,' Herr wrote in an essay for *Vanity Fair*, 'but he wasn't sure which war, and in fact, now that he mentioned it, not even so sure he wanted to make a war movie at all.'

Nevertheless, Kubrick asked Herr if he knew of any good books about the Vietnam War, which he didn't – indeed, having spent a year in Vietnam as foreign correspondent for *Esquire*, another seven years writing *Dispatches* – a book about his experiences in Indochina – and a further two years writing Martin Sheen's narration for Francis Ford Coppola's *Apocalypse Now* (1979), Vietnam was the last thing Herr wanted to think about. Over the next three years, Kubrick and Herr participated in what the latter has frequently described as 'one phone call lasting three years, with interruptions', until Kubrick discovered *The Short-Timers* – which, coincidentally, opens with a quote from Herr's *Dispatches* – bought the rights, wrote a long treatment of the book, and invited Herr to work with him on the script. 'Then we really started talking,' Herr recalled.

The script for *Full Metal Jacket* was created in a unique way: working from Kubrick's treatment, Herr wrote a screenplay in prose form, which Kubrick subsequently rewrote before passing it to Gustav Hasford, by now in London, for his own contribution. The script continued to evolve throughout the pre-production process, and through principal photography itself. The script dated 4 February 1985 is radically different from the one presented on screen. While still divided into three sections, set on Parris Island, in Da Nang, and Hué – Kubrick's beloved 'nonsubmersible units' – the screenplay remained in prose form, but with Private Joker's copious narration underlined. Although much of the dialogue and many of the scenes remained largely intact, the two separate sniper scenes from the latter half of the book were merged together.

Further additions to the script came with the casting of a former US Marines drill instructor, R Lee Ermey, as Gunnery Sergeant Hartman, known in the novel by the name Gerheim. 'I'd say fifty per cent of Lee's dialogue, specifically the insult stuff, came from Lee,' Kubrick told *Rolling Stone*. 'Lee came up with, I don't know, 150 pages of insults. Off the wall stuff: "I don't like the name Lawrence. Lawrence is for faggots and sailors." ' Ermey remembers at least one instance when his own improvisation wound up in the script, on this occasion, after he forgot his dialogue lines while in the midst of a tirade against Arliss Howard's Private Cowboy, and replaced it with one of his own invention: 'I bet you're the kind of guy that would fuck a person in the ass and not even have the goddamn common courtesy to give him a reach-around!' ('I'd love to take credit for those lines,' Herr told the producers of the documentary *Stanley Kubrick: The Invisible Man*. 'They're fabulous, fabulous lines – very true, really funny, great language, and it plays.') 'Drill instructors are very inventive,' Ermey explained. 'As a DI I could walk down a line of recruits and drop every third or fourth one of them to his knees, and you'd never catch me at it. Just give a little elbow, drop him like that.' Kubrick was clearly full of admiration for Ermey. 'Unless you're living in a world that doesn't need fighting men, you can't fault him,' he enthused. 'Except maybe for a certain lack of subtlety in his behaviour. And I don't think the United States Marine Corps is in the market for subtle drill instructors.'

Kubrick had initially wanted his regular cinematographer John Alcott to light *Full Metal Jacket*; when he turned it down for health reasons (he died in 1986), Kubrick hired Douglas Milsome, who, as Alcott's assistant for fifteen years, had been focus puller on *Barry Lyndon*, and second-unit photographer on *The Shining*. Similarly, without the option of working with the *Dr Strangelove* and *Barry Lyndon* production designer, Ken Adam, Kubrick turned instead to Adam's former assistant, the British-born designer Anton Furst. Furst had helped to realise the deep-space design of *Alien* (1979) and the fairy-tale fantasy of *The Company of Wolves* (1985), and, later, had won an Oscar for his extremely gothic Gotham City in *Batman* (1989). *Full Metal Jacket* arguably gave him his greatest challenge of all – bringing Vietnam to London.

Having spent half a lifetime, and most of his career, insisting upon absolute authenticity in almost every aspect of his films, Kubrick surprised many with his decision to make a film about the Vietnam War in the concrete jungle of East London. Nevertheless, as the actor Adam Baldwin explained to *American Film*, 'When you think of Vietnam, it's natural to imagine jungles. But [*Full Metal Jacket*] is about urban warfare. That's why London wasn't such a crazy location after all.' A Territorial Army base in Bassingbourne, a disused airfield in Enfield and a purpose-built army latrine at Shepperton Studios would serve as locations for the scenes set at the Marine Corps' training camp at Parris Island, South Carolina, while a former coke-smelting plant in East London – popularly known in the region as 'Beckton gasworks' – would double as the Vietnamese city of Hué, where the film's final scenes would be set. 'We worked from still photographs of Hué in 1968, and we found an area that had the same 1930s functionalist architecture,' Kubrick recollected. 'Now, not every bit of it was right, but some of the buildings were absolute carbon copies of the outer industrial areas of Hué. It had been owned by British Gas, and it was scheduled to be demolished,' he added, 'so they allowed us to blow up the buildings. We had demolition guys in there for a week, laying charges . . . Then we had a wrecking ball there for two months, with the art director telling the operator which hole to knock in which building.'

To add verisimilitude, two hundred living palm trees were shipped in en masse from Spain, along with thousands of plastic versions for the background; almost five thousand Vietnamese ex-patriates living in London were drafted in to populate the areas doubling for Phu Bai, Da Nang and Hué; murals, signs and advertisements were copied from photographs of the period, many of them taken by combat correspondents like *Full Metal Jacket*'s Rafterman. 'He never got the thin light of the Southeast England skies to match the opulent light over Vietnam,' Herr considered, 'but whatever could be dressed was dressed *à la* Kubrick, Stanley studying photographs of palm trees that he'd had taken in Spain, individually choosing from the thousands of trees which ones he wanted in his movie. Very meticulous guy, Stanley.'

The ability to locate his battlefield within a defined space, just as he had for *Paths of Glory* and *Spartacus*, gave the film's battle scenes a spatial reality that would have been difficult, if not impossible, to create within a studio backlot. 'One of the things I tried to do was give you a sense of where you were, [and] where everything else was,' Kubrick explained, 'which in war movies is something you frequently don't get. The terrain of small-unit action is really the story of the action,' he added, 'and this is something we tried to make beautifully clear: there's the low way, there's the building space. And once you get in there, everything is exactly where it was. No cutting away, no cheating.'

As always with Kubrick, there were frequent disagreements over the script, this time pointedly good-natured due to his and Herr's long and enduring relationship. Kubrick and Herr disagreed over a number of elements, most notably Kubrick's desire for voice-over (Kubrick won), and to end the film with Private Joker's death (Kubrick lost). 'He wanted Joker, the teenage hero of *The Short-Timers* and of his still-untitled movie, to die,' Herr stated. 'I didn't think so. "It's the Death of the Hero," he said. "It'll be so powerful, so moving." And he was genuinely moved by it. "We've seen it in Homer, Michael." ' Herr evidently persuaded Kubrick that Joker did not literally need to die, since the last vestiges of his humanity have been removed by the film's end – transformed into just another 'grunt', he is effectively dead already. 'I am in a world of shit,' he says, echoing Private Pyle's words in the Parris Island head, 'but I am alive, and I am not afraid.'

Production was typically tough on the young and relatively inexperienced actors – among the youngest Kubrick had ever worked with – many of whom found the director's penchant for filming a great many takes on almost every scene to be physically and psychologically demanding. Kubrick, who frequently claimed that such rumours were exaggerated, told Tim Cahill that his unusually high shooting ratio was largely due to actors who did not know their lines. 'What Stanley really didn't like is if you wasted his time,' Arliss Howard (Cowboy) stated. 'And what he considered to be time-wasting was if you didn't know your lines. One day we had to do this thing called the "Rifleman's Creed" where we laid on the bed and recited this speech, and we had to do it with a tiny speaker in your ear and do it to playback, which was very disorienting for me. We got to take sixteen and he said to me, "You're not prepared." And I said, "No, I know the thing – I'm just having trouble with this thing in my ear." And he said, "You don't know it if you don't know how to be able to do it with that in your ear." We got into an argument about how well I knew it, but I finally realized that he was absolutely right.'

'A lot of actors today get bad advice from teachers who tell them not to get locked into their lines, so you end up doing thirty takes of something,' Kubrick told Tim Cahill of *Rolling Stone*. 'Now, if the actor is a nice guy, he goes home, he says, "Stanley's such a perfectionist, he does a hundred takes on every scene." So my thirty takes becomes a hundred. And I get this reputation. If I did a hundred takes on every scene,' Kubrick added, 'I'd never finish a film.' The cinematographer Douglas Milsome corroborated Kubrick's story. 'There were occasions on *Full Metal Jacket* where we went a few more than twenty-five or thirty takes, but we usually didn't average more than ten to fifteen takes.'

Most difficult of all was the barrage of abuse and intimidation to which the actors playing Marine recruits were subjected by Ermey, both on and off camera. 'It was terrifying to those actors,' Ermey told the *New York Times*. 'My objective was intimidation. No one had ever invaded their private space. No one had ever put his head close to them. The first time I came up to Vincent [D'Onofrio], all he had to say was, "Yes, sir" and "No, sir" and he was so shocked he blew his lines three or four times.' As Matthew Modine told *American Film*, 'It was humiliating. I mean, it's not pleasant getting your head shaved once a week and getting yelled at by some guy for ten hours a day. There were times when just out of pure frustration you'd get angry with Lee. But there's some kind of bonding that happens and you can't really get mad at anybody,' he added. 'You don't get mad at the director, because he's trying to create an art form instead of just a film.'

With the cast pushing themselves to the limit, injuries were as common as they had been on *Spartacus* and *A Clockwork Orange*. The Steadicam operator, John Ward, was briefly replaced by Jean-Marc Bringuier after the propellor wash from a helicopter knocked him down as he was carrying his heavy equipment. Matthew Modine strained his shoulder on the assault course, although the injury has since been exaggerated to a broken arm. Most seriously of all, Lee Ermey – who had already taken time off after losing the use of his voice – was seriously injured when his Jeep ran off the road in Epping Forest. 'He broke all his ribs on one side,' recalled Kubrick, 'and he probably would have died, except he was conscious and kept flashing his lights.' Production was halted for four and a half months while Ermey recovered from his injuries; by the time principal photography was resumed, Kubrick had decided to reshoot a number of Ermey's scenes.

'It was as close to war as I ever want to get,' Dorian Harewood told *American Film*. 'And all the time, all that waiting around, turned us into a "unit" just like in the film. There we were in army garb, rifles in our laps, in the hot weather, sitting around in the dirt and rubble and waiting and waiting, and smoking and playing cards and being away from home and our wives for months. It *was* the army.' Kubrick got the joke. After spending the afternoon at a local gun club with Herr, no expert at marksmanship, Kubrick reportedly told him, 'Gee, Michael, I'm beginning to wonder if you've got what it takes to carry a rifle in my beloved Corps.'

**CASTING:** *Variety* announced Kubrick's intention to write, produce and direct his adaptation of *The Short-Timers*, already retitled *Full Metal Jacket*, in January 1984. The same report, drawn from a Warner Bros press release, noted that Kubrick would 'launch a nationwide search for new faces to play the Marines', inviting aspiring young actors to audition for the film. Advertisements placed in various publications asked for videotapes in which would-be 'grunts' performed a three-minute acting scene appropriate to a film about Vietnam, dressed in a T-shirt and casual trousers. Several key talent agencies were nominated as locations where such auditions might be filmed, and within a few months, Warner Bros had received 'about three or four thousand videotapes', eight hundred of which were personally reviewed by Kubrick.

Although several of these young hopefuls would win minor roles in the film, in the event, all of the leading roles went to established Hollywood actors, among them Matthew Modine (*Birdy*), Adam Baldwin (*My Bodyguard*), Arliss Howard (*The Day After*), Dorian Harewood (*The Falcon and the Snowman*) and Kevyn Major-Howard (*Sudden Impact*). Modine, whom Kubrick described as 'the kind of baby Gary Cooper and Henry Fonda might have had', spoke for many of the young actors when he told *American Film*'s Susan Linfield: '[Vietnam] was something I grew up with, and the more that I read and the more I try to understand, the less sense it makes. I just watched the war on television. Listening to the body count – you know, listening to the score. Who was winning. It was like a baseball game. We got ten casualties, they got a hundred. Oh, we had a good day.'

The emerging stage actor Vincent D'Onofrio was one of the few actors with no feature-film experience to be cast in one of *Full Metal Jacket*'s leading roles. Alerted to the audition process by his friend Matthew Modine, he rented a home video camera and made an audition tape of his own, and was rewarded for his trouble by being cast as Private Leonard Lawrence, a.k.a. 'Gomer Pyle'. There was just one caveat: the athletic six-footer would be required to gain around sixty pounds in weight, increasing his muscular frame to 280 pounds. 'I gained weight everywhere,' D'Onofrio told the *New York Times*' Leslie Bennetts. 'My thighs were tremendous, my arms were tremendous, even my nose was fat. I had a tough time tying my shoelaces, but this was the only way I could play Leonard, because I had to be meek-minded in the same way.'

Tim Colceri, a 36-year-old ex-Marine, had already been cast in the role of Gerheim/Hartman when Kubrick met R Lee Ermey, who had joined the Marines at the age of seventeen, and served as a drill instructor throughout the Vietnam War, until wounds from a rocket explosion ended his military career after eleven years. Although he had appeared in several commercials, and all three of the films on which he had served as technical adviser – *Apocalypse Now* (1979), *The Boys in Company C* (1979) and *Purple Hearts* (1984) – Kubrick did not feel that Ermey had the right stuff to play the brutal, sadistic, 'hard but fair' Parris Island drill instructor. Ermey decided a demonstration was in order. 'I wanted that role so much, I stole it,' he told *Empire* magazine's

Jake Hamilton. 'I thought the guy should have a personality; not be just some machine deriving pleasure from inflicting pain. So I turned up in my old Smoky Bear uniform and got my boys doing push-ups. I think I made quite an impression . . .'

Tim Colceri did not react well to the news that he had been replaced, much less by a real drill instructor with minimal acting experience. 'Maybe he should have got a real killer to play the other roles,' he commented sourly, 'then he could have dispensed with actors altogether.' He was, however, partly mollified with an alternative role as the cold-blooded door gunner who shoots Vietnamese citizens indiscriminately, yelling 'Ain't war hell?'

**THE USUAL SUSPECTS:** The composer Vivian Kubrick made a second uncredited appearance in one of her father's films, having played Dr Floyd's daughter in *2001*, and, here, a news-camera operator seen at the site of the mass grave filled with lime-covered bodies.

**THE PURSUIT OF PERFECTION:** Despite having decided to shoot a film set in Southeast Asia in the southeast of England, Kubrick insisted on absolute authenticity as far as props, weapons, uniforms and even vegetation were concerned. 'He quizzed me a lot about South-East Asia,' Kubrick's friend John Milius, who co-wrote *Apocalypse Now* (1979) with Michael Herr, told Peter Bogdanovich. 'He wanted to know every little detail: what the food was like, how the airport was, whether they lost your baggage. He was preparing himself as if he would go.' Milius recommended Fred Ropkey, a supplier of 'militariana' who was able to locate everything from small arms to big tanks. 'I thought six months later the guy was ready for a medal. Stanley just drove him nuts: "Are you sure the colour of these patches is the same as the last batch? I've been looking at them and I can see a difference." '

According to the military historian Lee Brimmicombe-Wood, Kubrick's efforts at re-creating the military hardware of the Vietnam era were mostly successful. 'Aside from some of the English settings, the movie is very authentic,' he says. 'When you watch it a couple of times, you get to notice things like the blacked-out English road markings in the Parris Island scenes. But the Sikorsky helicopters are authentic – they're not UH-1s, but the Marines weren't big on the Huey, preferring helos that can fit inside LCH hangars – as are the tanks (M-48s) and the small arms (the usual M-16A1s, M-60s, M-79s, and so on). To be honest,' he adds, 'much of this US kit, particularly the uniforms, has been available as surplus for years and there is little that would have been hard to replicate.'

The ubiquity of videotape since the shooting of *The Shining* made it possible for Kubrick to replay and review each take after it was shot – sometimes simultaneously on different monitors. 'On *Full Metal Jacket*, he had every take on a different television screen with a different tape unit,' Steven Spielberg told the producers of the documentary *The Last Movie*, 'and he would compare take one to take thirty-one with all these monitors and all these three-quarter-inch tape machines. He would just rave about how easy it is to compare performance on take five and take twenty-five, because he would have the monitors next to each other.'

## CLASSIC QUOTES

**Hartman:** 'There is no racial bigotry here. I do not look down on niggers, kykes, wops or greasers. To me you are all equally worthless.'

**Joker:** 'Is that you, John Wayne? Is this me?'

**Hartman:** 'Tonight you pukes will sleep with your rifles. You will give your rifle a girl's name. Because this is the only pussy you people are going to get. Your days of finger-banging old Mary Jane Rottencrotch through her purty pink panties are over!'

**Marines:** 'This is my rifle. There are many like it but this one is mine. My rifle is my best friend. It is my life. I must master it as I must master my life. Without me, my rifle is useless. Without my rifle, I am useless. I must fire my rifle true. I must shoot straighter than my enemy, who is trying to kill me. I must shoot him before he shoots me. I will. Before God I swear this creed. My rifle and myself are defenders of my country. We are the masters of our enemy. We are the saviours of my life. So be it, until there is no enemy, but peace. Amen.'

**Hartman:** 'Private Joker is silly and he's ignorant but he's got guts, and guts is enough.'

**Hartman:** 'A rifle is only a tool. It's a hard heart that kills. If your killer instincts are not clean and strong you will hesitate at the moment of truth. You will not kill. You will become dead Marines. And then you will be in a world of shit, because Marines are not allowed to die without permission!'

**Joker (VO):** 'Graduation is only a few days away and the recruits of platoon 3092 are salty. They are ready to eat their own guts and ask for seconds.'

**Joker:** 'Are those . . . live rounds?'
**Pyle:** 'Seven . . . six . . . two . . . millimetre. Full . . . metal . . . jacket.'
**Joke:** 'Leonard, if Hartman comes in here and catches us, we'll both be in a world of shit.'
**Pyle:** 'I *am* . . . in a *world* . . . of *shit*!'

**Hartman:** 'Now you listen to me, Private Pyle, and you listen good. I want that weapon, and I want it now. You will place that rifle on the deck at your feet and step back away from it. *What is your major malfunction, numbnuts? Didn't mommy and daddy show you enough attention when you were a child?*'

Colonel: 'You write "Born to Kill" on your helmet and you wear a peace button. What's that supposed to be, some kind of sick joke?'

Joker: 'No, sir.'

Colonel: 'You'd better get your head and your ass wired together, or I will take a giant shit on you!'

Joker (VO): 'My thoughts drift back to erect-nipple wet dreams about Mary Jane Rottencrotch and the Great Homecoming Fuck Fantasy. I am so happy that I am alive, in one piece and short. I'm in a world of shit, yes. But I am alive. And I am not afraid.'

**THEMES AND MOTIFS:** Many observers condemned *Full Metal Jacket* as misogynistic, principally because the only female roles in the film are the prostitutes and the sniper, but also because most of the references to femininity are obscene ('Eskimo pussy is mighty cold,' for example). In fact, a thorough exploration of the film from the masculine/feminine perspective reveals, as Australia's *Cinema Papers* suggested, that Kubrick intended to show 'that men destroy each other when they deny the female in themselves'.

Hartman, of course, is the surrogate father figure whom the recruits inherit when they arrive on Parris Island, and he attempts to instil in them the patriarchal values of brotherhood, and exclude women from the lives of the boys he is training to kill. 'When Hartman announces that their rifles will be the only pussy they'll get from now on,' Michael Pursell observed, 'he isn't just commenting on the exclusion of women from a male group, he's talking about the process of expunging women psychologically. His language dismembers women, absenting them even from the sexual act. He addresses the platoon as "ladies", using the female label as a sign of contempt until they qualify, at which point they are suddenly told they are brothers.' The killing of the recruits' feminine side, Pursell explained, is the gynocide that facilitates the genocide. Even the shooting of the female sniper is given strong overtones of rape, being preceded by Animal Mother's instruction to 'fuck her', and followed by an unnamed soldier's intonation of the words 'Hard core, man, fucking hard core.'

Like *The Shining*, *Full Metal Jacket* uses characters from children's stories and cartoons to emphasise the dichotomy between childish innocence (Danny Torrance; the new recruits) and circumstantial horror (the Overlook Hotel; Vietnam). Faced with Private Pyle's loaded rifle, Gunnery Sergeant Hartman says, 'What is this Mickey Mouse shit?' A second reference to Mickey Mouse comes at the end, when Sergeant Joker's adopted platoon sing the theme song to the Mickey Mouse Club – 'Who's the leader of the club that's made for you and me? M-I-C . . . K-E-Y . . . M-O-U-S-E!' A Mickey Mouse doll, along with a toy Snoopy from the newspaper strip created by Charles M Schulz, can also be seen in the offices of the *Stars and Stripes* at Da Nang (Snoopy turns up again in *Eyes Wide Shut*). The juvenile references are arguably a subtle way of reminding us that the marines are no more than boys; yet they carry the added subtext of cartoon violence, and of cartoon characters locked in a world in which the joke, ultimately, is on Joker and his comrades. It is also, remember, a booby-trapped stuffed toy which blows Lieutenant Touchdown to pieces.

One of the most crass pieces of exposition in any Kubrick film comes as Private Joker attempts to justify the incongruity of the peace button worn on his jacket with the slogan 'BORN TO KILL' written with marker pen on his helmet. Joker claims that it is a comment on 'the duality of man', but it is also clearly intended to represent the schizophrenic nature of the United States' role in Vietnam, as death-dealing peace-keepers who would destroy the country in order to save it. Intriguingly, the peace button is hidden from view by the weapon that Joker raises to kill the sniper.

**MUSIC:** The original score for *Full Metal Jacket* was the work of an unknown composer, 'Abigail Mead', using a Fairlight Series III and a CMI Series I, utilised, Kubrick told Alexander Walker, 'to avoid any prior musical associations that conventional orchestra instruments might bring'. The identity of the composer remained shrouded in mystery until 28 January 1988, when an article by Robert Koehler appeared in the *Los Angeles Times*, revealing that Mead was a pseudonym for Kubrick's youngest daughter, Vivian. After rejecting some Kodo-style Japanese drum music he had originally intended to use for the *Full Metal Jacket* trailer, Kubrick was so impressed by a piece of original music composed and recorded by his daughter that he asked her to write the entire score for the film. Vivian took her nom de plume from the family home, Abbot's Mead, changing the name 'Abbot' to 'Abigail', which Kubrick discovered meant 'a father rejoices'. 'He loves coincidences,' Vivian told Koehler, 'and he really loved this one.'

In addition to Mead's original music, Kubrick trawled through hundreds and hundreds of popular songs from such artists as the Rolling Stones, the Dixie Cups, Nancy Sinatra, Chris Kenner and Sam the Sham and the Pharoahs, in an effort to capture the spirit of the times. 'The Tet offensive was in '68,' Kubrick told *Rolling Stone*'s Tim Cahill. 'Unless we were careless, none of the music is post-'68. The music really depended on the scene. We checked through Billboard's list of Top 100 hits for each year from 1962 to 1968. We were looking for interesting material that played well with a scene.'

One of Kubrick's most unlikely, inspired and memorable choices was the juxtaposition of the Trashmen's surf tune 'Surfin' Bird' with the Marines' first combat scene. 'What I love about the music in that scene is that it suggests post-combat euphoria, which you see in the marine's face when he fires at the men running out of the building: he misses the first four, waits a beat, then hits the next two,' Kubrick enthused. 'And that great look on his face, that look of euphoric pleasure, the pleasure one has read described in so many accounts of combat. So he's got this look on his face, and suddenly the music starts and the tanks are rolling and the marines are mopping up. The choices weren't arbitrary.'

**POSTER:** The breathtakingly stark and simple poster image featured a painting of a Marine Corps field helmet, with several rounds of ammunition taped to it, the hand-lettered legend 'BORN TO KILL' from Joker's helmet, and the peace button that Joker wears on his lapel now pinned to the cloth covering the helmet. The painting was mounted against a stark white background for maximum impact.

**TAG-LINE:** Warner Bros' marketing department got creative and inventive with their poster tag-lines, with such gems as 'VIETNAM CAN KILL ME BUT IT CAN'T MAKE ME CARE' and 'IN VIETNAM THE WIND DOESN'T BLOW, IT SUCKS' as examples of the bold-face lines – many taken from the source novel – emblazoned over the poster image of Joker's helmet. Later posters featured the rather exaggerated claim that the film was 'ACCLAIMED BY CRITICS AS THE BEST WAR MOVIE EVER MADE' – a direct quote from a single reviewer, Toronto *Globe and Mail*'s Jay Scott.

**TRAILER:** The trailer begins with scenes of soldiers advancing into Hué City, cut to an ominously percussive piece of original music by 'Abigail Mead', over which Lieutenant Lockhart outlines the aftermath of the Tet Offensive: 'The enemy has very deceitfully taken advantage of the Tet ceasefire to launch an offensive all over the country. In Saigon, the United States embassy has been overrun by suicide squads. Khe Sanh is standing by to *be* overrun. We also have reports that a division of NVA has occupied all of the city of Hué south of the Pershing River. In strategic terms, Charlie's cut the country in half. The civilian press are about to wet their pants and we've heard even Cronkite's going to say the war is now unwinnable.' Cowboy ponders the news. 'Sir, does this mean that Ann-Margret's not coming?'

Cut to Joker standing before the 'poge' colonel. 'Whose side are you on, son?' he asks. 'Our side, sir.' 'Don't you love your country?' 'Yes, sir.' 'Then how about getting with the programme? Why don't you jump on the team and come on in for the big win?' 'Yes, sir.' 'Son, all I've ever asked of my Marines is that they obey my orders as they would the word of God. We are here to help the Vietnamese,' the colonel continues as we see a Vietnamese hooker, 'because inside every gook there is an American trying to get out. It's a hardball world, son. We've got to keep our heads until this peace craze blows over.' A captioned title appears, white lettering on a black background: 'Stanley Kubrick's FULL METAL JACKET', followed by a rudimentary credit block.

**WHAT THE PAPERS SAID:** 'Vietnam can kill me, but it can't make me care', ran one of *Full Metal Jacket*'s advertising tag-lines, a credo that neatly encapsulates the critical response to the film in the United States. 'After the first part reaches climax, the movie becomes dispersed, as if it had no story,' opined the *New Yorker*'s Pauline Kael. 'It never regains its forward drive; the second part is almost a different picture, and you can't get an emotional reading on it . . . This may be his worst movie,' she concluded. '[Kubrick] probably believes he's numbing us by the power of his vision, but he's actually numbing us by its emptiness . . . Moviemaking carried to a technical extreme – to the reach for supreme control of his material – seems to have turned Kubrick into a machine.' Less withering in its view, *Variety* was nevertheless unsure what Kubrick had been trying to achieve. 'Most of what's on view here has been seen before in some way or another, and is perhaps lacking that extra philosophical dimension that has marked Kubrick's greatest films. But this graphic portrayal of two levels of hell on earth generates considerable power via many riveting sequences, extraordinary dialogue, and first-rate performances.'

There were some positive reviews, however, most notably from the *Christian Science Monitor* – which, almost two decades earlier, had called *2001* 'the ultimate trip' – whose critic David Sterritt called it 'the most artful film yet made about the Vietnam war'. *Newsweek*'s Jack Kroll described the film as 'scorching you with the absolute chill of [Kubrick's] depiction of the war as a plague of corruption and dehumanization', while the *New York Times*' Vincent Canby likened the film to 'a series of exploding boomerangs. Just when you think you can relax in safety, some crazed image or line or event will swing around to lodge in the brain and scramble the emotions.'

In the United Kingdom, critics generally viewed the film far more favourably than their US counterparts. 'Black but obvious irony abounds, madness and racist bigotry are rampant, and a muddled moral message arises from the mire of a sprawling second half,' commented *Time Out*'s Geoff Andrew, but added that 'despite a certain stereotyping and predictability there are moments of gripping interest. Finally, however, Kubrick's direction is as steely cold and manipulative as the régime it depicts, and we never really get to know, let alone care about, the hapless recruits on view.' In the *Sunday Times*, Iain Johnstone described the film as 'shattering', and Kubrick as 'the cinema's master craftsman'. The BBC broadcaster Barry Norman, perhaps the country's most influential critic, called the film 'brilliant . . . [a] riveting condemnation of the Vietnam war'.

**CONTROVERSY:** 'I know there's going to be a lot of outraged and offended responses to this movie,' Michael Herr predicted prior to the film's release. 'The political Left will call [Kubrick] a fascist, and the right – well, who knows? I can't imagine what women are going to think of this film.' As it turned out, however, much of the editorial controversy over films about the Vietnam War had been covered by the films that, partly due to Kubrick's laconic scheduling, got there first. Besides, as Kubrick countered, 'I certainly don't think the film is anti-American. I think it tries to give a sense of the war and the people, and how it affected them.'

**BOX OFFICE:** *Full Metal Jacket* opened in the US on 26 June 1987, grossing a modest $5.6 million in its first ten days, and amassing a total US gross of $38 million after fifty days on release – an impressive return for a film with a declared budget of $17 million. Box office was particularly strong in Western European markets such as Germany, France, Italy and the United Kingdom, and it is probable that *Full Metal Jacket* eventually doubled its domestic gross overseas.

**AWARDS:** A year after Oliver Stone's *Platoon* (1986) had won four Academy Awards from eight nominations, *Full Metal Jacket* received just one Oscar nomination, in the category of Best Writing, Screenplay Based on Material from Another Medium. Kubrick's daughter Vivian was denied a nomination for her musical score, composed as Abigail Mead, on the basis that the music of the film was dominated by popular music from the period – despite the fact that Mead's original compositions comprised 22½ minutes, compared with 17½ minutes of pop music.

R Lee Ermey was also nominated for a Golden Globe award, in the category of Best Performance by an Actor in a Supporting Role in a Motion Picture. At the British Academy of Film and Television Arts (BAFTA) awards, *Full Metal Jacket* received two nominations, in the categories of Best Sound (Nigel Galt, Andy Nelson and Edward Tise) and Best Special Effects (John Evans). Kubrick also received the Luchino Visconti Award for his outstanding contribution to cinema, at Italy's David Di Donatello Awards.

**TECHNICAL ACHIEVEMENTS:** Slow motion was one weapon in the film maker's arsenal that Kubrick had seldom utilised before *Full Metal Jacket*. Now, he would use the technique for almost all of the film's death scenes, from Hartman's shooting at the end of the Parris Island sequence, through the Marine sniper victims in Hué, to the final revelation of the sniper's identity as she turns to fire on Joker. 'This wasn't just achieved by slowing the film down,' the cinematographer Douglas Milsome told *American Cinematographer*. 'We actually put the shutter of the camera out of phase with the movement of the film, which created a slight vertical strobe. As she was moving up and down and turning around, the flames seem to be standing still, and when she moved into the flames, they didn't move with her but seemed to bleed onto her face.'

**INFLUENCED BY:** Despite Kubrick's being almost the last of his contemporaries to direct a film dealing with the Vietnam War, it is difficult to pick out obvious influences on the film, since he was at great pains to deal with the subject matter in an entirely different way. Certainly, the scenes set on Parris Island are a far cry from the 'I'm hard on 'em 'cause I love 'em' drill instructors typical of the genre, as Kubrick himself pointed out to *Rolling Stone*'s Tim Cahill. Referring to Lou Gossett Jr's Oscar-winning role as a drill sergeant in *An Officer and a Gentleman* (1982), Kubrick said that, while he admired Gossett's performance, 'he had to do what he was given in the story. The film clearly wants to ingratiate itself with the audience. So many films do that.' *Full Metal Jacket*, however, did not.

DÉJÀ VU: There is something about the expression on Private Pyle's face, as Private Joker finds him in the bathroom, which recalls the equally maniacal visage of Malcolm McDowell's Alex in *A Clockwork Orange* and Jack Nicholson's Jack Torrance in *The Shining*. In fact, with a little interpretation, it is possible to watch *Full Metal Jacket* and compile a checklist of references made, covertly or otherwise, to Kubrick's earlier films:

- Kubrick's camera dollies back with Gunnery Sergeant Hartman as he walks along the line of new recruits, much as it does in the trenches as General Mireau inspects the troops of the 701st infantry in *Paths of Glory*;
- the recruits' mantra, 'My rifle is my best friend', recalls General Mireau in *Paths of Glory* telling one of Dax's men that the rifle is 'the soldier's best friend – you be good to it, and it'll always be good to you';
- the drums heard as the soldiers parade are uncannily similar to those sounded as a precursor to battle in *Paths of Glory* and *Spartacus*;
- as part of the recruits' training, they are seen fighting hand to hand, like gladiators from *Spartacus*;
- the segment of the film at the training camp ends, like *Spartacus*, with the death of the brutal instructor;
- Private Pyle shoots himself in a military bathroom, like General Ripper in *Dr Strangelove*;
- the attack on the Marine Corps base at Da Nang is strongly reminiscent of the assault on Burpelson Air Force Base in *Dr Strangelove*;
- a sweeping, second-unit helicopter shot of the North Vietnamese landscape is strikingly similar to the opening shots of *The Shining*;
- statements like 'We must keep our heads until this peace craze blows over' serve to make the 'poge' colonel a latterday version of *Dr Strangelove*'s Buck Turgidson;
- Cowboy's cynical assertion that the South Vietnamese 'would rather be alive than free – the poor dumb bastards' sounds like a mockery of *Spartacus*'s ideals;
- the incongruity of the 'Mickey Mouse Club' theme sung by the marines as they hump their way into battle recalls the closure of *Dr Strangelove* with 'We'll Meet Again'.

Kubrick was dismissive of at least two of the other parallels drawn between *Full Metal Jacket* and his earlier films. Several observers noted that *Paths of Glory* and *Full Metal Jacket*, two war films separated by thirty years, each closed with a scene in which a lone female appears amid a group of fighting men, proving their humanity in the former, and arguably signalling their dehumanisation in the latter. 'That resonance is an accident,' Kubrick demurred. 'The scene comes straight out of Gustav Hasford's book.' Other observers noted the appearance of an object strongly resembling the monolith from *2001* burning in the background as Cowboy dies in Joker's arms. 'It just happened to be there,' Kubrick responded. 'I'm sure some people will think that there was some calculated reference to *2001*, but honestly, it was just there.'

**INFLUENTIAL ON:** There can be little doubt that *Full Metal Jacket* has, in one respect or another, influenced virtually every war movie to follow it, although its occasional, superficial similarities to Barry Levinson's *Good Morning Vietnam* – the hardcore officer played by JT Walsh, the juxtaposition of sixties pop tunes with scenes of war – are coincidental, since both films debuted in 1987. There are stronger parallels between *Full Metal Jacket* and Steven Spielberg's *Saving Private Ryan* (1998), in which both the raw, hyperreal and bleached photography and the sniper sequence are examples of Spielberg's 'souveniring' his long-time friend's work. Spielberg also appropriated Kubrick's idea to keep the actors in a 'boot camp' atmosphere prior to principal photography, with a real-life drill instructor giving them a crash course in army life.

**SEQUELS AND REMAKES:** Although Gustav Hasford made what were described as 'minor revisions' to the text for a new edition published to coincide with the release of *Full Metal Jacket*, he once indicated that he had written a follow-up to *The Short-Timers*, entitled *The Phantom Blooper*. Intended as a direct continuation of the events of Hasford's first novel, the book saw Sergeant Joker change sides and become the leader of a Viet Cong commando group, further muddying his already skewed view of war, Vietnam-style. Despite the success of *Full Metal Jacket*, however, the book never materialised.

**KUBRICK GOES POP:** If the idea that music from *2001* could top the pop charts in 1968 seems fantastic today, no less bizarre is the fact that a rap version of Lee Ermey's drill-instructor diatribes, set to music by 'Abigail Mead' and the guitarist Nigel Goulding, made it to No. 2 in the UK Top Forty in 1987. The song is featured on the *Full Metal Jacket* soundtrack album, currently available on Warner Records (7599-25613-2), along with most of those used in the film – with the notable absence of the Rolling Stones' 'Paint it Black'.

'Full Metal Jacket' was not the only rap record to be made using dialogue from the movie. The X-rated rap artists the 2 Live Crew used a different dialogue sample on 'Me So Horny,' the opening track of their 1989 double album, *Nasty as They Wanna Be*. Kicking off with the Da Nang dialogue exchange between Matthew Modine and Papillon Soo Soo – 'What do we get for ten dollars?' 'Everything you want!' 'Everything?' 'Everything.' – the track uses a repetition of Soo Soo's line 'Me so horny – me love you longtime!' as its chorus. No credit for the sample is given on the vinyl album or CD versions.

Lee Ermey's unforgettable performance as the senior drill instructor, Hartman, may not have earned him an Oscar, but it gave his career a new lease of life – even if it meant repeating the same character, or variations thereon, in many other projects. As R Lee Ermey, he performed the voice of 'Sarge', leader of a platoon of plastic toy soldiers in *Toy Story* (1995) and its sequel, *Toy Story 2* (1999). In Peter Jackson's *The Frighteners* (1996), produced by a Kubrick fan, Robert Zemeckis, Ermey played a phantom drill instructor named Hiles, effectively an undead version of Hartman.

On television, Ermey played the Hartman-inspired drill instructor Sergeant-Major Frank Bougus in the 1995 pilot episode of the science-fiction series *Space: Above and Beyond*, in which he leads space marine recruits on a chorus of '1, 2, 3, 4/I love the Marine Corps', and references several of his famous *Full Metal Jacket* lines. The same year saw him voice the Hartman-like Colonel Hapablap in an episode of *The Simpsons*, 'Sideshow Bob's Last Gleaming' (#3F08), in which Ermey fires off his *Full Metal Jacket* line 'What is your major malfunction?' at Bart Simpson. In another *Simpsons* reference to *Full Metal Jacket*, featured in 'Dead Putting Society' (#7F08), Homer Simpson names his putter 'Charlene' – the name that Private Pyle gives his rifle.

In Disney's *Mulan* (1998), the dragon training the eponymous heroine for battle says, 'Let me see your war face!'

The bestselling novel *The Beach* by Alex Garland, the basis for Danny Boyle's 2000 screen adaptation, contains a number of references to Vietnam War films, including one to *Full Metal Jacket* in its opening line: '*Vietnam, me love you long time.*'

**CUT SCENES:** The screenplay dated 4 February 1985 shows a very different dénouement from that of the film, beginning just after Joker shoots the female sniper. 'Animal Mother takes a step, kneels, zips out his machete. With one powerful blow he chops off her head. He picks the head up by its long black hair and holds it high. He laughs and says, "Rest in pieces, bitch." Animal Mother laughs again. He walks around and sticks the bloody ball of gore into all their faces. "Hard? *Now* who's hard? Now who's hard, motherfuckers?" Animal Mother pauses, spits, throws the head into a ditch. He picks up his M-60 machine gun, lays it across his shoulders, struts over to Joker. "Nobody shits on the Animal, motherfucker. Nobody." Joker stares at him.'

The same version of the script ends with a montage of Joker the Marine running into battle with his rifle, intercut with an eight-year-old

Joker playing 'war' with a toy gun. The contrast continues until the grown-up Joker is cut down by machine-gun fire, whereupon the following description appears in the screenplay:

JOKER, <u>THE 8 YEAR OLD</u>,
CLUTCHES HIS CHEST IN MOCK
AGONY AND STARTS TO CRUMPLE TO
THE GROUND. HIS IMAGE WILL
SLOW DOWN UNTIL WE HOLD ON A
FROZEN FRAME, IN A POSE
SOMETHING LIKE CAPA'S FAMOUS
SPANISH CIVIL WAR PHOTOGRAPH
OF A MAN WHO HAS JUST BEEN
FATALLY SHOT BUT WHO IS
FOREVER SUSPENDED IN MID-FALL
BY THE CAMERA.
BUT THIS PICTURE IS OF AN
<u>8-YEAR-OLD</u> BOY.

Immediately following this moving image is a scene that takes place at Joker's funeral, at which the still-unnamed Marine's father, speaking with some difficulty, reads extracts from his dead son's notebook. 'I often think about . . . [pause] how things were when I was ten . . . I loved to lie in bed . . . before the sun was up . . . and before I was really awake . . . and think of the long, exciting day ahead. When the sky began to turn pink, and the great stillness outside gave way . . . to the rustling of trees and the sound of birds . . . I went downstairs . . . without waking anyone . . . and went out into the backyard. The air was fragrant and cold . . . and as I watched the sun slowly come up from behind the mountain . . . I could hardly contain my happiness. How little I knew of the world . . . beyond that garden . . . and our town.' Joker's father then reads some poetry by AE Housman, which his parents have chosen as his epitaph. 'Here we lie . . . because . . . we did not choose . . . To shame the land . . . from which we sprung . . . Life . . . to be sure . . . is nothing much to lose . . . But young men think it is . . . and we were young . . .' He closes the notebook, revealing Joker's peace button pinned to the front.

At one stage, according to the Warner Bros marketing executive Julian Senior, a long-time friend and confidant of Kubrick's, this scene would have appeared at the beginning of the film. 'Originally, the film began at Joker's funeral,' he explained. 'It was told in a flashback. But [Kubrick] felt it was wrong, that he'd be telling the whole story before you got a chance to see it. What's important is Joker's affirmation of life.'

Among the other scenes excised completely were two separate visits by Corporal Joker to a Captain January in Phu Bai, where the combat correspondent learns of – and attempts to reject – his promotion to sergeant, and later takes lessons in propaganda from his superior officer.

Tony Spiridakis (*Queens Logic*), who was cast as January, recalled how. 'His idea of a wonderful noble thing was to send the head of a gook back to his fiancée.' Spiridakis described January's scenes, taken straight out of *The Short-Timers*, as 'a whole middle third' of the film, in which Joker is disillusioned by the discovery that military journalism is pure propaganda, in which the truth is never used if a half-truth – or even an outrageous fabrication – will suffice. 'That was a fascinating part of the journey,' Spiridakis said, adding that Kubrick had the courtesy to tell him personally that his scenes had been cut. Much of January's dialogue from the second scene was, in the event, given to John Terry as Lieutenant Lockhart.

Rumours persist of a deleted scene in which the Marines play a grisly game of soccer with the head of the female sniper, whom Animal Mother decapitated with a machete in early versions of the script. The soccer scene does not appear in the novel, nor in any versions of the screenplay, and although it is possible that such a scene was improvised and even shot, its existence is almost certainly apocryphal.

TRIVIA: The phrase 'I am Become Death', written with marker pen on Animal Mother's helmet, is a quote from *Upanishads*, which has been connected with nuclear weapons ever since Robert Oppenheimer recalled the phrase while watching the Trinity atomic weapons tests.

The combat cameraman seen filming Cowboy's platoon is John Ward, who stepped in for *The Shining*'s Garrett Brown, Kubrick's first choice of Steadicam operator, when Brown declined the offer to work on the project due to prior commitments.

APOCRYPHA: 'Vincent D'Onofrio didn't like Stanley's "craziness look",' Lee Ermey informed Peter Bogdanovich, referring to the glowering expression on Private Pyle's face when Joker encounters him loading his rifle in the bathroom. 'He wanted to try it some other way. The problem with Vince was this was his first film, and he's telling Stanley Kubrick how he thinks this look should be. They stand there arguing. Stanley finally said, "Look, do it my way and we'll load back up and we'll shoot it your way." Well, when they shot it Vince's way they didn't have any film in the camera.' According to D'Onofrio, however, the incident never took place.

'While the anecdote is interesting,' he told the *New York Times*, 'it is false. I was much too young and inexperienced to have ever challenged a great film maker like Kubrick. 'When we were leaving the set the night before we shot the bathroom scene, Kubrick stopped in the parking lot and called out my name. He asked me if I knew what I was going to do the next morning. I answered that I thought I did. He said, "Good," and started to leave, but then turned back to me and said, "There is just one thing: it has to be big, it has to be Lon Chaney big." I carried that home in my mind that night and into the morning,' he added. 'Without that one sentence I don't think that my performance in *Full Metal Jacket* would have ever been remembered.'

**AVAILABILITY:** Full-screen (4:3) transfers of *Full Metal Jacket* are available in the United Kingdom on PAL VHS video (PES 11760) and in the United States on NTSC VHS video (WA 17371) and a Region 1 DVD (17372), which also features the theatrical trailer, as well as subtitles and dialogue tracks in English and French.

Although the first NTSC laserdisc (11760) featured a full-screen transfer of the film, the more recent version is one of the few formats on which a 'letterbox' (1.85:1) transfer – in line with the theatrically released version, but with a cropped image at the top and bottom of frame – can be found.

**EXPERT WITNESS:** 'We were a group of green actors mostly. He had his own private little war going on there. He didn't have a lot of respect for any of us. He would have us crawl in the asbestos and the coal dust and not care if we got hurt. I figured, get in there and get dirty. But a couple of guys got sick of it. We'd do a series of five or six takes and we'd go look at it on video playback, and he'd say, "Don't stand here. Don't go that far into the frame. See, you're out of focus here." He was very much concerned with what the picture looked like. I found after a couple of months that it was a great luxury to be able to work at that pace – you could do it as many times as he wanted. There was one scene where we were sitting on a wall and the tanks are firing off in the distance. We ended up doing that for three and a half weeks – one scene.' – the actor Adam Baldwin (Animal Mother), from an interview with Peter Bogdanovich, quoted in the *New York Times*, 4 July 1999.

**FINAL ANALYSIS:** I first saw *Full Metal Jacket* in 1987, in an East London cinema a few blocks from where the film was made. Its power was undeniable, yet after the screening I realised that I had been so blown away, appropriately enough, by the shattering impact of Pyle's murder-suicide, that I had retained little information about the second half. In retrospect, this initial reaction is a fair assessment of the film's biggest flaw: that the second half never fully recovers from the impact of the first. In this respect, it would be like spending the first half of *A Clockwork Orange* – whose basic theory, that killers are born (as in Joker's 'BORN TO KILL' motto) and not made, is in stark contrast to the views of *Full Metal Jacket* – with Alex up to his old tricks, and then spending the rest of the film with the 'cured' version, plodding through his humdrum existence with none of the fire he possessed earlier on. Thus, the lack of empathy we have for any of the characters – we laugh at Hartman's humiliation of Private Pyle and others, even as we try not to – leaves us, following the deaths of Hartman (whom we love to hate) and Pyle (whom we root for, as the underdog), without a hero.

As in his previous war films, *Fear and Desire* and *Paths of Glory*, and even *Dr Strangelove* and *Barry Lyndon*, Kubrick was fascinated with the military establishment and the effect its brutal machinations had upon the ordinary man, the supposedly acceptable insanities of the hierarchy routinely handed down to the field grunts, who vainly struggle to make sense of their orders. However, without having any one character to care about – even Joker turned against Pyle, his betrayal leading directly to his former friend's psychosis – we are left to watch as the last vestiges of humanity are stripped away from characters who, with very few exceptions, were not drawn as particularly human to begin with.

More interesting, perhaps, is Kubrick's view of those on the other side of the war. Although the enemy seem almost absent from the story – and tend to be presented as petty criminals, pimps and prostitutes when they do appear – the views of the disaffected and disillusioned marines are telling: they have lost all ideological illusions, such as that the war is being fought for freedom. Instead, the doorgunner tells Joker that all Vietnamese are essentially the same – 'Anyone who runs is VC. Anyone who stands still is well-disciplined VC.' – except for women and children, whom you don't have to 'lead' as much; Crazy Earl calls them 'the finest human beings we will ever meet'; Joker claims to have 'wanted to meet interesting and stimulating people of an ancient culture and kill them'. In Kubrick's wars, as in the real ones, there are no easy answers.

Whether *Full Metal Jacket* is as powerful an antiwar statement as *Paths of Glory* is debatable, but then comparing the two films is unfair: World War One may have been managed badly, but it was fought for a reason. In *Full Metal Jacket*, the soldiers do not know why they must fight, only that they must. Thus, Kubrick's examination of war had come full circle, because when your enemies look the same as your allies, each enemy killed is also a suicide – a point made more explicitly, but less effectively, in *Fear and Desire*.

**KUBRICK ON KUBRICK:** 'Vietnam was probably the first war that was run –.certainly during the Kennedy era – as an advertising agency might run it. It was managed with cost-effective estimates and phony statistics and kill ratios and self-deceiving predictions about how victory was the light at the end of the tunnel. The Americans in Vietnam were encouraged to lie. If a couple of shots were fired on patrol it was good to say that you'd killed two gooks and if you said two somebody would make it eight.' – quoted in the London *Observer*, 6 September 1987.

# Eyes Wide Shut (1999)

(Colour – 159 mins)

Produced and Directed by Stanley Kubrick
Screenplay by Stanley Kubrick and Frederic Raphael
Inspired by *Traumnovelle* by Arthur Schnitzler
Executive Producer Jan Harlan
Co-producer Brian W Cook
Assistant to the Director Leon Vitali

Lighting Cameraman Larry Smith
Production Designers Les Tomkins, Roy Walker
Editor Nigel Galt
Editor Foley Becki Ponting
Original Music by Jocelyn Pook
Györgi Ligeti 'Musica Ricercata II', Dominic Harlan, Piano
Dmitri Shostakovich from 'Jazz Suite, Waltz 2', Royal
Concertgebouw Orchestra conducted by Riccardo Chailly
Chris Isaak 'Baby Did a Bad Bad Thing'
Costume Designer Marit Allen
Costume Supervisor Nancy Thompson
Wardrobe Mistress Jacqueline Durran
Venetian Masks Research Barbara Del Greco
Hair by Kerry Warn
Make-up Robert McCann
Tom Cruise's Evening Wear Cerrutti (Paris)
Sound Recordist Edward Tise
Supervising Sound Editor Paul Conway
Re-recording Mixers Graham V Hartstone, AMPS, Michael A
Carter, Nigel Galt, Anthony Cleal
Production Manager Margaret Adams
Script Supervisor Ann Simpson
Assistants to Stanley Kubrick Anthony Frewin, Emilio
D'Alessandro
Casting Denise Chamian, Leon Vitali
Choreography Yolande Snaith
First Assistant Director Brian W Cook
Second Assistant Director Adrian Toynton
Third Assistant Directors Becky Hunt, Rhun Francais
Location Managers Simon McNair Scott, Angus More
Gordon
Location Research Manuel Harlan
Location Assistant Tobin Hughes
Supervising Art Director Kevin Phipps
Art Director John Fenner
Set Decorators Terry Wells SR, Lisa Leone
Draughtspersons Stephen Dobric, Jon Billington
Assistant Draughtsperson Pippa Rawlinson
Art Department Assistants Samantha Jones, Kira-Anne
Pelican
Original Paintings Christiane Kubrick, Katharina Hobbs

CAST: Tom Cruise (*Dr William Harford*), Nicole Kidman (*Alice Harford*), Madison Eginton (*Helena Harford*), Jackie Sawiris (*Roz*), Sydney Pollack (*Victor Ziegler*), Leslie Lowe (*Ilona*), Peter Benson (*Bandleader*), Todd Field (*Nick Nightingale*), Michael Doven (*Ziegler's Secretary*), Sky Dumont (*Sandor Szavost*), Louise Taylor (*Gayle*), Stewart Thorndike (*Nuala Windsor*), Randall Paul (*Harris*), Julienne Davis (*Amanda Curran*), Lisa Leone (*Lisa*), Kevin Connealy (*Lou Nathanson*), Marie Richardson (*Marion Nathanson*), Thomas Gibson (*Carl Thomas*), Mariana Hewitt (*Rosa*), Dan Rollman, Gavin Perry, Chris Pare, Adam Lias, Christian Clarke, Kyle Whitcombe (*Rowdy*

*College Kids*), Gary Goba (*Naval Officer*), Vinessa Shaw (*Domino*), Florian Windorfer (*Maître D' – Café Sonata*), Rade Sherbedgia (*Milich*), Togo Igawa (*Japanese Man #1*), Eiji Kusuhara (*Japanese Man #2*), Leelee Sobieski (*Milich's Daughter*), Sam Douglas (*Cab Driver*), Angus MacInnes (*Gateman #1*), Abigail Good (*Mysterious Woman*), Brian W Cook (*Tall Butler*), Leon Vitali (*Red Cloak*), Carmela Marner (*Waitress at Gillespie's*), Alan Cumming (*Desk Clerk*), Fay Masterson (*Sally*), Phil Davies (*Stalker*), Cindy Dolenc (*Girl at Sharkey's*), Clarke Haynes (*Hospital Receptionist*), Treva Etienne (*Morgue Orderly*), Colin Angus, Karla Ashley, Kathryn Charman, James DeMaria, Anthony Desergio, Janie Dickens, Laura Fallace, Vanessa Fenton, Georgina Finch, Peter Godwin, Abigail Good, Joanna Heath, Lee Henshaw, Atheeka Poole, Adam Pudney, Sharon Quinn, Ben de Sausmarcz, Emma Lou Sharratt, Paul Spelling, Matthew Thompson, Dan Travers, Russell Trigg, Kate Whalin (*Masked Party Principals*).

**UNCREDITED CAST:** Stanley Kubrick (*Elderly Man at Sonata Café Table*).

**TITLE SEQUENCE:** Three title cards appear in succession, in blocky, pastel-coloured text: 'TOM CRUISE', 'NICOLE KIDMAN', 'A FILM BY STANLEY KUBRICK'. Nicole Kidman, as Alice Harford, stands with her back to the camera, wearing a black sheath evening dress. With a hidden movement, the dress falls to the floor, revealing her to be naked underneath. In a second, the screen turns black, 'as if', as the critic Alexander Walker suggested, 'an eyelid had closed, or a shutter descended in one of those sex-shop peepshows'. A final title card follows: 'EYES WIDE SHUT'.

**SUMMARY:** A New York couple, Dr William Harford and his wife Alice, a failed art gallery owner, attend their friend Victor Ziegler's grand pre-Christmas party. Separated from her husband, who becomes the target of advances by two predatory models, Alice meets and dances with an older Hungarian man who attempts a seduction and tempts her upstairs. She declines. Bill, too, is called upstairs, to attend to a naked woman, Mandy, who has overdosed during a sexual encounter with the party's host. Bill revives her, and agrees to keep the incident a secret.

The next night, the couple share a joint and tease each other, and then argue about the previous night's flirtations. Incensed by Bill's belief that men are interested in her for only one reason, and that women are less likely to be unfaithful than men, Alice tells him of a sexual fantasy she had a year earlier, in which she was prepared to give up everything for one night with a naval officer she had not even spoken to. Called away on a medical emergency, Bill begins a sexual odyssey prompted by his visualisation of Alice and the officer making love: a dead patient's daughter declares her love for him; he meets and almost beds a prostitute; he resolves to crash an invitation-only masked ball/orgy at which an old school friend is playing piano; renting a costume for the purpose, he encounters two cross-dressing Japanese men in a sexual liaison with the proprietor's teenage daughter.

At the ball, he witnesses a baroque and rather bizarre ceremony leading to a sexual free-for-all. He is warned away by a masked woman, who tells him his presence may put his life in danger. Discovered and unmasked, he is about to pay the price for his encroachment when the woman offers to 'redeem' him, taking his place in whatever punishment might have been meted out. Bill heads home, where Alice tells him of a sexual dream which ended with Bill's humiliation. The following day, Bill retraces his steps, but is warned off his own search for answers. Later, he reads that Ziegler's 'friend' Mandy (Amanda Curran) has died, and visits her in the hospital morgue, strangely moved. Called to Ziegler's, he learns that his friend was present at the masked ball, as was Mandy, the girl who 'redeemed' him, but that the girl's death was unconnected with her punishment. Returning home, he tells Alice everything, and the two go Christmas shopping, emerging from their experiences wiser, their marriage stronger.

SOURCE: *Eyes Wide Shut* was adapted from – or 'inspired by', as the credits would have it – a 1926 novella by the Viennese-born author Arthur Schnitzler (1862–1931). The book was originally published in German as *Traumnovelle*, the literal translation of which – *Dreamstory* – loses the intended double entendre of 'traum' and 'trauma'. Kubrick encountered Schnitzler long before he read *Traumnovelle* for the first time, as the basis for the 1950 film *La Ronde*, directed by Kubrick's greatest cinematic influence, Max Ophuls. Most sources state that Kubrick was introduced to *Traumnovelle* itself by his Viennese-born second wife, Ruth Subotka. 'What struck Kubrick so much about *Traumnovelle* was that it would allow him to examine his own dark side, and one can speculate that he also saw it as a way to expiate his guilt,' suggested Kubrick's biographer, John Baxter, referring to Subotka's suicide in 1968. 'The author was from Vienna and was introduced to him by the wife who he thought for the rest of his life was the woman most suited to him.'

Like much of Schnitzler's work, *Traumnovelle* was a sexually themed, highly stylised and erotic – if not exactly explicit – story, exploring the relationships between couples and their sexual fantasies: Fridolin – like Schnitzler, a Viennese doctor – is happily married to Albertine, until the revelation of their secret dreams/desires threatens their marriage. 'It's a difficult book to describe,' Kubrick explained. 'What good book isn't? It explores the sexual ambivalence of a happy marriage and tries to equate the importance of sexual dreams and might-have-beens with reality . . . The book opposes the real adventures of a husband and the fantasy adventures of his wife, and asks the question: is there a serious difference between dreaming a sexual adventure, and actually having one?'

Enquiries were made after the screen rights by a former *Time* magazine critic turned screenwriter (*Strange Days*), Jay Cocks, who purchased the rights on Kubrick's behalf, on the basis that a relative unknown might obtain the rights for a more modest price than one of Kubrick's means. Kubrick initially tried to get the British writer David Cornwell – better known by his nom de plume, John Le Carré – to write the screenplay, as the former Warner Bros president John Calley told *Premiere* magazine: 'He thought Cornwell was the greatest dialogue writer. They had endless meetings about it. And David realized that he would never be able to subordinate his stuff to Stanley's stuff, so he decided not to do it. But they admired each other tremendously.'

**WORKING TITLES:** Kubrick's adaptation of *Traumnovelle* was originally announced under the title of the only English translation in existence at the time: *Rhapsody*.

**PRODUCTION HISTORY:** Kubrick first intended to film an adaptation of *Traumnovelle* after *2001*, as Christiane, Kubrick's widow, told *Sight and Sound*'s Nick James. 'Stanley was very interested and I didn't want him to be. Then Terry Southern gave him *A Clockwork Orange* . . . and Schnitzler was forgotten for a while. But he kept coming back to it. It's good that it took so long,' she added. 'By the time he was an old man he was in a far better position to make a film about the ultimate topic.'

Thus, when a Warner Bros executive, John Calley, announced Kubrick's imminent production of an adaptation of Arthur Schnitsler's (sic) *Traumnovelle* in April 1971, he was around a quarter of a century premature. Later the same year, however, the novelist and Oscar-winning screenwriter Frederic Raphael (John Schlesinger's *Darling* and *Far from the Madding Crowd*) published what might be considered a modern retelling of *Traumnovelle*, under the somewhat balder title, *Who Were You With Last Night?*. Nearly a quarter of a century later, in December 1995, Schnitzler and Raphael would converge again, as Warner Bros announced Kubrick's intention to direct an adaptation of *Traumnovelle* entitled *Eyes Wide Shut*, 'a story of sexual jealousy and obsession', with a screenplay co-written by Raphael. The stars, the studio said, would be Tom Cruise and his wife, the Australian actress Nicole Kidman.

Such was the veil of secrecy with which *Eyes Wide Shut* was shrouded immediately after Warner Bros' unexpected announcement that, by the summer of 1996, it was widely reported that Kubrick had abandoned the project in favour of another – not unexpectedly, given that he had made three other films since the original 1971 press release – after hearing of the director Brian De Palma's problems with Cruise during the filming of *Mission: Impossible*; the rumours persisted, however, to the extent that

Kubrick issued a press release declaring that pre-production was continuing, and that he had not spoken to De Palma for more than a decade. Raphael had delivered the first draft of his script just before Christmas of 1994, and continued to work on his adaptation – now transposed to present-day New York, although the film would be made in the United Kingdom – for several more months.

'Stanley was attentive to my pages, and alert to what he did not like,' Raphael wrote in *Eyes Wide Open: A Memoir of Stanley Kubrick*, 'but he admitted that he was making no contribution: "I wish I could give you some input, but I can't. I'm not a writer." ' Kubrick encouraged Raphael to minimise dialogue and think in voice-over, in order to maximise what could be seen on screen, enacted by actors, and developed during rehearsal. This was a methodology that had proven valuable for *Lolita*. 'Stanley favoured voiceover because it avoided all need to use dialogue to articulate how people felt or what motives they had.' In other words, Raphael added, 'Kubrick wanted to *show*, not tell. He preferred to leave motive or "psychology" to be divined by the spectator.'

Raphael delivered a further, 170-page draft of the script in March 1995, at about the same time that Kubrick began to woo Cruise. 'I read the script and flew immediately to where he was . . . and I landed on his property in this helicopter,' Cruise told the producers of the documentary *The Last Movie*. 'We discussed the script – did I understand this, was I confused about anything – but he first allowed me to talk. He didn't probe, really. And I took off in the helicopter and it was over too quickly for me. And I thought, "OK, this is going to be a great adventure in my life." ' The offer for Kidman to co-star opposite her husband came a year later, while she was in London finishing *Portrait of a Lady*. 'I said, "I don't even need to read the script," ' she recalled to *Rolling Stone*'s Nancy Collins. ' "If my character's got one line, one word, I'll play Alice." In fact, Tom and I both went into the movie saying, "You have us. All of us. We want to dedicate our lives to making this film." ' Kidman and Cruise both realised that they could invest aspects of their own relationship and their own understanding into the characters. 'Even though Stanley would say, "Well, that's just an added bonus," ' Cruise said, 'that was definitely something that he counted on and wanted.'

Meanwhile, work on the script continued. Shortly before Christmas 1995, Raphael was summoned back to Abbot's Mead, where he learned of the Cruise-Kidman interest, and was asked to read Kubrick's own, untitled, rewrite, which, like *A Clockwork Orange*, *Barry Lyndon* and *Full Metal Jacket* before it, rejected the traditional script form in favour of prose narrative. Raphael described Kubrick's 85-page draft as 'a blueprint of a movie [containing] only enough words to remind the director of what he means to do or have people say', and felt that the prose was 'jejune and without literary grace . . . almost gauche in its unpretentiousness', and, occasionally, 'embarrassing'. As Raphael noted, 'He had indeed digested my work, but its shape and much of its detail was there in his rescript.' Raphael set to work revising the new draft, still in prose form, in early 1996.

With Kubrick finally satisfied with the script, principal photography officially began on 7 November 1996, at locations that included the Rothschilds' country manor, Mentmore, London's Lanesborough Hotel and the mansion at Luton Hoo – where an excised scene from *2001* had been filmed three decades earlier – all of which were hosting scenes supposedly taking place in and around Manhattan, Kubrick's birthplace. 'Originally, Stanley wanted to shoot a lot in London streets and convert them – change the signs, add American cars,' the production designer Les Tomkins told *Premiere* magazine. 'But after extensive looking, and the problems of trying to shoot in London, we decided to build a certain amount of street on the lot at Pinewood [Studios]. That gave him much more freedom to play with his lighting.'

Tomkins says that the sets were revamped several times, at one point borrowing an idea from the *Titanic* (1997) director James Cameron: reversing all of the shop-front signs and 'flopping' the film to give an impression of greater geographical area. 'It worked brilliantly,' Tomkins said. 'But eventually I think [Kubrick] realized that he needed a little extra footage, and we did go out onto two streets in London.' That decision brought its own inherent problems, as Kubrick's daughter, Katharina Hobbs, told *Sight and Sound* magazine's Nick James. 'There's a scene in *Eyes Wide Shut* where Tom had to walk into a hospital,' she said, referring to a sequence filmed at the Chelsea and Westminster Hospital in London. 'Word got round, and within half an hour the police were having to put up cordons and people kept ruining the shot by shouting, "Tom, I love you!" ' Christiane, Kubrick's wife, added: 'Stanley watched it from the car and said it was just terrifying.'

A more intimate stage was set for the scene – a version of which would act as the film's ninety-second 'teaser' trailer – in which Bill and Alice, naked, begin to make love while standing in front of a mirror: only Kubrick, Cruise and Kidman were present on the set. 'Stanley shot it himself. We shot it for a day but set it up for days before,' Kidman told *Rolling Stone*'s Nancy Collins, adding that Kubrick played Chris Isaak's 'Baby Did a Bad Bad Thing' – the song played over the scene in the trailer and the film itself – to create the right mood. 'We shot a lot I wouldn't do for any other director,' she said later, at a packed press conference for the film. 'Kubrick wanted it almost pornographic,' she added. To avoid any unwanted nudity, however, both Cruise and Kidman had clauses in their contracts stipulating that they could veto any footage they deemed too revealing. Neither exercised them.

As always, Kubrick exercised his proclivity for multiple takes. 'Stanley always was waiting for something to happen,' Kidman recalled. 'He wasn't as interested in naturalistic acting as he was in something that, for whatever reason, surprised him or piqued his interest. That was when he'd go, "Ah, OK, now we're on to something." She continued, 'Sometimes he'd do ten takes, sometimes a lot more. But I'd always ask him for another. He'd say, "Nicole, you're the only actor I've ever worked with who's asked for another take." '

Kubrick's customary high take ratio – rumour had it he shot ninety-five different versions of Cruise walking through a door – suited several other actors, too. 'I loved the fact that you were able to work a scene again and again,' Alan Cumming told *Premiere* magazine, adding that, because the sound technician kept track of the slate numbers silently, 'you didn't go, "Oh, take 48, my God, this is terrible." You weren't bored, because every take was different.' Vinessa Shaw (*Ladybugs*), whose two-week stint as the HIV-infected hooker, Domino, turned into twelve months, voiced similar views to *Entertainment Weekly*. 'I remember one time, around three in the morning, I did my 69*th* take of a scene. I heard somebody say, "Wow! That must be a record." And then I ended up doing twenty more takes.' Like Kidman and Cumming, however, Shaw welcomed the opportunity to get the most out of every scene. 'It gives you a real sense of freedom. Doing a scene over and over, all of a sudden you see it as completely different. It gives you a chance to explore.'

Throughout the shoot, Kubrick continued to tinker with the script, rehearsing for hours before letting the cameras roll. 'We'd rehearse and rehearse a scene, and it would change from hour to hour,' Todd Field, who spent seven months playing the pianist Nick Nightingale, explained. 'We'd keep giving the script supervisor notes all the time, so by the end of the day the scene might be completely different. It wasn't really improvisation,' he added: 'it was more like writing.' This approach, coupled with the multiple-take ethos, led to casualties among the cast. The departure of the actor Harvey Keitel, originally cast as Victor Ziegler, in May 1997 led to extensive – and expensive – reshoots with his replacement, Sydney Pollack, an Academy Award-winning director whose films include *The Way We Were* (1973), *Tootsie* (1982), *Out of Africa* (1985) and the Tom Cruise vehicle *The Firm* (1993), and who had played small roles in such films as *Husbands and Wives* (1992), *A Civil Action* (1998) and his own *Random Hearts* (1999). 'My initial take on my part was very different from what Stanley wanted,' Sydney Pollack told Peter Bogdanovich. 'I came in with the idea of being tougher with the character of [Bill] because he had done something that I disapproved of strongly. And then Stanley had an idea of my wanting to manipulate him more and therefore be kinder, and he was very specific about how to communicate that.'

Another hasty casting replacement was required when Kubrick decided to reshoot the scene in which Jennifer Jason Leigh (*Single White Female*), as Marion Nathanson, declares her love for Bill Harford as her father lies dead. Leigh claimed a prior commitment to David

Cronenberg's *eXistenZ* (1999), and was replaced by Swedish-born Marie Richardson (*Best Intentions*), reputedly one of Ingmar Bergman's favourite actresses.

If the resulting delays irked Cruise – who, after a record-breaking five $100 million hits in a row, had not made a film since *Mission: Impossible* (1996), and would be forced to postpone that film's sequel in order to accommodate *Eyes Wide Shut* – he never complained. 'People kept saying, "Isn't Tom being driven crazy by the schedule?" the actor Thomas Gibson (Carl Thomas) recollected. 'I'm sure he had other fires and pots on the stove, but he knew that this movie was going to take as long as it took.' Cruise confirmed as much to *Time* magazine's Cathy Booth: 'We knew from the beginning the level of commitment needed. We felt honored to work with [Kubrick]. We were going to do what it took to do this picture, whatever time, because I felt – and Nic did too – that this was going to be a really special time for us. We knew it would be difficult. But I would have absolutely kicked myself if I hadn't done this.'

Even the Warner Bros co-chairman, Terry Semel, did not seem to mind the lengthening production schedule. 'He made the movie at a very modest price by today's standards,' Semel told Peter Bogdanovich of the $65 million production. 'He always shot with very small crews and very low daily rates. From time to time, he would decide to close down for a week or two and spend a little more time on the script or other aspects. So, economically, his process was terrific, since it didn't matter how long it took him to shoot because he was shooting at insignificant per-day rates. So there was no problem – no pressure on either himself or the studio.' As Sydney Pollack told *Time* magazine, 'Stanley had figured out a way to work in England for a fraction of what we pay [in the United States]. While the rest of us poor bastards are able to get sixteen weeks of filming for $70 million with a $20 million star, Stanley could get forty-five weeks of shooting for $65 million. He ensured himself the luxury of trying to work out something that's as complicated emotionally as this film was.'

By the time *Eyes Wide Shut* finally wrapped, the eighteen-week schedule had spread to fifty-two weeks over fifteen months. 'We shot for ten and a half months, but we were there for a year and a half. Sometimes it was very frustrating because you were thinking, "Is this ever going to end?" ' Kidman admitted. Cruise even developed an ulcer during production. 'I didn't want to tell Stanley,' he confided. 'He panicked. I wanted this to work, but you're playing with dynamite when you act. Emotions kick up. You try not to kick things up, but you go through things you can't help.' Kidman added, 'We were both dealing with jealousy and sex in a way that it was always lurking around.'

According to Kubrick's wife Christiane, the punishing schedule eventually took its toll on the director. 'He was very tired,' she recalled. 'But anybody would be who had worked such long hours. He was seventy, so to see him pale and tired seemed understandable. And he was looking forward to taking a rest. Nobody could have known,' she added. 'The heart attack was so massive, nobody could have done anything.'

When it came to publicising the film in the summer of 1999, the policy for cast and crew members was to keep their mouths wide shut. 'I can't talk about the plot,' Todd Field (Nick Nightingale) told *US* magazine. 'I don't even know if I'm *in* the [finished] film.' Even when they did talk about the film, most seemed to say nothing at all. 'The movie is whatever the audience takes from it,' Cruise told *Time* magazine. 'Wherever you are in life, you're going to take away something different.' Kidman: 'I don't think it's a morality tale. It's different for every person who watches it.' Pollack: '[It's] the story of a man who journeys off the path and then finds his way back onto it, a man who almost loses himself because something awakens a darker part of him, and he follows it against his own better sense. [When] he realises that what he's lived through was about values so far below what he's lived his life for, he's devastated.'

Kubrick himself remained tight-lipped about the film, a silence that his death from a heart attack on 7 March 1999 – just five days after delivering a final print to Warner Bros – would leave unbroken. 'Knowing how Stanley was such a perfectionist,' Kubrick's friend and former producer James B Harris told Peter Bogdanovich, 'he may have killed himself on this picture.'

**CASTING:** Kubrick did not always envisage Tom Cruise and Nicole Kidman in the central roles of *Eyes Wide Shut*: in fact, he had been considering the project for so long that Julie Christie had been an early possibility for the role of Albertine/Alice, as well as such husband-and-wife acting couples as Alec Baldwin and Kim Basinger (who had starred together in *Too Hot to Handle* and a remake of *The Getaway*) and even Steve Martin and Victoria Tennant (*The Man with Two Brains, LA Story*). Val Kilmer (*The Saint*) also reportedly sent the director some thirty unsolicited audition tapes, hoping to secure a role in *Eyes Wide Shut*. Kubrick was ultimately convinced that Cruise – who has three Academy Award nominations and $3 billion worth of box-office receipts to his name – and his wife, Nicole Kidman (*Dead Calm, Portrait of a Lady*), who met Cruise when they appeared together in *Days of Thunder* (1990) and later co-starred with him in *Far and Away* (1992), would make the ideal screen couple.

Other roles were filled by actors with a variety of different backgrounds. Thomas Gibson, a familiar face from his television roles in *Dharma & Greg* and *Tales of the City*, and a close friend of Cruise and Kidman since they appeared together in *Far and Away* (1992), was cast as Carl Thomas, Marion Nathanson's fiancé, without an audition; Kubrick had been impressed enough by his role in *Barcelona* (1994). Leelee Sobieski (real name Liliane Roudabeh Elzvieta Gloria Sobieski), then fourteen, was cast as the precocious, Lolita-like daughter of the costume-shop proprietor, Milich, after Kubrick saw an audition tape in which she acted the role of a girl about to have an abortion. 'He said, "You're the only actress I could see was thinking about what she was talking about," ' she told *Scene* magazine. Sobieski has since played critically acclaimed roles in *A Soldier's Daughter Never Cries* (1999) and the CBS mini-series *Joan of Arc* (1999), as well as appearing in *Deep Impact* (1998), *Never Been Kissed* (1999) and *Here on Earth* (2000).

Milich himself would be played by the Croatian-born actor Rade Serbedzija (*Before the Rain*, *The Saint*, *Mighty Joe Young*) under his Americanised name, Rade Sherbedgia. Although he originally auditioned – for Leon Vitali, whom he describes as 'first officer of General Kubrick' – for the part of the Hungarian Lothario Sandor Szavost, he was invited back two weeks later to try out for the role of Milich. 'We had terrible trouble when we started to shoot the film,' Serbedzija recalls. 'It was my first shot in the film, a very simple shot, when I am coming into my shop, and I'm turning on the lights and said, I think, two sentences. We had rehearsals, which [Kubrick] was shooting with a video camera. After a few times, he said to me suddenly, "It's not good, what you are doing." And I said, "Okay, what you want me to do?" He said, "I don't know. You are an actor." I said, "Okay, I'm an actor, tell me what you would like me to do." He said, "I don't know. Try again." ' They began the scene again, but still Kubrick was not satisfied, and called for a break. 'He asked me and Tom to come to his apartment, and he put my audition tape on TV, asking Tom and me to watch this. And they were watching this, and Stanley was laughing, saying, "Ah, what a guy! He is excellent!" And he asked me, "Do you know this guy?" And I said, "I think I know him." And he said, "Could you try it like him?" ' Serbedzija, an actor with more than sixty film credits and many international awards to his name, was furious.

'We started again, same day, and he still didn't like this,' he says. 'I was completely white, and I thought, "My God, you can be one thousand times Kubrick, I will leave!" And just in this moment when I wanted to tell this, it seems that he knew it, and he told me, "But I'm sure you can do this." We started again, shooting with the real camera, did three takes and that was it.' Serbedzija, who has since learned about Kubrick's similar maltreatment of Shelley Winters on *Lolita* and Shelley Duvall on *The Shining*, thinks he knows what Kubrick was doing. 'He knew that I am pretty good actor,' the actor reflects. 'He didn't want any of my old tricks.' Cruise was so impressed with Serbedzija that the two remained firm friends after filming was completed, and the producer-star created a role for him in *Mission: Impossible 2* (2000).

The Scottish-born actor Alan Cumming (*Goldeneye*), cast as the gay New York hotel clerk who makes eyes at Harford, also nearly didn't make it past the first day. 'I walked into this room, and there were Stanley and Tom Cruise,' Cumming told *US* magazine, 'and I went,

"Hello, I'm Alan." And Stanley went, "You were American in the [audition] tapes." And I went, "I know, I was acting." And he said, "Great." Actually, he didn't say "great," he just looked at me. And I went, "Oh, fuck, this is going to be a nightmare!" '

**THE USUAL SUSPECTS:** Leon Vitali, who plays the mysterious Red Cloak, had previously appeared as the impetuous Viscount Bullingdon in *Barry Lyndon*, and subsequently became a close friend, personal assistant and major domo to Kubrick. After acting as Kubrick's assistant on *The Shining*, *Full Metal Jacket* and *Eyes Wide Shut*, and supervising the casting of the last two, Vitali was honoured with his own storefront sign in *Eyes Wide Shut* – 'Vitali's'.

**CLASSIC QUOTES**
Szavost: 'Don't you think one of the charms of marriage is that it makes deception a necessity for both parties?'

Alice: 'Because I'm a beautiful woman the only reason any man wants to talk to me is because he wants to fuck me! Is that what you're saying?'
Bill: 'Well, I don't think it's quite that black and white, but . . . but I think we both know what men are like.'

Bill: 'Look, women don't . . . they basically just don't think like that.'
Alice: 'Millions of years of evolution, right? Right? Men have to stick it in every place they can, but for women . . . women it is just about security and commitment and whatever the fuck else!'

Alice: 'I first saw him that morning in the lobby. He was . . . he was checking into the hotel and he was following the bellboy with his luggage, to the elevator. He . . . he glanced at me as he walked past, just a glance. Nothing more. *But I could hardly move.* That afternoon, Helena went to the movies with her friend and . . . you and I made love, and we made plans about our future and we talked about Helena and yet . . . at no time was he *ever out of my mind*. And I thought if he ever wanted me, even if it was only for one night, I was ready to give up everything. You, Helena, my whole fucking future. Everything. And yet it was weird 'cause at the same time you were dearer to me than ever, and . . . and at that moment my love for you was both tender and sad.'

Alice: 'We . . . we were . . . we were in a deserted city and . . . and our clothes were gone. We were naked, and . . . and I was terrified, and I . . . I felt ashamed. Oh, God! And . . . and I was angry because I felt it was your fault. You . . . you rushed away to try and find our clothes for us. As soon as you were gone it was completely different. I . . . I felt wonderful. Then I was lying in a . . . in a beautiful garden, stretched out naked in the sunlight, and a man walked out of the woods, he was . . . he was the man from the hotel, the one I told you about . . . the naval officer. He . . . he just stared at me and then he just laughed . . . he just laughed at me.'

Bill: 'That's not the end, is it?'

Alice: 'No.'

Bill: 'Why don't you tell me the rest of it?'

Alice: 'It's . . . it's too awful.'

Bill: 'It's only a dream.'

Alice: 'He . . . he was kissing me, and then . . . then we were making love. Then there were all these other people around us . . . hundreds of them, everywhere. Everyone was fucking, and then I . . . I was fucking other men, so many . . . I don't know how many I was with. And I knew you could see me in the arms of all these men, just fucking all these men, and I . . . I wanted to make fun of you, to laugh in your face. And so I laughed as loud as I could. And that must have been when you woke me up.'

Ziegler: 'Bill, suppose I told you that . . . that everything that happened to you there, the threats, the girls . . . warnings, the last-minute interventions . . . suppose I said all of that was staged, that it was a kind of charade? That it was fake?'

**THEMES AND MOTIFS:** At the end of *Eyes Wide Shut*, Alice tells her husband that they should be grateful for surviving all of their adventures, 'whether they were real or only a dream'. She is sure, she says, but 'only as sure as I am that the reality of one night, let alone that of a whole life time, can ever be the whole truth.' Bill replies, 'And no dream is ever just a dream.' So are the events of *Eyes Wide Shut* supposed to represent reality, or a dream, or – as the title suggests – elements of both? And, if there is a point of departure from reality in which one or other of the characters, but presumably Bill, begins to dream, where is that point?

In an article for *Sight and Sound*, Larry Gross suggested that the first dreamlike thing that happens in *Eyes Wide Shut* is Bill's summons to Ziegler's bathroom to attend the girl who has overdosed. 'Harford, entering the scene late, is surprised along with the audience. He's not only "too late" to undo what has happened, he has no context in which to understand it. The scenario of being late for something important, being placed in a situation where we are ill-prepared or our proper role is difficult to discern, is described by Freud as the "examination dream".' Perhaps. Yet the slightly dreamlike state in which Bill and Alice each enter the party suggests that the departure from reality came even earlier: otherwise, why would one of the models ask Bill if he would like to go 'where the rainbow ends', only for him to find himself later at a costume shop called Under the Rainbow?

Gross suggested that another model of Freudian dream analysis, the 'anxiety dream', follows Alice's revelation of an unfulfilled sexual fantasy she had about a complete stranger a year earlier. 'Alice's story doesn't simply unearth Bill's capacity for jealousy,' Gross explained. 'More precisely, she reveals that her erotic feelings could have led her to destroy her marriage and family.' The moment this hypothetical death is postulated, Bill learns of the literal death of Lou Nathanson. 'Conveniently so, as in the way wishes are magically realised in dreams? Absolutely.' Bill's erotic odyssey, which begins with the suggestion of necrophilia that hangs over Marion Nathanson's confession of love – significantly, she also tells him, 'It's so unreal' – has all of the hallmarks of his taking revenge on Alice for her 'thought crime', yet his failure to capitalise on any of the proffered sexual opportunities suggests that his heart is not truly in adultery, and that it is his mind at work. This is exemplified by Domino, the prostitute with masks on the wall of her apartment, who says she would 'rather not put . . . into words' the sexual services she offers – a stark counterpoint to Alice, who uses the word 'fuck' at every available opportunity. In Bill's mind, Alice is lower than a whore.

The anxiety of Bill's waking dream, if that is what it is, reaches critical mass at his unmasking at the orgy. Being naked and vulnerable in situations in which others are not is a common anxiety dream, and one related subsequently by Alice to her husband after he has returned from a series of erotic escapades which closely resemble the events of her dream: she imagines herself naked, he is without a costume; she imagines hundreds of couples making love around them, something that Bill literally witnesses at the orgy; she dreams of Bill's humiliation, which Bill almost suffers after being unmasked. At this point, Bill's waking dream and Alice's literal one have become intertwined and almost indistinguishable from one another: it no longer matters which was reality and which a dream. The line between eyes wide open and eyes shut has become meaningless. Besides, as Alice concludes once her husband's revelations have sunk in, 'The important thing is we're awake now and hopefully for a long time to come.'

Like *The Shining*, Kubrick's earlier film about domestic dysfunctionality, *Eyes Wide Shut* contains a number of bathroom scenes, which offer hints of the potential nightmares that exist beneath the apparently calm surface of normality. The complacency in the Harfords' marriage is perfectly illustrated in the first bathroom scene, as Alice asks Bill how she looks, and whether her hair is OK, and each time he replies without looking at her. Victor Ziegler's bathroom sets the stage for the film's many juxtapositions of sex and death (see below), and also, as Larry Gross pointed out, 'reminds us of the greatest iconographic sexual/dreamlike/perverse bathroom in US cinema – the one in *Psycho* [1960]. And the bathroom where a butler helping Jack Nicholson clean up a drink he has spilled reveals slowly, with hilarious indirectness, that he is a murderous ghost in Kubrick's own *The Shining*.'

Sex and death – the continually juxtaposed themes of *Dr Strangelove* – are inextricably entwined in each of the encounters on Bill Harford's odyssey. Victor Ziegler's sexual encounter with the model Mandy almost ends in her death; Alice suggests that female patients whom Bill examines for breast cancer may be sexually aroused by him; Marion Nathanson's declaration of love comes within an hour of her father's death, indeed, his body is present in the room as she makes it; the playful prostitute who proffers casual sex, which, Harford later learns, carried the threat of death from AIDS; Harford's incursion into the underground world of the orgiasts threatens his life, after it has apparently claimed that of the mysterious woman who 'redeemed him'; Harford seems about to kiss the dead woman as she lies in a hospital mortuary. As Christiane Kubrick once said of *Eyes Wide Shut*, 'It has nothing to do with sex and everything to do with fear.'

MUSIC: In 1997, Jocelyn Pook became the latest collaborator to be invited to work on a Kubrick film after an out-of-the-blue telephone call from the director. Pook is a violinist and composer who had written music for avant-garde theatre and television, co-founded bands, released a solo album (*Deluge*, retitled *Flood* in the United States) and recorded with such diverse acts as Peter Gabriel, Massive Attack, the Cranberries and Nick Cave before Kubrick's call, which came after the director heard her music being played by the choreographer Yolande Smith, during rehearsals for the masked ball scene. In all, 22 minutes of Pook's music appears in the film, equivalent to that composed for *Full Metal Jacket* by Vivian Kubrick and therefore insufficient to qualify for an Academy Award nomination – although it was nominated for a Golden Globe.

Pook's compositions would accompany several classical pieces – by Dmitri Shostakovich ('Waltz 2 from Jazz Suite'), Frans Liszt ('Grey Clouds') and György Ligeti ('Musica Ricercata II'), whose music had also appeared in *2001* and *The Shining*. These classical recordings appear on the Warner Sunset/Reprise Records' soundtrack CD (9 47450-2), along with some seventeen minutes of Pook's original music, Chris Isaak's song 'Baby Did a Bad Bad Thing', and several big-band instrumentals – 'I Got It Bad (And That Ain't Good)', 'When I Fall in Love', 'If I Had You', 'Strangers in the Night' and 'Blame it on my Youth'.

POSTER: The American and European poster images for *Eyes Wide Shut* all feature a colour photograph of Cruise (bare-shouldered, eyes shut) kissing Kidman (bare-shouldered, eyes open and looking warily out of frame). The image is placed against a solid purple background, and – in early versions – surrounded by the baroque silver frame of the mirror in the couple's screen bathroom.

TAG-LINE: Although no copyline other than the powerfully enticing 'CRUISE KIDMAN KUBRICK' appeared on any of the posters promoting *Eyes*

*Wide Shut*, several critics' quotes were displayed in press advertisements following the film's release.

**TRAILER:** Such was the secrecy that surrounded the shooting of *Eyes Wide Shut* that Kubrick's own ninety-second 'teaser' trailer, unveiled at the ShoWest exhibitors' showcase in Las Vegas, created a media storm. Taken from a single scene, cut to Chris Isaak's grinding sex-and-rockabilly song 'Baby Did a Bad Bad Thing', the trailer begins with a naked Nicole Kidman standing before a mirror – the same, elegantly framed looking glass featured on the earliest posters for the film. She removes an earring, as Tom Cruise approaches her, at least half naked, touching her back and shoulder before cupping one breast in his hand and caressing it. He kisses her, eyes closed – or wide shut – as she turns towards the mirror with the same knowing look in her eye as Sharon Stone sported as she looked out over Michael Douglas's shoulder on the *Basic Instinct* poster.

**WHAT THE PAPERS SAID:** Kubrick's long-time friend Alexander Walker, the London *Evening Standard*'s resident film reviewer, and *Time* magazine's Richard Schickel, were the first critics to see *Eyes Wide Shut*, and both gave the film favourable previews: Walker termed the film 'an astonishing work made with masterly control and at the same time a humanity that this director's detractors have insisted he did not possess', while Schickel called it 'Kubrick's haunting final masterpiece' – a quote widely used to publicise the film. *Variety* was equally enthusiastic, with Todd McCarthy declaring *Eyes Wide Shut* 'a riveting, thematically probing, richly atmospheric and just occasionally troublesome work, a deeply inquisitive consideration of the extent of trust and mutual knowledge possible between a man and a woman'.

Most other critics were less generous. In the UK, the *Independent*'s Anthony Quinn called *Eyes Wide Shut* 'a dismal and overwrought piece of work', and suggested that the film, at turns, resembles 'a Ferrero-Rocher advert' or, at the orgy scene, '*Purgatorio* directed by Peter Greenaway'. *Sight and Sound*'s Charles Whitehouse suggested the scene 'feels like a stolid throwback to the more innocent times of Hammer horror or Roger Corman's Poe movies', and damned the film with faint praise: '*Eyes Wide Shut* is no masterpiece, but it is endlessly fascinating.' For *Time Out* magazine's Geoff Andrew, Kubrick's final film was 'perfectly watchable but neither shocking, erotic nor profound and actually rather silly . . . What starts as a study of a threatened marriage becomes a murky conspiracy mystery that's barely suspenseful or credible. That said, despite over-stretched scenes it is entertaining.'

Intriguingly, several periodicals allowed different reviews to offer diametrically opposed views of the film. The *New York Times*' Janet Maslin called it 'spellbinding', 'startling' and 'a brilliantly provocative *tour de force*', while her colleague Michiko Kakutani described it as 'a lugubrious, strangely static work . . . overly studied and stilted', which came as 'an unfortunate misstep at the end of a dazzling career'. The *Guardian* also neatly summarised both points of view, with Peter Bradshaw calling it 'superbly confident and absolutely captivating', while Duncan Campbell voiced the 'Emperor's new clothes' feeling of dozens of critics worldwide by pointing out that 'there is always a risk with films featuring masks that there is nothing underneath'.

**CONTROVERSY:** 'The first time [we saw the film], we were in shock,' Nicole Kidman told *Time* magazine's Cathy Booth. 'The second time, I thought, "Wow! It's going to be controversial." ' Nevertheless, despite the attempts of various journalists, critics and Internet buffs to provoke controversy about the sexually charged nature of *Eyes Wide Shut*, the most serious outcry resulted from Warner Bros' decision to digitally alter 65 seconds of the film, in response to the Motion Picture Association of America's (MPAA) decision to encumber *Eyes Wide Shut* with a crippling 'NC-17' rating, seriously damaging its box-office potential. Protests came from the Los Angeles Film Critics' Association and the New York Film Critics' Circle, each group issuing a statement declaring that the ratings board was 'out of control', having become 'a punitive and restrictive force, effectively trampling the freedom of American filmmakers'.

The studio also came under fire for agreeing to digitally alter the offending scene by superimposing shrouded figures in front of couples engaged in copulation, effectively obscuring the audience's view. The New York critics insisted that Warner Bros provide details of Kubrick's contribution to its decision, if any, noting that 'the process by which this bowdlerised edition of Kubrick's final film came into being has been shrouded in vagueness and misinformation'. Responding to the criticism, Warner Bros' co-chairman, Terry Semel, explained the studio's decision as one of company policy. 'We're not in the "NC-17" business,' he stated, adding, 'When one looks at *Eyes Wide Shut* perhaps there was not a huge difference between what would be an "R" [and] what would be an "NC-17".' Besides, as the film's publicist Pat Kingsley told *Premiere* magazine, 'Stanley said to me at one point, "This is an 'R' movie." He said, "There was a time when I thought about maybe asking for an 'NC-17', but that just limits it, and it could be misrepresented. I'm happy with an 'R'. I plan to make two minor adjustments in the movie, which will make it easier to get an 'R'." Very minor, he said.' Indeed, as Cruise – fiercely protective of Kubrick's vision – asserted, 'There is nothing in the picture that Stanley didn't approve.'

Despite the controversy over the cuts in the United States, there was greater outrage in India, where Warner Bros pulled the film altogether after protests from local censors regarding the use of holy scripture as part of Jocelyn Pook's music for the orgy scene.

**BOX OFFICE:** *Eyes Wide Shut* was released in the United States on 16 July 1999, earning a more than respectable $21.7 million on its opening weekend, on which it placed at the top of the box-office charts. Over subsequent weeks, the film went on to gross $55.6 million domestically, but topped the $100 million mark overseas, where it was seen without the 65-second digital alterations (see above). In Japan, *Eyes Wide Shut*'s $5.3 million bow gave Warner Bros its most successful opening week ever, and the film held the number-one spot in the UK, France and Italy for two weeks running, earning more than $10 million in each territory. In late November 1999, Warner Bros took out double-page advertisements in trade periodicals declaring that *Eyes Wide Shut* had earned a total of $155,655,000 worldwide, making it Kubrick's most successful film ever.

**AWARDS:** On 8 March 1997, Kubrick received the Directors' Guild of America's (DGA) coveted DW Griffith Award for lifetime achievement at its 49th annual awards, making him the 27th director to receive the accolade. 'The DW Griffith Award is the most prestigious artistic trophy given by the Directors Guild of America,' the DGA president, Gene Reynolds, said. 'In the judgment of a committee of ex-presidents, Stanley Kubrick is entitled to join the company of Orson Welles, David Lean, John Ford, Alfred Hitchcock, Elia Kazan, Akira Kurosawa and . . . Woody Allen.'

Although Kubrick asked Jack Nicholson to collect the award on his behalf, Kubrick also sent a videotaped acceptance speech, apologising for his absence, 'but I'm in London making *Eyes Wide Shut* with Tom Cruise and Nicole Kidman.' Kubrick went on to say of directing, 'although it can be like trying to write *War and Peace* in a bumper car at an amusement park, when you finally get it right, there are not many joys in life that can equal the feeling'.

The awards season for which *Eyes Wide Shut* would have qualified began in earnest with the announcement of a single nomination at the Golden Globe Awards: Jocelyn Pook for Best Original Score – albeit in a category crowded with eight other feature films. Although three of *Eyes Wide Shut*'s actors, Tom Cruise, Thomas Gibson and Leelee Sobieski, all received Golden Globe nominations for other projects the film received no Academy Award nominations at all.

**TECHNICAL ACHIEVEMENTS:** Despite the dream themes at the heart of *Eyes Wide Shut*, and the problems of trying to re-create New York in London – here, after all, was a director who had made a Vietnam War film on location in London – Kubrick strove for a level of reality that prompted *Variety*'s Todd McCarthy to compare the naturalistic lighting to the *natural* lighting of the 'Dogme 95' production *Festen*, a.k.a. *The Celebration* (1999). The Scottish actor Alan Cumming (*Goldeneye*) told *Premiere* magazine that Kubrick's desire for naturalistic conditions led to a momentary disagreement over make-up. '[Robert McCann] came to powder me at one point, and Stanley said, "What are you doing?" And I said, "Oh, it's all right; it's just the shining, Stanley" – 'cause I was a bit shiny. And we all just howled with laughter.'

**INFLUENCED BY:** While working together on the screenplay for *Dr Strangelove*, Kubrick and the writer Terry Southern had watched a pornographic film together, prompting Kubrick to say, 'Wouldn't it be interesting if an artist were to do this with beautiful, first-rate actors and good equipment?' The subsequent conversation led to Southern's 1970 novel *Blue Movie* (see Lost Worlds: The Films That Never Were), in which the film director King B, 'an artist whose responsibility for his work was total, and his control of it complete', sets out to make a pornographic film that will be erotic, beautiful and above all expensive. 'I've got to find out', says King B, 'how far you can take the aesthetically erotic – at what point, if any, it gets to be such a personal thing that it becomes meaningless.' Kubrick enjoyed the book, telling Southern, 'You've written the definitive blow job.' Did the ideas that sprang from that initial conversation with Southern, and lead to *Blue Movie*, inspire the creation of Kubrick's erotic masterpiece, *Eyes Wide Shut*?

According to Frederic Raphael, the orgy scene was partly inspired by a notorious sex party thrown – in the Vatican of all places – by the Duke of Valentino on 31 October 1501, with fifty courtesans in attendance. According to Richard Sennett's *Flesh and Stone*, quoted in Georgina Masson's *Courtesans of the Italian Renaissance*, 'they danced with the servants and others present, at first in their clothes and then naked ... The Pope [Alexander VI], the Duke, and his sister, Donna Lucrezia, were all present to watch. Finally, prizes of silk doublets, shoes, hats and other clothes were offered to the men who copulated with the greatest number of prostitutes.' After first researching the idea of a re-creation of a Roman orgy – which, as Raphael learned, owed more to early cinema than to actual fact – Kubrick and Raphael decided to use the Duke of Valentino's Hallowe'en party as the basis of the orgy scene, re-created by a mysterious and secret group of hedonists to which Ziegler might belong.

As further inspiration, Kubrick sent Raphael a batch of erotic photographs by the photographer Helmut Newton in order to prime the writer's imagination. 'Newton's photographs were divided between fantasies, set in extremely elegant surroundings,' Raphael wrote, 'and shots of whorish women in the style of stills from low-life documentaries.' In addition to the photographs, Raphael received reproductions of paintings and drawings by the Austrian erotic artists Egon Schiele and Gustav Klimt.

Oddly enough, Kubrick's widow Christiane remembered their first meeting, which took place shortly before Kubrick cast the young actress in *Paths of Glory*. 'I met him at a studio, and then he went to an enormous masked ball where I was performing. He was the only one without a costume. He was quite baffled.' Did Kubrick's memory of this event contribute to the masked-ball scenes in *Eyes Wide Shut*?

In his article for *Sight and Sound*, Larry Gross suggested strong thematic parallels between four films from European art cinema in the 1960s, which he believes influenced *Eyes Wide Shut*: Alain Resnais' *Last Year at Marienbad* (1961), Ingmar Bergman's *Persona* (1966), Luis Buñuel's *Belle de Jour* (1967) and Michelangelo Antonioni's *Blow-Up* (1966). 'In these four films the utterances of the central characters about their erotic desires obscure the comprehension they would elicit in more traditionally structured movies,' Gross explained. 'The same is true in *Eyes Wide Shut*. And . . . in all four films people of a certain privileged class travel in obsessive, repetitive circles through ominous landscapes with inexplicable symmetries and maze-like patterns, worlds so aestheticised, so overdetermined their reality is dubious. This is Kubrick's programme here.' Although Gross neglected to mention it, the pattern of Bill's unconsummated sexual liaisons suggests the difficulties encountered by the aristocratic protagonists of Buñuel's *The Discreet Charm of the Bourgeoisie* (1972) in their attempts to eat a meal, hampered by their own fantasies, their lack of purpose and their own discreet charm – Bill Harford, in other words, in a nutshell.

**DÉJÀ VU:** *Eyes Wide Shut* contains a number of subliminal similarities and small-scale references to earlier Kubrick films:
- the party sequence, bathed in a warm amber glow and aurally illuminated by a band, strongly echoes the bar scene in *The Shining*;
- Tom Cruise's intonation of 'Maybe because you're my wife!' recalls Jack Nicholson's utterances to his own spouse in the same film;
- the elderly corpse in the bed as Marion Nathanson makes her declaration of love recalls the occupant of the bed in *2001*;
- Milich's daughter, in attitude more than physical appearance, suggests that she has something of the Lolita about her;
- the orgy sequence recalls the carefully choreographed brawl in the mannequin factory in *Killer's Kiss*;
- a sign painted on the side of a building prominently features the name BOWMAN, another reference to *2001*;
- one of the patients cancelled by Harford is called Kaminsky, the name of one of the hibernating crew members killed by Hal in *2001*;
- the mortuary visited by Harford is located in wing C, room 114 – a subtle reference to the CRM-114 device from *Dr Strangelove*;
- a pile of Kubrick's own films, topped off with *Full Metal Jacket*, can be seen on the long table under the painting, just before Bill sees the mask on his pillow.

**INFLUENTIAL ON:** It is arguably too early as I write this to assess the true influence of *Eyes Wide Shut* on the cinema of the new century, but the *Guardian* reported in November 1999 that Kubrick's shooting style had already influenced the film's leading actor. 'Tom Cruise, it seems, has learnt something about power from Stanley Kubrick,' Tom Dewe

Matthews suggested. 'While Cruise merely played a role in *Eyes Wide Shut*, on the forthcoming *Mission: Impossible 2*, he is wielding his authority as producer and star. "Cruise has been his usual perfectionist self lately," one source from the set in Australia reported. "The director, John Woo, is too humble to argue, so he just does his best on each shot." Accordingly, the film's shoot has extended to Kubrickian proportions.'

A more palpable influence appeared on the next film from another *Eyes Wide Shut* alumnus, the actor-director Sydney Pollack's *Random Hearts* (1999). While not thematically similar – two strangers are united by chance when they discover that their spouses were engaged in an affair that ended with a plane crash – the film unfolds at a similarly languorous pace, and with a similarly dispassionate narrative, as Kubrick's film.

Nicole Kidman's discovery of Schnitzler through her involvement in *Eyes Wide Shut* almost certainly led to her taking the leading role in David Hare's acclaimed 1998 stage production of *The Blue Room*, based on Schnitzler's 1900 play *Reigen*. Intriguingly, *Reigen* was the story that formed the basis of Max Ophuls' 1950 film *La Ronde*, which first exposed Kubrick to Schnitzler's work. 'The ring' was, indeed, complete.

In October 1999, the veteran film maker Stanley Donen – who directed *Two for the Road* (1967) from Frederic Raphael's script, and co-directed *Singin' in the Rain* (1952), from which Kubrick borrowed the song sung by Alex in *A Clockwork Orange* – announced his plan to make a film based on Raphael's *Eyes Wide Open: A Memoir of Stanley Kubrick*. Donen, who introduced Kubrick and Raphael in the seventies, suggested that, rather than playing himself, Raphael – 'a great, great actor' – should play Kubrick, and that Tom Conti would be perfect for the role of Raphael.

**KUBRICK GOES POP:** The British radio station Heart 106.2 took a unique approach to its review of *Eyes Wide Shut*, dispatching two grandmothers to see it before giving their appraisal on air. 'There was too much sex . . . It made my eyes boggle,' one said. 'Three hours watching a load of old rubbish, really,' offered the other.

**CUT SCENES:** In his review of *Eyes Wide Shut*, *Variety*'s Todd McCarthy pointed out that the final hour of the film was 'saddled with an unnecessary stalking interlude and an overlong dialogue sequence between Bill and Ziegler', which Kubrick, who recut several of his earlier films after their initial release, might have trimmed if he had been alive to do so. In fact, only one scene of significance is reported to have been excised after it was filmed, as Rade Serbedzija explains: 'I had three scenes in the film [originally], and he cut one beautiful scene with Tom and me – very nice dialogue, I remember – where Tom was trying his costume and mask. It was the next scene after his daughter left the room, and they were in another room in front of mirrors, and he was dressed in his costume and trying his mask. I forgot the lines, but I think they were talking about his daughter. It was a really good scene.' Kubrick cut it, Serbedzija believes, because he did not want to show Cruise in his mask and cloak before the orgy itself.

**TRIVIA:** The Harfords' apartment was modelled on one in which Kubrick once lived in Manhattan. According to *Time* magazine's Cathy Booth, 'Kidman chose the books, the colour of the window shades, and even added the change Cruise always leaves by their bed at home. She populated it with her own things too, leaving her makeup in the bathroom, tossing her clothes on the floor.' 'By the end,' Cruise told Booth, 'we felt as if we lived on that set. We even slept in the bed.'

When Milich's daughter whispers in Bill's ear – recalling Lolita whispering to Humbert Humbert in Kubrick's earlier film – she is saying, 'You should have a cloak lined with ermine.'

The password for the orgy, 'Fidelio', is from the latin root for fidelity, one of the film's principal themes. It is also the title of a Beethoven opera, *Fidelio, or Married Love*, first performed in Vienna in 1806.

Alice can be seen watching *Blume in Love* (1973) on television, while a video copy of *Rain Man* (1988) can be glimpsed in the Harfords' bedroom.

Frederic Raphael claims that the WASP-ish name Harford, no obvious relation to the original novel's Jewish name Scheuer, was a contraction of the name *Harrison Ford*, whom Kubrick said Bill should resemble.

Kubrick and Arthur Schnitzler were both the sons of Jewish doctors.

**APOCRYPHA:** As always with a Kubrick production, the rumour mill continued to seethe with activity, bolstered now by the Internet, which reported, as filming progressed, a number of inaccuracies: that Cruise and Kidman played psychologists or psychiatrists; that Leelee Sobieski played their screen daughter; that Cruise kissed a corpse, and spent one scene in a dress; that Kidman was taught how to inject heroin for another scene; that the fashion photographer Helmut Newton had been engaged to shoot production stills; that John Malkovich was among the supporting actors; that the replacement of Harvey Keitel with the actor-director Sydney Pollack was a studio-engineered move to place a Warner Bros spy – not to mention a respected film maker who had previously directed Cruise in *The Firm* (1993) – on location.

Perhaps the most tantalising – and libellous – allegation came when the British tabloid the *Star* reported that Cruise and Kidman had to be instructed in the intimate behaviour of a married couple by a pair of sex therapists. The couple sued – and won – because, as Kidman told *Rolling Stone*'s Nancy Collins, 'not one tiny element of that story is true. There were no sex therapists. What happened on screen happened because the three of us worked on this together, with no outside people coming in. In fact, we have a legal affidavit from the two therapists [named], saying they never did a thing.'

**AVAILABILITY:** *Eyes Wide Shut* is available in the United States as an NTSC VHS and a Region 1 DVD. *Eyes Wide Shut* is also available on video and DVD in the United Kingdom. DVD editions feature the theatrical trailer.

**EXPERT WITNESS:** 'Because Tom is in every scene in the movie, they had a very different relationship, a very private one. Stanley really understood Tom. And me. He said that Tom was a rollercoaster and I was a thoroughbred . . . He also directed us very differently. He allowed me more freedom. He and Tom worked very closely together on the character, while with me he'd say, "You can ad-lib." He loved to improvise – then he'd go write it. With Peter Sellers in *Lolita*, he'd have two cameras going, because he said you'd only get it a couple of times and you better have the cameras on. He was like that with me, too. He'd say, "Now you can play." And I would.' – Nicole Kidman to Nancy Collins, quoted in *Rolling Stone*, 8–22 July 1999.

**FINAL ANALYSIS:** A mere six months of analysis of one of Kubrick's films can rarely bring to light every possible nuance, interpretation, meaning and significance – particularly in the case of a film that the director had in mind for three decades, and appeared twelve years after his previous film, and several months after his death. Kubrick's absence from the director's chair may have paled into insignificance next to the coincidental returns, in the same year, 1999, of the directorial exiles George Lucas and Terrence Malick, whose films *The Phantom Menace* and *The Thin Red Line* ended directorial droughts of 22 years and 25 years respectively. Without the benefit of hindsight with which Kubrick's earlier films can be evaluated, we face the odd position of being able to assess a work of art that probably needs some years to fully appreciate, yet one that the death of the artist has given immediate significance for which it would not necessarily qualify if it had been made by a more prolific film maker, or if it had not proved to be his final endeavour.

At first viewing, *Eyes Wide Shut* is compelling, fascinating, erotically charged and faintly preposterous; descriptions that can all be applied to the orgy sequence, which perhaps too closely resembles the sacrifice in *Interview with the Vampire* (1994) – an association which Cruise's presence in a long black cloak does nothing to dispel. The choice of fantasy, rather than infidelity, as the catalyst for the potential breakdown of the Harfords' marriage is an intriguing one: it arguably speaks much more to married couples than a *Fatal Attraction*-style film in which one or the other partner in a marriage has been unfaithful. With Alice's indiscretion given the reduced status of a 'thought crime', Bill's ability to avenge himself is removed, and he is unable to consummate his own confused sexual desires – even when several genuine opportunities present themselves, along with the false ones.

Part of the fascination with *Eyes Wide Shut* amid the late-twentieth-century cult of celebrity was, as Kubrick knew it would be, the casting of a real-life married couple in the leading roles. Yet when the veneer of interest provided by their celebrity status has been stripped away, along with their clothes, the question becomes one of performance: are their acting chops up to the parts? For Tom Cruise, who is obliged to carry the film by virtue of the fact that he appears in almost every scene of it, there is a get-out clause that states that, since his character is lost in a nocturnal world of which he assumes much but knows little, he can be excused for acting like a fish out of water – or an actor out of his depth. With Nicole Kidman, who disappears for an hour or two in the middle of the film, the question of acting ability sits squarely on the test of three scenes: one in which she is drunk, another in which she is stoned, and a third in which she has just woken from an upsetting dream. In each, her performance ranges from the theatrically stunning (no one in the auditorium dares cough during her speech) to acting-class amateurish (several in the auditorium laugh during her speech) without ever really coming down on either side. In other words, both actors escape from their experiences in much the same way that their characters do.

Without the baggage, Kubrick's final film would almost certainly have been seen as a mature, radical, thoughtful but ultimately slight story about the near-collapse of a marriage precipitated by a sexual confession. Unfortunately, in the wake of Kubrick's death, and given the length of time for which Kubrick had been attempting to bring the story to the screen, it is required to be so much more than it can ever be, at least for the foreseeable future. In time, critics may well come to appreciate the film in ways they have not yet thought to do, as they have done with so many of Kubrick's earlier films. Until then, while not exactly the equivalent of Domecq Double Century sherry ads to the director of *Citizen Kane*, *Eyes Wide Shut* has the unenviable role of the flawed masterpiece that closes the career of the master film maker.

**KUBRICK ON KUBRICK:** '[Schnitzler's] plays are, to me, masterpieces of dramatic writing. It's difficult to find any writer who understood the human soul more truly and who had a more profound insight into the way people think, act, and really are, and who also had a somewhat all-seeing point of view – sympathetic if somewhat cynical.' – quoted in an unpublished interview with *Horizon* magazine's Robert Emmett Ginna, circa 1960.

# Lost Worlds: The Films That Never Were

'When he read over and over how few films he made, he would be very depressed,' Kubrick's widow, Christiane, said of her late husband. He would say, 'Yes, I wait always too long in between [films] because I want to get it right.' Here are the films Kubrick considered but did not make.

## The Burning Secret

Kubrick and his producing partner James B Harris came across Stefan Zweig's novel, the story of a child who conceals his mother's affair from his father, while looking for a project with which to follow *The Killing*. Novelist Calder Willingham (*Paths of Glory*) scripted the adaptation, but by the time he had completed a first draft, the Kubrick-Harris-MGM deal had expired. 'It's a good story but I don't know how good the screenplay was,' Kubrick told Michael Ciment. Andrew Birkin, one of Kubrick's assistants on *2001*, eventually directed a film version in 1988, with Faye Dunaway and Klaus Maria Brandauer.

## ?

'A few years [after *The Killing*] I wrote an incomplete screenplay about Mosby's Rangers, a Southern guerrilla force in the American Civil War.' Kubrick said about the untitled project, based on research done by Civil War expert Shelby Foote.

## The German Lieutenant

Korean War veteran Richard Addams wrote this script for Harris-Kubrick after the release of *Paths of Glory*, but the partnership did not pursue the project.

## I Stole $16,000,000

Kubrick and Jim Thompson collaborated on this script for Bryna Productions after the release of *Paths of Glory*, which Thompson co-scripted. Based on the autobiography of Herbert Emerson Wilson, a notorious safecracker who served time in San Quentin prison. 'It was written for Kirk Douglas, who didn't like it,' Kubrick recalled, 'and that was the end of it.'

# The Authentic Death of Hendry Jones, a.k.a. One-Eyed Jacks

Impressed by *The Killing* and *Paths of Glory*, actor and would-be producer Marlon Brando met with Kubrick and Harris in 1957 to discuss their potential collaboration on a boxing film or a western. Unable to reach agreement on the former, they turned instead to Charles Neider's 1956 novel *The Authentic Death of Hendry Jones*, a thinly disguised reworking of the Billy the Kid legend. Sam Peckinpah had scripted an adaptation of the novel, which Brando's Pennebaker Films owned, and on 12 May 1958 Kubrick signed on to direct the film for Paramount Pictures.

Kubrick, dissatisfied with the script, persuaded Brando to fire Peckinpah and hire Calder Willingham (*Paths of Glory*) to rewrite it, a move that perturbed the studio. Although Karl Malden, with whom Brando had worked on *A Streetcar Named Desire* (1951) and *On the Waterfront* (1954), had been cast along with Mexican actress Pine Pellicer (*Macario*), the proposed start date slid further and further back, as Kubrick and Willingham stalled at page 52 of the script – now entitled *One-Eyed Jacks* – struggling to accommodate Brando's frequent changes of direction.

Finally, on 21 November 1958, Kubrick was politely fired, later issuing a statement claiming to have resigned 'with deep regret,' due to his 'desire . . . to commence work on *Lolita*'. After approaching Elia Kazan (*On the Waterfront*), Sidney Lumet (*12 Angry Men*) and several other directors without success, Brando directed the film himself. It was released in 1961. In 1973, Peckinpah directed his own version of the story, *Pat Garrett and Billy the Kid*.

## Childhood's End

Planning his science fiction 'film of mythic grandeur' in 1964, Kubrick was intrigued by the far-reaching themes of Arthur C Clarke's 1954 novel, in which the arrival of alien spaceships paves the way for Mankind's destiny among the stars. The book was already under option by writer-director Abraham Polonsky (*Force of Evil*), but Kubrick's interest led to his collaboration with Clarke on the project which would become *2001: A Space Odyssey*.

## Blue Movie

Although Kubrick never seriously considered directing an adaptation of Terry Southern's 1970 novel about an acclaimed director's efforts to make a pornographic film with a big budget and big stars, the novel was inspired by a conversation between Kubrick and Southern prompted by the viewing of rushes from a pornographic film during their collaboration on *Dr Strangelove*. When Kubrick passed on the offer to direct, the project was set up at Warner Bros in 1974, with Mike Nichols in the director's chair and Julie Andrews in the leading role. The deal broke down, and although the project was briefly considered by David Lean, the film never materialised.

## Napoleon

Kubrick's MGM-backed epic about the French emperor was due to go before the cameras in the winter of 1969. 'Napoleon himself once remarked what a great novel his life would be,' he told Alexander Walker. 'I'm sure he would have said "movie" if he had known about them.' Of his planned 'bio-pic', Kubrick told Joseph Gelmis, 'This will not be just a dusty historic pageant but a film about the basic questions of our own times, as well as Napoleon's,' he added, noting that some forty thousand infantry and ten thousand cavalry would be used for the biggest battles. Regarding the 'tremendous problem' of finding an actor to play L'Empereur from emergence to exile, Kubrick initially considered Al Pacino, though the project came far closer to fruition with Ian Holm, and then Jack Nicholson, who remained interested in playing Napoleon long after Kubrick abandoned the project in favour of another eighteenth-century story, *Barry Lyndon*.

## Inside The Third Reich

In 1971, Andrew Birkin, one of Kubrick's assistants on 2001, scripted an adaptation of *Inside the Third Reich: The Secret Diaries* – the autobiography of Hitler's architect, Albert Speer, whose role in the Nazi war effort led to a twenty-year prison stretch at Spandau. Despite Kubrick's interest in making a film about the Nazis (see below), Kubrick told Birkin, 'I'm Jewish – I can't get involved in this.'

## Perfume

After *The Shining*, Kubrick considered returning to the eighteenth-century setting of *Barry Lyndon* for an adaptation of German author Patrick Süskind's bestselling novel *Perfume*, about a sociopathic perfume maker who creates scents so powerful that those who smell them lose their will.

## Aryan Papers

In 1991, Kubrick bought the rights to Louis Begley's novel *Wartime Lies*, the story of a young Jewish boy named Maciek who is forced to flee Poland with his beautiful aunt Tania when the Germans invade, and later becomes involved in the black market. Although Warner Bros announced Kubrick's intention to adapt the novel as *Aryan Papers* in April 1993, locations were scouted, and Julia Roberts and Uma Thurman were mentioned for the role of Tania, Kubrick eventually abandoned the project, probably because of its similarity to the critically acclaimed *Schindler's List*, released later the same year.

## AI

An acronym of 'artificial intelligence', *AI* was Kubrick's long-gestating science-fiction fable – inspired in equal parts by Brian Aldiss's 1969 short story 'Super-Toys Last All Summer Long', which Kubrick optioned in 1982, and *Pinocchio*. Set in a flooded future Manhattan in which only the tops of the tallest buildings protrude from the oceans (cf. *Waterworld*), the project was developed for many years before being set aside until special effects were sufficiently advanced to do justice to Kubrick's elaborate ideas. Steven Spielberg's *Jurassic Park*, released in 1993, convinced Kubrick that the time had come – and that actor Joseph Mazzello might be the perfect choice to play the artifically intelligent android at the heart of the story, co-scripted by Kubrick with science-fiction writers Aldiss, Sara Maitland and Ian Watson.

By this time, Kubrick had already consulted several British make-up artists and special effects technicians – including director Chris Cunningham, who later turned Björk into a perfect robot for the music video 'All is Full of Love'. Now his many conversations with Spielberg led him to invite Industrial Light & Magic's Dennis Muren and Ned Gorman, two of *Jurassic Park*'s Oscar-winning effects team, to his St Alban's home to find out if it would be possible to create a completely computer-generated character – perhaps with Joseph Mazzello's voice – to fill the role of the boy. Kubrick eventually decided to film *Eyes Wide Shut* before *AI*, and his death on 7 March 1999 meant that his bold second science-fiction film seemed unlikely to be made.

Then, in March 2000, director Steven Spielberg – whom Kubrick had spoken of as an ideal director for the project – confirmed rumours that he intended to bring *AI* to the screen in, appropriately enough, the year 2001. 'Stanley had a vision for this project that was evolving over eighteen years,' Spielberg said of the Warner Bros-DreamWorks SKG co-production, which he would direct from his own screenplay adaptation of Kubrick's 80-page treatment. 'I am intent on bringing to the screen as much of that vision as possible,' he added, 'along with elements of my own.'

# Index of Quotations

## Day of the Fight

## Flying Padre

## The Seafarers

## Fear and Desire

## Killer's Kiss

## The Killing

## Paths of Glory

## Spartacus

83    'The censors weren't quite sure . . .' Douglas, *The Ragman's Son*.
83    'I owe you a movie . . .' Douglas, *The Ragman's Son*.

Special thanks to Kirk Douglas and 'April N Paris' for permission to quote from *The Ragman's Son*.


## Lolita

88    'It was a hardback and we only had one copy . . .' Harris, quoted in *Stanley Kubrick* by Vincent LoBrutto.
89    'I was instantly attracted to the book . . .' Kubrick, quoted in an unpublished interview with Robert Emmett Ginna, circa 1960.
90    'absolutely first-rate' Vladimir Nabokov, quoted in *Playboy*, January 1964.
90    'I went to a party . . .' Kubrick, quoted in *Stanley Kubrick Directs* by Alexander Walker.
90    'My first reaction to the picture . . .' Nabokov, *Lolita: A Screenplay*.
90    'The novel itself seems to have aroused . . .' Shurlock, quoted in *The Cutting Room Floor* by Laurent Bouzereau.
91    'You couldn't make it . . .' Harris, quoted in *BFI Film Classics: Lolita*.
91    'The day the contracts were delivered . . .' Harris, quoted in 'Stanley Kubrick: A Cinematic Odyssey,' *Premiere*, August 1999.
91    'When Peter was called to the set . . .' Kubrick, quoted in *Peter Sellers: The Authorized Biography* by Alexander Walker.
91    'The most interesting scenes . . .' Oswald Morris, quoted in interview by Bob Baker and Markku Salmi, *Film Dope*.
92    '[Peter] seemed to be acting . . .' Shelley Winters, *Shelley II*.
92    'Whenever I complained . . .' Shelley Winters, *Shelley II*.
92    '[She] was very difficult . . .' Morris, quoted in interview by Bob Baker and Markku Salmi, *Film Dope*.
92    'if the girl looked like a child . . .' Shurlock, quoted in *The Cutting Room Floor* by Laurent Bouzereau.
92    'We knew we must make her a sex object . . .' Harris, quoted in *Kubrick: A Biography* by John Baxter.
93    'it wasn't because mothers kept their daughters away . . .' 'She is a natural actor . . .' Kubrick, quoted in *Look*, 1962.
93    'No doubt about it . . .' Nabokov, quoted in *Stanley Kubrick: A Biography* by John Baxter.
94    'In *Lolita*, Stanley wanted me to speak . . .' Peter Sellers, quoted in 'The Strange World of Peter Sellers,' *Rolling Stone*, 17 April 1980.
94    'Dennis and I and one other guy . . .' 'two or three weeks' Bob Gaffney, quoted in *Stanley Kubrick* by Vincent LoBrutto.
99    '*Lolita* is the saddest . . .' *Time*, 10 October 1960.
99    'an occasionally amusing but . . .' Anby, *Variety*, 22 June 1962.
99    'turned into a film about . . .' Michael Davie, '*Lolita* Fiasco,' *Observer*, 17 June 1962.
99    'It is clear that Nabokov . . .' Stanley Kauffman, *New Republic*, circa 1962.
99    'She looks to be . . .' Bosley Crowther, *New York Times*, circa 1962.
99    'Have the reviewers looked at . . .' Kael, KPFA Broadcast, *Partisan Review*, Fall 1962.
99    'style and treatment . . .' Beckley, '*Lolita*: The New Movies,' *New York Herald Tribune*, 14 June 1962.
99    'the outsider who is passionately committed . . .' Kubrick, quoted in 'Film Fan to Film Maker' by Jonathan Stang, *New York Times Magazine*, 12 October 1958.
100   'The protagonists of *Paths of Glory* . . .' Kubrick, quoted in the *New York Times*, 17 October 1959.

100 'The film was successful . . .' 'If I realised how severe the limitations . . .' Kubrick, quoted in *Eye*, August 1968.

101 'If one of the new directors . . .' Mason, *Before I Forget*.

102 'If I realised how severe . . .' Kubrick, quoted in a 1972 issue of *Newsweek*.

103 'Between the age limits of nine and fourteen . . .' Nabokov, *Lolita*.

103 'Whatever opinion one may have . . .' unsigned letter from the Motion Picture Association of America (MPAA), December 1960.

103 'that the man is fucking Lolita . . .' 'The succeeding dialogue . . .' Shurlock, quoted in *The Cutting Room Floor* by Laurent Bouzereau.

104 'was originally done with Peter in full drag . . .' Harris, quoted in 'Stanley Kubrick: A Cinematic Odyssey,' *Premiere*, August 1999.

104 'I don't even know . . .' Harris, quoted in *Stanley Kubrick* by Vincent LoBrutto.

## Dr Strangelove or: How I Learned to Stop Worrying and Love the Bomb

108 'The ideas of the story . . .' 'The decision to ignore this dire warning . . .' Kubrick, quoted in *Kubrick* by Michael Ciment.

109 'The decision to ignore this dire warning . . .' Kubrick, quoted in *Kubrick* by Michael Ciment.

109 'I started work on the screenplay . . .' Kubrick, quoted in *The Film Director as Superstar* by Joseph Gelmis.

110 'slightly irreverent story . . .' Kubrick, quoted in the *New York Times*, 31 December 1962.

110 'He told me he was going to make a film . . .' Terry Southern, 'Notes from the War Room,' *Grand Street*, Issue 49, 1993.

110 'One morning, three weeks later . . .' Ken Adam, quoted in *Screencraft: Production Design and Art Direction* by Peter Ettedgui.

110 'I doodled various shapes . . .' Ken Adam, quoted in *Screencraft: Production Design and Art Direction* by Peter Ettedgui.

111 'I had designed a circular light fitting . . .' Adam, quoted in *Stanley Kubrick* by Vincent LoBrutto.

111 'Just tell Stanley that New York . . .' Mo Rothman, quoted in 'Notes from the War Room' by Terry Southern, *Grand Street*, Issue 49, 1993.

111 'During shooting many substantial changes . . .' Kubrick, quoted in *Stanley Kubrick: A Film Odyssey* by Gene D Phillips.

111 'I used to kid [Kubrick] by saying . . .' George C Scott, quoted in *Playboy*, December 1980.

111 'It was minimal . . .' Southern, quoted in *Smoke Signals*.

111 'Stanley's idea was to have a black glove . . .' Sellers, quoted on *The Steve Allen Show*, 1964.

112 'Dear Stanley . . .' Sellers, quoted in 'Notes from the War Room' by Terry Southern, *Grand Street*, Issue 49, 1993.

112 'When Sellers arrived on the set . . .' 'Stanley had set such store by [Sellers'] acting . . .' Southern, quoted in *Smoke Signals*.

113 'Kubrick remembered Slim Pickens . . .' Southern, quoted in *Smoke Signals*.

113 'I was going to do them *all* . . .' Sellers, quoted in 'The Strange World of Peter Sellers,' *Rolling Stone*, 17 April 1980.

113 'When you are inspired . . .' Kubrick, quoted in *Peter Sellers: The Man Behind the Mask* by Peter Evans.

113 'He got fed up . . .' Hattie Proudfoot, quoted in *Arena: The Peter Sellers Story*.

113 'On the first day of shooting . . .' Hayden, quoted in *Newsweek*, 3 January 1972.

114 'It was so amazing that through a technical flight magazine . . .' 'I had no idea of what a missile would look like . . .' Adam, quoted in *Stanley Kubrick* by Vincent LoBrutto.

128 'He used to talk in a strange little voice . . .' Sellers, quoted on *The Steve Allen Show*, 1964.

129 'badly ripped dupes . . .' Kubrick, quoted in 'The Rolling Stone Interview with Stanley Kubrick' by Tim Cahill, *Rolling Stone*, 27 August 1997.

## 2001: A Space Odyssey

135 'It wasn't placed . . .' 'Other titles which we ran up . . .' Clarke, *The Lost Worlds of 2001*.

135 'the proverbial good science fiction movie . . .' Clarke, *The Lost Worlds of 2001*.

135 'of mythic grandeur . . .' 'the reasons for believing . . .' 'the impact (and perhaps even lack of . . .' Kubrick, quoted in *The Lost Worlds of 2001* by Arthur C Clarke.

136 'After various false starts . . .' Clarke, *The Lost Worlds of 2001*.

136 'It was just as well . . .' Clarke, *ibid*.

136 'Thereafter (we thought) . . .' Clarke, *ibid*.

137 '*Journey Beyond the Stars* is an epic story . . .' Kubrick, quoted in MGM press release, 23 February 1965.

138 'While you were acting . . .' Robert Beatty, quoted in *The Making of Kubrick's 2001* by Jerome Agel.

138 'cars and buses going by . . .' Clarke, quoted in the 1996 documentary *Stanley Kubrick: The Invisible Man*.

138 'People were saying, "How are you going to shoot that . . .' Stuart Freeborn, quoted in 'Stanley Kubrick: A Cinematic Odyssey,' *Premiere*, August 1999.

139 'We never got into the film's philosophical message . . .' Keir Dullea, quoted in 'Stanley Kubrick: A Cinematic Odyssey,' *Premiere*, August 1999.

140 'He was on the set with us . . .' Dullea, quoted in 'Keir Dullea' by Lowell Goldman, *Cinefantastique*, June 1994.

142 '[Hal] is far, far more human . . .' Clancy Sigal, quoted in '*2001*: An Informal Diary of an Infernal Machine,' *Town*, July 1966.

142 'Well, what can I say?' Alex North, quoted in sleeve notes to *Alex North's 2001 The Legendary Score*.

143 'wrote and recorded a score . . .' Kubrick, quoted in *Kubrick* by Michael Ciment.

143 'For me, *2001* was ruined . . .' Jerry Goldsmith, *ibid*.

143 'negroes and people with beads' quoted in 'The Rolling Stone Interview with Stanley Kubrick' by Tim Cahill, *Rolling Stone*, 27 August 1997.

144 'The first reviews of *2001* . . .' Kubrick, *ibid*.

144 'A major achievement in cinematography . . .' review of *2001* in *Variety Movie Guide 1999*.

145 'either an exercise in transcendental meditation . . .' review of *2001* in *Life*, reprinted in *The Making of Kubrick's 2001* by Jerome Agel.

145 'uncompromising slowness . . .' quoted in *A Year in the Dark* by Renata Adler.

145 'It's fun to think about Kubrick . . .' Kael, "Trash, Art and the Movies," *Harper's*, February 1969.

145 'A characteristically pessimistic account . . .' Andrew, *Time Out Film Guide: Eighth Edition*.

145 'beautiful to watch . . .' 'Kubrick's greatest achievement . . .' review of *2001* in *Sight and Sound*, quoted in *The Stanley Kubrick Companion* by James Howard.

146 'Wally [Veevers], I think, was principally responsible . . .' Douglas Trumbull, quoted in 'An Effects Odyssey' by Dan Persons, *Cinefantastique*, June 1994.

147 One of the first tasks . . .' 'just absolutely the utmost . . .' 'I worked out a technique . . .' Trumbull, quoted in 'An Effects Odyssey' by Dan Persons, *Cinefantastique*, June 1994.

147 'This was a breakthrough in technical wizardry,' Martin Scorsese, quoted in *A Personal Journey with Martin Scorsese through American Movies* by Martin Scorsese and Michael Henry Wilson.

## A Clockwork Orange

162 'The filming sessions were conducted . . .' Burgess, *You've Had Your Time: The Second Part of the Confessions*.

162 'I bought this yard of it . . .' McDowell, quoted in 'Stanley Kubrick: A Cinematic Odyssey,' *Premiere*, August 1999.

163 'So I got under the cold shower . . .' McDowell, *ibid*.

163 'At the end of the film . . .' Adrienne Corri, quoted in 'Stanley Kubrick: A Cinematic Odyssey,' *Premiere*, August 1999.

163 'If McDowell hadn't been available . . .' Kubrick, quoted in 'A Clockwork Utopia' by Andrew Bailey, *Rolling Stone*, 20 January 1972.

166 'After all, man is the most remorseless killer . . .' Kubrick, quoted in *Newsweek*.

167 'I think that his version . . .' Kubrick, quoted in *Kubrick* by Michael Ciment.

167 'Suddenly the idea popped into my head . . .' Kubrick, quoted in 'Interview with Stanley Kubrick regarding *A Clockwork Orange*' by Philip Strick and Penelope Houston, *Sight and Sound*, Spring 1972.

169 'a painless, bloodless, and ultimately pointless . . .' Andrew Sarris, 'Films in Focus,' *Village Voice*, 30 December 1971.

169 'brilliant, a tour de force . . .' Vincent Canby, '*A Clockwork Orange* Dazzles the Sense and Mind,' *New York Times*, 20 December 1971.

169 'Literal-minded in its sex and brutality . . .' Kael, 'Stanley Strangelove,' *New Yorker*, 1 January 1972.

169 'a sexless, inhuman film . . .' Geoff Andrew, *Time Out Film Guide: Eighth Edition*.

169 'most cynical and disturbing . . .' review of *A Clockwork Orange* in *Monthly Film Bulletin*, 1972.

169 'chilling and mesmeric adaptation . . .' Derek Malcolm, *Guardian*, 13 January 1972.

169 'brilliant piece of cinematic art . . .' John Trevelyan, quoted in *National Heroes* by Alexander Walker.

170 'lead to a clockwork cult . . .' Maurice Edelman, 'Clockwork Oranges are Ticking Bombs,' London *Evening News*, 27 January 1972.

171 'really quite frightening . . .' Burgess, *You've Had Your Time: The Second Part of the Confessions*.

170 'If they dressed like Alex . . .' McDowell, quoted in the 1996 documentary *Stanley Kubrick: The Invisible Man*.

170 'Because *A Clockwork Orange* played with the background of England . . .' Christiane Kubrick, quoted in 'At home with the Kubricks' by Nick James, *Sight and Sound*, September 1999.

170 'There was a concentrated group . . .' Anya Finney, *ibid*.

171 'The simplistic notion . . .' Kubrick, quoted in the 1996 documentary *Stanley Kubrick: The Invisible Man*.

170 'Stanley was very insulted . . .' Christiane Kubrick, quoted in *The Last Movie*.

171 'It's up to Warner Bros . . .' Christiane Kubrick, *ibid*.

171 'It's not exactly high . . .' Anya Finney, quoted in 'At home with the Kubricks' by Nick James, *Sight and Sound*, September 1999.

171 'Two or three years ago . . .' Julian Senior, quoted in *Empire*, February 2000.

172 'the production company that had originally bought the rights . . .' Burgess, *You've Had Your Time: The Second Part of the Confessions*.

172 'I think Stanley Kubrick is the best . . .' William Friedkin, quoted in *Stanley Kubrick: A Biography* by John Baxter.

173 'I wanted to find a way . . .' Kubrick, quoted in *The Film Director as Superstar* by Joseph Gelmis.

173 'Every character save Alex . . .' Kevin Jackson, 'Real Horrorshow,' *Sight and Sound*, September 1999.

174 'The government eventually resorts to . . .' Kubrick, quoted in *Kubrick* by Michael Ciment.

## Barry Lyndon

191  'The fact that Stanley thinks . . .' Calley, quoted in *Time*, 15 December 1975.
191  '*Barry Lyndon* was one of Warner Bros' biggest grosses. . .' Kubrick, quoted in 'How I Learned to Stop Worrying and Love *Barry Lyndon*' by John Hofsess, *New York Times*, 1 November 1976.
191  'the only one that did poorly . . .' Kubrick, quoted in 'The Rolling Stone Interview with Stanley Kubrick' by Tim Cahill, *Rolling Stone*, 27 August 1997.
192  'He was very vulnerable. . .' John Milius, quoted in 'What They Say About Stanley Kubrick' by Peter Bogdanovich, *New York Times*, 4 July 1999.
192  'With this lens. . .' Kubrick, quoted in *Kubrick* by Michael Ciment.
193  'Stanley just treasured his equipment. . .' Ed DiGiulio, quoted in *Stanley Kubrick* by Vincent LoBrutto.
193  'Stanley wanted to make direct reference. . .' Adam, quoted in *Kubrick* by Michael Ciment.
193  'began to search through a book. . .' O'Neal, quoted in 'Stanley Kubrick: A Cinematic Odyssey,' *Premiere*, August 1999.
193  'On the surface. . .' Scorsese, quoted in the 1995 documentary *The Century of Cinema: A Personal Journey with Martin Scorsese through American Movies*.
194  'Costume drama is difficult. . .' David Mamet, quoted in 'The Winslow Man' by Jonathan Romney, *The Guardian*, 27 August 1999.
194  'In the book, Barry is pensioned off. . .' Kubrick, quoted in *Kubrick* by Michael Ciment.
194  'The function of the scene . . .' Kubrick, *ibid*.

## The Shining

197  'It was important to establish an ominous mood . . .' Kubrick, quoted in *Kubrick* by Michael Ciment.
198  '*The Shining* didn't originate . . .' Kubrick, *ibid*.
198  'to make the world's scariest movie . . .' Kubrick, quoted in *Stanley Kubrick* by Vincent LoBrutto .
199  'He wanted to pare [the novel] down . . .' Diane Johnson, quoted in 'Stanley Kubrick: A Cinematic Odyssey,' *Premiere*, August 1999.
199  'Very early on, I decided . . .' Kubrick, quoted by John Hofsess in *New York Times*, 1 June 1980.
200  'I had never done that many takes . . .' Barry Nelson, quoted in 'Stanley Kubrick: A Cinematic Odyssey,' *Premiere*, August 1999.
200  'In one scene . . .' Scatman Crothers, quoted by Jack Kroll, *Newsweek*, 26 May 1980.
200  'When I saw the film . . .' John Boorman, *The Emerald Forest Diary*.
200  'It looks fake, it really does . . .' 'I honestly don't think . . .' 'we're fucking killing . . .' Kubrick, quoted in the 1980 documentary, *Making the Shining*.
200  'From May until October . . .' Shelley Duvall, *ibid*.
200  'Stanley's demanding . . .' Jack Nicholson, quoted in *Stanley Kubrick* by Vincent LoBrutto .
201  'the most eccentric and rather over-the-top [takes] . . .' Gordon Stainforth, quoted in *Stanley Kubrick: A Biography* by John Baxter.
202  'Stanley had a really good way of speaking to me . . .' Danny Lloyd, quoted in 'Stanley Kubrick: A Cinematic Odyssey,' *Premiere*, August 1999.
203  'The concept of the ghost . . .' Kubrick, quoted by Stephen King in *American Film*.
203  'the psychological states of the characters . . .' Johnson, quoted in *Stanley Kubrick: A Biography* by Stephen Baxter.
204  'the artistic satisfaction . . .' Johnson, quoted in *Stanley Kubrick: A Biography* by John Baxter.
206  'the first epic horror film . . .' Jack Kroll, 'Stanley Kubrick's Horror Show,' *Newsweek*, 26 May 1980.

## Full Metal Jacket

## Lost Worlds: The Films That Never Were

All other quotes are from author's own interviews.

# Picture Credits

**First Section**

| | |
|---|---|
| Page 1 | Both The Kobal Collection |
| Page 2 | Private collection (top), The Kobal Collection (bottom) |
| Page 3 | Both The Kobal Collection |
| Page 4 | The Ronald Grant Archive (top), private collection (bottom) |
| Page 5 | The Ronald Grant Archive (top), private collection (bottom) |
| Page 6 | The Ronald Grant Archive (top), private collection (bottom) |
| Page 7 | Both private collection |
| Page 8 | Both The Kobal Collection |

**Second Section**

| | |
|---|---|
| Page 1 | Both private collection |
| Page 2 | Both The Ronald Grant Archive |
| Page 3 | Both The Kobal Collection |
| Page 4 | The Kobal Collection (top), private collection |
| Page 5 | Private collection (top), The Kobal Collection (bottom left), private collection (bottom right) |
| Page 6 | Both private collection |
| Page 7 | The Kobal Collection (top), private collection (bottom) |
| Page 8 | Both The Kobal Collection |

# Bibliography

Agel, Jerome. *The Making of Kubrick's 2001.* New York, New American Library, 1970.

Baxter, John. *Kubrick: A Biography.* London, HarperCollins, 1997.

Beahm, George. *The Stephen King Story.* London, Little, Brown, 1993.

Bettelheim, Bruno. *The Uses of Enchantment: The Meaning of Importance of Fairy Tales.* London, Thames & Hudson, 1996.

Bizony, Piers. *2001: Filming the Future.* London, Aurum, 1994.

Boorman, John. *The Emerald Forest Diary.* New York, Farrar, Straus and Giroux, 1985.

Bouzereau, Laurent. *The Cutting Room Floor.* New York, Citadel Press, 1994.

Burgess, Anthony. *A Clockwork Orange.* London, William Heinemann, 1962. *You've Had Your Time: The Second Part of the Confessions.* New York, Grove Wiedenfeld, 1990.

Chase, Chris. *How to be a Movie Star, or a Terrible Beauty is Born.* New York, Harper & Row, 1974.

Ciment, Michael. *Kubrick.* New York, Holt, Rinehart and Winston, 1984.

Clarke, Arthur C. *2001: A Space Odyssey.* New York, Signet, 1968. *2010: Odyssey Two.* St Albans, Herts, Granada, 1982. *The Lost Worlds of 2001.* New York, New American Library, 1972.

Condon, Paul, and Jim Sangster. *The Complete Hitchcock.* London, Virgin, 1999.

Corliss, Richard. *BFI Film Classics: Lolita.* London, BFI, 1994.

Curtis, Tony, and Barry Parris. *Tony Curtis: The Autobiography.* New York, William Morrow, 1993.

Dougan, Andy. *Martin Scorsese: The Making of His Movies.* London, Orion, 1997.

Douglas, Kirk. *The Ragman's Son: An Autobiography.* London, Simon & Schuster, 1988.

Elley, Derek. *Variety Movie Guide 1999.* London, Boxtree, 1999.

Ettedgui, Peter. *Screencraft: Production Design and Art Direction.* Hove, RotoVision, 2000.

Evans, Peter. *Peter Sellers: The Man Behind the Mask.* New Jersey, Prentice-Hall, 1968.

Falsetto, Mario. *Stanley Kubrick: A Narrative and Stylistic Analysis.* Connecticut, Praeger, 1994.

Fast, Howard. *Spartacus.* New York, Modern Library, 1951.

Gelmis, Joseph. *The Film Director as Superstar.* New York, Doubleday, 1970.

George, Peter. *Dr Strangelove or: How I Learned to Stop Worrying and Love the Bomb.* New York, Barnes & Noble, 1999.

Gimple, Scott M. *The Simpsons Forever! A Complete Guide to our Favourite Family . . . Continued.* London, HarperCollins, 1999.

Hasford, Gustav. *The Short-Timers.* New York, Harper and Row, 1979.

Howard, James. *The Stanley Kubrick Companion.* London, Batsford, 1999.

Jenkins, Greg. *Stanley Kubrick and the Art of Adaptation.* North Carolina, McFarland, 1997.

Kael, Pauline. *Playing for Keeps: 30 Years at the Movies.* New York, Dutton, 1994.

Kagan, Norman. *The Cinema of Stanley Kubrick.* New York, Holt, Rineheart, and Winston, 1972.

Katz, Ephraim. *The Macmillan International Film Encyclopaedia, Third Edition.* London, Macmillan, 1998.

King, Stephen. *The Shining.* New York, Doubleday, 1977. *Danse Macabre.* New York, Everest House, 1981.

Kubrick, Stanley, Michael Herr and Gustav Hasford. *Full Metal Jacket* (Screenplay). New York, Knopf, 1987.

Kubrick, Stanley, and Frederic Raphael. *Eyes Wide Shut* (Screenplay). New York, Warner, 1999.

LoBrutto, Vincent. *By Design: Interviews with Film Production Designers.* Connecticut, Praeger, 1993. *Stanley Kubrick.* New York, Donald I Fine, 1997.

Mason, James. *Before I Forget*. London, Hamish Hamilton, 1981.

Mazursky, Paul. *Show Me the Magic*. New York, Simon & Schuster, 1999.

Mathews, Tom Dewe. *Censored*. London, Chatto & Windus, 1994.

Nabokov, Vladimir. *Lolita*. New York, Fawcett, 1959. *Lolita: A Screenplay*. New York, McGraw Hill, 1974.

Nelson, Thomas Alen. *Kubrick: Inside a Film Artist's Maze*. Bloomington, Indiana University Press, 1982.

Phillips, Gene D. *Stanley Kubrick: A Film Odyssey*. New York, Popular Library, 1975.

Pickard, Roy. *Oscar Stars from A to Z*. London, Headline, 1998.

Polito, Robert. *Savage Art: The Life of Jim Thompson*. New York, Knopf, 1995.

Pym, John. *Time Out Film Guide: Eighth Edition*. London, Penguin, 1999.

Raphael, Frederic. *Eyes Wide Open: A Memoir of Stanley Kubrick*. New York, Ballantine, 1999.

Richmond, Ray. *The Simpsons: A Complete Guide to Our Favourite Family*. London, HarperCollins, 1997.

Sammon, Paul M. *Future Noir: The Making of Blade Runner*. London, Orion, 1996.

Schnitzler, Arthur. *Dream Story*. London, Penguin Books, 1999.

Scorsese, Martin and Michael Henry Wilson. *A Personal Journey with Martin Scorsese through American Movies*. London, Faber and Faber, 1997.

Silver, Alain and James Ursini. *The Noir Style*. New York, Aurum Press, 1999.

Starr, Michael. *Peter Sellers: A Film History*. London, Robert Hale, 1992.

Stork, David G (ed.). *Hal's Legacy: 2001's Computer as Dream and Reality*. Massachusetts, MIT Press, 1997.

Sylvester, David. *Moonraker, Strangelove and Other Celluloid Dreams: The Visionary Art of Ken Adam*. London, Serpentine Gallery, 1999.

Thackeray, William Makepeace. *Barry Lyndon*. Oxford, Oxford University Press, 1984. *Vanity Fair*. London, Pengun, 1994.

Trumbo, Dalton. *Additional Dialogue*. New York, Evans and Company, 1970.

Ustinov, Peter. *Dear Me*. London, Heinemann, 1977.

Walker, Alexander. *National Heroes: British Cinema in the Seventies and Eighties*. London, Harrap, 1985. *Peter Sellers: The Authorized Biography*. New York, Macmillan, 1981. *Stanley Kubrick Directs*. New York, Harcourt Brace Jovanovich, 1972.

Walker, Alexander, Sybil Taylor and Ulrich Ruchti. *Stanley Kubrick, Director*. New York, Norton, 1999.

Winters, Shelley. *Shelley II*. New York, William Morrow, 1984.

Wyke, Maria. *Projecting the Past: Ancient Rome, Cinema and History*. London, Routledge, 1997.

Youngblood, Gene. *Expanded Cinema*. New York, EP Dutton, 1970.

# Supplemental Credits

The following notes are additional credits that did not appear in the opening or major end credits.

## Spartacus

Camera Operator Harry Wolf
Assistant Directors Foster H Phinney, James Welch, Joe Kenny, Charles Scott

## A Clockwork Orange

Casting James Liggat
Hair Stylist Olga Angelinatta
Make-up Artists Barbara Daly, George Partleton, Freddie Williamson
Assistant Director Derek Cracknell
1st Assistant Director Dusty Symonds
Boom Operator Peter Glossop
Dubbing Mixer Eddie Hoben
Sound Recordist John Jordan
Dubbing Mixer Bill Rowe
Stunt Arranger Roy Scammel
Wardrobe Supervisor Ron Beck
Assistant Film Editor David Beesley
Electrician Best Boy Lou Bogue
Propety Master Frank Bruton
Assistant Film Editor Peter Burgess
Location Manager Terence A Clegg
Grip Tony Cridlin
Camera Operator Ernie Day
Production Assistant Andros Epaminondas
Assistant Camera Laurie Frost
Prop Men Peter Hancock, Tommy Ibbetson
Assistant to Producer Jan Harlan
Production Co-ordinator Mike Kaplan
Continuity June Randall
Production Secretary Iris Rose
First Assistant Editor Gary Shepherd
Gaffer Frank Wardale
Construction Manager Bill Welch

## Barry Lyndon

Written for the Screen, Produced and Directed by Stanley Kubrick
Based on the Novel by William Makepeace Thackeray
Music Adapted and Conducted by Leonard Rosenman from Works by Johann Sebastian Bach, Frederick The Great, Georg Friedrich Handel, Wolfgang Amadeus Mozart, Giovanni Paisiello, Franz Schubert, Antonio Vivaldi
Irish Traditional Music by The Chieftains
Executive Producer Jan Harlan
Associate Producer Bernard Williams
Production Designer Ken Adam
Photographed by John Alcott
Costumes Designed by Ulla-Britt Søderland, Milena Canonero

Editor Tony Lawson
Hairstyles and Wigs Leonard
Art Director Roy Walker
Assistant to the Producer Andros Epaminondas
Production Accountant John Trehy
Assistant Accountants Ron Bareham, Carolyn Hall
Production Managers Douglas Twiddy, Terence Clegg
Germany Production Manager Rudolf Hertzog
Unit Managers Malcolm Christopher, Don Geraghty
Location Liaisons Arthur Morgan, Colonel William O'Kelly
Assistant to the Producer Andros Epaminondas
Producer's Secretary Margaret Adams
Production Secretaries Loretta Ordewer, Pat Pennelegion
Assistant Directors Brian Cook, David Tomblin, Michael Stevenson
Continuity June Randall
Casting James Liggat
2nd Unit Cameraman Patrick Carey
Colour Grading Dave Dowler
Camera Operators Mike Molloy, Ronnie Taylor
Focus Puller Douglas Milsome
Camera Assistants Laurie Frost, Dodo Humphreys
Camera Grips Tony Cridlin, Luke Quigley
Gaffer Lou Boge
Chief Electrician Larry Smith
Assistant Editor Peter Krook
Germany Art Director Jan Schlubach
Assistant Art Director Bill Brodie
Set Dresser Vernon Dizon
Property Master Mike Fowlie
Propman Terry Wells
Prop Buyer Ken Dolbear
Construction Manager Joe Lee
Painter Bill Beacham
Drapesmen Richard Dicker, Cleo Nethersole, Chris Seddon
Costume Makers Gary Dahms, Yvonne Dahms, Jack Edwards, Judy Lloyd-Rogers, Willy
   Rothery
Hats Francis Wilson
Wardrobe Supervisor Ron Beck
Wardrobe Assistants Gloria Barnes, Norman Dickens, Colin Wilson
Make-up Ann Brodie, Alan Boyle, Barbara Daly, Jill Carpenter
Hairdressing Susie Hill, Joyce James, Maud Onslow, Daphne Vollmer
Choreography Geraldine Stephenson
Sound Recording Robin Gregory
Dubbing Mixer Bill Rowe
Sound Editor Rodney Holland
Sound Editor's Assistant George Akers
Gambling Adviser David Berglas
Historical Adviser John Mollo
Fencing Adviser Bob Anderson
Candlelight Photography Lenses Made by Carl Zeiss
Lenses Adapted for Cinematography by Ed Di Giuilio
Stunt Arranger Roy Scammell
Armourer Bill Aylmore
Horsemaster George Mossman

## The Shining

Production Accountant Jo Gregory
Production Assistant Emilio D'Alessandrio
Production Secretaries Pat Pennelegion, Marlene Butland
Producer's Secretary Margaret Adams
Location Research Jan Schlubach, Katharine Kubrick, Murray Close
Assistant Directors Brian Cook, Terry Needham, Michael Stevenson
Continuity June Randall
Casting James Liggat
2nd Unit Photographer Douglas Milsome
2nd Unit Photography MacGillivray Freeman Films
Camera Operators Kelvin Pike, James Devis
Focus Assistants Douglas Milsome, Maurice Arnold
Camera Assistants Peter Robinson, Martin Kenzie, Danny Shelmerdine
Grips Dennis Lewis
Gaffers Lou Bogue, Larry Smith
Video Operator Dan Grimmel
Special Effects Alan Whibley, Les Hillman, Dick Parker
Assistant Editors Gill Smith, Gordon Stainforth
2nd Assistant Editors Adam Unger, Steve Pickard
Décor Artist Robert Walker
Set Dresser Tessa Davies
Draughtsmen John Fenner, Michael Lamont, Michael Boone
Property Master Peter Hancock
Propmen Barry Arnold, Philip McDonald, Peter Spencer
Prop Buyers Edward Rodrigo, Karen Brookes
Construction Manager Len Fury
Drapes Barry Wilson
Master Plasterer Tom Tarry
Head Rigger Jim Kelly
Head Carpenter Fred Gunning
Head Painter Del Smith
Wardrobe Supervisors Ken Lawton, Ron Beck
Wardrobe Assistants Ian Hickinbottom, Veronica McAuliffe
Make-up Artist Barbara Daly
Title Design Chapman Beauvais
Titles National Screen Service
Colour Grading Eddie Gordon
'20s Music Advisers Brian Rust, John Wadley
Sound Recording Ivan Sharrock, Richard Daniel
Boom Operators Ken Weston, Michael Charman
Dubbing Mixers Bill Rowe, Raye Merrin
Sound Editors Wyn Ryder, Dino Di Campo, Jack Knight
Hotel Consultant Tad Michel

## Full Metal Jacket

Production Accountant Paul Cadiou
Assistant Accountant Rita Dean
Accounts Computer Operator Alan Steele
Production Assistant Steve Millson
Assistants to the Producers Emilio D'Alessandrio, Anthony Frewin
Producer's Secretary Wendy Shorter
Production Runners Michael Shevloff, Matthew Coles
Continuity Julie Robinson

Aerial Photography Ken Arlidge, Samuelsons
Follow Focus Jonathan Taylor, Maurice Arnold, James Ainslie, Brian Rose
Camera Assistant Jason Wrenn
Grips Mark Ellis
Louma Crane Technician Adam Samuelson
Steadicam Operators John Ward, Jean-Marc Bringuier
Chief Electrician Seamus O'Kane
Modeller Eddie Butler
Editing Trainee Rona Buchanan
Special Computer Editing Programs Julian Harcourt
Art Directors Rod Stratfold, Les Tomkins, Keith Pain
Assistant Art Directors Nigel Phelps, Andrew Rothschild
Art Department Research Anthony Frewin
Set Dresser Stephen Simmonds
Property Master Brian Wells
Prop Buyer Jane Cooke
Chargehand Prop Paul Turner
Standby Props Danny Hunter, Steve Allett, Terry Wells
Propmen R Dave Favell Clarke, Frank Billington-Marks
Dressing Props Marc Dillon, Michael Wheeler, Winston Depper
Construction Manager George Crawford
Assistant Construction Manager Joe Martin
Standby Construction George Reynolds, Brian Morris, Jim Cowan, Colin McDonagh, John
    Marsella
Supervising Painter John Chapple
Painters Leonard Chubb, Tom Roberts, Leslie Evans Pearce
Riggers Peter Wilkinson, A R Carter, T R Carter
Plasterers Dominic Farrugia, Michael Quinn
Stagehands David Gruer, Michael Martin, Stephen Martin, Ronald Boyd
Title Design Chapman Beauvais
Laboratory Contact Chester Eyre
Sound Transfers Roger Cherrill
Technical Adviser Lee Ermey
Unit Drivers Steve Coulridge, Bill Wright, James Black, Paul Karamadza
Catering Location Caterers
Nurses Linda Glatzel, Carmel Fitzgerald
Action Vehicle Engineer Nick Johns
Armourers Robert Hills, John Oxlade, Hills Small Arms
Helicopter Pilot Bob Warren
Helicopters Sykes Group


## Eyes Wide Shut

Production Associate Michael Doven
Production Accountant John Trehy
Production Co-ordinator Kate Garbett
2nd Unit Production Manager Lisa Leone
Venetian Masks Research Barbara del Greco
Assistant to Mr Kubrick Emilio D'Alessandro
Cinematography (Second Unit) Patrick Turley, Malik Sayeed, Arthur Jaffa
Camera Operator Martin Hume
Camera Assistants (2nd Unit) Carlos Omar Guerra, Jonas Steadman
Focus Pullers Rawdon Hayne, Nick Penn, Jason Wrenn
Clapper Loaders Craig Bloor, Keith Roberts
Camera Grips William Geddes, Andy Hopkins

Steadicam Operators Elizabeth Ziegler, Peter Cavaciuti
Steadicam Operator/2nd Unit Assistant Director Jim C McConkey
Gaffers Ronnie Phillips, Paul Toomey
Best Boy Michael White
Electricians Ron Emery, Joe Allen, Shawn Wjite, Dean Wilkinson
Video Co-ordinator Andrew Haddock
Stills Photography Manuel Harlan
Digital Visual Effects/Animation Computer Film Company
Back Projection Supervisor Charles Staffell
Set Decorators Terry Wells Sr, Lisa Leone
Production Buyers Michael King, Jeanne Vertigan, Sophie Batsford
Property Master Terry Wells Jr
Tom Cruise's Evening Wear Cerrutti (Paris)
Titles Chapman Beauvais
Music Contractor Peter Hughes
Music Consultant Didier De Cottigniers
Choreography Yolande Snaith
Sound Maintenance Tony Bell
Sound Re-recorded at Pinewood Studios
Sound Editing Sound Design Company
Editor Foley Becki Ponting
Camera Technical Adviser Joe Dunton
Medical Adviser Dr CJ Scheiner
Journalistic Adviser Larry Celona
Cameras Arriflex Arri
Dialect Coach (Nicole Kidman) Elizabeth Himelstein

# Index